[Teilhard de Chardin's] religious faith was the soul of his scientific effort and of his intellectual quest. Few priestly lives, I imagine, have been so completely a single, integral life . . .

Père Teilhard had the boundless, extravagant, ingenuous ambition to give the modern world to Jesus Christ; for he had an experience that he felt was an exemplar, and he did not believe that he had any right to keep that experience to himself.

At a time when a gulf seemed to be widening between the most living elements in the modern world and the Church, when those men whose passion for scientific research or for the advancement of man was most intense were turning away from the Catholic faith, Père Teilhard had met with an experience that was directly contrary.

Few men in his generation have shared so deeply and with such passion in the hopes, the efforts, the boundless ambitions of his time. There was no field of thought or action in which he found himself a stranger. But while the appreciation of earthly values was turning so many others away from the religion of their childhood, Père Teilhard's faith, with its roots deep in the past of a Christian family, and humbly maintained in strict loyalty to the observances of his Order, was confirmed by that same appreciation. The modern world, as a vital experience had shown him, had need of Jesus Christ, and could be saved only by Jesus Christ.

Such was Père Teilhard's message, as old as Christianity, but lived with such intensity that it was as though he had himself discovered it.

Excerpt from an address given by Père René d'Ouince, S.J.*

* Pages 311–14.

D1225031

The Religion of Teilhard de Chardin

HENRI DE LUBAC, S.J.

TRANSLATED BY RENÉ HAGUE

IMAGE BOOKS

A DIVISION OF DOUBLEDAY & COMPANY, INC.
GARDEN CITY, NEW YORK

Image Books edition 1968
by special arrangement with Desclee Company, Inc.

Image Books edition published September 1968

Originally published in French under the title
La pensée religieuse du Père Teilhard de Chardin
(© 1962 by Editions Montaigne, Paris)
This English translation © 1967 William Collins
Sons & Co., Ltd., London and Desclee Co. Inc.,
New York.

TO THE MEMORY
OF A GREAT CONTEMPLATIVE
PÈRE CHARLES NICOLET
(1896–1961)
WHO WAS A DEVOTED FRIEND
OF PÈRE TEILHARD, AND WAS
CONSUMED BY THE SAME FIRE

CONTENTS

ACKNOWLEDGEMENTS

It is a pleasure to thank all those who have so unselfishly helped me by allowing me to see unpublished papers, providing me with valuable suggestions, reading my manuscript, and in other ways. In particular, I am grateful to Mgr Bruno de Solages, M. Joseph Teilhard de Chardin, Mlle Jeanne Mortier, Mlle Alice Teilhard-Chambon, Mme M. Madaule, M. Claude Cuénot, M. l'abbé Gaudefroy, and to my colleagues, R. Père Blaise Arminjon, Pères Louis Barjon (author of an important book, as yet unpublished, on Père Teilhard), René d'Ouince, Henri Bouillard, François Russo, Christian d'Armagnac, Edgar Haulotte, Henri Mogenet, Régis Araud and Auguste Demoment.

THE RELIGION OF
TEILHARD DE CHARDIN

Chapter 1

THE ESSENTIAL CORE

It is only too easy to dismiss, in a writer's thought, anything
that makes no special appeal to us, to minimize or even completely overlook its importance. This may lead us, in all good
faith, to distort the whole meaning of his work, even if any
analysis we include is itself accurate. Numerous examples
could be quoted of the operation of this unconscious mechanism of choice and rejection, among them that great field of
study, of cardinal importance in the history of religious
thought, represented by the biblical exegesis of the Fathers of
the Church. This rests in its entirety on a keen perception of a
relation, unique of its kind, the relation of the two 'Covenants'
or the two 'Testaments'. There we have the key without which
it cannot be properly understood. And yet how often has it
been treated, even by historians of repute, with little or no
mention of that key relationship: the reason being that the
personal interest of those historians, or the general interest of
their period, lies elsewhere. Much can be learnt from what
they say, but the essence of the subject is left in the dark,
while all the non-essential is presented with a deceptive clarity.
Only a few years ago a work with the title *The Letter and the
Spirit*,[1] dealing solely with the principles of biblical exegesis
as developed during the first centuries of Christianity, gave not
the least hint that this relation between letter and spirit was,
for the ancient exegetes, primarily and precisely the relation
between the Old Testament and the New.

Another example of this same unconscious mechanism may
be found in a number of recently published studies of the
work of Père Pierre Teilhard de Chardin. His writings undoubtedly form one whole in a way that those of few other
thinkers do, and the imprint of his own personality can constantly be recognized in them. Nevertheless (leaving aside his
purely technical scientific papers) one can, roughly speaking,

divide them into two parts. The first, in which the line of thought is still scientific or, one might prefer to say, philosophical, is developed from the data of experimental science; the second, more strictly mystical and religious, is often explicitly based on the data of Christian revelation. Central to the first is *The Phenomenon of Man*, to the second, *Le Milieu Divin*. It is evident that for all the importance of the former in Père Teilhard's eyes, he constantly regarded it as necessarily leading on to the latter. He continually endeavoured, sometimes with more success, sometimes with less, to bring the two together without confusing one with the other; and it is in fact the transition from one to the other that raises the nicest problems in interpretation. To study the first part in isolation, or almost in isolation, without a warning—or without first reminding oneself—that it represents an incomplete study and is no more than a methodological abstraction, is to mutilate Teilhard's thought. However exact the analyses offered, and however profound the interpretations, it still distorts the thought by putting forward as a complete view what is only partial and still preliminary.

This mistake becomes particularly serious when an attempt is made, using only what material can be found in the first part of Teilhard's work, to reconstruct the whole, or practically the whole, of his religious thought. We have Teilhard's own warning that beyond the furthest point to which the effort we devote to reflecting on scientific data can lead us, 'we can see no further, and our argument must cease'; and he goes on to say, 'except in the case of the Christian who, drawing upon an added source of knowledge, may advance yet another step'.[2] What is more, this continuation of the first in the second is much more than a supplementary rounding-off; in the two parts we have distinguished within Teilhard's work, the second is not 'a sort of appendix, to be detached at will'; in other words, while theology (in the wide sense of the word) is not 'all-invading' in Teilhard, no more is it simply an appendage, for the universe he describes and contemplates 'ultimately holds together' (as Pastor Georges Crespy has well noted) 'only from on high'.[3]

Even when readers include *Le Milieu Divin* in their attention, they may still apply a similar type of exclusive dichotomy. Their own concern is with the quest for a doctrine or mystical teaching applied to human action and they are accordingly pleased to find in the book chapters that seem to offer what they are looking for and to give body to what they feel in only a vague way. Dazzled by the rich store they find in *Le Milieu Divin*, they can see no further: and yet a mere glance at the table of contents would have been enough to show them that they have stopped short at the initial stage and have only broken through the first crust. They have not found their way to the heart of Teilhard's mystical teaching.

While such interpretations are partial in the sense of incomplete, others are partial in the sense that they show partiality. We need not concern ourselves with a number of detractors of Teilhard, in whom emotion has blunted intelligence: but you find the writer who, when he quotes Teilhard, is looking primarily for something that will encourage him in his own personal line of inquiry. Or the man again who, reading that religion should teach man 'first to recognize, love and serve the Universe with passion', adopts the thought and gives it his own interpretation, as though 'first' meant a priority in value and not simply the first term of a dialectic or the first stage in a training in religion. In one such recent work, while the writer expresses the warmest admiration for Père Teilhard's thought, he nevertheless presents it in a light that makes it unrecognizable. The picture of *Le Milieu Divin*, in particular, is a complete travesty, so that any reader who expected to get at least some first idea of the book would be utterly misled. He would not obtain even a distant glimpse of what Père Teilhard meant by the *milieu divin*.[4] And the reason for this is that the author, having no concern for the spiritual problems that were vital to Père Teilhard, is interested only in making him serve his own purposes.

Fortunately, other studies, some presenting a synthesis, others dealing with particular points, are more objective: and since the present work was begun, they have been multiplying. These I have found more useful, and I make no claim to offer a substitute for them or to carry them further in the particular line they have chosen. I shall make little attempt, except incidentally, to examine Père Teilhard's scientific ideas or the various ramifications into which they are pursued. Not, indeed, that I in any way underestimate their importance, but because every writer must have his own end in view. Moreover I cannot forget the many passages in which he tells us what was for him the essential thing. As a small child he already had 'the passion for the Absolute'; and he already sought this Absolute, 'this beatifying Object', 'everywhere' and 'unceasingly'. 'The story of my interior life,' he wrote in 1918, 'is the story of this quest, directed towards more and more universal and perfect realities. Fundamentally, my deep-seated natural impulse, the *nisus* of my soul, has remained absolutely inflexible as long as I can remember.' In another of his first essays, as yet unpublished, he hailed the Faith that transports man 'beyond all that man's eye has ever seen or his ear has ever heard', and towards the end of his life he could still write 'A certain love of the invisible has never ceased to be active in me'.[5] This faith and this love did not remain silent. They developed into a spiritual teaching and thus became the soul, the organizing principle, and the pole of all his thought. 'Mysticism,' he said, 'is the Science of Sciences'; it is the 'great science and the great art, the only power capable of synthesizing the riches accumulated by other forms of human activity'.[6] For Teilhard, mysticism is the only means we have for examining the Real in its 'prodigious magnitude'.[7] Moreover, in his view, 'the mystical vibration is inseparable from the scientific vibration':[8] 'To read the Secret of the Real . . . , to find its source: the scientist's quest, however positivist he may claim it to be, is coloured or haloed—or rather is invincibly animated, fundamentally—by a mystical hope.'[9] On more than one occasion he did not conceal his desire to feel himself 'free to forget a little the scientific aspects of nature, and return to a more direct study of their continuations in mysticism'; it was these latter, he confessed, that 'fascinated' him more than anything.[10] Père Teilhard never believed that science was a 'sufficient goal for life'. Specializing in geology, he enjoyed finding in following that discipline 'a contact with the Real' that was calculated to 'arouse' and 'foster' it, and a 'working on the Real' that enabled him to share in 'man's endeavour' and operate the alliance he advocated 'between the man and the Christian'. At the same time he realized that 'some quite different experience might have had the same results' for him,[11] and he was by no means completely satisfied with it. The thousands of kilograms of 'precious objects' that he brought back from his distant geological expeditions were of passionate interest to him, but he was even more interested in the 'smallest spark of true mysticism' he had managed to discover.[12] His research work, which he loved, provided his platform and his career, but he said again and again, and with increasing emphasis as he grew older, 'I feel that the basic interest of my life is wandering elsewhere.'[13] 'The real interest of my life' is the effort towards 'a plainer disclosing of God in the world'. That, he writes again, 'is my only true vocation',[14] for 'the whole human problem comes back to the love of God'.[15]

We must be equally careful to remember that for Teilhard 'the true mystical science, the only one that counts'—because the only one whose interest was 'ultimate'—was 'the science of Christ through all things',[16] and that this ardent conviction culminated in another, the belief that Christ is to be found in the Church in which he lives; that that Church, 'the Christic pole of the earth', is 'phyletically essential to the fulfilment of Mankind';[17] that Christianity is only fully itself when it is accepted in all 'the cold rigour of its Catholic demands'; and that for each one of Christ's faithful 'to be a Catholic is the only way of being fully a Christian and a Christian through and through'.[18] There is, then, no form of conformism in Teilhard; nor is this simply an apologetic approach. It is the very soul of his soul, and it shows us what constitutes the essential core of his work.

It is on this, accordingly, that our attention will be concentrated, on the spiritual teaching of Père Teilhard de Chardin. (A study of his spiritual life can be attempted only later.) Circumstances have, no doubt, influenced me in choosing this aspect. I cannot, indeed, flatter myself that I was one of Père Teilhard's disciples nor have I ever undertaken, as he did, any personal research in the field of exact science. Like many others, my own interest has centred on the past of Christianity, seeking to recover from it a number of traditional values that our own time, too unadventurous or too feverishly restless, was in danger of losing. Alone, Père Teilhard looked ahead, to proclaim Christ to generations born into the age of science, and to work in Christ for the triumph of man's adventure. While both tasks are necessary, the second, which obviously calls for more qualifications, also involves more risks. It gives new life to more things, and it is open to more uncertainty. Thus it is that, on more than one occasion, I have addressed questions to Père Teilhard, either verbally or in correspondence, that, addressed to anyone younger or less great a man than he, would have been called objections; and the answers I received, often illuminating, were not always such as to discourage any comment. Over a period of more than thirty years, my contacts with him were marked from the very beginning, as he wished them to be, by confidence and complete openness of mind; thus I was able to follow the development of his thought, in its very hesitancies and withdrawals, until a long interview in the summer of 1954, which took place in the Paris he loved, revisited for a few days just before he sailed for America for the last time, some months before his death. A careful reading of his manuscripts and of many intimate letters has confirmed me in my belief that I am not likely to be mistaken about what was most firm and constant in the general direction of his thought. This, as I see it, is what I propose to express. I have no intention either of offering a panegyric or of in any way adjusting Père Teilhard's views. Whenever it seems useful so to do, I shall be at pains to point out, so that they may be better understood, how his ideas evolved, how he shifted his point of view or even adopted a new terminology. As we proceed, it will be necessary to correct the misunderstandings that have accumulated around a number of points in his teaching. At the same time I shall, so far as possible, allow Père Teilhard to give his own explanations and interpretations, by making use of the texts of various types that have been available to me.

Unless one approaches Père Teilhard's work with preconceived ideas in one's head, his admirable simplicity of mind facilitates such an undertaking. He described himself, modestly but truthfully, as 'a man trying to express frankly what lies at the heart of his generation'.[19] In his writings, as in his personal relationships, the only diplomatic art he used was 'the diplomacy of candour'.[20] His method was not, any more than Buddha's of old, that of 'giving away nothing'. 'It would be a mistake to conclude that there was an exoteric and an esoteric Teilhard.'[21] His most 'confidential' memoranda were generally addressed to his superiors, sometimes to them alone, either to draw their attention to some aspect of the religious situation or to have his own views checked.[22] On several occasions he sent directly to Rome some of what he considered his most important essays, solely, he said, in order to keep higher authority abreast of 'all the principal developments of *his* thought'.[23] What is more, one never finds in Père Teilhard, as one does in others, any dualism between writer and man, between theories expressed in writings addressed to some unknown reader and his own personal reflections or confidential communications to his friends. Taking the whole of his work, one must, no doubt, distinguish (as we shall see) writings that differ in nature, in value and in scope. Nevertheless, whatever their type, there is never any hidden implication to be found in them, never a false profundity to be unmasked or a clever trick of language to be on one's guard against. We do not have to distinguish between what should rightly be called his real 'system' and the series of 'concessions' or 'precautions' that some critics have been too ready to attribute to him whenever one of his ideas threatened to upset the hard and fast framework—an over-simplified travesty—in which they had made up their minds to enclose his teaching. He does not even make use of the excessive refinements of accuracy that might on more than one occasion have served effectively to protect himself against the one-sided interpretation of readers who do not fall naturally into the rhythm of his inquiry. He always assumes that the reader is his friend, anxious to join him on the road; and with such a reader, as with himself, he has but one idea: to see and make others see, to understand and make others understand; always to find the most exact way of expressing what he thinks, feels, and *sees*.

From time to time the force behind his conviction is so

strong that it breaks out into phrases of striking intensity, as in the words that conclude his last essay, *Le Christique*: 'It is enough for the truth to appear one single time, in one single mind, for it to be impossible for anything to prevent it from spreading universally and setting all ablaze.' At times his conviction is expressed with a missionary ardour and in prophetic accents that some have been inclined to consider almost intemperate. It was, however, accompanied in Père Teilhard by a modesty that prevented him from ever believing that he had seen the whole truth, or even had been able, in spite of his continually renewed efforts, to get across the little truth he had seen.[24] 'Of course,' he once said, after being questioned at length about the relations between science and theology, 'I cannot claim to clear this up for you. I am feeling my way, just as you are. All I shall ever be able to do is to give you a number of suggestions. But, surely, it is upon this hesitant, shared work of those who believe that God sends down the truly creative action of his light.'[25] For all the assurance of his tone, his successive essays, each completing and correcting one another, never did more than seek (again in his own words) to define 'a possible line of approach to one of the aspects of the truth'.[26] Père Teilhard did not simply accept advice, supervision and correction, but went out of his way to seek them: and this not only from his superiors or proved masters, such as Père Léonce de Grandmaison for example, but even from younger and less experienced colleagues.[27] He was, he said, the first to realize how much in his 'attempts at explanation' was 'approximate and inadequate', and, if given the opportunity, he was ready to recognize that his way of expressing himself could at times have been 'defective'.[28] Several times, again, when he re-read one or other of his writings, it happened that he himself judged them severely; and it would be a mistake to use them all in the same way, not distinguishing those in which, on Père Teilhard's own admission, the thought was tentative or fumbling or the expression over-hasty,[29] from those more mature productions in which he was more sure of himself, in particular those he published himself or wished to have published.

Moreover, he assures us that 'in spite of certain appearances' he was not trying to present 'any fixed and self-contained system'. In 1919 he had written: 'The somewhat hazardous or over-systematized points in my "doctrine" are, in fact, of only secondary importance to me: it is not nearly so much ideas that I want to spread abroad as a *spirit*', and he prayed that this spirit might always come to him from 'the good spirit'.[30] He never wavered in this general attitude. Whenever, later, he systematizes, he is only trying, he says, 'to come a little closer to, and express a little more fully, the ever-elusive foundation of what *he* feels, of what *he* sees, of what *he* lives'.[31] Continually, therefore, we have to go back to an initial intuition that unremitting thought can never exhaust or even fully express. 'Even when the form of Père Teilhard's writing is most finished, its power of emphasis, its impact, one might say, comes from the first spark that kindled the whole.'[32] And this remains true even when his thought is most ambitious, in those writings which are remarkable both for the strength of their structure and for the compactness of their content. Père Teilhard does not claim to do more than present a 'fascicle of axes of progression' or to mark out certain 'lines of penetration along which there opens up for us an immensity of hitherto unexplored reality'.[33] If the truth of things can be defined as 'the total coherence of the Universe in relation to each point within it', it is evident that truth about things 'is arrived at by systematizing'. For the rigorous inquirer, that is an essential. At the same time he knows that it is always a hazardous undertaking. The construction of the system can never be perfect; once it reaches a particular critical point, it may even, through a law similar to that of diminishing returns, have the effect of shutting out and impoverishing rather than gathering together and unifying. Père Teilhard was well aware of this. Thus, at the very moment when he was building up a system, he could assert, 'Absolutely speaking, I do not believe in any system.'[34] All that we have just said obviously holds good more particularly in connexion with spirituality than in any other field. We shall find that Père Teilhard gives us his spiritual doctrine by opening his soul to us. The many writings in which he does this are all of a more or less intimately personal nature; and the full substance of what they contain could not be completely assembled—or, at any rate, all their subtleties of meaning be retained (except for Père Teilhard himself) in his more systematically constructed essays.

In his spiritual writings Père Teilhard was always more concerned to define an interior attitude than to lay bare the dogmatic foundations. These do, indeed, emerge in many of his writings and are given considerable prominence, but they were not the object of a study in any way comparable to that we find in *The Phenomenon of Man* or *Le Milieu Divin*. Nevertheless, everything holds together as one whole. Life presupposes thought. A spirituality can be understood and judged only in its relation to the sum total of truths on which it is based. That is why it has been necessary to widen, without abandoning, the point of view I have already explained; and this study, whose original intention was to present only Père Teilhard's spiritual doctrine, has necessarily developed into an examination of his religious thought.

Of the whole body of his work we may say, in the words of Père Édouard Boné, that 'it was written in a spirit of boldness' and presented 'in a spirit of humility'.[35] It is the work of a man of faith who offers men his vision of Christ. It is a very personal vision, but one that sees the one Christ of the Gospel and the Church. 'His integrity,' says Père Teilhard, 'is more to me than the colours in which I see him'; and, in even stronger words, 'I am determined to sacrifice everything rather than allow Christ's integrity to be impugned, either personally or in my environment.'[36] He wishes to speak only 'in the hope of serving Christ', 'with absolute trust in him and acceptance of his will before all else'.[37] Similarly, it would be false to his spirit to be at pains to justify him at all costs, whatever form of expressing himself he adopted, just as it would be to force any particular expression in such a way as to extract from it propositions that are obviously contradicted by the whole tenor of his thought. These elementary precautions should be borne in mind as we set out to join Père Teilhard, independently and yet sympathetically, in the various stages of his journey. To do so will be even more important when, later, we shall have to stand back a little and obtain an over-all view in which sympathy must not be allowed to rule out criticism.

Chapter 2

LE MILIEU DIVIN

'Oh! how much I would have liked to have met the St. Ignatius or St. Francis of Assisi that our age so sadly needs! What a wonderful dream—to follow a man of God along a free, fresh road, impelled by the full force of the religious life-sap *of his own* time. Often I pray to God that I may be the ashes from which will arise, for other generations, the great blaze that our own looks for in vain.'

It was thus that Pierre Teilhard de Chardin wrote to his friend Auguste Valensin on New Year's Eve, 1926. It was in this frame of mind that for the last two months he had been devoting his leisure, in Tientsin, to writing *Le Milieu Divin*. Five years earlier, he had already confided this dream to the same friend, in words that explain just what he was planning. 'I dream,' he wrote, 'of a new St. Francis or a new St. Ignatius, who will offer us the new type of Christian life (at once more involved in and more detached from the world) that we need.'[1] The book he was now engaged on, therefore, was no improvisation. It had been slowly maturing in his mind. As early as 1916, when he was at the front, he had made up his mind to 'systematize *his own* interior life',[2] and in 1917 he had written a complete short treatise, *Le Milieu Mystique*, which is a sort of first draft of *Le Milieu Divin*—somewhat clumsy in places, but less impersonal and more closely attached to his own experiences. Back from the war, he communicated the substance of this in a series of lectures and spiritual retreats given between 1920 and 1923. Such, for example, was a three-day retreat attended by a group of Ecole Normale students, and recalled by Jacques Perret.[3] Père Teilhard had been using the phrase *milieu divin* for a long time.[4] It was on 7 November 1926 that he finally wrote: 'I have finally decided to write my book on the spiritual life. I mean to put down as simply as possible the sort of ascetical or mystical teaching that I have been living and preaching so long.'[5]

It will be, he says elsewhere, 'a sort of little treatise on spirituality': 'My plan is to produce something easy somewhat in the form of a prayer; I want to put my whole heart into it.'[6]

The book was finished during March 1927 and sent to Père Charles at Louvain. On several occasions Père Teilhard had reason to believe that publication was imminent. The Jesuits at Louvain wanted to include it in their series *Museum Lessianum*. Several official reports on it were favourable.[7] After he had been asked to elucidate a number of points he was told that the book was going to be printed, and then that it was actually being printed. Then, after a long silence, and waiting for further reports, the revised manuscript was again sent back from Tientsin to Louvain, in the spring of 1932. Until November there were still hopes of its appearance; but in December the plan had to be dropped.[8] However, copies of the manuscript circulated, and Père Teilhard had the satisfaction of knowing that it was warmly welcomed by a number of his fellow-Jesuits, including even some of his seniors.[9]

In *Le Milieu Divin* he had incorporated the fruit of an intense spiritual life, evidence for which is contained, apart from *Le Milieu Mystique*, in a series of personal notes; and he had thought over the problems with equal concentration. In 1919 he had had long conversations about them, in Paris, Lyons, and Jersey, with his superiors and colleagues, and towards the end of the year he had sent a first batch of spiritual writings, through their common friend Père Valensin, for critical examination by Maurice Blondel.[10] On this occasion, he was not setting out to write a learned treatise; all he wished to do was to express himself 'in simple, incontestable terms, with no evident appeal to any philosophical system', and in a form 'as devoid of systematized views as possible';[11] and to indicate the nature of the book he added the sub-title, 'An Essay on the Interior Life'.

The description—in words Père Teilhard was constantly using[12]—was eminently appropriate. One should not look in *Le Milieu Divin* for an exposition of abstract doctrine. It is clearly neither a complete moral treatise nor a methodical handbook of ascesis. Such works are, indeed, indispensable, and the *Milieu* cannot take their place, nor was it in any way intended that it should. Again, it does not offer anything that resembles a rule of life; nor is it any more concerned with historical philosophy or theology—except in so far as it recalls the main lines of Christian thought in that connexion. Père Teilhard constructed in it no plan for the organization of the world; he was not trying to expound any strategy or lay down any social or apostolic tactics. What he was concerned with was the most personal and most intimate aspect of life. His subject is the Christian questioning himself about his interior attitude as he confronts both the world and God. For each man, the problem is *his own soul*; for, mindful of the Gospel warnings and dismissing over-nice doubts that stem from a misconception, Père Teilhard had no hesitation in believing and asserting that, for each one of us, all problems centre on and culminate in the problem of saving his own soul.

We should not look for more, then, in *Le Milieu Divin*, but, equally, we should not look for less. The prospects it opens up for us are vast; they are not only cosmic but divine, and therefore infinite. Nevertheless, the daily practical immediateness of the spiritual problem is not thereby neglected, nor lost in considerations of a different nature. The work is, in the proper sense of the word, an exhortation. It calls on us not only to think, but to act, to be, and to recollect and look into ourselves. The message that runs through it is 'Put your hand to the plough'.[13] In this characteristic lies its first great merit. It saves it from an over-intellectual enthusiasm, and at the same time discourages any attempt to make factious use of it. Minds of the most different types can derive profit from it; but only those will really get into it, understand it, meditate on it and love it, who feel at least an initial desire for the 'interior life' and who have not allowed themselves to be befogged in advance by the disparagement of which it is the victim.

Although it is a book of spirituality, *Le Milieu Divin* does not, moreover, put forward a new spirituality, at least if the adjective is used in a rather forcible and provocative sense.

No doubt, compared with many other writings in Christian tradition and in our own time, it introduces a new element. That is undeniable; it is admitted and even emphasized. However, the new element is not in itself of the spiritual order—

nor is it of the order of theory. It is the registering of a fact, and indeed a massive fact—one that Père Teilhard felt before many other men, with exceptional intensity, and then expressed and interpreted in his own way, but the world-wide evidence of which no one can henceforth be blind to. In these last centuries the universe, as seen by man, has expanded prodigiously. Copernicus and Galileo brought the discovery of space, and now we have the discovery of time:[14] not only, or principally, the immensity of time, analogous to that of space—not only the twofold abyss of Past and Future, following on the twofold Abyss of the infinitesimal and the immense—but, if one may use the word, its fecundity. Whatever the truth about a celebrated hypothesis, of which Père Teilhard was not an ardent supporter, we see the universe as expanding within time.[15] Creation 'is an act co-extensive with the duration of the World'; it 'has never ceased'; it unfolds like 'a great continuous act, spaced out over the totality of time; it is still going on, and the World is constantly, even if imperceptibly, emerging a little further above nothingness'.[16] Duration, therefore, is not what it was commonly believed to be until our own time: it is not a sort of 'homogeneous magnitude, divisible at will' nor 'a time-container in which the years are stored', nor 'the permanent framework of certain divergent or circular diversifications'. It is a time 'measured by the development of global Reality'; in other words, it is 'the axis of a sort of cosmogenesis'.[17] It is much more internal to beings than it used to appear, or, to put it in another way, beings are much more internal to it. It permeates 'the very ultimate fibres' of their essence. Its role, in consequence, appears to us both infinitely more vast and infinitely more profound. It has taken on a positive significance for us. Through duration there is in fact a 'growth of the world' which becomes manifest to our investigation 'as a specific Whole, endowed with a power of organic development'.[18]

Thus the Universe has acquired a further dimension: organicity. 'Like children who come to appreciate depth and perspective, we have just come to perceive' this 'new dimension'.[19] 'Under the influence, unconcerted but convergent, of the natural, historical and physical sciences, in countless subtle ways, the concept of Evolution has been weaving its web around us.'[20] Combined with and closely related to this discovery, we have the staggering advances in technology, the natural consequence of the modern 'scientific explosion',[21] which themselves are producing an immense step forward for our species. 'What are the most glorious victories of life in the past compared with the rising tide of modern civilizations? What eruption can compare with the explosion of man?' This has profoundly modified the idea of man's relation to nature. It is a revolution 'much greater than the revolution in astronomy at the time of Galileo'.[22] At the same time as man discovered the scope and power of cosmic ties, he discovered that social organization could become equally extensive and powerful; and as he recognized that he was much more deeply rooted in the development of the universe than he imagined, so he became more conscious of his own strength, potentialities and responsibilities, and of the value of his action. His action can no longer seem 'completely satisfactory to him unless it is carried out in union with the fulfilment of all cosmic perfection'.[23] Man has really begun to understand that he is not and cannot be a mere onlooker in the immensity of Evolution. He now sees that he has a collective work to carry through in this world and on this world. He knows that this world, as such, has a future and that it is he who is building up that future.[24]

As happens whenever centuries-old habits of thought are upset, we find ourselves faced with a crisis. The majority concentrate their attention exclusively on external transformations, on 'the mutation of human societies', and, accordingly, on the social crisis. This latter, however, is of only secondary importance, and though Père Teilhard was by no means indifferent to it, he very soon acquired a deeper understanding of the true nature of the crisis; 'the present crisis', he continually insisted, 'is a spiritual crisis'.[25] When we look back on the last fifty years, who could now fail to see that he was right? And who, among thinking men, would be so rash as to deny the extreme gravity of the crisis? The notion of 'organic time' has forced us to alter nearly all our ways of looking at things. It has 're-ordered the whole field of our experience'.[26]

Such a change must have repercussions, and it has made itself 'felt effectively even in what is most deeply religious in the soul'.[27] There again, a sort of mutation is at work. For some time already, at an accelerated pace, 'something is happening in man's consciousness. It is the beginning of another sort of life'.[28] As one might expect, Christian consciousness is feeling the repercussion of this 'collective awakening'. Some are dangerously elated; others are no less dangerously depressed. It is at once a gain in value and an anxiety. For many it is a 'bewitchment' that draws them away from the God of Scripture, the only living God, to worship a 'sort of Divinity entirely immanent in the World',[29] and that in consequence may well drive them back into despair. To others, on the contrary, it brings intense suffering, which makes them steel themselves against it; the defensive reflex it provokes distorts their faith, and makes it barren and narrow, and it may well cut them off from living humanity.

In *Le Milieu Divin*, Père Teilhard is trying to help both these groups. He wants to show them the road of true fidelity. Allowing for the new situation, and accepting the truth which emerges from it, he speaks to all men, telling that 'without mixture, without confusion the true God, the Christian God' alone can overcome the crisis in our hearts, because 'the star for which the world is waiting' is not some new *Fatum*; it is, and can only be, 'the Christ himself in whom we hope'.[30] Once again, then, a Christian has risen up, strong in his own experience, to tell his fellows that Jesus Christ exists for them, that he exists for all men and that he alone, today as always, is the 'truth of Life'. In the burning words of a man who lives intensely the adventure of his own age, he re-tells in his own way, and has no desire to do anything but re-tell, 'the Church's eternal lesson'. With an emphasis that demands attention, he communicates what 'is most traditional in Christianity's teaching, Baptism, the Cross, and the Eucharist'.[31] He shows that its power of universal assimilation is still unimpaired, still fresh, and continually increasing in step with the increase we see in the world of nature.

Thus Père Teilhard tells us that if we wish to give new vigour to our minds, we must steep ourselves in tradition.

From many quarters today we hear, in the Church, a demand for a 'spirituality for lay folk'. It is a legitimate demand, if we are thinking of a form of Christian life independent of the particular practices and mentality found in the monastic or priestly state. It may, however, disguise an ill-advised demand, if that form of life is conceived as being specifically based on different principles, requiring different sources of nourishment, determined by a different fundamental attitude, or directed towards a different ultimate goal. There cannot be two parallel types of spirituality within Christianity.[32] Just as there is but 'one Lord, one Faith, one Baptism', and for all Christians but 'one body and one spirit'; and just as there is first of all but one human nature and as but one Gospel has ever been proclaimed, so in all the variety of times, circumstances, and inclinations, there is but one Christian vocation, founded on one and the same hope and producing one and the same life.[33] It is this fundamental vocation of the Christian that *Le Milieu Divin* insists upon, this hope that it announces, and this life that it presents to all men. It seeks to present the vocation in all its urgency and in all its beauty, with nothing that would particularize it, and nothing that would weaken it: and at the same time, by the way in which the emphasis colours the exposition, it constantly makes full allowance for the new and permanent element that has been added to man's consciousness and that must be included.

While *Le Milieu Divin* is not written specially for priests or religious, neither is it addressed to some exceptional class of intellectual or 'seeker'. Ten years earlier, Père Teilhard was writing: 'If you judge me worthy, Lord God, I would show to those whose lives are dull and drab the limitless horizons opening out to humble and hidden efforts: for these efforts, if pure in intention, can add to the extension of the Incarnate Word a further element, an element known to Christ's heart and gathered up into his immortality.'[34] He believed that the joy to be found in doing one's duty and in submission to Providence 'can ultimately replace all others, by which I mean that it can make us find life passionately interesting even in the most commonplace and tedious setting'.[35] He was equally convinced that 'even though we cannot control our inspiration and understanding', yet, in answering the invitations of grace, we always have 'the resource of intensifying our intention and faith', and that 'in that direction our strength is immense . . . the humblest effort, exercised with the loving consciousness of acting (physically) *in Christo* has (and this is a fundamental law for the Christian) a repercussion on the real fibres of the world that no purely "human" force could produce'.[36] When he came to write *Le Milieu Divin*, his idea and plan remained unchanged.

Père Teilhard himself, no doubt, was 'pre-eminently a scientist'. At that time, and for years before, he had, as Père Boné has rightly noted, 'an acute sense of the world of science' and of the 'demands of scientific research'.[37] In 1916 he had paid tribute to the 'sacred flame of Research'. In 1918 he set himself the task of showing his contemporaries that 'Research directed towards the World and truth is an absolute duty'.[38] In *Mon Univers* he had welcomed the ideal of a future that would see 'the unanimous quest for the truth' realized on earth. On several later occasions he returned to this problem, which seemed to him to become of increasingly capital importance.[39] He showed how scientific research, 'originating as a childish diversion', had 'become the serious, central, vital occupation of adult man', 'the form in which God's creative power is disguised and operates most intensely in the Nature we live in'.[40] So strongly did he feel this, that he went so far as to see concentrated in 'today's rising tide of Research' the whole approach he dreamed of for all mankind. He demanded from the Seeker a real death to his own self, and he promised him, as the cost of his ennobling task, 'interior agonies and persecutions'.[41] He heralded or at least openly wished for the 'decisive hour' that was to inaugurate a 'capital phase of History', that in which 'the Spirit of Discovery would absorb all the vital energy contained in the Spirit of War'.[42] In the evening of his days he wrote still another note on 'Research, Work, and Adoration', addressed to priests whose special vocation committed them to a career similar to his own.[43] At the same time he did not fail to give a warning against a certain 'mystique of Research' that claimed to be self-sufficient, pointing out that the enthusiasm and devotion it arouses, as in the case of 'social mystiques', are 'hard, cold, grim, incompletely productive of happiness' because 'no precise peak and, what is more serious, no lovable object is offered for them to adore'.[44] On this occasion, in writing this short but 'frankly impassioned' book,[45] Père Teilhard had a more universal aim. He was at pains to 'include nothing esoteric',[46] in other words anything addressed only to the expert. He wished to speak as a Christian, for every Christian who is in any degree affected by the crisis of our age. In it he shares his own experience, lived in faith, with his fellow-men, inside or outside the fold. He invites them to join him not on some 'difficult peak reserved for a few chosen souls' but on 'the solid platform built up by two thousand years of Christian experience', whence he will direct their eyes towards God.

Many other essays were to follow *Le Milieu Divin*. Those which can, in view of their purpose, most appropriately be considered with *Le Milieu Divin* are *Le Coeur de la Matière* (1950) and *Le Christique* (1955). Both these, however, are much more concentrated, even though they cover a much wider field. *Le Coeur de la Matière* has a frankly autobiographical flavour, and in it the 'psychological' point of view is dominant. In *Le Christique* Père Teilhard was trying to concentrate his whole teaching in the final form it had arrived at. He does this in a systematic form and from a point of view that he calls 'energetic'. In writing each of these, he still had *Le Milieu Divin* in mind, so much so that when he refers to them he speaks as though they might have been second and third versions of the original work.[47] Nevertheless, his intention was not that they should supplant the 'mystical' point of view of the *Milieu*, but should express 'the same fundamental vision': the vision that he always found if he looked deeply into himself, always 'exactly the same', to be contemplated 'with the same sense of wonder'.[48] Père Teilhard never followed up his plan of rewriting *Le Milieu Divin* itself under the new title of *Sacrement du Monde*. His intention had been to elucidate a number of points that he now felt that he saw more clearly or 'in a slightly different light'.[49] These new changes of emphasis, however, will emerge from later writings we shall have occasion to quote. Even allowing for them, what Père Teilhard once wrote in answer to a friend's inquiries still remains true: '*Le Milieu Divin* is precisely me.'[50]

Chapter 3

THREE MAIN LINES OF FORCE

Like every powerful work, *Le Milieu Divin* suggests count-less different lines of thought, that present themselves to our reflection as so many paths to be followed. We cannot hope to follow them all, nor to cover every idea the book contains, nor even to sum up its development or condense its substance. A number of points will emerge more precisely as we proceed. In this chapter we may confine ourselves to pointing out three main lines of force, of particular importance;[1] and these may serve to correct for us three misconceptions that today enjoy a considerable vogue. Thereby, in its very boldness, the traditional character of Père Teilhard's thought will be apparent.

1. In any number of expositions of Christianity, treatises, exhortations and programmes, the work of Jesus Christ and his Church is presented as hardly more than the means of en-suring for the human race some modicum of 'happiness' on our planet. Men dream of 'a better world': an admirable dream, indeed. But they seem to make it the ultimate end of the Creation and Redemption. There is a readiness to admit—somewhat illogically, perhaps—that to achieve this there must be an *élite* of devoted men, strangers to any egoism and armed with all the virtues of the Gospel. But the effort to reflect on the destiny of man and the universe is hardly carried beyond that point. The problems of social organization are, indeed, grave; they are urgent; they present the Christian conscience with more than one imperative demand, to which no man can be deaf. But if we allow these problems to hypnotize us, our faith may well be thereby distorted. Is the Gospel made to make the world comfortable for us, or only to be practised ultimately in a city that has become the ideal city? Too prag-matic a concern for man's future overshadows both the present need for the absolute at every moment of our existence and

the thought of an eternal beyond all time. Anyone who abandons himself, without counterbalancing considerations, to such concern tends to confuse, as Lammenais did, 'the transformation of society' with 'the establishment of the kingdom of God'.

This tendency is common to all ages, but today its threat is particularly serious. With the majority, no doubt, it is less a matter, by the grace of God, of real confusion or exclusion than of oversight. At the same time it is regrettable that there should be such a contentment with truths that are too incomplete, too hasty or ill-ordered. The Abbé Jules Monchanin, who was in touch with Père Teilhard, has rightly denounced 'this reversal of perspective, by which the Church is taken to be finally directed towards the world, instead of the world towards the Church'.[2] In fact, it sometimes seems as though the divine teaching of Jesus Christ and his work itself were simply a recipe to be used to achieve a purely human result. It seems, too, as though people were afraid to face the ultimate problem in its full rigour, inescapable though it is—the problem that dominates everything—as if men feared to see universal death looming over the horizon. In thought, we remain within the limits of this world, of which we are told, nevertheless, that 'it passes away'; and because we have not from the beginning looked at the world in its essential relation to what is beyond the world, our view of it and at the same time our view of man remains superficial.

This, indeed, is a state of affairs hardly calculated to ensure even the temporal happiness of man. Père Teilhard, on the other hand, had the courage boldly to face the ultimate end, and to appraise everything in its light. He had the courage to say again and again—'in season and out of season'—that 'the term towards which the earth is moving lies not merely beyond each individual thing but beyond the totality of things'.[3] He states with urgency the problem of the ultimate end of each being and of the world: an end that must be at once dissolution and transition, death and transfiguration. His whole line of thought, pursued in the light of faith, culminates in an 'expectation of the Parousia'.[4] Realizing, as we all do, that 'since Jesus was born, and grew to his full stature, and died', the world has remained outwardly unchanged, that it has not reached a state of rest but 'that everything has continued to move forward' just as before, he concludes, again as every believer concludes, that this is 'because Christ is not yet fully formed'[5]. Such a conclusion by no means leads him to under-estimate the value of human action. What he wishes to do, on the contrary, is to rouse us from the spiritual torpor induced by too short-term action. 'Expectation,' he says, 'is the supreme Christian function . . . successors to Israel, we Christians have been charged with keeping the flame of desire ever alive in the world. Only twenty centuries have passed since the Ascension. What have we made of our expectancy?'[6] Père Teil-hard's thought, accordingly, is essentially eschatological. In this it never varied, and it is no surprise, in the year of his death, to find him writing in his retreat notes, 'I am going to meet him who comes.' Proper attention has not always been given to his views on the natural and terrestrial future of man, as developed in his writings that deal with the philosophy of science; others have confused all forms of eschatological thinking with the cataclysmic mentality. In both cases the re-sult is a complete misunderstanding by which, at times, Père Teilhard is taken to stand in direct opposition to eschatological thinkers. It is true, indeed, that he rejects 'the short-term an-ticipations' of certain 'modern apocalyptics', seeing in them only an 'outbreak of illuminism'.[7] Nevertheless, his eyes are constantly fixed on the ultimate consummation. He continually bears in mind the 'ultimate term of the Historic', and never, it would seem, ceases to ask, with St. Augustine, whether 'any end can await us other than to attain the Kingdom that will have no end'.[8]

Thus it is that, precisely because he looks beyond the world, he can already distinguish in the heart of the world the *Milieu Divin*.

2. To the believer who lives by his faith, this world is not one-dimensional. It has a mysterious background. It is not opaque, but ever increasingly transparent. Here Père Teilhard coincides with one of Newman's favourite themes. He was very fond of Newman, and when in Oxford looked for any-thing connected with him;[9] he admires the 'breadth, freshness, and realism' of his views, with which his own mystical attitude

gave him a kinship. Everything in this world, things and events, and human relationships, had for Père Teilhard a sacramental character. When some years later he was thinking of treating the subject of *Le Milieu Divin* with a slightly different emphasis, he proposed, as mentioned earlier, to give the new essay the title 'Sacrament of the World'; and if we wish fully to understand what was in his mind here, we must take it as what it actually is, a contemplation that derives all its luminosity from prayer.[10] For the Christian whose eyes are open, there is nothing in the world that does not make God manifest. Everything in the world can lead to God, the 'ultimate point' upon which everything converges: everything and, more particularly in the first place, what constitutes our constant daily portion—work. And this does not mean only the (humanly speaking) specially privileged work that makes a man feel that he is 'making history', as some are immoderately fond of putting it; or, again, makes him feel that he is helping to raise higher the continually growing structure of science. It means all human work without distinction, from the humblest household task to the most spiritual activity. In this order, no instrument is specially favoured: God 'is at the tip of my pen, my pick, my brush, my needle, of my heart and of my thought'.[11] 'God awaits us every instant in our action, in the work of the moment'; his 'all-embracing Providence shows me, every moment, throughout the day's vicissitudes, the next step to take, the rung to climb'. Even more does 'the fire of the divine Presence' kindle those who are united in charity. In the phrase of St. Ignatius—and as a Jesuit, at home in the *Spiritual Exercises*, Père Teilhard, we feel, was impregnated by his spirit—the believer concentrates on the only thing that matters: to see God in all things, in every being; to see him 'wherever he may be'.[12] He looks for God in every action and in every love—and yet nothing is God to him save God alone.

In so far as the Spirit of God gives him the 'light of heaven', it already becomes for him, in a vision that we may call mystical but that is none the less a vision of faith, 'perceptible and attainable in the crystalline transparency of beings. But the Christian wants only this light; and if the light is extinguished . . . then even the most precious substance is only ashes in his sight'.[13] He has found the 'way of divinizing everything',[14] without being satisfied with anything other than God. While others disperse their interests and let their minds roam abroad, he recollects himself and is subject neither to the constraining complexities of affections nor to aimless dissipation of thought.[15] He has read the secret of the world, for it is not hidden in any part of the world: it is 'wherever we contrive to see the transparency of the world', and 'the heights' where God dwells 'are not inaccessible mountains but a more profound sphere of things'.[16] Henceforth, it is no longer that he knows, with abstract knowledge, but *sees*, so to speak, 'with the unclouded vision of contemplative faith, that nothing exists, in an absolute mode, outside God'.[17] Such a man, in short has come to dwell in the divine Milieu, the mysterious other side to the universe, which has nothing in common with the so-called 'astral milieu' or other pseudo-mystical fantasies of those 'who look for mystery at the phenomenal level'; this Milieu 'is involved in things and at the same time higher than things'.[18] It is 'the universal Milieu', which, in its entirely spiritual vastness, is 'in reality a centre'. In other words, he has found—still to continue seeking him—Him for whom he had, before he could give Him a name, acquired a 'zest' and 'irresistible need',[19] 'the Uniquely sufficing',[20] 'the unique principle of activity', 'the one thing that is necessary',[21] beyond the transparencies in which he is mirrored.[22]

It is from this that such a believer derives that 'sort of higher indifference (a passionate indifference) that comes from clinging, in all things, to what is above all'. From this comes the 'surrender to' and 'constant communion with, the divine will', which sustains the most active life and brings about its internal unity in the complex network of events it is involved in.[23] It calls for constant practice and effort to attain this position. Unlike those literary mystics who, with too little sacrifice, give themselves the feeling that they are 'in touch with the divine' the believer cannot escape 'the inexorable necessity of renunciation'.[24] He can, indeed, for so his calling as a man demands, explore things, measure and conquer them; but it is always in order to 'extract from them, and refer to God, all the essence of beauty and spirituality they contain', nor does he ever do more than 'pass through them'. Thus it is 'God alone' that he passionately seeks 'in the heart of every substance and every action'.[25] We may put it another way and say that while he still attaches value 'to things', it is 'in absolute dependence on God's presence in them'.[26] He is immersed 'in the great, peace-giving, intensity of the divine Omnipresence'.[27]

If a man explains such matters to us, dealing with them again and again from different angles; if he succeeds in making them not only intelligible but what one might almost call tangible; if he can teach us to 'pass through' all things, with one's eyes fixed on the 'beyond' and the 'above'; if he holds out a brother's hand to help us across the sacred threshold of detachment even in the most deliberate use of things; if we may say all this of him, surely we must agree that he is a master of the spiritual life? Anyone who is familiar with the *Spiritual Exercises* of St. Ignatius will have no difficulty in recognizing in Père Teilhard's teaching an echo, enriched by modern overtones, of Ignatius's *Foundation*:[28] or more exactly, perhaps, a restatement or mystical transposition of it in the spirit of contemplation *ad amorem* in which the *Exercises* reach their peak.

Those who follow such a master will find that they are effectively protected against a second misconception which Père Teilhard often exposed: it is one that threatens so many deeply reflective souls, spontaneously mystical, who come to lose themselves in the object they divinize. Fortified by a purer and nobler experience, Père Teilhard forewarns such souls against the 'enchantments of the earth'.[29] He does not weaken nor constrict the enthusiasm that drives them on, as overhuman counsellors do: what he does is to prevent it from being bogged down. He saves it and frees it, and gives it added strength, by showing it its term. He offers them a true concept of Transcendence, which is not absence nor exteriority, but Presence that fills to overflowing and transfigures. More accurately, perhaps, and more forcibly than other writers who have used these same formulas, he shows them in God at once the Heart and the Beyond of all things; for in the convergent and dynamic universe of his concept, the Heart lies beyond, and the Beyond lies at the heart of all. By making them share, through a spiritual contagion, in this feeling, he makes them understand that 'the effort required of our fidelity must be consummated *beyond a total transformation* of ourselves and of everything surrounding us'.[30] It is a stimulating prospect, a vision at once austere and warm: a principle of serene activity that can never be a prey to discouragement. 'The vast setting of the universe might be engulfed or wither away or be taken from me by death without my joy being diminished. Were creation's dust, which is vitalized by a halo of energy and glory, to be swept away, the substantial Reality wherein every perfection is incorruptibly contained and possessed would remain intact: the rays would be drawn back into their Source, and there I should still hold them all in a close embrace.'[31]

3. The question now arises whether an effort is all that is required, even one stimulated and sustained by grace, one carried to its peak of 'Christian perfection'.[32] Is nothing required but action carried out in a spirit of holiness? Such a belief would be a further misconception. It is common to many men to good will, sincere but as yet by no means fully spiritual Christians. It is the specifically modern form of the Pelagian error, which may be called the activist misconception.[33] It has often been said that *Le Milieu Divin* expounds a 'mysticism of action'. While that is partly true, as a complete assessment it is utterly false. The first part of the book has the resonance of a hymn to action, exalting its human value when understood in a Christian sense. Père Teilhard, however, is quick to warn the reader. With action, even when perfectly pure and detached, the divine Milieu is only at the 'first stage of its development'; at this stage 'we are still only half-way along the road which leads to the mountain of the Transfiguration'.[34] To tend towards God alone through all things, is not truly to attain him. A higher price has to be paid for the divinization we are promised, and 'all that human activity can do' in this field 'is humbly to make itself ready and accept'.[35]

What we now have to do (and in this the whole tradition of spirituality is with us, restated all the better by being expressed in less familiar and freer terms) is to recognize in ourselves, as coming from God, the part that should be played by 'passivities': it is a more important part than that played by activities —'immeasurably the wider and deeper part',[36] and the most indispensable. While there are indeed 'forces that cause the earth to grow greater' there are others that cause it 'to die'; and these latter, which always have the last word, are at work in each one of us. Both have to be accepted; both have to be passionately loved; but the latter more than the former, because they alone have the power to carry us 'to the bosom of God'.[37]

There are, no doubt, 'passivities of growth' which we accept without distress, because we can see that they pave the way for or maintain our own effort, and make it bear fruit. More menacing to our nature and at the same time more fundamental are the 'passivities of diminishment'. These are our 'true' passivities. On all sides we come up against obstacles, and everything continually ends in a setback. Life would indeed present a sorry picture, if we did not look beyond the external appearance. 'Man is always torn by the separations which set distance between bodies, which set the impossibility of mutual understanding between souls, which set death between lives. Moreover, at every minute he must lament that he cannot pursue and embrace everything within the compass of a few years. Finally, and not without reason, he is incessantly distressed by the crazy indifference and the heartbreaking dumbness of a natural environment in which the greater part of individual endeavour seems wasted or lost, where the blow and the cry seem stifled on the spot, without awakening any echo.'[38] It can finally be summed up in one word: Death. Death is the shadow that makes all existence a gift to be dreaded.[39] It is the total obstacle, the impassable boundary, the final checkmate. And we know that when it has destroyed us, it will swallow up our universe and destroy with it anything that might remain of our work.

Nevertheless, while all this is 'the source of most mysterious and most profound pain', for the Christian it is still only 'a surface desolation'. We must break through superficial appearance, and 'establish ourselves in the divine *milieu*'.[40] We must accept all these hostile forces in a spirit of faith and so convert them into 'blessed passivities'.[41] We must understand that 'everything that happens is worthy of adoration'.[42] Like the Apostle Peter who in his old age 'was carried where he did not wish to go', let us, when we have done our best, gladly allow ourselves to be led unresistingly by what seems to us to be simply 'the determinism of the world', but is in reality 'the hand of God upon us'.[43] We must realize that the soul beings to know God only when it is *really* forced to suffer diminishment in him.[44] We must agree to place ourselves under 'the dominating arms of the cross' and there remain; hidden in it, we must learn to understand 'the constructive value of suffering'; we must discover 'with extreme intensity, the force that raises up the world'; all that has to be done is to 'release' this force.[45] We must value above all what death is converted into 'by the influence of the divine omnipotence coming down upon our faith'. Jesus Christ conquered death 'not only by suppressing its evil effects, but by reversing its sting'. Henceforth, 'its fatal power to decompose and dissolve will be harnessed to the most sublime operations of life'. It is death, and death alone, the supreme passivity, that—once it is not only suffered but accepted and loved—will finally 'make the very depths of our being appropriately receptive'; it will bring us into the state that no activity could achieve for us, 'the state organically needed if the divine fire is to descend upon us'.[46]

Chapter 4

CHRISTIAN OPTIMISM

If we ask whether this doctrine is one of optimism, we must answer that it is, in the sense that it is a conquering of pessimism. There is, however, a vast difference, all the difference in the world, between pessimism so overcome and natural optimism. To fail to distinguish between the two would argue a great lack of human, and still more of Christian, experience. Optimism, at least when it is initially present without facing any dilemma or answering any question, 'can avoid being naïve only at the cost of becoming hypocritical'. With this, Teilhard's thought has nothing in common. The more we consider it the more (as M. André Rousseaux has said)[1] do we find that it is governed by the theological virtues. If, taking the final balance, Teilhard seems to be resolutely and triumphantly optimistic, his optimism is 'Christian'; and when we speak of 'Christian optimism' the words should not be given too facile an interpretation, positive though their content certainly must be. The optimism that Père Teilhard professed and constantly retained in spite of everything represented in him a victory of Faith.

Nevertheless, in this connexion a legend—the word is Père Teilhard's—has come to be accepted, and it is fairly commonly believed that the 'optimistic' views he taught are the fantasies of a man who paid little attention to the hard facts of life, or were the fruit of a happy temperament, or the effusion of a noble soul that could not bear to look evil in the face:[2] unless, indeed they were unconsciously dictated to him by memories, too hastily transposed to a new context, of his religious training. Even some intelligent writers have come to believe this. For example, in the Abbé Henri Bars's little book on *Trois Vertus-Clefs*, we read, in the chapter on hope: 'Père Teilhard asked too much from anthropology, because he had first instilled into it a strong dose of Christian hope. One of his scientific colleagues came close to suggesting this when he said one needed theological hope if one was to concur with Teilhard de Chardin's optimistic inferences.'[3] Later, we shall try to distinguish the element of truth in that verdict. If we examine it more closely, we shall find that only a single passage is quoted in support, as representing in Père Teilhard's thought too facile a conclusion from what he claims to be scientific evidence. This passage comes not from the *Phenomenon of Man* or some similar work, but from *Le Milieu Divin*. Here Père Teilhard was making no claim to base himself on scientific anthropology, nor to be making inferences, for the latter in fact were paralogisms or extrapolations. He was speaking quite explicitly in the name of theological faith and hope: he was referring to Christ's work, and the virtue of his 'painful Incarnation' which prepares the world for the day of the Parousia.[4]

Whatever over-hasty interpreters may also say, the consideration of evil in all its forms holds a prominent position in Père Teilhard's work. As early as 1915 he was writing a study of evil.[5] We shall deal a little later with the problem of moral evil and sin. Suffering was a subject often treated by Père Teilhard, and it would be no exaggeration to say that it lies at the heart of his thought. Earlier, we quoted a passage from *Le Milieu Divin*, which, removed from its context and expressed in a different style, might have been attributed to some gloomy existentialist. Others could be quoted—for example that in which he meditates on the misery of Job. In 'The Mass on the World' he speaks of 'pouring into the chalice of Christ the bitterness of all separations, of all limitations, and of all sterile fallings-away'.[6] An essay, dated 26 February 1927, examines at length the fact of suffering as 'the evil of the multitude': 'Multiplicity of the flesh, dualism of human nature, the very complexity of the soul in which, at its highest peak, the dust of a world that as yet has hardly taken on solidity, shudders and shakes: the misery of our own personal multitude within us . . . and the misery, too, of the universal multitude around us—a misery so overwhelming and shattering that it drives to the verge of despair any being that experiences it.

'Tired of irretrievably exhausting his impetus against the

walls of an opaque body—and of never finding in sensible experience (always superficial) *the secret of anything*—and of
being unable to find anywhere, in the dark places of his soul,
the way through that leads from one mind to another—he begins to sigh for death, for death, maybe, will give back mo-
bility to his soul and restore its initial community.

'We carry within us, as a continuous deep vibration of
which our individual agonies and intoxications are passing
harmonics, the dull, gnawing *pain of the individuation* by
which the separation of beings is maintained and their plurality persists.'[7]

Although the expression is still somewhat clumsy—so much
so that Père Teilhard himself admitted that it 'may even seem
Manichean'[8]—what he is describing in that passage is a profound feeling of the sorrow inherent in man's condition as we
know it. It is a feeling that goes far beyond even the most
acute perception of all that the common feeling of men calls
suffering. For this sorrow is tied up with 'individual' existence;
it is one of the aspects of consciousness, and the two necessarily grow in step with one another. This, we know, was the
basis, exaggeratedly real, of Buddha's teaching.[9] Père Teilhard did not proceed from this, as did Buddha, to the denial
or rejection of personality, the positive principle of which he
was later, on the contrary, at pains to establish. Here he is
chiefly alive to what constitutes the shadows of our present
situation, the individuality in which he wishes to consider, like
so many mystics, only the negative aspect. Even in his *Esquisse
d'un Univers personnel*, written in 1936, he emphasized the
sombre side of existence. 'True sorrow,' he wrote, 'came into
the world with man, when, for the first time, a reflective consciousness found that it could be a witness of its own diminishment.' 'Man's disquiet,' he said again, 'is linked with the very
appearance of reflection,' and if it is true that we are moving
towards a type of reflection that is becoming continually more
'socialized', then it cannot but drive deeper into each one of us
a 'fundamental anguish'. A universe in process of 'involution'
and 'interiorization' is also, and 'in virtue of the same process',
a universe that meets pain and suffering.[10] Much later still,
we have these moving words: 'To a perfectly clear-sighted ob-

server, who watched it for a long time from a great height, our planet, the Earth, would at first appear blue from the oxygen in its atmosphere; then green from the vegetation that clothes it; then luminous—and ever more luminous—from the intensification of thought on its surface: but it would also appear dark—and ever more dark—from the suffering that grows in quantity and acuteness in time with the rise of consciousness as the centuries pass by.

'Yes, the more Man becomes man, the more deeply engrained—in his flesh, in his nerves, in his mind—and the more serious becomes the problem of Evil: evil that has to be understood, and evil that has to be suffered.'[11]

Such passages are obviously no rhetorical flights nor lessons in academic philosophy. Their essential note is found again in countless confidential communications: 'The more conscious life is, the more full of pain.'[12] 'What a strange and sad thing life is, isn't it?'[13] 'I feel it more and more, the world, is a great and terrible thing.'[14] This was for Père Teilhard a fundamental theme; it was the background of melancholy and nostalgia that he shared with so many great souls;[15] it was the underlying anguish that he was too circumspect always to show but could not always hide.[16] Those who are at all familiar with Père Teilhard's life will know what a tapestry of trials was unceasingly woven upon the framework of that basic distress. Among many others, we need only quote this passage from a letter written from Tientsin on New Year's Eve, 1926: 'I have been watching, with what was half melancholy, the last sun of 1926 setting, a ball of red, over the marshy flatness of the Cheli. I feel that life is rapidly running down; and at the same time, I count myself happy that that is so (since it is the only possible end to certain conflicts). I often feel afraid, because the further I go on, the further the horizon towards which we are going becomes shrouded in mist. Is that again my own small way of bearing the sorrow, that is to say redeeming the doubts, of the world?'

With Albert Schweitzer Père Teilhard might well have said (though qualifying the adverb with some elucidations) 'the world is inexplicably mysterious and full of suffering'; but, again with Schweitzer, he would have been quick to add, with

more justifiable conviction: 'My knowledge is pessimistic, but
my willing and hoping are optimistic.'[17] With Claudel, too,
he could have said: 'What matters today's chaos and its distress, since it is the birth of another thing?'[18]

For Père Teilhard, then, suffering, 'that same suffering that
kills and decomposes, is necessary to the being in order that
it may live and become spirit . . . The mechanism of creation
demands it'. Nature itself 'lets us discern in her an almost
heart-rending effort towards light and consciousness'.[19] And
man cannot allow himself to be trapped in 'what brings immediate and facile satisfaction'. 'The whole of a first, pleasant
and tempting unification' must be shattered.[20] As for truth, it
'advances through minds that pay for its birth and growth, in
suffering'.[21] Even in the achieving of results that are still natural and terrestrial, there is nothing that so resembles a 'way of
the Cross' as the stages of progress in being or knowledge.[22]

'The harsh law of creation.' 'The painful waste-product of
the operation that forms us.' Emotionally, if we follow our
natural reaction, we cannot accept it without revulsion, for,
judging simply by experience, the term to which it leads us,
happy though it may appear to be or we may anticipate it to be
in the future, can be only a relative and impermanent term:
nor is it one that we can love. Thus every natural (as opposed
to supernatural) solution to the problem of happiness, if it
offers itself as a 'happy ending', has to face objections that are
'terribly, cruelly, just'.[23] Père Teilhard, it is true, reacted
against 'the existential fear'; he proclaimed his 'faith in the
future'.[24] He fought passionately against the scepticism of the
indifferent, of people who regard themselves as 'enlightened'
and of those who simply wished to follow the line of least resistance. He criticized the 'immobilism' of common sense and
routine, as he did all forms of cynical intelligence.[25] When
he was back in Paris in 1946, after those long years in Peking,
he stood up to the 'existentialist' wave that was then at its
height: and it may well be that some have judged him too exclusively in the light of his vigorous reactions at that time. He
rejected the pessimism of 'the experimental scientist who is
depressed by the rigidity of living forms and their violent
egocentrism', as he did that of the 'materialist who sees Man-

kind falling into decay, or caught in a physiological cleft stick between the contradictory tendencies of its vital organism and its brain'; nor would he accept 'religious pessimism' in which he saw a 'distortion' of Christianity. In short he rejected all forms of pessimism, whether secular or religious.[26] And this he did with increasingly firm conviction. On two occasions at least his writings were directly aimed against the pessimism of scientists. It was in reply to Sir James Jeans's 'completely despairing' *The Universe around us* that, in 1938, he wrote his *Esquisse d'un Univers personnel*; and it was with a similar desire to supply a cool and collected answer to M. Jean Rostand's short *Ce que je crois* that he composed his last essay in synthesis, 'The Singularities of the Human Species', which was published after his death, in 1955, in the *Annales de Paléontologie*.[27] He concluded by putting forward an 'optimistic structure of the Universe';[28] but while he constantly proclaimed his optimism, we must distinguish in what sense and under what conditions and at what cost he had made his decision.

In the first place we should look at the man himself: in finally adopting an optimistic attitude he was not following a natural bent. So far as the narrow limits of human experience allowed him to see, the future held no smile for him. He was more familiar with the 'charm, always tinged with melancholy, that makes us look back to what is past'; he found that he had to resist 'the bitter-sweet tendency to become emotional about the past'. His heart ached at the thought of the number of things that 'were threatened by the remodelling of society in which we are caught up'. He had no illusions about 'the first wave of enslavement, of levelling-down, of ugliness and catastrophes' that accompanied 'the rise of the collective'. Already, he said, 'it strikes us in the face'. It was only by a great effort that he overcame these feelings and said 'the future is finer than any past'[29]; and it was only by faith that he maintained against them 'the vigorous conviction that happiness and life lie ahead of us, in God'.[30] That last remark leaves no more to be said; but it will be worth our while to examine, with Père Teilhard, its content in detail, and see just what he meant by 'future' and 'ahead of us'.

He despised and was revolted by the 'dingy milleniarisms'—those visions of the future dear to so many hawkers of ideologies—too ready to play the demagogue, 'in which a golden age (i.e. an age of abundance) makes a boringly unattractive appearance'.[31] He criticized more than one form of 'neo-humanism' for failing to distinguish between the grand idea of a 'maturing of Mankind' and these pitiful fantasies. He went so far as to castigate, in this sort of longed-for 'euphoria', in this 'expectation of a well-being that is confused with fuller-being', 'an atmosphere as penetrating and unhealthy as that of the theosophists' dissolution'.[32] The true maturing that the facts seemed to him to justify us in anticipating, appears in the prospects he opens to us not as a state of 'rest' but as one of 'tension'. He was well aware, moreover, that to rely too much on 'man's goodness' is to expose ourselves to 'bitter disappointments'. Reflecting on the manufacture of the hydrogen bomb, 'the fruit of the physicists' admirable tenacity', he 'bows', though 'with regret, to this evidence that War is still more effective than Peace in forcing men to think.'[33] He unmistakably affirmed his scepticism of the 'evolutionary humanism' of his friend, the non-Christian scientist Julian Huxley.[34] In the 'world's astonishing adventure' he saw a drama, in the course of which man advances only through successive crises, each step forward being paid for by 'a vast series of disorders and sufferings'. Each crisis, with the hazards it holds, is more truly dramatic 'than all the self-centred and morbid fancies of contemporary existentialism'; finally, the progress achieved will be no true progress unless spirit finally emerges from the adventure as the undisputed victor.[35]

Even when once he believed that 'heart-breaking Entropy' had been neutralized (how, we shall see later), he still saw Evil appearing: in many different forms 'it seeps out through every nook and cranny, through every joint and sinew of the system in which I have taken my stand'.[36] He experienced that 'essential distress characteristic to a particle lost in the universe', a distress that 'makes human wills founder daily under the crushing number of living things and of stars'.[37] He shared with Baudelaire a sickening disgust with an earthly experience that is essentially superficial.[38] Nothing that is hu-

man could allay in him 'the pain of isolation'.[39] He had 'a
sharp and concrete "realization" (he uses the English word)
of the utter vanity of human effort unless there is both a natural and a supernatural *emergence* of the universe towards
some immortal consciousness'.[40] At the same time, he felt
with equal force 'how much *in itself* exploration of the earth
sheds no light on, points out no *issue* to, life's most fundamental problems.[41] 'I feel,' he continues, 'as though I am going round and round an immense problem without getting to
the heart of it. And I know, too, that the wider the problem
seems to grow before my eyes, the more clearly I see that its
solution can be sought only in a "faith" beyond all experience.
We must break through and go beyond appearances; never
perhaps more than now has their veil seemed to me so "without seam".'[42]

'Which is the right way?'[43]

'By what road can we escape?'[44]

We can already see the fundamental temptation beginning
to assert itself: It is the temptation to lose heart, and in it lies
the great threat to Evolution. Père Teilhard spoke of it so
often with such emphasis and was at such pains to neutralize
it, that he must have experienced it personally, and painfully.
Will man be able to preserve 'the passion for growth'? Will
he even retain the mere 'will to survive'? 'No external pressure,
however powerful, could prevent him from throwing up the
sponge, even with an abundance of energy still available, were
he, unhappily, to lose interest in, or despair of, the movement
that is urging him on.'[45]

'When it reflects upon itself, the consciousness of the individual acquires the formidable property of being able to foresee the future, in other words, to foresee death. And at the
same time it recognizes that to collaborate any longer with
life's effort would become psychologically impossible, if something—that something being what is best in its work—could not
succeed in escaping total destruction . . . As applied to the
individual the idea of *total* death may not, when first entertained, prove too great a shock; but extend it to the whole of
mankind in its unity, and our minds revolt.'[46] There is no
future of man that can maintain our will to live unless, when

the ultimate end is reached, there is 'some issue that opens into indefinite freedom'.[47] In this lies the whole formidable problem of Action. From the objection itself, Père Teilhard extracts an initial, though not a complete answer, when he distinguishes within this power of despairing reflection a 'demand for irreversibility'; and it is in this sense that the Abbé Bars could speak of Père Teilhard's 'inferences'. The nature of these will have to be examined, and the reader may then judge their soundness. For the moment, two comments may help us to see the basis of Père Teilhard's optimism.

In the first place, by whatever method he concluded that this 'demand for irreversibility' is valid, the value he attributed to it is not affirmed as a proposition of impersonal metaphysics. However rational he may have wished it to be, it still remained for him in the order of faith.[48] 'Faith in a meaning and a term for man's restless activity'; faith 'in the meaning assumed by all things, even diminishments, in the eyes of the man who believes in God's universal animation of all that happens'; faith, he adds, which 'provides the only issue'; 'blind and absolute faith'; faith to which, 'at all costs, we must cling.'[49] 'Confidence in the world' can be restored only by 'faith in a supreme centre of personalization, of convergence, and of cohesion, in which alone salvation for the Universe can be conceived'.[50] Secondly (and the passages just quoted have already hinted at this), no belief that is of the purely natural order, however firmly based it may be in reason, can be sufficient at this juncture. It could never, Père Teilhard believed, succeed in completely overcoming practical pessimism in real life. For it is not enough to understand the necessity of suffering: if we are willingly to accept suffering, nothing can take the place of the 'astonishing Christian revelation', which shows us that, 'provided it be accepted *in the right spirit*, it can be transformed into an expression of love and a principle of union'. There is, then, nothing Utopian, no unwarranted inference, no giving way to an instinctive desire to escape too harsh a reality, in this recourse—which has reason, too, behind it—to the light of supernatural faith. But, 'when the believer has penetrated into Christ, the world loses for him its multiplicity, its burden, its harshness and bitterness. Flesh and spirit still suffer—but

the faith of the sufferer discloses in his very suffering the
prodigious spiritual energy generated by the Cross'. On the
other hand, 'once my faith, unhappily, grows weak, the light
is immediately extinguished, everything disintegrates'.[51] Père
Teilhard was entranced by 'the miracle, constantly renewed for
the last two thousand years, by which it is possible for suffering
to be Christified'. He gazes on the figure of the Crucified, he
hears his voice echoing 'from the depth of the night'.[52] He
listens, and believes that 'until they at last dissolve in a loftier
atmosphere, the sombre clouds that envelop us may be transfigured'.[53]

'Though the phenomena of the lower world remain the
same—the material determinisms, the vicissitudes of chance,
the law of labour, the agitations of men, the footfalls of death
—he who *dares* to believe reaches a sphere of created reality in
which things, while retaining their habitual texture, seem to
be made out of a different substance. Everything remains the
same so far as phenomena are concerned, but at the same
time everything becomes luminous, animated, loving.'[54]

It is not, however, simply a question of knowledge. The
believer must still pray, so that he may not succumb 'to the
temptation to curse the Universe and its Maker'.[55] What happens, in fact, is that in faith, a divine strength, along with light,
is transmitted to him. Strength is given him, not only to put
up with, but 'warmheartedly' to accept—even to desire and
almost beg for—what he would otherwise spontaneously turn
away from with loathing—because he thinks of the unsullied
fruit that it will bring him: 'Lord, in order that the spirit may
ever be resplendent in me, that I may not yield to the temptation that ever lies in wait for the overbold, and that I may
never forget that you alone are to be sought through all
things—you will send me, at times that you know best, privation and disappointments, and sorrow.'[56] He has continual
need for prayer, for if suffering and heart-rending are, as we
have seen, 'the harsh law of creation', they are also, and in
more subtle forms that call for a more interior and more active acceptance in the believer, the law of all moral life and of
all spiritual progress. Here again, 'every forward step' in this
spiritual journey brings with it an 'anguish', the perpetual

'anguish of feeling that there is a threat to what is most intimately one's own self'. At all levels there is always this 'pain of metamorphosis'.[57]

'To become unified and concentrated upon itself, the being must break many sensible attachments. To make itself one with others and give itself to them, it must encroach upon those intimate personal intellectual and emotional reserves that it most jealously guards. To enter into a higher life, by centring itself upon another self, it must destroy its own preliminary unity. This can mean only one thing, that at all levels of the formation of being, creative synthesis involves detachments—every aggregation being accompanied by a segregation. The moral effect is necessarily accompanied by suffering and sacrifice. That is why, in every moral condition, perfection is inseparable from suffering, and the highest life is attained through a dying. Death (which means disintegration) accompanies every change for better or worse. However, while in the case of some (which it leaves permanently disintegrated and diminished) the death is *ad mortem*, in the case of others (those it reintegrates as it disintegrates them) it is a transition (the only true issue) that leads to a new life.'[58]

Whether we regard that as optimism or not depends upon the meaning we attach to the word. We know that Père Teilhard accepted it unhesitatingly. He would even have it be an absolute.[59] But when he uses the word, it is seldom that the context does not make it perfectly clear that we cannot apply the term 'optimist' to him in an unacceptable sense. He welcomes the 'irresistible rise of a Christian optimism'; he says that he has 'made up his mind to fight to the bitter end for the birth and triumph of Christian optimism'.[60] We should note the adjective: for Père Teilhard it is the optimism that every Christian should profess. He explains it as 'the message and watchword, that he dreams of publishing far and wide'—as he wishes his Church herself to do—'after two thousand years, in a nativity of the universal Christ'.[61] For every individual, as for the whole of Mankind, this optimism is the confidence that comes from faith. 'I still can see only one answer: to keep pressing on, in ever-increasing faith.'[62] Had he not 'pulled himself together', he would sometimes have been tempted 'to abandon to its own sort of suicide this ridiculous world that destroys its finest products'.[63] However, he reacted against this tendency. Even the most painful trials in his personal life produced 'no bitterness', he confided to a friend on one of these distressing occasions, but simply a 'firm optimism, founded specifically on the vast and unique potentialities of God and the Gospel'.[64] Whenever a new blow fell or he seemed to be faced with an insoluble dilemma, he still hoped, he said, 'to overcome the obstacle *through the power* of optimism and fidelity'.[65] A month before his death he wrote, again, 'I am more optimistic than ever'—and this he said after reminding himself of 'the Presence of God'.[66] He had already said the same in *Le Milieu Divin*: we are enveloped in darkness, more charged with menace than promise: but for the Christian the darkness is lit up and animated by 'the divine Presence': 'The immense hazard and the immense blindness of the world are only an illusion to him who believes', and 'the more threatening and irreducible reality appears, the more firmly and desperately must we believe'.[67] Again, we should re-read this passage in a note-book in which, during one of his retreats, he put down his intimate thoughts: 'May the risen Christ keep me young, for the greater glory of God. Young—which means optimistic, active, smiling, clearsighted; because trials and old age lead to Him; because trials and old age will affect me only in so far as they bring me close to Him.'[68]

How, then, should we sum up Père Teilhard's optimism? No one, surely (no believer, that is), could reasonably see it as anything but a victory of Faith.

Chapter 5

MEDITATION ON DEATH

The total obstacle, the supreme check, the evil that more than any other horrifies man, is death. We have already seen the role attributed to death in *Le Milieu Divin*. Even if Père Teilhard had not treated the subject on many occasions in his other works, his treatment of it in the *Milieu* would in itself make us wonder when we read this comment (it comes from a writer whom one would be prepared to respect, but who seems deliberately to have adopted an over-controversial tone), 'Verily, I say unto you, let us warm ourselves and take comfort in the breath of Evolution'. And the writer goes further, emphasizing his irony in a note '. . . for tomorrow we die. The irony of this, however, comes from the Wisdom of God (Isaiah, 22. 13) not from Père Teilhard. Perhaps, though, God's point of view is too "individual" or "imaginative" for Evolutionism'.[1]

Tomorrow, indeed, we die. Père Teilhard did not wait for this ironic reminder, on the morrow of his death, to reflect on that truth—and, first of all, to *feel* it:

'The more we look into the depths of ourselves, the more does our introspection multiply, to our horror, the bonds of the Incurable and the Irreparable. Necessity snakes in from all sides to attack our bodies and our souls. Every day it builds up a further network of even more numerous nervures in the initially youthful and plastic tissue of the future. And all these lines of rigidity have a common integument: the fundamental obligation imposed on us of living without having wished to do so; and they all converge upon one and the same inescapable centre, Death.

'Seen in the future death is the epitome of all that terrifies and dements us, and the common element that underlies them all . . . One must have passed under the shadow of death if one is to realize all the loneliness, danger and terror that surrounds our advance into the Future. . . . Those who have not been within a hair's-breadth of death have never completely seen what lay before them. Others—those whom an overpowering terror has forced to raise their eyes and look time straight in the face; have often succumbed to fear even in the middle of their passage between the abysses on either hand; and it can happen that they are so overcome that they feel they must be lost.'[2]

That passage dates from October 1918. In its somewhat romantic form, common to much of Père Teilhard's youthful work, it is not difficult to recognize the still vibrant echo of his war experiences. Some thinkers of that period, Léon Brunschvicg, for example, were at pains to exclude any existential element from their systems, as though they might be guilty of some indecency. Père Teilhard, on the contrary, introduced his personal experiences into the fabric of his intellectual reflection; what was more, death became one of its central themes, so much so that there would be no exaggeration in presenting the whole body of his work as one long meditation on death.

This meditation was foreshadowed in a 'fantasy' dated 15 January 1918. 'Rather a crazy fantasy', he said many years later,[3] but nevertheless 'a serious one', echoing an original subtitle. It is a sort of vision, or apocalyptic poem with many overtones, which proves that our species has not entirely lost its capacity to create myths. It is an astonishing piece of work, to which the heading 'for tomorrow we die' would be far more appropriate than it is to the controversial article quoted at the beginning of this chapter. It is entitled 'La Grande Monade' and was published in 1960 in the second of the *Cahiers Pierre Teilhard de Chardin*.[4] The editor rightly describes these ten short pages as a 'generating cell', and it would be well worth while to provide them with a minutely detailed commentary. Over thirty years later, Père Teilhard himself quoted 'La Grande Monade' as evidence of his discovery, during the Great War, of 'the organicity of collective magnitudes'.[5] Here we shall confine ourselves to what is, in fact, its dominating theme, Death—collective Death.

It is at night, during the war, and a sentry sees the moon rising 'over the crest of the neighbouring trenches'. 'Hail, symbolic star!' As he watches it, he thinks to himself that the star which bears us, like the moon he is watching, detached itself long ago in space; and then that, after long ages, man one day appeared on it; in a heroic campaign, man gradually extended the strands of his network over the whole surface of the globe. A series of continually more serious crises marked his progress, but the time came when the human mass formed one single bloc. This was when the fluid mass 'set'; and from this resulted the 'great Monad' (the first name for the Noosphere). It is this great Monad that the narrator now sees rising 'above the torn and blackened earth'. He watches it ascending in glory. He hears the cry of triumph that rises from all these elements that have at last found unity. Before his eyes, man's earth is celebrating the unity it has won. But what thoughts does this arouse in the mind of the sentry? (By a tacit fiction, God is still absent from this universe.)

'. . . And I myself felt fear, and dizziness seized hold of me, when, gauging the narrow limits within which the radiant globe was enclosed, I suddenly became conscious of the uncurable isolation in which the glory of Mankind is lost.

'Hitherto, men have always lived in the shadow of human realities greater than themselves . . . That evening, when I saw the single solid unit in which we are now all on the verge of being included, I had the impression of *emerging* and standing outside our race, and of overlooking a closed whole; and I felt as though all of us, clinging together, were floating away into the void . . .

'Man has man to be his companion. Mankind is *alone*. I saw the frontiers of Mankind; I saw the blackness and emptiness that surrounds the Earth.'

There is no denial, then, of progress. Its decisive step is even envisaged as coming tomorrow: and this is no imaginary vision, but a serious prophecy. Even during the 'great schism' of the world war, 'the plan of a universal civilization' is taking shape. Men are going to be proud of the work they have done. They are going to give themselves up to worshipping the power they have tamed. Their song of triumph is already echoing through the heavens. But Père Teilhard remains calm and unmoved. He looks further ahead, and he sees that already it will not be long before the great Monad will know 'the anguish of feeling itself shut in'. As yet there has been no catastrophe. For the thinking Monad, final death has not yet come into sight. But already, from seeing itself now drifting helplessly into the spiritual void, from feeling heavy upon itself the 'burden of a final and total isolation', heavier than any cataclysm, is being born a distress that is worse than death. Would any 'optimist' have read this in our future?

Supposing, however, that to escape this anguish, Mankind succeeds in finding some end for itself; supposing that it 'can attain the idea of a specific and integral *human effort*, in which all its members co-operate. Let us suppose—or hope —that, conscious of their solitude, men finally 'begin to love one another'[6]—'unless they rend one another', adds our prophet, though for the moment he leaves that hypothesis aside . . . Then, indeed, the single-minded star rises over the horizon; then, the disc of the great Monad concentrates and grows bright in the sky, and follows its unfaltering path straight to the zenith. This time, triumph is indeed at hand. But at that very moment, the first picture, the real picture, again forces itself upon the dreamer as he awakes—the moon over the trenches. Again it is the moon that rises and forces us to look upon its dead face:

'When the last spasms that are now convulsing civilization seem to our descendants as distant and irrelevant as the invasion of this corner of France by the first nomads seem to us— then, O Moon, you will rise over a Mankind that has concentrated on its ideal of progress, as tonight you rise over these smoking trenches—the same moon that will rise over our great-grandchildren. And over the living who, their day's work done, are wrapt in sleep, as over those who keep watch at night, you will shed your sad smile.

'Pale, icy, moon, will those who then look on you, men living in the fulness of their strength on this ageing earth, will they understand the final meaning of your speechless face?

'The ascetic sets before his eyes the funereal picture of a whitened skull.

'What does your wan face, burnt-out star, hold up for all

ages to see, tell us again, if not that Mankind grows, fettered to a corpse?

'Work, you seem to be telling us, work to your utmost, O men, to make your dwelling lovely and a fit habitation, throw yourselves passionately into the search for what is hidden and the creation of beauty. For what awaits you, too, you and your works, is the frozen immobility of my rigid shell.'

There are, perhaps, two ways of understanding this silent discourse. 'Is it a challenge, O Moon, implacable mirror of our future, that you offer us, or is it rather our final lesson that we should read?'

If it is a challenge, surely Mankind should accept it. We shall force our barriers, we shall launch our ship on the ocean of space and let the earth sink behind us. We shall, if need be, migrate from planet to planet. From star to star, as they begin to burn out, we shall carry the flame of life. But how will this profit us? Could the last star be less doomed to death than our earth? 'What Titan would prevent Matter from continuing its inexorable contraction and closing in around us? The day will come when the Earth too, like a huge fossil, will sink back into one bleached mass. There will be no more movement on its surface, and in it all our bones will be held.'[7]

'It is not a challenge, then, to a mad duel that comes down to us from the heavens when the nights are clear. . . . It is a final warning.' There is but 'one single issue towards the fuller life, and that is Death'. It is the acceptance of Death, through the trust we put in the Author of life:

'Like a haze that trembles and vanishes, a small portion of released spirit rises up and evaporates around the Earth: it is the soul of the dead. The adult and mature spirit of the great Monad will have to follow the same road . . .

'The only true death, the good death, is a paroxysm of life. It is won by the desperate effort of the living to become more pure, more one, more tensely striving to break out of the place in which they are confined.

'Happy the World that is to end in ecstasy.'[8]

We cannot set limits in advance to man's cosmic exploits. The whole of space lies open to him.[9] But his release from death will never come about by his physical migration in space.

Spirit will have, without regret, to abandon the remains of life to space, and, when it is mature, escape to join not another visible star in which it would again be imprisoned, and which when its turn came would itself die, but the 'higher, boundless unity of the universe', the 'unique circle' that 'embraces the whole spirit and holds nothing prisoner'.

'O wonder-charged centre, O vast sphere, O God!'[10]

Here the suggestive power of the myth is derived to some extent from this perpetual transition from material space to a spiritual space: from the perception of visible things to the evocation of invisible realities. At the same time, Père Teilhard is conscious, when speaking of the latter, of the linguistic incoherence into which he is forced. How can one picture this sphere which is at the same time a centre? What is this circle that has no containing circumference and that embraces without imprisoning? And yet how could the divine reality be patient of representation? Were it possible to represent it, it would no longer be the wonder that it is. In such a context coherence expressed in terms of the senses would be a contradiction. Such a reality takes us outside our element. 'At the most, there are times when a breath, coming we know not whence, passes through our soul. . . . But, consider this—What could infinitesimal beings, dwelling on the molecules of our bodies, understand of our personal life, or even of the life of one of our cells?'[11] Of one thing, in any case, we can be certain: without this Being, as marvellous as it is incomprehensible, no *issue*, no 'emergence' is possible—there can be, as the Buddhists say, no 'door into the open'. Without it we are 'shut in'.[12] Without the reality of the living God, there is no prospect either for mankind or the individual other than total death.

'And our endeavour, carried to its fruitless limit, fades like a passing wrinkle.'[13]

Take away faith in God, and the only life that is left is full of hazard and lived in despair. There may be minds that believe that 'death appears as the hard-won victory of the species over the individual', and that can accept this without demur on the grounds that 'the individual is simply a generic, determined, being'.[14] To these Père Teilhard answers that so to sacrifice the individual to the species is to rob the species of its reality, and that its 'hard-won victories' can lead it only to its own defeat. It would be an acceptance of a ludicrous 'article of faith' to believe in 'an issue for the World' and 'a salvation for the individual', 'in the direction of some higher form to be attained by Mankind', if that higher form itself was necessarily ephemeral. Others, again, are not so lost in dreams of the future. Sometimes they 'bow to a fashionable agnosticism; sometimes they are attracted by the deceptive appeal of stoicism and the ideal of the most complete lack of self-interest. These imagine that they can accept without qualms the idea that the duration of thought upon the Earth is no more than momentary'. If, however, they can placidly envisage the defeat that the others could not bear to contemplate, it is because 'they delude themselves by never having got to the bottom of the meaning of the words "the total death of the Universe".'[15]

The growing pressure, then, of human totalization brings this effect with it: that, precisely in virtue of the clarity with which they see things, men are in danger, and continually more so, when they see that they are about to be 'caught up in' 'a single bloc', of being the victims of three 'essential fears': 'fear of being lost in a world so great and so full of indifferent or hostile beings that Humanity seems positively to have no more importance in it'; 'fear of being henceforth and for ever *reduced to immobility*' in a stabilized zoological group; and finally the supreme 'fear of being *shut in*, imprisoned, within an irremediably closed world in which, even if it were not lost or arrested at present, humanity could not help striking tomorrow, when it reaches the peak of its trajectory, against an impassable barrier of reversibility which would force it to fall backwards'. Such, then, is the fate to which the very progress of our consciousness would seem to condemn us more and more inevitably. 'Fear of not being able to make itself understood. Fear of no longer being able to move. Fear of not being able to get out. A triple fear betraying at the heart of each thinking element in the Universe the same obstinate wish to be distinguished, completed, saved.' It is a triple and at the same time a single wish, and the science of our day cannot dispel it. It can only, through its Godless bias, convert it into despair.[16]

After devoting much thought to 'this fascinating and deathly front line' of the war,[17] Père Teilhard constantly returned to this theme, so strongly did he believe that he could see in it some of the essential characteristics of man's condition, and that the feelings that it aroused were in a profound sense his own. He wished that he had the time to develop it in a book, of which he once wrote to a close friend that it would be 'rather like the book of his own life':

'I dream of a sort of "Book of the Earth", in which I would let myself write not as a Frenchman, nor as an element in any pigeonhole, but simply as a man, or as a "terrestrial". I would like to express the confidence, the ambitions, the fulfilment, and at the same time the disappointments, the anxieties, and the sort of dizzy confusion, of the man who becomes conscious of the destinies and interests of the whole Earth (of the whole of Mankind). I would not try in this book to reconcile my views with any of the currents of accepted ideas, but simply to express what I feel: I would like it to bring out my faith in human work and human unity—and my anger against the walls and ceilings that still divide up spiritual fragments whose destiny is to form one—and the disappointment we feel when we see ourselves imprisoned on a globe whose limited interest is becoming exhausted—and the anguish we know when we see ourselves alone, all together, in the midst of stellar space.'[18]

There would have been a natural sequel to the book he planned; and we have, in fact, its substance in papers that were actually written. For there are men—Christ's disciples—who proclaim themselves to be the bearers of a message or, what is more, the custodians of a force, that holds what is required to preserve faith in 'human work and human unity'. The issue, they say, has been revealed to them. They believe in the vivifying power of death. They do not pursue the chimera of some spatial or temporal liberation, but maintain that through Faith man can conquer what is inevitably determined.[19] Would it not be as well to check their credentials and listen to their teaching, which is the message of the Gospel? Then, perhaps, if we again reflected on our human condition, we might be in a better position to find this issue that 'opens up for consciousness in the heart of things'; hope of 'an escape in depth' might take root in us and flourish.[20] And then, 'as though by magic' our 'terror of Matter and Man' will be 'transformed, reversed, into peace and trust'; we shall feel that we are already, in principle, 'freed', for there is indeed a World-heart.[21]

Under the influence of this 'operative faith', the whole of human effort will regain its value for us, as being the essential preparation of the elements that will be subjected to that grand Alchemy or final transfiguration, that looks towards eternal Life.[22] We shall, no doubt, never become completely insensitive to that other sort of 'terror' we experienced, when we have to leave the realities of experience for the Realities of faith, which 'have not the same sensibly perceived consistence'. At the same time, perhaps, when each one of us turns back to consider his own self and his own individual death, when he gazes at the 'dizzy abyss' that opens up inexorably at his feet, we may all become better able to master the 'horror of falling back through death into the cosmic forces'; and since death is to hand us over 'totally to God', it may be easier for us to surrender ourselves to death 'with great love and abandonment'[23]. Thus we may be able to use to good purpose the example Père Teilhard offers us in the prayer he includes in *Le Milieu Divin*[24] and 'The Mass on the World'.

'It is a terrifying thing to have been born: I mean, to find oneself, without having willed it, swept irrevocably along a torrent of fearful energy which seems as though it wished to destroy everything it carries with it.

'What I want, my God, is that by a reversal of forces which you alone can bring about, my terror in face of the nameless changes destined to renew my being may be turned into an overflowing joy at being transformed into you.'[25]

How mistaken, then, it is to say, as has been said, that Père Teilhard 'minimizes death' by reducing it 'to purely biological considerations', or that he advocates an attitude that falls short of 'Christian resignation'. Can one fairly say that the views we have just been examining propose a 'biological and cosmic serenity' that is unworthy of a Christian? No doubt, the whole range of Christian thought on the subject of death cannot be exhausted by one individual Christian thinker. Nevertheless, we must agree that to see death as Père Teilhard saw it is indeed to see it with the eyes of a true Christian. In speaking as he did of death, he was repeating with St. Paul, and with the same tone of triumphant faith, the tone in which he himself spoke at the moment of his own death: 'The last enemy that shall be destroyed is death. For Christ has put all things under his feet.'[26]

Chapter 6

THE BASIS IN TRADITION

We have spoken of death as the absolute obstacle, the final stop; but this is only what it appears to be, and we added that, through Faith, death is in reality the perfect passivity: it is the door that opens on to transfiguration.

Passivity is one of Père Teilhard's key notions. It dominates even that of the divine milieu, as is immediately evident from the order in which the book treats them.[1] So long as the various forces that act upon us, independently of us, and in spite of us, are still external and still something that we have simply to endure, neither the forces themselves nor the fact that we come up against them and have to endure them can rightly be called passivities. Whether they affect us from outside or from within, they are still 'neutral, ambivalent and hostile influences'.[2] Passivities—as the very word indicates—are such only when they become *ours*: ours, by virtue of an initial acceptance or assumption, a ratification by the will; or at any rate from the moment when, reflected on by us and echoing in us, they cease to exercise their pressure simply as brute force, and present themselves to us as an actual interior state and as an attitude of obedience and love proposed to our freedom. They then become in a true sense *our passivities*, without ceasing to be other than us; and the operation that God effects in us through them cannot be replaced by any activity that we ourselves could initiate. 'To allow God, when it so pleases him, to grow within us, and, by death, to substitute himself for us: that is now our duty; that, if one may use the word, is our opportunity; and that is the only attitude that can finally bring salvation.'[3]

There are obvious differences in the points of view, but Père Teilhard's 'passivities' are analogous, in their functions of purifying and finally of divinizing, to the 'nights' of St. John of the Cross. Père Teilhard himself, in a letter that sets out the principles of his spirituality, refers in connexion with 'passivities' to the necessity of a 'passing through the night'.[4] They represent the negative, dark phase of God's work in us, the phase of trial. It is only by a complete misunderstanding that the omission of sin from the list has been commented on with regret, or that it has been asserted that 'this theory of passivities is most unsatisfactory in its treatment of sin'.[5] Passivities begin to play their part, in Père Teilhard's system, once the 'Christian perfection of human effort' has been achieved, when the maximum possible 'detachment through action' has been attained; he fosters a 'cult of passivities'; he 'offers' himself to them; he 'encourages them with all his power';[6] he calls them 'blessed', and says that they must be 'loved passionately'; and 'cherished'; it is through them 'that Christ eminently transforms into himself' what 'we have tried to develop for him';[7] they ensure 'the divine Presence' in us; they are 'full of sweetness' and 'worthy of adoration', because 'it is through them that God becomes paramount in us';[8] finally they are the 'royal road' by which we penetrate to the heart of the divine Milieu. This, surely, is sufficient answer to the charge of confusing sin and passivity.[9]

In the case of the 'divine Milieu', again, there is an analogy that we cannot overlook. It has more than one feature in common with the 'Kingdom of God' in the Gospels. Like the Kingdom, it is there that we find the marvellous element in our wretched universe, which initially is the only universe that our physical senses can recognize. Again, like the Kingdom of God, it has been with us since all time, even though our natural blindness has, practically always, made us exiles from it. We cannot in reality either construct the divine Milieu, any more than we can the Kingdom, nor obtain it for ourselves, even though it grows in some way as it is more fully perceived, since those who perceive it then become part of it.[10] It is the 'mystical Milieu' of which Père Teilhard himself wrote that 'it does not constitute a finished zone, in which beings remain static once they have been able to enter it. We should call it not precisely God, but the Kingdom of God'.[11] It is of this Milieu again that he says in another essay, 'Only the bold can enter into the Kingdom of God, already hidden henceforth in the heart of the World'.[12] If through our efforts we collaborate with the work of the Creator, yet we discover and enter into the divine Milieu, we 'migrate' to it (to use another of Père Teilhard's words)[13] only by the adherence of our will to the Will of God:[14] and that even though we act 'boldly', as the Gospel urges us, and use 'violence'. Further, as the Kingdom of God is within us as well as around us, so the divine Milieu surrounds us on all sides, 'so intimately and profoundly that nothing can make it apparent to us.'[15] Only a faith that is rooted deep in our lives can introduce us to it. 'Present in, and exercising its attractive force in the inaccessible depths of every creature', it nevertheless continually eludes our grasp, withdrawing 'always further bearing us along with it towards the common centre of all consummation'. And, if we are to plunge deep into the Milieu, and there remain for ever, the final great passivity must intervene: this is the apparent annihilation which is the 'supreme gateway of Life';[16] it is the total 'ecstasis' in which the night is finally and for ever changed into light, so that henceforth all we have to do is to 'submit to the light of God'.[17]

Nothing, perhaps, brings out more clearly the rich store of tradition that nourishes Père Teilhard's spirituality than the predominance in it of these two key ideas.[18] He sang the praises of cosmic evolution as carried further by human activity, but at the same time he was the herald, without in any way contradicting himself but speaking at a deeper level, of a mysterious reality that is always an integral gift, and the apostle of the passive life that alone allows integral access to that reality. 'Divinization of activities', 'divinization of passivities', and 'the divine Milieu' are the three successive, linked, parts of *Le Milieu Divin* that indicate an essential order of progress—that looks forward to the Parousia. Again, as with every spiritually minded representative of Christian tradition, the Cross and its mystery occupy a central position in Père Teilhard's thought. Before theorizing about the Cross, he draws the essential foundation of his teaching from contemplation of it. On a Good Friday, he wrote: 'I've been struck by the insistence with which the Church constantly repeats the final refrain *"Christus factus est obediens usque ad mortem crucis"*. That is obviously the exact and profound significance of the cross: obedience, submission to the law of life—and to accept everything, in a spirit of love, including death, there you have the essence of Christianity.'[19] When the Christian seems finally to have lost the battle, it is through the Cross that he triumphs in Christ. When he seems to sink into death, in reality 'he rises up into the light', the light of God that is in the first place the 'light of the Cross'.[20]

Thus, if we get to understand Père Teilhard's work with some accuracy, we find that his thought is very different from that sometimes attributed to him by a conventional interpretation, published too hastily, and based on evidence that is incomplete or ill understood. In his first writings, Père Teilhard himself had no thought of saying anything that differed substantially from what so many who treated 'similar' themes had been saying for 'twenty centuries'.[21] Nevertheless, he may later have laid himself open to misunderstanding. In treating religious problems from the point of view derived from his speculations as a scientist, he was obliged to do so from a particular angle that was necessarily incomplete. His constant concern with apologetics was to exaggerate this tendency. Even when addressing Christians, he normally assumed that they were familiar with the Church's immutable teaching, and concentrated rather on making them realize the religious repercussions of a new human spirit that he sought to proclaim. He did not continually, and wearisomely, expound to all and sundry the immutable laws of that 'personal sanctification' of which he had clearly said that every man, if he wishes to be true, must secure it for himself 'before considering others' and 'in order to do so'.[22] Nor did he on every occasion lay bare the intimate depths of his own being; an increasing modesty, strengthened by an increasingly objective attitude, held in check the lyricism of his first intensely personal writings. Not all those, accordingly, who came into contact with him can flatter themselves that they penetrated his secret. Even in his autobiographical reminiscences one feels, for all their clarity, that his dominating concern is to rediscover the essential features of his interior life and of his thought which paved the way to the synthesis he later constructed.[23] In his passion for complete sincerity, he was nevertheless subject to the laws that make every way of expressing a thought more an individual way of so doing, the more it avoids banality. Later in life, again, he may, in spite of his efforts to prevent himself, have allowed himself to over-systematize. As his scientifico-religious views became more cut and dried, it can sometimes have had the effect of narrowing rather than, as he thought, widening his spiritual horizon. This we shall consider later. However that may be, a letter dating from 1931 sheds light on what was then, and so remained, his over-all plan. 'The Christian attitude,' he writes, 'has long been established; but there has never been any "critique" of it (as, for example, there has been a critique of knowledge).'[24] His 'critical' essays, accordingly, might be more successful or less successful, but in either case the substantial reality of dogma is in no way impaired. It always remained for Père Teilhard the initial datum, representing what, being recognized by faith, can never be questioned. 'Realism,' he says himself, 'is the life of his whole mystical system.' If he considers some theology too 'verbal', too out of touch and specialized, if he criticizes it for ending in leaving Christianity 'adrift in an artificial atmosphere', it is because he is urging it to return 'to the best currents of Catholic tradition', where it will regain its practical vigour and mastering strength.[25] As we shall see later, this is just what he himself was to do more often than he realized. Although Père Teilhard's work was begun at a time when modernism was at its height, it never, even when some of his conclusions are questionable, acquired any taint of modernism.

Le Milieu Divin does not set out to be, any more than any other of his writings did, an exposition of doctrine. As in the case of any number of other works that deal with apologetics or spirituality, it is not put forward as some form of advanced catechism or theological summary; it is difficult to understand, accordingly, how anyone could criticize it, for example, for making only a brief reference to baptism or for not going thoroughly into the problem of predestination.[26] Nevertheless, the doctrinal basis of the spirituality Père Teilhard teaches often comes to the surface, so much so that the book takes the reader to the heart of Christian dogmatics. 'By revealing an original fall,' it tells us, 'Christianity provides our intelligence with a reason for the disconcerting excess of sin and suffering at certain points. Next, in order to win our love and secure our faith, it unveils to our eyes and hearts the moving, unfathomable reality of the historical Christ in whom the exemplary life of an individual man conceals this mysterious drama: the Master of the World leading, as an element of the world, not only an elemental life but (in addition to this and because of it) leading the total life of the universe, which he has shouldered and assimilated by experiencing it himself.' By the death of Jesus on the Cross, which is at once symbol and reality—effective symbol and exemplary reality— each one of us is called on to understand that 'the term of creation is not to be sought in the temporal zones of our visible world'; each one of us is invited to join this 'folly of Christianity' which makes him, as soon as he sets out, break, in a sense, with the world, and tends to 'uproot' him 'from everything perceptible on earth'.[27]

The reader will no doubt have noted in this passage, in the sentence that refers to the 'historic Christ', the ease and sureness of touch, theologically speaking, with which a writer who was not a professional theologian summed up in a few lines a whole exact doctrine of the mystery of the Incarnate Word: and this is accompanied by an equally admirable strictness and simplicity in the expression of faith. To those who sought to look on him, whether to praise or blame him, as something of an innovator, he had already replied in advance that his religion 'in no way represents a compromise between Christianity and the modern world'.[28] It is true, no doubt, that, sometimes over-boldly, he wished for 'a re-fashioning' of some Christian 'forms of representation' and 'attitudes' in order 'frankly to Christify Evolution'; he may, too, have been over-confident in his hopes of such re-fashioning; but in this there was not the least intention of weakening or diluting the substance of the faith. On the contrary, he could say of himself that he was 'a long way from feeling disturbed in his Faith' by such prospects. He truly adhered, with all his soul, to the unique Revelation, with no desire either to add anything to it or to reduce it, to select from it or to modify it, in any essential. He knew that, in his very humanity, the historic Christ 'is not only perfect Man, ideal Man, but total Man, he who gathers together in the depths of his consciousness the consciousness of all men'. His thoughts turned on 'the unapproachable secret of Christ's agony' and 'the incomparable virtue of his death on the Cross'. He knew, too, that the 'current of grace released historically by Jesus Christ is propagated only by being borne on a living tradition'.[29] He recognized, 'in the living thought of the Church the reflection, adapted to our evolutionary situation, of the divine thought'. It is 'not by way of pure inference, but by adherence to an affirmation from on high', which is thus passed on to him, that he 'affirms the fact of the Incarnation'.[30] If he liked Péguy, and took pleasure, during the 1914 war, in feeling that he was close to him, it was primarily because Péguy, in his *Eve,* had succeeded in paying a worthy tribute to Christ's 'carnal cradle'.[31] He worshipped 'the Child of Bethlehem'.[32] He invoked with fervour the intercession of 'her whom God chose to set above the World and the Church as a never-fading nimbus',[33] in whose heart we 'relive the mysteries—so that the whole of dogma becomes familiar, concrete, and real, in Mary'.[34] He knew and asserted that 'to suppress the historicity of Christ, in other words the divinity of the historic Christ, would be to bring about the instantaneous evaporation into the unreal of all the mystical energy accumulated during the last two thousand years in the Christian phylum. Christ born of the Virgin, and the risen Christ: these two form an indivisible whole'.[35]

'For God and the World to form one in the Pleroma, God had first in some way to *break his circle* and so admit and sublimate our imperfections . . . On our side, we too have to make a similar effort if it is to be possible for us to be enclosed in the higher circle that draws us: this is our death and our mortification.'[36] Those words, written *currente calamo,* bring to life again the most central affirmation of faith: it is through the self-abasement, the 'kenosis,' and humiliation of the Word that man is enabled to rise above his condition; God was made man that man might become God. Through the historic Incarnation of the Word, the transcendent became 'to some degree immanent'.[37] By his Passion, followed by his Resurrection, Christ became 'universal'; his assimilative power is henceforth exercised in the formation of his mystical body. These are the three stages that Père Teilhard, in common with Christian tradition, distinguishes. He described them again, to reaffirm their indissoluble connexion, in his last effort to proclaim Christ, written only a few days before, on the evening of Easter Sunday, 1955, he left this world to return to Christ: 'It is easy,' he explains to the Gentiles to whom he sought to bring the light of his faith, and with whose mistaken interpretations he was familiar, 'it is easy to criticize in abstract this paradoxical mixture of "primitive anthropomorphism, mythical marvel and gnostic boldness" in which you imagine our belief consists. But the remarkable fact remains, I insist, that the combination of those three elements (strange though it may seem) *holds* together—that it *works*— and that you would only have to weaken the reality (or even the realism) of a single one of the three components present for the flame of Christianity immediately to be extinguished.'[38]

This is the very line of argument used by St. Paul: '. . . Christum, Dei virtutem; Fides . . . in virtute Dei.'[39]

The universal 'diaphany' of Jesus, the 'wonderful diaphany that has transformed everything in *his* eyes',[40] thus depends entirely on his first 'manifestation', his 'epiphany' localized in time and place. No doubt, once this mystery has been recognized, there is, within the unity of the faith, more than one way of living. Christian spirituality, one though it is, can be lived in a number of different ways in the wide embrace of the one Church. The way followed in ancient times is not precisely that of St. Bernard, or St. Francis of Assisi, or of St. Ignatius Loyola. For his part, Père Teilhard was not inclined, in an effort of retrospective imagination, to dwell too much on the sensible aspects of the Gospel. Here again, he was following St. Paul, who said that 'though we once regarded Christ from a human point of view, we regard him thus no longer'.[41] Such an attitude, which is by no means confined to Père Teilhard,[42] would be more frequently endorsed by tradition than might be imagined. For example, in the commentary on St. Matthew's Gospel, by Saint Paschasus Radbert, abbot of Corbie in the ninth century, we find: 'It is pure folly to look in a confined or hidden place for him who fills all things, who will one day overturn all things and shed his light on each one of them.'[43] Earlier, Origen, whose thought owed much to a study of St. Paul, had written in his *Periarchon*: 'Christ is everywhere. He permeates the universe, and we should no longer think of him as in that constricted state he accepted for love of us, nor imprisoned in the limits in which a body like ours enclosed him; he was willing to assume that body during his sojourn among us on earth, and was therefore in a way a prisoner in that place.'[44] Such statements, moreover, do not rule out for Origen any return in spirit to the letter of the Gospel story. The same is equally true of Père Teilhard, even though he sometimes showed too hasty an inclination in practice to identify meditation on the gospel story with an exclusive consideration of the humanity of Christ or the particular characteristics of his life on earth.[45]

Nevertheless, there is no disjunction between the one state of Christ and the other: it is always the same Christ. This assertion is found first in a number of passages in which Père Teilhard's own highly personal attitude may be seen, as for example in this noble passage on the hands of our Saviour.

'*In manus tuas, commendo spiritum meum.* To the hands that broke and gave life to the bread, that blessed and caressed, and were pierced—to the hands that are as our hands, of which we can never say what they will do with the objects they hold, whether shatter them or care for them, but whose whims, we may be sure, are full of kindness and will never do more than hold us in a jealous grasp—to the kindly and mighty hands that reach down to the very marrow of the soul—that mould and create—to the hands through which so great a love is transmitted—it is to these that it is good to surrender our soul.'[46]

Père Teilhard makes the same point more theoretically, with equal force. However far we may be led by the Spirit 'into the divine spaces opened up by Christian mysticism, we never depart from the Jesus of the Gospels'. The light of the divine Milieu 'radiates from a *historical* centre'; it is transmitted to us 'along a *traditional and solidly defined axis*', in other words it starts from the contact of God and man that was made manifest 'in Jesus Christ', from the 'tangible and verifiable event' of his life and teaching, as communicated to us from generation to generation by the tradition handed on by those who first witnessed it, and accepted by us in its fulness.[47]

Thus, all that is professed as dogma, far from being left as abstract, becomes a living part of the spiritual life. Père Teilhard liked to speak of the mystical Christ, the cosmic Christ, the universal Christ, but at the same time he was equally anxious to remind us that this Christ 'has neither meaning nor value in our eyes except as an expansion of the Christ who was born of Mary and died on the Cross.'[48] He realizes that we must not allow 'the human reality of Christ to vanish in the superhuman or evaporate into the cosmic'. 'I find myself,' he says, 'so placed that I cannot breathe outside Our Lord— and I realize that without his historic and traditional Revelation Our Lord completely disappears.'[49] Although his universal Christ is subject to no 'accidental and restrictive particular qualification', he is none the less 'strictly defined'. He is that same Christ whom 'the Gospels show us, St. John especially. He is the Christ of St. Paul, the Christ in whom the great mystics lived', and whom he wishes regretfully that the Schoolmen had made more a part of their lives.[50] He is Christ the King, understood in his plenitude.[51] Such, he says again, 'is the universal nature of the Christ of history'. Some readers may, perhaps, be disconcerted by such a thought or by the ways in which it is expressed; they would, however, be equally disconcerted by the teaching and the very language of Scripture, if habit had not now made them so familiar. Such readers would do well to consider, for example, how fantastically unheard-of was the identification of one particular concrete individual, who had just appeared on earth, with the logos who 'was with God and was God', or with the principle that holds together all beings in the cosmos. In this connexion Mgr Maurice Nédoncelle has written, 'Our persons and the world that shelters them can find their centre in the person of the Incarnate Word. There is no reason why one should not hold that this conviction is a faithful reflection of the Prologue to St.

John's Gospel and of the corollaries St. Justin long ago deduced from it.'[52]

It is in the mystery of the Eucharist that Père Teilhard found the vital synthesis of these aspects of the Christ who was to him always one and the same Christ. Devotion to the Eucharist was one of the features of his interior life.[53] It gave vigour to his religious thought, and one can recognize in him something similar to what may be found in other Christians who lead the spiritual life, a development of mystical life that starts from the Host.[54] The 'theological disputation' he took part in at the conclusion of his studies, in 1912, was concerned with the treatise on the Eucharist, and he recorded his pleasure at the choice.[55] During the First World War, he felt keenly the deprivation of the sacraments and 'the prolonged mass-less days' that came with periods of active fighting and some spells in the front line. It was then that he adopted the habit of making up for it by saying Mass in spirit, as layfolk are urged on similar occasions to make a 'spiritual communion'. One fruit of this was his meditation Le Prêtre (1918). It represents the first draft of what was later to be 'The Mass on the World', when scientific expeditions into the heart of the desert were again to involve a similar deprivation.[56] This is a subject that has often been strangely misunderstood. In the Eucharist, which is the central mystery, Père Teilhard contemplates both the extension of the Incarnation of the Word and the promise of the world's transfiguration. Here again his faith is as realistic as it is lively. He accepts the dogma literally; but his realism cannot be satisfied simply by the literal expression of the revelation. He knows that the dogma calls for more than formal adherence from us, and that while orthodoxy of belief is essential, it is not a wall which pulls the Christian up short, but the foundation and support of his impetus. In other words, he knows that the mystery is fruitful; he strives in prayer to get to the bottom of its meaning, and he meditates on its effects. He seeks, accordingly, 'worthily to interpret the fundamental position that the Eucharist holds in the economy of the world'. He considers its 'extensions'; following the liturgy and a number of ancient writers, he sees that it already contains what it effectively signifies. Thus it is that, in his own way, he spontaneously rediscovers something of the fullness of tradition that our age was by way of forgetting. 'The Host is like a burning hearth from which its flame radiates and spreads.' The priestly function extends to the growth of the mystical body and the consecration of the cosmos. This is what Pastor Georges Crespy, in an analysis of these passages, has called 'eucharistizing, that is to say the movement by which the Host assimilates mankind and the entire universe'.[57] 'From the particular cosmic element into which he has entered, the activity of the Word goes forth to subdue and draw unto himself all the rest.'[58]

Nevertheless, Père Teilhard did, during a later period, speak of a 'Super-Christ', proportioned to a 'Super-mankind', as he spoke of a 'Christian super-evolutionism'.[59] Towards the end he made more frequent use of such expressions, with the prefixes 'super', 'hyper' and even 'neo', and one might well think that they were somewhat unfortunate. Père Teilhard himself had all along recognized that such words might be given 'an unacceptable meaning' and he used them at first only with diffidence.[60] It should, however, be recognized that from the point of view of dogma they introduce no innovation into his thought. His explanations of them are unmistakably clear. 'By Super-Christ I most certainly do not mean another Christ, a second Christ, different from and greater than the first. I mean the same Christ, the Christ of all time, disclosing himself to us in a form and in dimensions, with an urgency and an area of contact, that are magnified and given new vigour.' *Christus semper major*—a phrase that has a very Ignatian flavour. For, 'we cannot continue to love Christ without discovering Him more and more',[61] and if Christ thus grows greater for us, 'he does so while still remaining what he was or, more correctly, *in order to* remain what he was'.[62] When, therefore, he chooses this term, 'Super-Christ', he does so, he tells us again, solely 'to indicate the "extra" magnitude assumed for our minds by the Person of Jesus, in step with our mental appreciation of the super-dimensions of the World and Mankind'.[63] He uses the word 'to maintain Christ at the head of Creation'. He seeks thereby to 'give traditional Christology additional vitality and bring it closer to our own age'.[64] *Ad majorem*

Christi gloriam. In this, as in what he said about the extensions of the Eucharist and in other connexions too, *securius loquebatur*—he expressed himself with insufficient care. What St. Augustine said about the ancient Fathers of the Church could be applied in this case, too: so entranced was Père Teilhard by his faith that it never crossed his mind that some readers might so misunderstand him as even to doubt his faith.

Nevertheless, we must admit (though in this there is no longer any question of his orthodoxy) that such modes of expression and the concern they evidence seem to proceed, at least in appearance, from the attribution of excessive importance to the material dimensions of the world. Père Teilhard wished to 'dissolve the mirage of Matter';[65] through the notion of his 'third infinite' (the 'infinite of complexity') he sought to rid us of what he called the Pascalian obsession of the 'two abysses', to teach us the 'gesture'—as he puts it—that will enable us to 'overcome the illusion of Quantity'.[66] Might one not think, however, that in this connexion Père Teilhard himself was somewhat subject to the spatial illusion? 'If he is to be Alpha and Omega, Christ must, without losing his human dimension, become co-extensive with the physical immensities of Duration and Space.'[67] We need not be held up by his use of 'extension', since on several occasions Père Teilhard explained it by the idea of 'omnipresence', and elsewhere put it better when he said, 'We must magnify Christ without limit, that is to say we must take him to the actual *organic centre* of All.'[68] But whatever the dimensions of the All may be, whether in extension or in complexity, surely its 'organic centre' and 'the universal bond' are such as they are, once and for all? Nevertheless, beneath the inadequacy of the expression, a powerful idea was seeking to emerge, and details of language should not prevent us from recognizing its value: that idea centres on the more rigorous organicity recognized in the universe, its temporal development in cosmogenesis, and its ultimately spiritual nature. In this we have a new illumination that gives the Christian a better understanding of the Pauline teaching on Christ, and that gives it a more urgent immediacy, while at the same time it introduces into it 'a further dimension' which develops it into a Christogenesis.[69]

Even though Père Teilhard never arrived at a systematic Christogenesis, he at least focused attention upon it. In this recognition (somewhat one-sided though it may have been) of one of the essential needs of contemporary Christian thought, he coincided with Maurice Blondel, who once wrote to his friend Victor Delbos: 'As mankind grows greater, so Christ is exalted. And the never-ceasing task of the philosopher and the apologist . . . is to show that he, Christ, is greater, beyond all comparison.'[70] For his part, Père Teilhard could write: 'That I magnify Christ above all is literally the only thing that can be held against me.' We find the essence of his vision in a passage he wrote out, towards the end of 1918, two days before Christmas, in a little room at the seminary in Strasbourg after long meditation under the vaulted roof of the cathedral: it is 'the Christ who is *more real* than any other reality in the World, the Christ who is everywhere present and everywhere growing, the Christ who is the ultimate determining force and moulding principle of the Universe'. In his earnest desire for interior sincerity, Père Teilhard was later to ask himself: 'Is this still indeed the Christ of the Gospel?'; and what helped to reassure him was, he tells us, the fact that 'in me, the increasing illumination is accompanied by love—and by abandonment of self in one greater than I'.[71] Similarly, he could write to his General, in 1951: 'I can truly say—and this in virtue of the whole structure of my thought—that I now feel more indissolubly bound to the hierarchical Church and to the Christ of the Gospel than ever before in my life. Never has Christ seemed to me more real, more personal or more immense.'[72] The year before he had, in fact, included in his essay *Le Cœur de la Matière* a prayer to 'Christ ever greater', whom he saluted as 'Lord of consistence and union', 'Lord of my childhood and of my end.'

To sum up, then: there can be no doubt that, in Père Teilhard's thought, 'so far from eclipsing Christ, it is only in Christ that the Universe finds the guarantee of its consistence'.[73] There is no blurring of the Person of the Incarnate Word or of the historic reality of Jesus of Nazareth, no danger of their vanishing before some collective being or before the mystery of the Universe. It is not 'evolution' that draws Christ to itself, there to incorporate him. On the contrary, for Père Teilhard, unshaken in his faith (and at the same time in full conformity with the essential strands of his own thought) it is the 'risen Christ of the Gospel' who, standing 'above the Creation' he is one day to 'consummate', 'incorporates in himself the evolution that some would seek to set in opposition to him';[74] and that is why we can and must say that the whole 'evolutionary effort . . . may be reduced . . . to the development of a Love'.[75] As early as 1918 he had written, in a pregnant sentence that still retained the warmth of vivid personal experience (and whose full meaning the reader would do well to search out): 'the Universe takes on the form of Christ', and, further, 'O mystery! He who makes himself manifest in it, is Christ crucified'.[76]

Chapter 7

THE PHENOMENON OF MAN

We may well wonder how such an intellectual structure could sometimes be so misunderstood as to induce the belief that it deliberately blurred part of Christian dogmatic teaching or allowed itself to be drawn into a distortion of the spiritual orientation of Christianity. If, however, we look at the several causes that lie behind the misconception, it will not seem so surprising; and in considering those that seem to be the most important, we shall not overlook such of them as may be attributed to Père Teilhard himself. The mistake seems to have originated in the first place in an appraisal of the total synthesis that was made immediately after reading such essays in the philosophy of science as *The Phenomenon of Man*. An inevitable respect for scientific method, as we have already pointed out, made it impossible for such writings to give a complete picture. This is a point of cardinal importance and calls for closer examination.

One can, and indeed, as Père Teilhard said, one must 'assail the real from different angles and on different planes'.[1] He himself did so from two angles or on two principal planes. He explains this, with the utmost simplicity, in two intimate letters. The first is dated 22 August 1925, and was written at the time he was thinking of writing the book that eventually appeared as *Le Milieu Divin*. 'I am gradually collecting the elements of a "divinization" of the Earth which will continue, *ad usum Christianorum*, the "hominization" that I have not yet shown you, but which is written *ad usum gentilium*.' The second letter is much later in date. Père Teilhard had on several occasions re-drafted, in various forms, the sketch to which he had given the name 'hominization'.[2] He had now got together all the elements of *The Phenomenon of Man*, and on 25 May 1938 he wrote to the same friend, Père Auguste Valensin: 'I am beginning work, first as a rough draft, on a fairly long book about Man . . . I shall be careful to stop short of Religion—the Church door, but not the sanctuary.'

He could hardly have expressed his intention more clearly. It is a perfectly clear warning that there are two parts to his work: they are distinguished by their aim and in consequence by their method, and it is useless to look in one for what can be found only in the other. Let us, therefore, determine more exactly what Père Teilhard was trying to do in *The Phenomenon of Man*.

If we wish to understand any written work, we must first decide to what type of literature it belongs. What Biblical experts tell us about the different compositions that make up the Bible applies to every form of literature. More precisely, when we are dealing with a work of wide intellectual range, it is important first to determine as strictly as possible its formal object and method. That is why historians have devoted so much attention to investigating, for example, Origen's *Periarchon*, or St. Anselm's *Proslogion*, or St. Thomas Aquinas's *Summa contra Gentiles*. The number of works that call for such treatment increases every year.

These elementary remarks assume more importance if one considers, in the first place, the demands that have been common to the finest minds ever since Descartes taught us (or reminded us of) the rules for methodically conducting thought, and secondly, the extreme differentiation between modern disciplines of knowledge. In commonplace, everyday writing, or with writers of no particular distinction, it often happens that the whole book is a medley. The thought may be brilliant or ingenious; but it has no rigidity of structure; it moves from one type of consideration to another, through some artificial connexion, without checking the source of every assertion that is made. It leaps from one field to a completely different one. One might say that it borrows anything that comes to hand. It is a very different story when we come to a book such as *The Phenomenon of Man*, a masterly work conceived by a great mind that attached the utmost importance to the rigorous development of its thought. If, then, we are not to misunderstand its over-all significance and aim, we must place it in its proper context. In other words, failure to do so will mean that we both exaggerate its significance and at the same time reduce it to the commonplace, and thereby are guilty of a double betrayal.

This preliminary study of a book is in itself a task of some difficulty: in fact, the more indispensable it is, the more difficult it is too. No great effort is needed to decide in what category one would place a book on modern history or a chemistry textbook, for example, and so find out exactly what one may expect from it. But whenever we have to deal with something that bears the stamp of an individual personality, with a new contribution to make, with a work that enriches the store of human knowledge, with a work that in no matter how small a way may rightly be called creative, then we meet a completely fresh problem in interpretation, since the work in question must always to some extent clash with normal methods of classification and accepted distinctions in acquired knowledge.[3]

Nevertheless this difficulty is very much lessened if the author has made his own position clear; and this is so in the case of Père Teilhard. Even though some effort is still required to understand the explanations he gives, at least the explanations are there, and in themselves are remarkably precise. They call for no speculation or deduction on our part. They solve the preliminary problem for us. For the moment, that problem is not to determine whether the explanations provided justify the method; nor is it to determine how we should judge the content of the book. It is not even the problem of discovering whether, and to what extent, its conclusions, and the chain of reasoning from which they are derived, are an extrapolation from the initial position; nor of deciding whether, and to what extent, its conclusions belong to philosophy or to some other field, rather than to positive science in the strict and exact meaning of the word.[4] The whole problem is confined to discovering from what source the author draws the substance that nourishes his thought, what is the nature of the materials he uses, on what ground he takes his stand, and what is his personal outlook; and, in consequence, what, in his own mind, should be the nature and scope of his conclusions.

On these points Père Teilhard's own statements leave room for no doubt or even, essentially at least, the least possibility of ambiguity. The synthesis represented by *The Phenomenon of Man* (and this holds good for his other writings of a similar type) does not in any degree belong to the order of metaphysics—at any rate if we allow the word its now classical meaning; nor, *a fortiori*, does it belong to the order of theology. This it utterly rules out. It is built up on the jealously preserved ground of objective scientific observation.[5] This does not mean that wider reflection does not play its part; but such reflection is exercised exclusively on facts that are judged to be scientific in order, with a view to bringing out 'the mutual relationships and underlying significance'. The strictness of its method will not allow any recourse to a different order of knowledge; it does not recognize nor wish to recognize any heterogeneous contribution, from no matter what source. This is what gives the book its strength—at least in principle, for we are not, for the moment, concerned with an appraisal of the result, nor with possible shortcomings in the execution of the plan—and this is at the same time what defines it, by which I mean that it determines its limits. These limits are recognized, are positively and resolutely intended. However much it may differ from a work of purely analytical research, and to whatever lengths the effort to attain a synthesis may be carried, *The Phenomenon of Man* is determined to remain from beginning to end in the 'field of experience'.[6]

Père Teilhard himself sums this all up in the first paragraph of his Preface:

'If this book is to be properly understood, it must be read not as a work on metaphysics, still less as a sort of theological essay, but purely and simply as a scientific treatise. The title itself indicates that. This book deals with man *solely* as a phenomenon; but it also deals with the *whole* phenomenon of man.'[7]

Solely the phenomenon, but also the whole phenomenon: Père Teilhard, in using that phrase, had in mind readers whose perception, even though sometimes acute, seemed to him to be lacking in range, so that they were often blind to some facts of great importance. He hoped to make them realize at last 'the pre-eminent significance of man in Nature' and 'the organic nature of humanity'. This wider view of the phenomenon

could not but be arguable, and we may in fact wonder up to
just what point it is possible, without overstepping the limits
of strictly positive science, to find room for such an idea as
the 'within of things',[8] or to introduce the synthesis at the
conclusion of analytical recordings. These are problems that,
later, we shall at least have to broach, but that we can leave
aside for the moment. Without distorting or impairing the
meaning of the phrase we quoted, Père Teilhard might well
have reversed it for the benefit of those who might be tempted
to read too much into his thought and thereby falsify it, or to
look to him for what he neither could nor should offer them
in this book: he could have reminded such readers that while
it deals with 'the *whole* phenomenon' at the same time it deals
'*solely* with the phenomenon'.

The whole phenomenon, indeed; Père Teilhard, in fact, had
'a profound sense of totality'. In him, to use an expression of
Pope Pius XII, philosopher and scientist collaborated in 'har-
monious unity'[9] to enable him mentally to embrace very comprehensive wholes. This enabled him to examine the phenomenon with an insight that penetrated into its inmost depths.
Again, however, it is the depths of the phenomenon as such
with which his thought is concerned. He is dealing with the
totality of the phenomenon, in other words he is always dealing with a sum-total of 'experiential relationships' and 'laws of
recurrence'. Everything is contained again in a certain sphere,
which itself is situated, or rather has to be situated, within a
wider totality. It is a question of then transposing a certain
'order', in its integral totality, into another 'order'. When Teilhard said '*solely* the phenomenon', he knew perfectly well
what he was saying.

He continues, in the same preface: 'The pages which follow do not attempt to give an explanation of the world, but
only an introduction to such an explanation. Put quite simply,
what I have tried to do is this: I have chosen man as the centre,
and around him I have tried to establish a coherent order of
antecedents and consequents. I have not tried to discover a
system of ontological and causal relations between the elements of the universe, but only an experiential law of recurrence.' Beyond this, there is 'ample room, room that must be

filled, and that is waiting for' other orders of reflection, which will have to be developed from different principles and along different lines.[10] These involve fresh tasks, which are much more than a mere continuation of his own. Père Teilhard is not concerned with these in *The Phenomenon of Man*; he is leaving them aside, he says, 'of set purpose'.[11] He goes to the limit of what scientific observation, as understood by him, forces him to accept or suggests to him. That takes him a very considerable distance, but to go further he would have to appeal to principles of a different nature: and that would not mean embarking on an extension of his own work but undertaking a new and entirely different type of work. He could, indeed, had he wished, have introduced those principles obliquely, by some sort of surreptitious device, but his cunning in so doing (or his failure to realize what he was doing) would have robbed his work of all impact for minds that are not easily satisfied. The convincing force of an organized train of thought is not to be judged by the width of the field it covers, but by its rigour—and that is the same thing as its honesty. Ultimately, it derives, therefore, from its recognizing and respecting the limits proper to it.[12]

Père Teilhard had too truly scientific a mind not to see this, and to say so. At the same time, his thought was so personal and his soul so avid for the truth that it was impossible for him not to construct within himself, and for his own satisfaction, a more complete synthesis. Passionately devoted though he was to the search for scientific truth, he fully realized that if a man could be satisfied only by an understanding of the Real, it was impossible for any positive science to enable him to get to the bottom of it. 'I feel,' he once wrote, 'how much the explanation of the World in itself sheds no light on, and opens up for us no issue to, the most fundamental of life's problems.'[13] He knew that beyond science, or, if you so prefer it, outside or beyond even metaphysics, there lies another source of knowledge with which man, in his present condition, cannot dispense: it is the source that throughout our history has sprung from a divine revelation to open our eyes to the essential basis of our being and to our divine destiny. He had, within himself and for himself, achieved a living synthesis between this supernatural order and the conclusions or indications that emerged from his scientific synthesis; and he did his best, as we shall see, to achieve it within a growing unity. Much as he respected the distinction between different disciplines—and careful though he was not to confuse 'the planes and sources of knowledge', or justifiably to allow 'an illegitimate contamination of the phenomenal plan by the metaphysical'[14]—he was equally resolute in refusing to allow them to stand in an isolation that destroys the unity of man. It was for this reason that he added an epilogue to *The Phenomenon of Man*.

The word 'epilogue' was used of set purpose. It is not, we should note, a supplementary chapter, or an extra digression, or an appendix, or even a final winding-up. It is something much more central to the book than the two first, much more important than an appendix, and of quite another order to that of a winding-up. To use Père Teilhard's words again, his purpose is to establish a 'cross-check'. Here he appeals directly to evidence that the sciences he has so far been dealing with did not and could not provide. In this final approach, accordingly, there is no confusion either of domain or of method. He is inviting the reader again to consider the evidence so introduced, in its phenomenal aspect; he is asking him to observe, within human history, 'the *Christian phenomenon*, rising upwards at the heart of the social phenomenon'.[15] The former is not introduced, at its own level, as any inference from what has already been said. It is, in the fullest sense of the word, a new contribution, a new datum, recognized as such. He could not have found a better way of making it clear that if Christianity is not to be an illusion it must be specifically supernatural. There was no need for Père Teilhard to develop, in *The Phenomenon of Man*, the whole content of this new datum—a content that must necessarily be accepted, if the hypothesis of the illusory nature of Christianity is rejected. This content is no part of what he has called 'the phenomenon of man'. He is simply hoping that the reader will add to his observation of the phenomenon of man an observation of the Christian phenomenon, that he will recognize an unmistakable 'coincidence' between the final requirements derived from his study of the former, and the fundamental affirmations imposed by an examination of the latter; and that from this will emerge the light of a 'final vision', which will be the truly complete vision—but ultimately can be a vision only of faith.[16]

This is the same process as that which Père Teilhard had already spoken of in a lecture he gave in 1921 on 'Science and Christ': 'Science alone,' he then said, 'cannot discover Christ—but Christ answers the wishes that are formed in our hearts by the schooling of science.' We find it again later, in 1944, in his 'Reflections on happiness', in which he urges his listeners not to look for what one may call the 'Christian impulse' in a natural extension of the 'terrestrial impulse', but to synthesize the two.[17] Later again, in 1948, he introduces the same process at the conclusion of the 'phenomenological' part of his important essay *Comment je vois*. 'Let us,' he says, 'accept, at least as an initial hypothesis, that the Christian phenomenon, the religious current that we can observe in history, is in fact the bearer of a revelation; if we do so, we shall find that "thereby many characteristics of the structure and general progress of the Universe become clarified and more exactly defined", and that "all sorts of practical determinations emerge that are as valuable from the point of view of our speculations as they are from that of our action".'[18]

We see, then, how careful Père Teilhard was not to confuse either the different types of literary expression or the different disciplines of knowledge, even though, like every thinker with a new contribution to make, he had his own way of distinguishing them and combining them. In *The Phenomenon of Man* (being well aware of the misconceptions the reader of such a book might fall into) he was particularly careful to dispel any such mistake by giving ample explanations. 'Take any book about the Universe,' he says in the Preface, 'written by one of the great modern scientists, such as Poincaré, Einstein or Jeans, and you will see that it is impossible to attempt a general scientific interpretation of the Universe without *giving the impression* of trying to explain it through and through.'[19] Some of the scientists he refers to may, indeed, have done more than 'give such an impression', but Père Teilhard, for his part, was anxious to avoid the least appearance of so doing. We must realize, too, that there was a special reason why he should be so careful. In *The Phenomenon of Man*, as in a number of similar essays, he was proposing to study man 'from outside as he might appear if seen through some fantastic telescope from the planet Mars'; but he then hoped to guide his reader, in successive stages, 'through the objective, to a discovery of the interiority of the personal, and through the human mass, to that of its value'[20] —and these are notions that are not normally found in scientific works, even when they present a synthesis. While, however, he widened so extensively the field of the 'Phenomenon', he introduced nothing into it except in so far as he believed that he could show that it was, in one way or another, 'externally perceptible'.[21] As he himself said later, when analysing the 'hominizing phenomenon of reflection' and its consequences, he is determined not to leave the 'naturalist' or 'empirical' point of view. He wishes to proceed 'on strictly positivist lines',[22] his only aim being 'to develop a *homogeneous* and *coherent* perspective of our general extended experience of man'.[23] This careful definition, which is but one of many, is not, as one critic has too lightly assumed, no more than a 'theoretical precaution'. Even if such principle cannot always be applied without some degree of self-deception (which we shall have to estimate so far as is possible) they nevertheless reflect on the whole a wise and rigorous methodological requirement and a clear view of the limitations it entails.[24] If Père Teilhard's works are read with no more than cursory attention or without full realization of their importance, it is impossible to understand them at all. When he was lecturing at the Sorbonne on 'the human zoological group' he used constantly to insist that 'hominized matter' is the 'only direct object of the scientific interest'.[25] He will always be careful to distinguish 'the arrangement of phenomena' (or in other words their interconnections and successive relationships) from their 'underlying causality'. 'He may perhaps venture into an ultraphysics' in order 'to knit together as harmoniously as possible the sum of our experiences', but, he insists, one must not look for 'any metaphysics' in such developments.[26] As early as 1923 he wrote an essay on 'Homi-nization' which was a first draft of what was to be the great work of his mature years. In this he urged his readers to ac-company him in his effort to obtain 'as objective a view as possible of Humanity . . . considered as a *phenomenon*', warning them that a very considerable effort would be re-quired.[27] The event proved how right he was. A number of readers have regretted not being able to find in *The Phe-nomenon of Man* a direct affirmation of the great propositions of traditional metaphysics. This is in fact evidence of their having failed to make the effort in question and of not having understood the nature of the book, in spite of all the author's warnings. Others have even hoped to find in it, if not the principal teachings of faith, at least a place clearly reserved for them. This demand is equally unjustified and goes even further; what is more, 'by confusing the terms of reference' it does violence to the supernatural character of the Christian mystery. If original sin, or the Redemption, are revealed truths, it would be a most improper presumption, as absurd as naturalistic, to claim to include them in the 'homogeneous and coherent' sequence of exclusively objective experience.[28] Some readers, however, can never understand that if they wish to obtain everything from one particular author or to find everything in one particular book, they will never find anything to satisfy them unless they confine their reading to platitudes. And some critics whose orthodoxy is too ready to take offence reach the point where they lose sight of the application of the elementary principles of the Faith.

Chapter 8

SCIENTIST, PROPHET AND MYSTIC

The Phenomenon of Man has not been the only book by Père Teilhard to be the subject of misguided interpretation. *Le Milieu Divin*, too, has given rise to uneasiness. Even apparently attentive readers have been doubtful of its Christian integrity. Had they been more familiar with the preliminary work that led up to it and the confidential communications that shed light on its origin, they would have been less disturbed in their minds. It nevertheless remains true, given the twofold character, at once prophetic and mystical, that is deeply imprinted in the book, that a misunderstanding was from the outset almost inevitable.

This misunderstanding reappears, in fact, whenever a believer, who is sensitive to a certain maturing of consciousness, realizes before the majority of his fellow-Christians what is the problem to be solved in a situation that is so far without precedent, what is the chief obstacle to be overcome or what new evidence has to be included, if we are to ensure not only the maintenance of traditional faith in a climate that tends to close in on itself in order to shelter it, but also its assimilative power and its increasing influence on men's minds. Initially, the very effort he makes is taken for a deviation. He is looked upon as being—what is only too often true of others— led astray by 'novelty'. This is a radical misunderstanding, even though it may sometimes be encouraged by some awkwardness in expression or some fumbling in his search for the truth: it is a misunderstanding that was in fact foreseen by Père Teilhard himself and allowed for in advance, when he pointed out, actually in *Le Milieu Divin*, the 'external resemblance' '*so often found in things opposite*'.[1]

The only half-perceptive observer, who sees only the danger and imagines that the only possible reaction is to go strictly on the defensive, cannot understand the man who can see the causes of the evil, who can distinguish the emergent value that may be extracted, purified and retained, and who thus uses the weapon that appeared about to deal him a death-blow to co-operate in a new development of truth. If a man has not understood the meaning of a question, if the question has not yet been formulated for him—or even never will be formulated—then he cannot understand the timeliness or even, indeed, the meaning of the answer given.

Thus has come about a misunderstanding in connexion with the spirituality of *Le Milieu Divin*. It is similar to the misunderstanding we find also, in some minds, in connexion with the philosophy of man, as expressed in *The Phenomenon of Man*.

One of the essential contributions of the latter is in fact the new and highly effective support it lends to the great affirmations of the philosophy of the primacy of the spirit and of Christian tradition, through an *empirical* study of the special properties that make up the fact of the 'human zoological group'.[2] 'Man's unique value as the spearhead of life'; the definitive significance of 'the threshold of reflection'; the transcendence of human intelligence over animal psychism; life's 'transformation in depth', 'revolutionary transformation', through 'hominizing metamorphosis'; the 'change, from animal to man, not only in degree but in nature, that results from a change of state'; 'the trans-experiential gap of which we can say nothing in terms of science but beyond which we find ourselves transposed to an entirely new biological level'. These, and many similar expressions, are what strike the unsophisticated reader. He reads again, in the same book, that the appearance of man, in which we see effected the emergence of 'discontinuity upon the continuous, of mutation upon evolution', brings about 'a transformation that affects the state of the whole planet'; that 'through hominization, in spite of its insignificance as an anatomical leap, it is a new age that is inaugurated'; that 'in reality it is another world that is born', that the 'earth grows a new skin', and that 'what is even more, it finds its soul'. Père Teilhard tells the reader that 'even in its phenomenal nature' such an event is utterly prodigious, that Man is truly the 'hub of the universe', 'the solution of all of which we can have knowledge'.[3] If the reader, moreover, has had some scientific training and some familiarity with scientific publications, all these expressions come to him with the impact of an unaccustomed newness. If he appreciates how well founded they are, a revolution takes place in his mind that affects the whole concept of man he has been taught to accept.

Such a reader is accustomed, in fact, to hearing exclusively about the 'insignificance' of the phenomenon of man, which is treated 'as an accident or incident in nature'. He knows that 'man came silently into the world'. He has been told that man is no more than 'one further term in the series of animal forms', that he is 'just one of the innumerable attempts of the cosmic stuff to infold upon itself'. He cannot deny that the zoological originality of the human is extremely slight: in the classification of living forms this group can only with difficulty be regarded as constituting a new family; 'it is a mere twig detached from the branch of the Primates', from which 'it is hardly separated anatomically'—and so on. Long ago Linnaeus had taught him that in the genus of which he is simply a species, the chimpanzee represents another species. With this basis of material considerations, which it is not difficult to make sound most impressive, he is periodically and forcibly reminded, as though it were a definitely established truth capable of refuting permanently the ancient illusions of the philosophies of the spirit, that nowhere in the world of life is there 'any hiatus or rapture'. It would therefore be 'illogical and dishonest' to seek to accord to man, in relation to other living forms that approximate to him, any 'essential' privilege; what man 'adds to the animal is, in short, very inconsiderable in comparison with what is already animal', and if there is 'a mystery that is proper to man', that mystery is 'of no great importance by the side of the massive mystery of animality';[4] finally, life itself in all its forms is 'only a local and ephemeral accident', a paltry 'unforeseeable by-product of evolution'.[5] Those who think differently, we are told, and consider they are entitled to 'special treatment', display a ridiculous self-satisfaction; they are reactionaries, unable to realize the consequences of the now centuries-old fall of geocentrism, and still more those that modern science obliges us to accept; they are, again, infatuated by 'the naïvely anthropological concept of a world whose only purpose is to be a halo for our planet, in other words for ourselves'.[6]

It must be very difficult for the reader in question not to come to believe in the end that he would not attach so much importance to the human species in his picture of the universe, if he were not the judge of his own case. And then he suddenly comes upon an astonishing book, written by an undeniable scientist and a convinced evolutionist, which sets out 'to break the spell of this false evidence'.[7] It reverses the perspective. It shows the reader that he would be wrong to 'allow himself to be intimidated by the reproach of anthropocentrism'.[8] Throwing off 'pre-conceived anatomical judgements', it brings out that 'by one of those strange inhibiting effects that so often prevent us from seeing what is under our eyes, it is, in fact, the very closeness of the phenomenon of man that blinds us to its formidably special character'.[9] Gradually the reader's mind becomes accustomed to this new way of looking at things; he finds that the book, confining itself, too, as a matter of method, to a study of the phenomenon as such, introduces him to a 'neo-anthropocentrism', to what one might call an anthropo-centrism of movement,[10] which sweeps away, in the name of science, the 'false modesty of scientists'. It forces the reader to recognize, always from the empirical point of view, the unique paradox of the human species and the unrivalled magnitude, 'the staggering magnitude', of the fact of man.[11] While making him realize how deeply 'man is rooted in the universe', Père Teilhard also shows him 'how unmistakably all preceding life is refashioned in man on a new and higher plane'.[12]

'It was essential,' he goes on to explain, 'that in the nine-teenth century a generation of scientists should concentrate on disclosing mankind's roots in the animal world and so con-nect the human genetically with the general evolution of mat-ter. Now, however, that this preliminary work of matching up the two has been done, it is the physical nature of the "hominization-leap" that is becoming the important part of the phenomenon. From this point of view, it is no longer enough (and would be unscientific and absurd) to continue

to treat man as a mere compartment *within* the animal kingdom'.[13]

Thus Père Teilhard, simply by using a method that has
been scientifically renewed, helps us to reinstate man in his
former dignity. He shows us man 'transcending all the categories of Linnaeus' classification, and all earlier forms of biological evolution'.[14] He allows us to recognize in him the
'physical realness of thought, which is stronger than (or rather
includes in its own self) all the boundless properties that a
century of research has attributed to matter'.[15] Man is no
longer merely at the centre of nature, as he was in the fixed
geocentric system (although the metaphor of a centre is still
appropriate),[16] but at the growing-point or peak, man is
seen to be 'a specific summit', 'the terrestrial head of a universe that is in process of psychic transposition', 'the key to
evolution', 'the structural keystone of the universe',[17] 'the
leading-shoot of the tree of life', 'an arrow shot into the
centre of a universe in process of concentration', 'the leading wave of a universe that lights up as it concentrates upon
itself'.[18] That is what man is. Such a being can once again,
without either arrogance or stupidity, believe himself to be the
'supreme achievement of the organizing power of the cosmos'.[19] Once again he can recognize in himself the creature
made 'in the image and likeness of God' that Christian tradition had taught him to see. The human mind 'was suffering
from the trauma of the too sudden, and still too recent, impact
of the realities of evolution'. Père Teilhard is at hand to provide a cure by making men understand that the old picture
of man, which had rescued him from his 'metaphysical dizziness', can be restored to him by the very science of evolution, in its full truth, 'in an even more real and profitable
sense'.[20]

A philosopher or theologian has only to acquire some
familiarity with the present situation in science and the type of
thinking that prevails in many scientific circles, to recognize
these characteristics of man, and to realize the boldness of the
concept, and, in the present scientific context, its revolutionary novelty. He will agree, with Étienne Borne, that in Teilhard's works, 'man's originality comes out with far more

emphasis than it does in Bergson', and that his thinking represents 'a decisive victory over the vague romanticism of the indefinite' of current evolutionary systems.[21] He can see, with Pastor Georges Crespy, that the result of all Père Teilhard's efforts 'to re-include the human object in the sum of scientific objects' has been to disclose 'what is specifically proper to man, and irreducible in him', and he will agree with Pastor Crespy in saying that Père Teilhard's view of things, far from minimizing the fact of man, gives it its true dimensions.[22] With Père Christian d'Armagnac, he will congratulate himself on finding in this scientist who is also a Christian 'the presentation of the whole of the scientific evidence in such a way as clearly to bring out, without venturing into metaphysics, the different levels of the real and their emergence from one another'.[23] With Père Joseph Maréchal he will recognize the kinship between this philosophy of science and Thomism, whose principles entail the possibility 'of a natural science not only of the human body but also of the whole man'.[24] With Père De Tollenaere, he will find in the 'hominizing leap', as described on the phenomenal plane by Père Teilhard, 'the most authentic reflection of what philosophers call the creation of the human soul'.[25] On the other hand, if the reader has little idea either of the influence of science on the whole body of our thinking or of the positivist habits of thought of our own day, or of the real continuity-factors presupposed by the fact that our species has its roots in the universe, or of the limitations that are inherent in every study of the phenomenon as such (even if understood in the wide sense)—then such a reader will be blind to the value of what we have been considering. As he reads, his attention is directed to only one of two sides of the 'paradox' that is presented.[26] In spite of all the book tells him about 'additivity', 'orthogenesis', the 'essential leap ahead' and so on,[27] it seems to him to emphasize only a 'simple continuous development'. It is in vain that Père Teilhard tells him in set terms that 'the union of one pleiad in a monad of higher order is not a simple resultant of the material properties of the elements' harmonized with one another; that 'it involves a complete re-casting and ends in the formation of a new substance'; that this latter presupposes on each occasion 'a completely new principle of union (or soul) that encloses an addition of higher unity'; that in relation to all other living beings 'the thinking being belongs to a new and higher order, for which we have to be careful to allow its own place in the structure of the world'; that, in consequence, 'at the level of reflection, a threshold or critical point is crossed, and something completely new appears'; and finally that what we are considering is 'a great revolution'.[28] However often such a reader is told these things, he still persists in thinking that the author is trying to show him 'each successive state of the world . . . deduced entirely from the preceding state, with no new addition'. He may be shown that there is indeed a difference between one state and the other, but for him it is only a superficial difference brought about by 'what is simply a new arrangement of the elements already in existence'.[29] As Bergson said of Spencer's system, he criticizes Teilhard's system for not living up to its name of evolution, in that it maps out something that is by no means a real development or true genesis. When he reads of the 'discontinuity of continuity' he retains only (as one finds sometimes when listening to an echo) the final syllables—continuity. When he is asked to see in the newly appeared being 'a knot whose strands have been for all time converging from the four corners of space',[30] he fails entirely to understand that, according to this Teilhardian concept, 'the *elements* of a thing are not the *constituents* of that thing, but of the appropriate *substructures*',[31] and that new 'synthesis' means a great deal more than 'simply new arrangement'.

At the same time a reader who makes such demands is surprised, as we have seen, not to find in such a book expositions of a metaphysical or religious order which would in fact be entirely out of place, and their absence seems to him to amount to a half-denial of them. He is distressed when he looks in vain for words that are familiar to him from his textbooks of philosophy or his catechism. He cannot see that 'the continuity recognized by science is phenomenal', that it 'concerns perceptible appearances, not hidden structures', and that it is 'compatible with a passage from one degree of being to another'.[32] Nor, again, can he see that when Père Teilhard invites him to appreciate the 'reflection' of the divine action by following a line of experiential observation,[33] and makes him 'see' in a real sense that the 'appearance of thought renewed the face of the earth'[34] he is offering him something infinitely more valuable than if he had confined himself to reproducing, out of context, the classical assertions or arguments. Time and time again Père Teilhard points out that he is 'assailing the real' from the scientific and not from the metaphysical or religious angle, and that he must accordingly leave to others the final interpretation of what is hidden *under the phenomenal veil* of a revolutionary transformation'[35]— but this reader distrusts these explanations and they fail to reassure him.

The same thing happens, *mutatis mutandis*, with readers of *Le Milieu Divin*. Just as *The Phenomenon of Man* takes over the idea of universal evolution and restates it completely in such a way as to restore to man his dignity, so *Le Milieu Divin* takes over the idea of universal evolution as continued in man through collective human work, and again restates it in such a way as to emphasize man's attachment to God alone. This was a subject we broached at the beginning of the preceding chapter and will examine more closely in the next.

When we consider this matter, it is difficult not to feel that a double prophetic instinct guided Père Teilhard in the development of his theme. It did not, indeed, make him infallible, nor could it ensure that he was always convincing. It could not make up for the inevitable narrowness of his personal point of view. Still less, however, could it have guaranteed him against false interpretations, as M. Nicolas Corte, not without a certain humour, has noted—in connexion, in fact, with the point we are now concerned with.[36] It is the fate of the prophets to be misunderstood, at least initially.

Père Teilhard was a scientist of the first order and had reflected deeply on the new evidence provided by science; but he was in addition, and integrally with his science, not a theologian nor a philosopher, strictly speaking, but a mystic.

He was, indeed, much less unfamiliar with the problems of theology than has been said. He had studied them for four years, at the Jesuit scholasticate of Ore Place, under teachers whose reputation was solidly established.[37] Among his fellow-scholastics were such men as Pierre Rousselot, Joseph Huby, Auguste Valensin, Pierre Charles, and Victor Fontoynont, and it is clear that he was certainly up to their level since he was chosen three years in succession to expound and defend the classic theses in the formal 'disputations'.[38] If we are to understand him properly we should not, therefore, introduce as an explanation some shortcoming on his own part or in the teaching he received, but simply remember the general situation in theology at the beginning of this century. He was quite justified in writing, as he did in a confidential moment: 'I couldn't help thinking of the abyss that divides the intellectual world I was in and whose language I knew, from the theological world of Rome with whose idiom I am also familiar.' And on another occasion: 'Professors of Theology would do well to have a spell of what I am doing now. I am beginning to think that there is a certain aspect of the real world as closed to some believers as the world of faith is to unbelievers.'[39] It was, no doubt, a good thing, and even necessary, that he was not a professional theologian, since it enabled him more easily to take an over-all view of the theology of his time and to appreciate better a number of fundamental problems that professional theologians were not in a good position to see. However, it is true enough that he soon became 'singularly indifferent to academic questions'[40] and that his own 'method of interior meditation in depth' on the dogma of faith, which resulted in the spiritual teaching found in *Le Milieu Divin*, owes nothing to academic theology.

Still less was Père Teilhard a metaphysician: and still less did he wish to be one, at least in his general habit of thought, so that he can hardly be called one at all. It was not that he denied the value of all metaphysics—although he was somewhat mistrustful of what he called 'abstract metaphysics' or '*a priori* geometric synthesis'.[41] The parallel that some have sought to establish in this connexion between his vocabulary and that of Marx itself seems to us somewhat 'deceptive'.[42] It was simply that his competence lay in another field. He knew this and generally took his stand upon it. In comparison with that of his friend Père Auguste Valensin, whose advice he valued greatly, he described his own 'intellectual position' as 'more empirical, more modest, closer, too, to the scientific approach'.[43] On another occasion he said, 'I am neither a philosopher, nor a theologian, but a student of the "phenomenon", a physicist in the ancient Greek sense'.[44] He recognized that, because of its synthesizing character, his 'general scientific interpretation of the universe' could indeed be taken already as a 'hyperphysics' or, as we saw earlier, an 'ultraphysics': but he always insisted that it was not yet a 'metaphysics'.[45] At the same time, this does not mean, as we shall see later, that his work cannot ultimately have a 'metaphysical' (or ontological) value more real than that of many metaphysicians.

'I am to my very marrow,' he once said, 'sensitive to the real, to what is factually so. My concern is to discover the conditions for such progress as is open to us and not, starting from first principles, some theoretical development of the universe. This bias means that I'll always be a philistine to the professional philosophers; but I feel that my strength lies in the fidelity with which I obey it. . . . Others can bring me into line with the principles, if they can.' He knew that metaphysics is something other than, and more than, an extension of science or an organizing of its results—even though, at every period, it must also draw from it the nourishment that too often, it seemed to Père Teilhard, it lacked. No doubt, too, the speculations of some metaphysician friends, always concerned, according to him, 'with what might have been or might not have been', seemed to him to be somewhat 'misleading' or at any rate 'shaky'.[46] Towards the end of his life, his work became increasingly specialized, he was moving in almost exclusively scientific circles, and becoming more familiar with the empiricism of English-speaking scientists; and old age was bringing its inevitable hardening of outlook. All this combined to make it more difficult for him (as in the case of many others) to understand the metaphysicians' approach to a problem: and this was at the very time when, in view of his passion for total synthesis, it would have been the most valuable to him. This accounts, for example, for his being too ready to criticize systems of philosophy of the spirit and studies dealing with the transcendental subject, as individualist thinking, or 'solipsism' or 'introspection in isolation'. These limitations meant that, while he appreciated better than anyone how deeply evolutionary theory had affected our mental system, he himself was unable fully to achieve the new equilibrium that should emerge from it.[47] 'Non omnia possumus omnes.'

The essay in which he carried furthest, and with the most rigour, his attempt to systematize—*La Centrologie* (1944)—is inspired by Leibniz's *Monadology*, both in its literary presentation and in its 'dialectic'. He expressly refers to it, even though he opposes it; he too is trying to produce 'in the form of linked propositions, an essay in universal explanation'; even in this case, however, he disclaims any attempt at 'abstract metaphysics', at an 'extra-temporal metaphysics of being'. His intention throughout is to appeal only 'to a law of experiential recurrence, verifiable in the field of the phenomenon'.[48] He would have been ready to accept, and indeed would have liked to see formulated, 'some generalized ontology' that would be at the same time an understanding of faith, embracing the evidence on being implied in the dogmas of the Trinity and the mystical body.[49] For his own part, however, whatever the object to which his thought was applied, he would prefer to express it 'in some sort of phenomenology'. We should, in fact, take his work as a whole as a 'phenomenology of nature', and understand that 'it remains in continuity with science, in the strict meaning of the word: continuity in method and even in the object considered, though taking into account the changes that method and object undergo at the scale of the whole'.[50] Père Teilhard felt that it was in this, from the scientific point of view, that his originality consisted. Here he was very much on his own ground and could communicate his own special emphasis—disconcerting though it might be to more than one scientist or metaphysician, not to mention the theologians. This is a point to which we shall have to return. While as a scientist himself he had a claim on the attention of his fellow-scientists, even the theologians and metaphysicians (professions to which he did not fully belong) cannot avoid concerning themselves with the problems he raised and cannot but profit from his suggestions.

If Père Teilhard was neither metaphysician by vocation nor theologian by profession, he was certainly a mystic. Even this, however, was contested. According to M. Roger Mehl, the value of Teilhard's work consists in that, like the work of Albert Schweitzer, it offers us a 'rational optimism that keeps us from adventuring into the world of mysticism'.[51] There is, of course, some ambiguity in this remark. If we are correctly to understand its meaning, we must allow for the pejorative sense commonly attached to the word mysticism in a certain Protestant tradition: for if there is any way of thinking that may rightly be called mystical, it is undoubtedly that of Père Teilhard. He himself is constantly using the word. Mysticism is for him, we may remember, 'the great Science, and the great Art'; its domain is 'immense and polymorphous';[52] 'it is the need for, the science and the art of attaining, simultaneously and each through the other, the Universal and the Spiritual';[53] it constitutes the synthesis and the unified peak of all mental activities. This is a concept very close to the old idea of theology as the Queen of the Sciences, dating from the time when theology still meant a practical knowledge of the divine. Even in such a book as *The Phenomenon of Man*, Père Teilhard says that he wishes to bring about 'the conjunction of reason and mysticism'; elsewhere in the same book he refers to that 'Resonance to the All', that 'fundamental vibration' experienced by the mystics 'in the expectation and awareness of a great Presence'.[54] Behind this lies a fact of which he was well aware and which he was not afraid to assert. We find him doing so at the end of a fine passage in an essay in scientific synthesis that he would have liked to see published: 'far from tending to discover a new god, science only goes on showing us matter, which is the footstool of the Divinity. One does not draw near to the Absolute by travelling, but by ecstasy.'[55]

Père Teilhard was a mystical thinker, but he was even more truly a mystic.[56] He was one of those 'souls that have a vision' that is by nature free from 'the countless ties of modern conventions'.[57] From his earliest childhood he had been possessed by a 'passion for the Absolute'. In a number of autobiographical passages he has described the chief characteristics that this passion successively assumed in him. Innate in him were two interior attitudes, the basis of the mystical impulse, which, 'for lack of a better word', he called the 'sense of Plenitude' and the 'sense of Unity'.[58] He had a lively feeling that 'the multiplicity of evolutions into which the world-process seems to us to be split up is in fact fundamentally the working out of one single great mystery'.[59] Since about 1916, which was the time when he had finally learnt to look into himself, the impact of his interior experience comes through in many of his writings. In 'The Mass on the World', whose perhaps somewhat exaggerated lyricism takes us outside all normal literary forms, he wrote: 'I thank you, my God, for having in a thousand different ways led my eyes to discover the immense simplicity of things . . . Through the the awakenings of spirit I owe to the successive initiations, gentle and terrible, which you caused me to undergo, I have been brought to the point where I can no longer see anything, nor any longer breathe, outside that *milieu* in which all is made one.'[60] Again, in 1926, a few days before starting to write *Le Milieu Divin*, he wrote: 'I pray to God that he may preserve in me this deep-rooted zest, this sort of lucid intoxication, that makes me drunk with the joy of Being, quaffed as though from some perennial spring. Sometimes, when I am immersed in rocks and fossils, I experience a nameless bliss in remembering that I possess, in one total, incorruptible and loving Element, the supreme Principle in which all subsists and has life. "Per quem omnia semper bona creas, vivificas, sanctificas et praestas nobis . . .", we say at Mass. What science and what philosophy could compare with the knowledge of that Reality—and above all with its perception, however modest and embryonic it may be?'[61]

If rationally analysed, there is always, we must recognize, an element of ambiguity in the language of the mystics. This is not because it is always imprecise, but because what is precisely expressed is not what we expected; not so much because its emotional basis causes it to be 'excessive' but because it contains an essential paradox. The mystical paradox—which is not theological inexactitude, nor a verging upon the poetic[62] —expresses the dialectic of an interior world which is foreign to pure intellect. What is more, it is seldom that true mystics can avoid meeting, at the outset, with an opposition from many religious-minded men that is stronger than the opposition false mystics have to face. This is because, with the true mystics, we feel that we are getting out of our depth;[63] because they seem to jeopardize more of the things we customarily accept; and because, at the same time, we feel obliged to take them more seriously.

We may conclude this examination of the chief reasons for the resistance with which Père Teilhard's work met, and which it still meets, by adding that, as happens with every scientist who turns the light of philosophy upon the evidence of his own field of science, Père Teilhard sometimes expressed views that contained a considerable element of hypothesis, more considerable, indeed, than he would have admitted. Of such views—in particular on man's future upon this planet—some will say that they border on the Utopian: nor, as we shall see in a later chapter, would I contradict this. At the same time, he was indulging in no Utopian dream when he saw (as he was one of the first to do) that our world is in process of unification and closing-in upon itself at an accelerated rhythm, and that this must inevitably introduce urgent and hitherto unknown problems.[64] No one, we must admit, could have been less dazzled by a false Utopian issue, when we remember how quick he was to realize the serious threat contained in the chief form the Utopia of this century takes, the myth of the 'Golden Age in the future'. He pointed out the power it had over men's minds in spite of the weakness of its intellectual basis—and yet, astonishingly, it is this Golden Age that he has been accused of promising.[65] It may well be true that all his own hypotheses did not share an equally sound foundation, but this is a risk that may occur, or even inevitably be inherent, in every important attempt to extend our knowledge, in every fruitful intuition, and in every progress. That this should be so will surprise only those who have no effective knowledge of the life of the mind and the conditions that govern it.

On the other hand, it is quite true that the conceptual analyses in Père Teilhard's essays are sometimes defective, even when their contribution is most valuable. Their language, although more precise than some have allowed, is moreover strongly characterized—and increasingly so—by a certain professional turn of mind. It was in the context of the natural sciences, a 'context intensely and passionately a part of his life', that 'he began to reflect on the great questions that interested him: the categories, notions and terms used in such reflection bear the mark of the scientific environment with which he was familiar'.[66] This made it easier for him to appeal to readers who shared the same scientific training, but at the same time was responsible for certain corresponding misunderstandings. This trifling fault, irritating though it is for some readers, should not blind us to the very deliberate technical approach found in some parts of his work: nor should it be confused with what was, on the contrary, one of the main strengths of his whole body of work, and may be seen in his best passages—'the invention of a new language, which was not simply a terminology in which to clothe new ideas, or a brilliant command of imagery, but a style of thought which, as we find in the greatest writers, is so closely attuned with what a period is looking for as completely to coincide with it, and whose appeal lies precisely in that correspondence'.[67]

Le Milieu Divin, however, is free from hazardous speculations and questionable phraseology. All one can detect in it is some details of literary presentation and some shades of sensibility that have not worn too well, but even these do not detract from the still striking immediacy of the thought. It could also, no doubt, be said that as an exposition of the spiritual life it is incomplete. That, however, is the price that has to be paid for any markedly personal piece of work. Considering, moreover, that it is an answer to a particular situation, it was doubly inevitable that it should emphasize some aspects at the expense of others. Even so, this in no way distorts the message it presents. It was conceived in its entirety in the light of faith; over a long period, before it was written, all his life and reflective power were put into its substance; later, he realized himself that it could truthfully be regarded as an expression of his own self: that being so, we can understand through *Le Milieu Divin* the full significance and orientation of the whole of Père Teilhard's work, and it is for that reason that it occupies a central position in this study.[68] Of the whole of that work, however, we may say with Père Teilhard that its effectiveness lies not so much in 'a philosophy that may be more or may be less expert' as in the overpowering evidence it offers of a man completely attuned to the ideas and interests of his own time, telling us how he has found 'the correct balance of his interior life' and thereby 'a limitless peace and growth of personality'.

Chapter 9

THE ELEMENT OF NOVELTY

Even in Père Teilhard's religious and spiritual writings, and even in the book that holds a central position among them, *Le Milieu Divin*, the part played by 'novelty' is undeniable. It is this that provides the vital thrust, that, we might say, gives it bite. It does not, however, lie in the domain of the things of faith. As we have seen, it belongs to the domain, always by nature more or less flexible, of what must be illuminated by faith, assimilated or 'incorporated' by faith,[1] lived in faith. Indolent or timid minds who turned away from any such novelty would be in danger of betraying faith itself by initiating a fatal mental divorce: the 'fundamentalist' attitude is a mere caricature of attachment to Catholic tradition. At the same time, we have to ask what reaction such a novelty, even if it is a necessary one, may have on the exercise of the life of faith; how it is interpreted, how far it is taken, and how it is assimilated by the believer.

In this case, the new element—whose basis, we must remember, is not a mental construction but an inevitable affirmation—is the part attributed to man and his work in the setting of a dynamic vision of the Universe.

'Time, that embraces the whole world, is itself embraced in its ruin and is lost as it flows on.' That remark from Guillaume Du Vair's *Traité de la constance*[2] is a good expression of the idea of time and the world's progress that was accepted for many centuries, and until recent times. 'For the ancients time is, in theory, negligible, since the duration of a thing brings out only the degradation of its essence.'[3] The ephemeral and catastrophic aspect of duration, which Péguy comparatively recently emphasized so strikingly,[4] and which Père Teilhard himself described on more than one occasion,[5] cannot, indeed, be denied, though it is not the only aspect. If time 'makes us grow old', if it wears out everything, if it disintegrates and corrupts, it is even more true that it builds. At every moment the Universe is being formed and is growing. It is this perpetual and universal genesis that is expressed by generalized evolutionism.[6] 'All empirical reality is by nature historical.'[7] Accordingly, just as we may not limit evolution in the past by making it begin only with life, so we cannot now halt it at the threshold of the human world. All it has done since the appearance of man is to adopt a new method.

Even those who accepted the idea of a material and biological evolution could look on the appearance of reflective consciousness as the end of a process. For Père Teilhard it simply marked the end of a long preparatory phase, and should more correctly be regarded as a beginning. 'A world that *is being born* instead of a world that *is:* that is what the phenomenon of man suggests, indeed compels us to accept, if we are to find a place for man in this process of evolution in which we are obliged to make room for him.' Through the collective effort of human generations, taking over from nature's vital impetus, a future is being developed. 'Life, in emerging into Thought, did not come to a stop . . . the ship that bears us is still making headway.'[8] Cosmogenesis is being continued in an anthropogenesis. 'It is thus entirely by its tangential envelope that the world goes on dissipating itself in a chance way in matter. By its radial nucleus it finds its shape and its natural consistency in gravitating against the tide of probability towards a divine focus of mind which draws it onward.'[9] 'Beneath the universal turmoil of beings, something is being made, something that is indeed celestial but that is initially within time. Nothing here below is lost for man of man's toil.' Nor, indeed, will anything of it be lost for ever in the beyond. What takes on form throughout duration, even though it is fated to perish in the form it takes on, cannot be pure vanity: for it cannot be doomed simply to nothingness.

Are we justified in seeing in man an extension of evolution that may go so far as to transform him in his very being? We may let that question stand for a moment. In any case, it is for man in some way to continue the creation, to coincide with the views of the Creator by spontaneously collaborating in the work that was begun without him and on his behalf.[10] Each one of us, in his natural activity, collaborates in a vast *opus* 'which infinitely transcends, while at the same time it narrowly determines, the perspectives of his individual achievement: that *opus* is the completing of the world'.[11] To use an analogy that is not to be found explicitly in this form in Père Teilhard himself, but which would seem to be an accurate expression of his thought,[12] we may say that everything that mankind produces, in any order, that has real and communicable value, constitutes a sort of enlargement of his own being, an extension and improvement of his organism, a vast collective body built up by the succession of human generations and no less summoned to resurrection than each of our individual organisms.[13]

We are all familiar with the prolonged resistance, on the part of many theologians, to any idea of biological evolution. It is partly accounted for by the attitude, often anti-Christian, not to say materialist, of those who put forward the theory. Père Teilhard recognized this. The first generations of transformists 'combined with their often masterly insights a great deal of defective explanation and false philosophy'.[14] Moreover, the theologians could find nothing about evolution in the Bible, just as their seventeenth-century predecessors could find nothing about heliocentrism. For the most part, it never occurred to them, any more than it did to the latter, that men can only have the science of their own time, and that Revelation cannot alter it in any way. The light it sheds is of a different order. In Père Teilhard's youth this fixed-species mentality was still very prevalent. There would have been nothing unusual in this, had it not been accompanied by an obstinate hostility to any form of research that might upset it. It drew from him some ironical reflections, in which one can detect a certain amount of resentment, unusual in Père Teilhard:

' "Nothing moves," a first Sage will say. "The eye of common sense sees it and science confirms it." "Philosophy shows that nothing can move," says a second. "Religion forbids it —nothing must move," says a third.'[15]

It was in connexion with the human body that resistance was particularly obstinate. This was to be for many years the principal reason for the opposition shown by a certain number —'not a few', says Fr. Gustave Weigel[16]—to Père Teilhard's activities. He did, it is true, receive support from a certain number of his fellow-Jesuits, as he did in Louvain circles, where Canon Henri de Dorlodot (who died in 1929) welcomed and warmly encouraged him. In his early days, Père Teilhard referred on several occasions to the writings of the latter, who aimed at showing what support for Darwinism could be found in patristic tradition (particularly in the thought of St. Gregory of Nyssa and St. Augustine), and in the great scholastic philosophers for a 'Christian naturalism'.[17] Nevertheless, apart from a few notable exceptions, the great majority of theologians were not with him. Far from it—just as in the twelfth century the 'ignorant' doctors opposed the investigations of Guillaume de Conches, for example, so in those days most theologians were unwilling to admit that God could have created the human body *per naturam operantem*.[18] In the thirties one could still read, in the earlier editions of one of the most approved and widely read treatises, which represented and guided the commonly accepted opinion, that 'God created the body of the first man from inorganic matter'; and this proposition had long been taken to be founded not only on the authority of Scripture and on theological arguments, but even on philosophical reason and, what was more, on scientific facts.[19] Thus all the arguments, whether of the natural or supernatural order, combined to condemn every form of biological transformism, either as certain error or at least (if hedged with precautionary reservations) as extremely rash, and that even when strictly confined to the physical body and seen in a spiritualistic and finalist perspective. We should remember, too, that when the *Évolution régressive* of G. Salet and L. Lafont (a book that is fairly typical) appeared in 1943, a postscript by the well-known Père Le Floch asserted that the authors had demonstrated the 'futility of transformist theories' and that we could now 'abandon for ever the pseudo-science of evolution'.[20]

In August 1950 the encyclical *Humani Generis* was published. Its purpose has not always been fully understood, but one thing it did was to remind theologians, or encourage them to use more circumspection, telling them that the Church's *magisterium* did not forbid inquiry into 'whether the human body was drawn from already living matter'. As some of its most responsible commentators immediately pointed out, this was 'positively to allow much greater freedom of research in this connexion than had been conceded until very recent times by the majority of textbooks of theology'.[21] It was an encouragement to develop an 'evolution' that was already, though with some diffidence, taking shape.[22] The only point on which the position of the *magisterium* was still rigorous—though even on this it was not committed to a definitive, irrevocable verdict—was that of 'monogenism'. On this point, however, Père Teilhard's scientific presentation avoids any, at least immediate, difficulty. 'It is impossible,' he explains, 'to put your hand on the real beginning of anything . . . It is of the very nature of human emergence that' it escapes scientific investigation 'in its concrete reality'.[23] Monogenism, therefore, and polygenism are notions 'that by their nature lie outside science, in as much as they cannot be verified experimentally'. In other words, 'the scientist can offer no direct proof that the hypothesis of an individual Adam is untenable'. At the same time, when Père Teilhard explained the scientific reasons which suggest that that hypothesis is less probable, he was doing no more than fulfilling his duty as a technical adviser without encroaching on the domain of theology, and it is well that qualified scientists should continue to do so.[24] As for transformism itself (of which the encyclical says that it must not be condemned as contrary to dogma), and the degree of probability to be accorded to the theory, it would appear that we may safely apply to them what Père Dominique Dubarle recently said about geocentrism and seventeenth-century theology: the transition from what the latter called hypothesis 'to the affirmation of the truth of the picture presented by science is not effected by the application of any particular proof and in the form of an irresistible argument: it is effected through an unshakeable reversal of accepted certainties in minds that have become sufficiently familiar with scientific thought and its solid acquisitions'.[25] We may now hope that the future attitude of theologians will show more than negative discretion and prudence. It may well be, in fact, that it will gradually be realized that 'evolutionary outlooks are more in accord with the tenor of Revelation itself' than was the former fixed-species mentality, since in the former 'mankind's progress towards the end of all time and the Kingdom of God finds a setting more co-natural to it than the cyclic universe in which theological thought has for centuries been accustomed to situate it'.[26] It is not too much to hope, then, that the successors of those who long ago so bitterly opposed Galileo and more recently Saint-George Mivart will be concerned to avoid such unhappy conflicts, the responsibility for which, as has been said,[27] was in any case shared to a large extent by both sides. But what is even more important, let us hope, too, that even though it may not be necessary for them to go all the way with Père Teilhard, they may profit from his work in a positive way. 'Contemporary science is transforming the appearance of nature under our very eyes, and theology cannot afford not to take this event into account. . . . The Church is so sure of the truth of faith that she sees in each advance of science the sure promise of a corresponding progress in the intellection of faith. . . . The better we understand nature, the better we shall know God.'[28] This was said by a Catholic Thomist, Étienne Gilson: the spirit of his words is precisely the spirit of the great doctor whose tradition he follows, and we know that another great interpreter of St. Thomas, Père Sertillanges, thought on the same lines. What the latter had said about the possibility and necessity of a synthesis of Thomist philosophy and evolutionary teaching had been a great consolation to Père Teilhard.

On 4 February 1934, he wrote to Père Sertillanges from Peiping:

'I have just been reading your excellent little book, *Dieu ou Rien*, which has just landed upon our distant shores. Let me tell you how delighted I have been with it. You are beginning at last, and in a tone so measured and authoritative, to make people hear the word that for so long I have dreamt of hearing echoing openly through the Church. If Christianity

. . . often finds it so difficult to maintain its true place in the minds of believers and also to attract the Gentiles, it is chiefly because it sometimes *appears* to underrate or fear the greatness and unity of our universe. And now at last one feels in your book an impassioned sympathy, completely un-partisan, with the World's work; a spirit of God breathes in it, nourished by the spirit of the Earth.'

It was not only that Père Teilhard was 'concerned to show how' the evidence of science 'leaves open the approaches to dogmatic truths',[29] or how 'the heaven of science' has not obscured 'the heaven of theology'.[30] His purpose was not simply to defend the truth of the faith against those who maintained that it had been disproved by the appearance of transformism. What had to be done now, he said, was 'to take the offensive' by showing that transformism, which some even within the Church considered was 'as anti-Christian by nature' in fact well qualified to provide 'an excellent basis for Christian thought and action'.[31] His thought, however, reached even further afield. As we have just seen, it did not stop short at an examination of biological evolution strictly so called, nor was it confined to a study of the past. '*The past*,' he wrote, in a phrase whose importance had rightly been emphasized, '*has revealed to me how the future is built*.'[32] It was increasingly on the 'building' that the enthusiasm of his quest was to be concentrated. 'What is past is dead and no longer interests me.' 'I am continuing to explore the past as faithfully as before, but there is no doubt that henceforth my interest is *quite definitely in what lies ahead*.'[33] That repeated admission dates from 1936. Much earlier, in 1916, he was feeling that 'in its broad outline, the history of life on earth has given us all one expected of it' and that the time had come 'to get to grips with matter, organic life, collective life, and to master it, subject it to experiment, make it give up its secrets and its power'. The future already 'fascinated' him. Later, he was to express himself more forcibly: 'I am now feeling a new sort of nausea with the study of the past . . . I have definitely made a right-about turn to the front.'[34]

What Père Teilhard sees ahead is in the first place 'that all men are made, by virtue of their natural situation, for collaborating' in one and the same task. Is not, he asks, 'this idea of a total human task to be accomplished the inevitable corollary of a totalized mankind?' He believes, accordingly, in 'the value of the human phyletic effort'.[35] To anticipate such a development could hardly in itself be called rash. 'In this perhaps,' says Père Olivier Rabut, 'we have his master-concept and the one most fruitful in practical application.'[36] It reaches out ahead of the situation that is emerging from 'the present technological fact' and it is this, no doubt, that so enormously strengthens its persuasive force. For this techno-logical fact 'represents a separate *order*, essentially new in re-lation not only to the civilization of the hand-tool but also to that of the first machine . . . Collective work is governed by an underlying hidden aim, and animated by an impulse, whose target is a conquest of the cosmos. It is not simply a question of organizing the earth to serve man and increase his well-being, but of effecting a complete re-fashioning of nature, in answer to a rational demand'.[37] It has 'become a matter of loyalty and "conscience" to strive to extract from the world all that the world can hold of truth and energy. (*There must be noth-ing* in the direction of more-being that remains *unattempted*)'. The Creator's ordinance, 'Fill the earth and subdue it' is re-peated today with a new significance of which Père Teilhard's writings are an exhilarating echo.[38]

In this lies the explanation and the basis of the spiritual thesis of *Le Milieu Divin*, as expressed in the most emphatic part of its message, which tells us that God is to be sought not by rejecting created beings but through them. What has to be done is 'without making the smallest concession to "nature" but with a thirst for greater perfection, to provide nourishment for'—so that it may continually grow stronger—the power both of giving and of detachment.[39] This means that the 'striving towards detachment' must be intensified even at the heart of 'the spirit of conquest'.[40] Such, in Père Teil-hard's view, was the new form that must be assumed by Christian humanism, if it is not to become a mere survival but remain faithful to its duty of Christianizing the neo-humanism of today.[41] He knew very well that what he was urging was liable to be misunderstood, and he was concerned to make sure that in his own case it should not become a source of error. On several occasions, accordingly, he was at pains to vindicate it by expressing it with greater accuracy. He was already doing so in December 1919, when he was in correspondence with Maurice Blondel. In Père Teilhard's view, it would matter little that the omnipresent action of Christ in him should assume 'the character of a break with, and extinction of the visible world' rather that of a 'transformation'. What he urges, then, is not a lesser degree of detachment; it is not a compromise between love of the world and love of God; it is not a sort of 'middle' way.[42] More emphatically, it is not an alternation from time to time between the two, rather like a new Ecclesiastes, as though there were a time for enjoyment and a time for abstention in order later to find better enjoyment. It might seem superfluous to say this, but it must be said, since an equally mistaken interpretation, backed by a reference to André Gide's *Ménalque*, has been put forward in all seriousness in a book addressed to the general reader.[43] Père Teilhard's way, which he calls 'the way of synthesis',[44] is one of austerity in both its phases, for the first phase itself is characterized by 'effort' and 'tension', and both phases are not exclusive of one another, following one another in time, but opposite and conjoint moments of a single dialectic. To seek God 'through all things' is, by definition, not to come to rest in anything. Within one and the same act that can be 'incredibly rich and simple', 'the spirit of detachment and the spirit of conquest', as also 'the spirit of tradition and the spirit of adventurous inquiry, meet together, correct and ennoble one another'. It is one 'deliberate act of transition' that is divided into two acts only by analysis.[45] Or again, it is a 'rhythm with countless variations', 'a twofold and yet single movement', or, as he says elsewhere, 'one alternating movement'. It represents 'two phases of the soul's breath —or two components of the impulse by which the Christian life uses things as a springboard from which to mount beyond them'.[46] These two components are always, more or less, fused in the unity of 'a single disinterested effort', even though one can distinguish in the life of every one of the faithful, as in that of the whole history of the Church, suc-

cessive or varying periods when one component is more dominant than the other: such dominance, however, is more in
the type of life adopted as a 'vocation' than in the substance
of an attitude that always remains fundamentally the same.[47]
It is simply, as we can see more clearly today, that there is
for the Christian 'a way of becoming very detached by so
attaching oneself to that element in the world that breaks
away and becomes divinized' in such a way that at every
moment he is borne onwards by creatures and at every moment leaves them behind, in a continual acceptance of them
and a continual detachment from them.[48]

With a slightly different aim in view, Père Teilhard adopts,
too, an idea found in St. Thomas Aquinas, for whom natural
love is not only the basis but already in some way the analogue
of charity. Thus the first phase of the act in which, as we have
seen, the Christian attitude is integrated may be considered as
the natural analogue of the second:

'Anyone whose aim, in conquering the earth, has only
really been to subject a little more matter to spirit has, surely,
begun to take leave of himself at the same time as taking
possession of himself. This is also true of the man who rejects
mere enjoyment, the line of least resistance, the easy possession of things and ideas, and sets out courageously on the
path of work, inward renewal and the ceaseless broadening
and purification of his ideal. And it is true, again, of the man
who has given his time, his health, or his life, to something
greater than himself—a family to be supported, a country to
be saved, a truth to be discovered, a cause to be defended.
All these men are continually passing from attachment to detachment as they faithfully mount the ladder of human endeavour.'[49]

It is a difficult road for anyone who wants to follow it
perfectly, more difficult than the way of an external and material detachment—which, moreover, cannot but be relative
and brings with it, too, its own misconceptions. It was in any
case the only way that seemed to Père Teilhard capable, for
men as a whole, engaged in the common callings of life, of
doing justice to all the divine ordinances. For further authority, he would have had to look no further than the *Spiritual*

Exercises of St. Ignatius, where he treats of the 'use of crea-tures' in the *Principle and Foundation*, of which, as we have seen, Père Teilhard offers a mystical interpretation. It is in fact because he loves God and in order that he may love him better, and it is in so far as he loves and seeks to love more, that he sees the Christian 'happily compelled to participate in all the endeavours, all the anxieties, all the aspirations and also all the affections of the earth—*in so far as these embody a principle of ascension and synthesis*'.[50] However, as this passage shows, the way that he sought so earnestly to mark out was taking on for him an increasing urgency. If, in fact, the use of creatures is imperative in order that every man may fulfil the duties of his state, then the new responsibility that has now been laid on mankind as a whole gives this imperative a further sanction. 'Starting with man, who is the term and consciousness of evolution, it was the forces of invention that began to take in hand the reins of progress.' In our day, man is realizing this for the first time; and he has never felt 'his fearful responsibility' so forcibly as now, 'when the whole sub-human cosmos begins to stir in response to his call, like a giant awakened from sleep'.[51]

Père Teilhard was keenly aware of this new responsibility, and this is reflected in some of his wartime thoughts:

'The more I think of it . . . the more I feel the necessity of defining and organizing the *total* natural human effort . . . I can't believe that the world was given to man simply to *keep him busy*, as if it were a wheel to turn. . . .

'It seems to me that man has a fundamental obligation to draw from himself and from the earth everything they can give; and this obligation is all the more urgent in that we are completely ignorant of what limits—perhaps still very far-distant—God has set to our natural powers . . . I cannot be-lieve that by opening up for us the prospect of a more divine life, God dispensed us from pursuing the work of creation, even on its natural plane.'[52]

We can now, perhaps, understand more clearly the paradox of the 'impassioned indifference' that he put forward as his watchword.[53] There must be indifference, because 'God alone' must be the object of the whole of our love; but it must be impassioned, because the task that God sets us is so great that we must give the whole of our selves to it. In our quest for 'the one thing that is needful', every slackening of tension and every halt to obtain some human enjoyment, is a weakness. Generally speaking, however, we shall not practise perfect detachment if we fail to apply ourselves to—or rather attack—with all our energies, and in line with our own particular calling, the work that has to be done. We have continually to raise our sights. 'Without deviating into any naturalism or Pelagianism the believer finds that he can and must, as much as and *more* than the unbeliever, develop a passion for the progress of the earth, which is a necessary condition for the consummation of the Kingdom of God. *Homo sum.—Plus et ego.* And nevertheless the elevating force of detachment remains unimpaired.'[54]

Such, then, was Père Teilhard's central intuition; he realized and asserted that he was at once a 'child of earth' and a 'child of heaven', and saw with complete clarity that renunciation and asceticism 'play a capital and definitive part in the construction of the new Universe'.[55] It was an intuition that was, indeed, not so much a solution to the problem of life as an intuitive appreciation of the problem itself. Or one might say that even if the general lines of the solution were indicated, a series of new problems (as constantly happens) arose; and year by year, not always with the same success, new essays were devoted to their elucidation. How are we rightly to effect 'the explicit fusion of the Christian life with the "natural" life-sap of the universe, or communion with God through the earth'?[56] How are we day by day to realize in practice this 'reconciliation of progress and detachment, of the passionate and legitimate love of the earth at its greatest and the single quest for the Kingdom of Heaven? How can we be as Christian as no other man is, and yet more man than anyone'?[57] How are we to establish 'in the depth of our hearts the alliance between the passion for the World and the passion for God'?[58] How can we effect, 'in the heart of each one of us, the living synthesis between the movement of the Gospel (Faith in God) that ascends towards the Above, and the modern movement of forward progress towards the Ahead'?[59]

How can one unite 'these two powerful currents, of human progress and the greater charity, between which the impact of man's religious energies are today divided'?[60] All they seek is 'to combine and complete one another'; but we still have to work to 'make ready this great event' by setting out to discover 'a unified impulse of worship in which will be joined and mutually exalted both a passionate desire to conquer the World and a passionate longing to be united with God: the vital act, specifically new, corresponding to a new age in the history of Earth'.[61] In other words, we have to find, more through life itself than through reflective effort, 'a new way of expressing holiness'.[62] We have to discover some 'new attitude', and it is no use looking to the saints of the past either for explicit approval or for condemnation of it, 'since the problem of human progress, as we see it today, *did not exist for them*'. But 'what is necessary—and sufficient—is to be able to recognize their specific act of perfection transposed', as we have just seen, 'into terms of our present outlook'.[63] It is thus that, in new conditions, 'the immutable axis of holiness' will have to be preserved in the Church.[64]

It was apostolic fervour as much as an inner compulsion that was behind Père Teilhard's desire to carry out this plan. Distressed by the evident 'rupture' he was well placed to observe between 'Christianity and natural progress', his ambition was to see 'a legitimate reconciliation—and how fundamental this is!—between those who worship Christ and those who worship the world'—and by the latter, he adds, he means 'those who are possessed by an overpowering and disinterested passion to make life greater'.[65] Thus the 'energies' that appeared 'so menacing' would be converted into a 'new flood' which would 'bring new life to the old underlying stream of Christianity', while the Christian faith would bring salvation to the combined whole of man's spiritual dynamism by raising it up with it in its ascent towards the divine.[66] Since about his thirtieth year, the idea, or to use his own word, the 'consciousness' of universal evolution, had been growing stronger in him 'not so much as an abstract notion as a presence', until 'it filled the whole of *his* interior sky', and this consciousness was influencing him in the same direction.[67] As early as 1917 he was feeling that 'spirit itself is still in process of creation, *de limo totius naturae*—if not as regards the spirituality of individual souls, at least as regards their hitherto unknown types and characteristics, and in their social synthesis.[68] Put forward originally with some diffidence, this view was to become more emphatic and extensive. It was to give him an increasing interest in, almost an obsession with, what lay ahead. He no longer had simply to face the almost classic problem of combining the cultivation of natural gifts with the urgent demands of Christian detachment. The 'robust common sense' of his 'spiritual father' in Jersey during his juniorate, Père Troussard, had once given him the practical solution to that problem, leaving to Père Teilhard himself to find later the theoretical confirmation of the line he suggested to him: this was when, in his youthful desire for perfection, Père Teilhard had thought it was his duty 'seriously to consider the possibility of giving up the science of petrology'.[69] It may, it is true, have always been the same problem, but in any case it came to him on a wider scale and with a new and more acute urgency. Henceforth Christianity 'was faced with an absolutely new situation' and had to 'match the new curve' adopted by time in such a way as to 'discover the values of this world *below the level of God*', while humanism would have to find room for a God above the level of this world.[70]

It was by no means a simple task, and to undertake it called for considerable courage. Moreover, it would certainly take very little to make it a complete failure. We may wonder whether Père Teilhard was always successful in expressing the problem correctly. When he speaks of a 'twofold vision' that must be brought into one, or of 'two components' that must be combined, of an 'alliance' to be concluded, of a synthesis, or even a 'fusion' to be effected, there is nothing, I believe, in such expressions that could disturb anybody. His 'unified impulse of worship', however, could be more open to misunderstanding. The phrase comes, we should note, in a lecture given in Peking in 1940 on 'the possible basis of a universal human creed', to a mixed audience, to whom, as the title suggests, he was outlining only the first stage of the spiritual journey. During those years of semi-isolation in Peking, a possibly too personal interest in apologetics may have conflicted in him, though without impairing it, with the mystical impulse of the preceding period. As he became more deeply conscious of the significance and 'necessity of irreversibility', his obsession with the Ahead became increasingly dominant. The need for interior unity expressed itself more and more, progressively found more satisfaction in, and even to some degree became converted into a tendency towards an intellectual systematizing.[71] Nevertheless, he was perfectly aware, and was always to insist, that the Ahead would be no more than a mirage without the initial and abiding presence of the Above. He knew well, and continued to assert with equal emphasis, that this Ahead, as such, was not promised for all time. In his own interior life, the solution of the great vital problem remained correct: there is any amount of intimate evidence to confirm this, in particular that of the notes he made during his annual retreats, when he always drew new strength 'from deep within the circle of the Presence'. Until the very end he could have repeated what he wrote in 1929 about all 'the centres of attraction' that might, throughout the course of his life, have had the power to draw him away from his faith. 'One after another, by the help of God, these various centers have either faded away into nothingness or, in most cases, have gradually come to coincide with the great figure of Jesus Christ . . . one single Light has absorbed all the others.'[72] Nevertheless, it must be admitted that the writings of his last period contain traces of a somewhat over-simplified prophetic attitude.

Here again, no doubt, we may say that he was faithful to himself. As he had written in 1923, in 'The Mass on the World', 'All joy and all achievement, the very purpose of my being and all my love of life, all depend on this one basic vision of the union between yourself, my God, and the universe'—so, in 1950, he wrote in *Le Cœur de la Matière*, 'From the depths of the cosmic future, as from the heights of heaven, it was still God, it was *always the same God* who was calling me', and in the general context the meaning of those passages is unmistakable. However, the substitution of 'cosmic future' for 'Universe' is not the only characteristic that distinguishes the second quotation. He now seems to envisage 'a new Faith, in which are combined the upward-striving Faith in a transcendent and the propulsive Faith in an immanent', and if we are to accept these and similar passages without demur, we should perhaps bear in mind the indisputable correctness of the author's intention. We shall then agree, and rightly, that when he spoke of a 'super-Christ', he expressed himself with insufficient care. We may remember, too, that he was writing with the consciousness of his inability completely to solve a problem in which so many other problems were involved, which was always with him and in which he was coming more and more to recognize the chief preoccupation of his life. 'I have always offered myself to Our Lord as a field for experiment, so that, to some small degree, he may effect in me the fusion of the two great loves, of God and of the world—a fusion without which, I am convinced, there can be no Kingdom of God.'[73] On another occasion he said: 'It is a great release no longer to prize anything but the truth, and to be convinced that sooner or later Our Lord will bring together in synthesis within himself the whole of this truth and all our clumsy or feeble efforts to attain it.'[74]

The fusion he so wished for could be obtained on the spiritual plane only if it could be effected at the same time on the doctrinal plane. In other words, only if there should become manifest 'a coherent prospect wherein . . . the deepest and most powerful currents of human consciousness may converge and culminate: . . . the currents of learning and religion'.[75] For Père Teilhard, this prospect is already here. He believes that he has not only expressed the 'undeniable need' but also found the effective intellectual means of 'saving and mutually intensifying the warmth of an ultra-personal God and the immense organicity of the fantastic cosmogenesis whose emergence we are witnessing'. He found the means through the study of St. John and St. Paul and of the Greek Fathers,[76] from whom he drew the ideas he expressed in his Christology—and for that reason his writings should encourage modern exegetes and theologians to give more continuous attention to texts whose doctrinal richness has not been sufficiently exploited. 'It is impossible for me,' he said in 1920, in

Mon Univers, 'to read St. Paul without seeing, beneath his words, with dazzling clarity, the universal and cosmic dominance of the Incarnate Word.'[77] Again, he asks: 'Is not the basis of Catholic dogma aimed at furthering and explaining the union of creatures in God through Christ?'[78] 'By a direct extension of his theandric attributes' and without his historic reality being thereby destroyed, the universal Christ 'makes the transcendent immediate—he unifies the Multiple by differentiating it—he makes it possible to complete what already is and to conquer what one already holds—he detaches us from the World by attaching us to it'.[79] He is 'the physical centre of final determination and true consistence imposed on all of creation that is to survive'.

The 'cosmic sense', therefore, must be combined with the 'Christic sense'.[80] 'The two poles of the World', the external and the internal, the tangible and the intangible, must be 'brought into contact'.[81] Today we have a new force at hand to effect this. 'In the old days, for Our Lady to be loved passionately' it was necessary for man 'to become, in the form of the Christian, more refined, sensitive, and human'. Similarly, 'if they were to love the great universe and feel the need to embody Christ in it, men had to make a prolonged effort of observation, thought and self-mastery'.[82] For the Christian of today who considers the evolution of the world and understands its significance, 'instead of the vague centre of convergence envisaged as the ultimte end of this process of evolution, the personal and defined reality of the Word Incarnate, in which everything acquires substance, appears and takes its place'.[83] And if such a Christian looks somewhat more closely, he will finally perceive 'a wonderful conjunction of a Christ directly seen as *evolver*, and a positively recognized cosmic centre to evolution'. He sees the brilliant emergence of 'the astonishing, emancipating, harmony between a religion that is Christic, and an evolution that is convergent, in type'.[84] The Apostle's statement, *in quo omnia constant*, to which Père Teilhard continually refers, without interpreting it simply according to the letter, then finds its natural expression for him, if it is to retain its realism, in faith in 'the Person of Christ, the principle and *soul* of evolution'. Knowing that Christ is the 'First-born and the Head' he concludes from this that 'in him and through him all things have been launched, hold together and are consummated'.[85] It is in this form, if it is to remain unimpaired and to retain all its force, that faith 'in the plenitude, beauty and kingship of Christ' must today be expressed.[86]

'Christ is not some extra feature added to the world, an embellishment, a king such as we crown, the owner of a great estate . . . He is the Alpha and the Omega, the Principle and the End, the foundation stone and the keystone, the Plenitude and the Plenifier. He is the one who consummates and the one who gives consistence to all things. To him and through him, the interior life and light of the world, is effected, in pain and labour, the universal convergence of all created spirit. He is the one single centre, precious and stable, that shines out at the summit, still to come, of the world, in diametric opposition to the dim and eternally shrinking regions into which our science ventures when it travels down the road of matter and the past.'[87]

One can understand, then, how Père Teilhard could write to his friend the Abbé Henri Breuil: 'Fundamentally, my real interest in life is moving irresistibly towards a more and more intense concentration on this basic question of the relations between Christ and "hominization".'[88] Here he was simply repeating in different words what he had written thirty years earlier in the first draft of his *Mon Univers*:

'I long with all my strength for the elements of truth universally believed and professed by the Church, concerning the universal presence of God and of Christ, to be at last considered as one whole, with no dilution of their substance.'[89]

Shortly afterwards, at the beginning of his scientific career, we find another repetition of the same wish:

'The Lord has taken me along roads so unexpected that I am counting on him to use me for his greater glory. If only I may in some small way serve this great cause—the only cause I really have at heart—of the deliberate fusion of the Christian life with the "natural sap of the universe".'[90]

Chapter 10

EVOLUTION AND FREEDOM

Numerous and emphatic though they are, it would nevertheless be a great mistake to be satisfied with the general terms
Père Teilhard uses when he is speaking of 'conjunction', or
'convergence', and even 'fusion', or of 'coincidence' and 'harmony' between Christ and the Universe, between the two
great zones of being, the natural and the supernatural. He had
no intention, when using such expressions, of suggesting any
confusion of the two. The reservations we have expressed are
far from implying that all he did was to clothe a naturalist
thought in Christian terminology. If he establishes a certain
organic relationship between the evolution of the cosmos and
the growth of the mystical body, or if he sets out to 'explain the
bonds that link together genetically the Kingdom of God and
human effort',[1] it is not in order to suggest to us that the two
terms of the equation are basically identical. The reader
will already have realized this. Because a line of thought points
to unity it does not necessarily point to uniformity, nor must
it necessarily involve an over-simplification. In spite of the
impression that may be given by some of the abrupt short-
cuts in the argument, Père Teilhard did not absorb the supernatural in nature nor reduce eternal life to a human future:
a point that we shall have to examine more closely. Nor, as
this chapter will show, did his dynamic, evolutionary concept
of the universe cause him to profess an optimism, based on
the inevitability of progress, that would destroy all man's
freedom.

In Père Teilhard's view, a double victory is assured. The
first is the victory of Spirit over matter. Spirit was born into
the universe with man, and can never perish. 'Whatever apparent elements of impermanence there may be in life, and
however impressive its involvement in spatial limitations and
the forces of disintegration, one thing is as certain as can be

(because it is as certain as the world itself): Spirit will always continue to succeed, as it has hitherto succeeded, in getting the better of determinisms and chance. It represents the indestructible portion of the Universe.'[2] 'The ebb of entropy' will be overcome 'by the rising tide' of Noogenesis.[3] Evolution is irreversible. 'The temperature of the Noosphere' is constantly rising: in other words there is 'an intensification of consciousness'. The universe is developing personality. Everything is rising 'towards an ultimate peak.'[4] A second victory, involved in and conditional upon the first, is equally assured. This is the victory of the risen Christ, whose Pleroma will one day be accomplished; and although the assurance we receive from our Faith 'leaves all the anxieties attendant upon the human condition, on their own level, still alive in the heart of the believer', at the same time it strengthens and sanctions our assurance of the victory of Spirit. For the Christian, man's 'biological success' must be much more than a probability: it is an absolute certainty.[5]

Nevertheless, this in no way means that every individual automatically shares in this double victory, or that the victory of Spirit in him is his own personal victory and the guarantee of his beatitude. The culmination of the universe is one thing, the salvation of the individual is quite another.[6] What happens is that cosmic evolution, continued by man, 'rebounds', but only to proceed in completely different conditions. Increasing complexity means increasing 'freedom'. 'Man', the final product of planetary evolution, is both supremely *complex* in his physico-chemical organization (measured by the brain), and, considered in his psychism, *supremely free and conscious.*[7] Similarly, the Noosphere, which in its initial significance is a reality with which we are already presented, is also, in a second sense, and predominantly, an ideal to be realized morally and by the use of our freedom. Just as suffering is the 'shadow' that lies over the ascent towards the 'improbable', so moral transgression is the 'hazard' that threatens it. Hominization means 'the appearance of morality and the crisis it involves'; and it is for that reason that Anthropogenesis, 'surrounded as it is by dangers', is a drama.[8]

Père Teilhard is continually warning us of this, in terms

that vary with the subject and point of view of each particular essay but that are fundamentally the same. 'Starting with man, the cosmos is built, physically, by moral values.'[9] In other words, 'in man' evolution 'becomes interiorized', which means not only that it becomes more conscious but also that it thereby acquires a 'moral'—even a 'mystical'—character (since 'the measure of an ethical system is its capacity to develop into mysticism'), and takes on freedom; and that again, it is clear, does not mean that men will do good as the result of a compulsive impulse, but (a very different thing) that the good is presented to them as a moral imperative. Thus 'morality and holiness take on an essential organic significance in the economy of universal development'. With man, life entered the age of 'reflective freedom'.[10] What had been until then a blind urge towards an 'infallible progress' became 'the power of reflective organization' and 'a progress that may be accepted or rejected'; and the effective achievement of that progress can consist only in a 'rise into the improbable through the triumph of freedom'. Thus 'to emerge into the domain of intelligence' is, by definition, to emerge into the domain not only of 'foresight' but also 'of freedom'.

This liberty of man is exercised, it is true, and 'manifested only through and by means of a closed circle of physico-chemical and physiological determinisms', but only 'a superficial examination' would fail to see in this anything more than a 'fantastically complicated mechanism'. It is true, again (and this is a point that, like Père Teilhard himself, we shall have to consider), that there are a technological and cultural progress, a progress of 'socialization' and intelligence that in themselves do not belong to the moral order, and constitute the natural conditions for the maturing of the universe. 'We may say without hesitation . . . that it would be easier to halt the revolution of the earth than it would be to prevent the totalization of mankind.'[11] It was with this type of progress that, in many of his writings, Père Teilhard generally found that he had to deal. He realized, as each one of us can do, whether believer or unbeliever, that such progress does not depend on the inner dispositions of those who bring it about. Evil itself, as we know, exists in the world 'like the slave who draws the water'.[12] God, said St. Augustine, realizes his work of justice *etiam per malos nescientes*,[13] and as the saying goes, even the devil has his uses. That is why 'there is a certain glamour about *daring* evil: when it's successful it seems to provide its own excuse'; in that, however, Père Teilhard adds, there is 'an organic sophism' which 'it is important to clarify precisely and expose'.[14] Here, though with a more modern emphasis, he echoes what was in Fénelon's mind when he said, 'God has often promised that the impious shall accomplish his designs even through crimes',[15] or Malebranche's explanation that 'though God uses the impious and the demons even for the carrying out of his designs, since everything, even disorder, enters into the order of Providence', yet it is equally true that 'disorder always remains disorder'.[16] At the same time, in spite of the disorder that persists and the evil that is not neutralized, the progress of the world, in the sense just defined, is assured, and that even though there can be any number of partial setbacks. It does not, however, follow from this (as has sometimes been too hastily concluded from Père Teilhard's explanations) that by the very fact that the world advances, becomes organized and unified, evil is 'in process of being re-absorbed'.[17] This type of optimism (though shared by some illustrious theologians)[18] was not Père Teilhard's. In other words, such a progress should not be confused with the positive attainment of an end. It is only a condition of that attainment, and while it constitutes a 'force', it is 'the most dangerous of forces'.

Thought, 'by the very fact of its appearance', is already, for the living stem, an element of disorganization; it 'necessarily marks an organic crisis of life'. The triumph of Spirit over Matter could thus become in the end the most crushing defeat for men, and one would then have to apply to it that terrible saying 'better that he had never been born'—which means that it would have been better had Noogenesis been destroyed by entropy. In fact, 'under the influence of isolated egoisms' the universe remains 'liable to disintegrate into a dust made up of grains of freedom'.[19] The temptation to lose heart, which always threatens our species, as we shall see more clearly in a later chapter, is not the only temptation. 'Nothing can prevent man-the-species from growing still greater, (just as man-the-individual . . .) so long as he preserves in his heart the passion for growth': but this growth, or progress, does not contain its own end.[20] It is 'designed to enable a considered action to proceed from the will of mankind, a wholly human exercise of choice'.[21] It will thus turn out to have been, according to the way the choice is made, 'for good or for evil'. This mental prospect is so much part of Père Teilhard's habit of thought that he instinctively uses such words as 'ambiguity', 'risk', 'choice', 'option', 'alternative', or again 'conversion', 'temptation', 'possible check', 'danger of perversion', etc.[22] A number of the titles or sub-titles to some of his essays emphasize even more the structural importance in his teaching of such an idea: thus we have 'the Option', 'the Grand Option', 'the Cross-roads', 'the Hour of Decision', 'the Choice of Road', 'the Rise of Freedom'.[23]

Teilhard had the perfectly justified feeling that human liberty 'appears everywhere' and even 'increases everywhere' in his universe.[24] He believed that anyone who adopts his evolutionary outlook must realize this with special force, when he sees 'the greatness of his responsibilities increasing almost to infinity before him'.[25] A number of his interpreters have appreciated this. For example Dr. Paul Chauchard speaks of freedom as 'being at the heart of Teilhard's thought'.[26] In spite of this some readers have appeared to believe that he suppressed freedom, or at any rate failed to take it into account. They suggest that between Christian teaching and Teilhard's optimism there is the 'fundamental difference' that the latter takes mankind's ascending progress towards ever greater happiness and virtue as assured in advance. In reality, the only infallible progress asserted by Père Teilhard is one not in happiness or virtue but in consciousness and 'tension'. It may be well at this point to anticipate another misunderstanding that might be suggested by the very passages in which Père Teilhard was in fact trying to show the transition from the order of biological necessity to that of moral freedom. After having attempted to establish that the 'era of active evolution did not end with the appearance of the human zoological type', he adds that in man a new factor comes in as 'a *necessary* condition for the preservation and heightening of his powers of invention and purposive thinking'. The new condition that will henceforth be necessary is 'ethics', whose 'rules' are bound to become increasingly imperative: 'the pursuit of human knowledge cannot be carried in concrete terms beyond a certain stage without this power of reflective arrangement becoming *automatically* charged with internal obligations' while at the same time it engenders around itself 'an entirely new atmosphere of spiritual needs'.[27] A hasty reader of these explanations (which are not in fact quite so clear as they might be) might well remember only the two words we have italicized (*necessary* and *automatically*) without noting the object that they qualify.[28] It is possible to overlook that what is asserted thereby is precisely the necessity for the intervention in the kingdom of man of *moral* freedom, and in consequence the automatic increase, in step with the progress of knowledge, of moral *obligations*, or the refinement of moral consciousness.[29]

'If progress is to continue it cannot do so unaided.' It is man's free will that is given the duty of 'ensuring the final success of an effort that has lasted for millions of years.'[30] Even though Père Teilhard's thought in this connexion may, perhaps, be somewhat open to question, it is not, in fact, a negation of, nor a threat to freedom. On the contrary, the idea he puts forward is that man's freedom can subsist only by becoming deeper or, we might say, by doubling itself, in such a way that the influence of the consequent risk is also bound to become greater. This idea may already be found in a number of passages we have just quoted. 'Evolution,' he says again, 'in virtue of the mechanism of its syntheses, is continually charged with a greater measure of freedom'; and 'the more forceful the energy, the more misguided and dangerous may be its ebullience'.[31] It is true, indeed, that he first recognizes without question the necessity for a personal option on the part of each individual throughout the course of human history, which will determine his own particular destiny; in referring, for example, to the 'life-giving power' of the Host, he notes that this power 'conflicts with our free will'; in Christ he sees 'the sword that mercilessly cuts away such of the body's members as are unworthy or decayed';[32] because Christ, he explains, 'is the one who unites, he is also the one who separates and judges'.[33] If he speaks, as we shall see he does, of a 'common option', he reminds us on several occasions that what he says of it holds good in the same way for each individual option; since, for all our common solidarity, each one of us is none the less charged 'with his own responsibilities, and his own incommunicable possibilities . . . It is *we* who save ourselves or lose ourselves'.[34] Nevertheless, the cosmological viewpoint adopted in the majority of his writings leads him generally to look at things in their evolutionary and collective aspect. He then sees the freedom of the insufficiently socialized individual as still 'elementary'.[35] He envisages the necessary and specially formidable option that will have to be made at the end of time by a humanity that has attained the fullness of its collective consciousness,[36] and by that very fact has reached also 'the apogee of its responsibility and freedom'.[37] After the 'individual's fundamental choice' will come 'the *common option* of the mass of mankind'.[38] A day must come, he believes, when men 'will have finally become conscious of their common unity and their intimate links with all the rest of the universe, and will hold in their hands the plenitude of their soul, to cast it freely into the divine centre'. It is then that the final option will be made, in the form of a world's choice between revolt and worship.[39]

Such, Père Teilhard once wrote to a friend, was 'the only form of millenarianism that *he* could entertain'.[40] At the same time the form in which it is expressed is tentative, and varies from time to time. Under the single term 'common option' at least two different concepts can be distinguished. Both are clearly formulated at the end of *The Phenomenon of Man*. One might suppose, says Père Teilhard, that 'as the earth draws to its close, evil will sink to a minimum'.[41] A second hypothesis, however, is possible, which fits in with the 'general curve' of his thought, and which he puts forward with more vigour:

'But there is another possibility. Obeying a law from which nothing in the past has been exempt, evil may go on growing alongside good, and it too may attain its paroxysm at the end in some specifically new form.

'There are no summits without abysses . . . Are we to foresee man seeking to fulfil himself collectively upon himself, or
personally upon a greater than himself? Refusal or acceptance
of Omega? A conflict may supervene . . . Universal love could
only vivify and detach finally a fraction of the noosphere, to
consummate it—the part which decided to "cross the threshold", to get outside itself, into the other. *Ramification once
again for the last time*.'[42]

In short, 'tomorrow, as yesterday and already today', the
energy man disposes of, whatever its strength, can even so
'produce discord by its operation'. For the reason he indicates, Père Teilhard regards the second hypothesis as the
more probable. It is, moreover, the hypothesis that he more
generally puts forward—though he sometimes tries to persuade
himself, on sociological grounds and even on grounds of probability and statistical necessity, that the most compact mass
will take the right road. This, indeed, can hardly be held
against him. In any case, his intention in so doing is in no way
to 'minimize the uncertainties inherent in our choice'.[43]

Moreover, 'this crisis of human activity is, by its nature, as
old as man'.[44] And thus it is that Père Teilhard sees in each
generation the same 'ambiguity', still identical even as it grows
more pronounced, of human progress. It is this progress that
he sees as the source of 'the heroic temptation of all times,
that of the Titans, of Prometheus, of Babel and of Faust; that
of Christ on the mountain; a temptation as old as Earth itself,
as old as the first reflective awakening of Life to the awareness
of its powers'. If the advent of modern science under the aegis
of materialism has encouraged the 'falsely scientific idea that
we have become gods', this is simply a revival. of 'the ancient
pride of the legendary Titans'.[45] Thus every generation of
mankind has to make the same choice, in different forms, between 'arrogant autonomy and loving excentration', between
'revolt and adoption'.[46] In every generation 'the two opposite
principles draw to themselves their faithful'.[47] 'Rejection of
being, or acceptance of being'—these, in other and eminently
classic, terms are the two alternatives of the dilemma; and,
according to the direction chosen by free will, such can be the
two contradictory effects of the same 'unanimously won pos-

session'; here we have 'the two opposite directions' in which
each one of us can set out 'upon a single road'. Thus man's
existence is always a 'struggle'.[48] No one can decline to make
'the decision that Life demands from our reflective activity',
the 'grand option' presented to us in such formidably simple
terms.[49] If, accordingly, there is a 'spirit of the Earth' that,
once again, cannot fail to emerge from it as from its 'matrix',
that 'ambiguous term' can, in fact, denote two opposite
spirits. It can mean both 'the Promethean and Faustian spirit,
the spirit of autonomy and isolation', which 'locates the secret
of our destiny in a certain power, inherent in mankind, to
fulfil itself by its own forces', and it can also mean 'the Christian spirit, the spirit of service and of giving', which 'even in
its constructive effort reaches out towards union with a God
who holds us up and draws us, through all the forces of the
world in evolution'. This 'spirit of the earth' can be as much a
'spirit of force' as 'a spirit of love'; and between these two
conflicting spirits, between these two converse aspects of the
whole of being, or between these two rival peaks to be climbed,
mankind must inevitably make its choice—or be divided.[50]

There can be no doubt, then, that Père Teilhard recognizes
a 'close connexion between the development of human faculties and their capacity to love God'.[51] A capacity for love,
however, is not effective love: it is also a capacity for the
opposite. 'To advance still further', in the first place through
'hominization' and later increasingly through 'humanization'
(both processes being themselves conditioned by technological
progress) evolution became 'morally ordered'. It acquired a
moral character[52]—and that character becomes more and
more pronounced, in the sense that the choice between good
and evil becomes more and more clear-cut and in consequence
more and more grave.[53]

'Justice will one day set its seal upon the Act' that will decide between the alternatives of 'revolt and adoration'. And
all things will be made new.[54]

Even so, Père Teilhard's line of thought does not stop short
at this point. He envisages more than the possibility of moral
evil, involved in freedom. A more practical examination of
the matter, and one more illuminated by the light of faith,

had shown him the reality of such evil. He noted in his diary, on 29 November 1947: 'A moral fault: *to be obtuse to evil (and absorbed in one's own part)* [the italicized words are in English] and to underestimate the forces of evil (= danger of failure for terrestrial evolution).' In a letter of 2 January 1952, he remarks on 'the more important place occupied in my thought by an explicit consideration of evil': in fact, that consideration had always occupied a very prominent place. He had never been 'blind to all that is most characteristically Christian in the Christian outlook'.[55] In *The Spiritual power of matter*, he had used the form of an allegorical story to show man overcome by 'a confused feeling that the force which had swept down upon him was equivocal, turbid, the combined essence of all evil and all goodness', and then realizing that 'according to the way a man surrenders himself to it, the whirlwind will either drag him down into the darkness of its depths, or lift him up into the blue skies'.[56] The nature of such a book as *The Phenomenon of Man* did not, of course, allow him to treat all the aspects of the problem, and the same may be said about many of his other writings.[57] *Le Milieu Divin*, however, could deal with it more explicitly; and this in fact it does, even though, as a sort of 'treatise on perfection', it is addressed to the Christian who is already committed to the road of salvation. We find in it a vigorous and impressive treatment of evil, not only the evil of suffering or of physical death, but what one might call the supreme evil, the evil that wars with God, sin. The whole of the last section of part three, with the significant heading, 'the outer darkness and the lost souls' (in contrast with the divine Milieu), is devoted to a bold and forceful treatment of sin.[58]

In that section, there is no playing-down of even the most severe Gospel teaching. We are shown the forces of evil at work in the universe, and these are not confined to impersonal forces that act as a brake or lead men astray: all around us, so that we feel them mingling with the 'luminous presence of God', there are 'vague presences, evil beings, malignant things'. For 'evil is as it were incarnate' or 'substantialized' in some beings: 'rebellious elements', 'refractory elements', whose soul is the 'soul of perverse light, corrosive and poisonous'. Under their influence, as Scripture tells us, the end of all time will be marked by a 'profound schism'.[59] Since the beginning of our species, a 'mysterious original defect' has intervened, to 'complicate and aggravate' man's dramatic situation, and it is to the burden of that defect that we have to attribute so many of the 'disconcerting excesses of sin' that we cannot fail to see.[60] The genesis of the world continues throughout our history, but it is accompanied by a 'immortal wastage': 'there is not only *nether*—there is also *outer* darkness'. And so we are urged to reflect seriously on the 'mystery of damnation'. We must measure the 'void' that is produced in the 'mystical body' by the defection of fallen souls, and realize how 'the damned are excluded from the luminous aspect' and 'beatification of the Pleroma'. 'Exiled though they are from love', they are none the less still maintained in being by the universal presence, but this is 'for their unhappiness'. 'At the heart of their immortal substance' they suffer 'the conscious agonies of an eternal decomposition'. Such can always be the fate of any one of us: in being summoned to 'aggregation', we run the risk of 'segregation'. On the last day Christ will reject those who have made themselves 'factors of dissociation'. So long, then, as our life on earth continues, we must reflect on 'the ever-threatening gravity' of a summons that goes unheard.[61] Hell exists; it is a 'structural element of the Universe'. Its existence, it is true, can in no way impair the plenitude of the divine Milieu, any more than the reality of creation can add to the being of God; but it is none the less true that a terrible possibility remains, and our fear of it can be overcome only by prayer and hope:

'Jesus, you are the centre towards which all things are moving: if it be possible, make a place for us all in the company of those elect and holy ones whom your loving care has liberated one by one from the chaos of our present existence and who are now being slowly incorporated into you in the unity of the new earth.'

'. . . the two death-bed agonies: 1. Will Jesus be there? 2. Will he accept me or reject me? . . . *Domine, include me (ne excludas me).*'[62]

It is difficult, with this evidence before us, to understand how a critic could write, in connexion with Père Teilhard, 'In his system, evil is confused with the various natural forms of inertia that man and the world are confronted by in their forward progress.'[63] This is true neither of the evil of suffering, nor of the evil of sin. Père Teilhard spoke in fact of 'a sort of ontological slope (or inertia) in virtue of which participated being tends continually to fall back into multiplicity': a 'slope' that many other thinkers have noted, but which his evolutionary view of the universe led him to analyse afresh. Again, he showed how, under the influence of sin, this tendency becomes more pronounced, until it becomes a 'positive tendency to retrogression', with the result that natural plurality, in which there is no evil, is changed into a disordered complexity 'the source of all evil and all corruption'. But what he did not do was to identify either the initial tendency or its later aggravated form with sin itself. The 'disordered complexity' he describes is produced, he says, in unmistakable terms, 'in society or in ourselves by the wrong use of our freedom'.[64] Similarly, he is careful to distinguish the rational creature's 'original weakness' from its 'first culpable acts'.[65] A sufficiently attentive reading will remove any temptation to look for his whole teaching about evil in a number of statements about the evil, that, he tells us, belongs to the 'order of statistics' or that may be completely explained by the mechanism of 'evolutionary creation': those statements are designed simply to indicate the general conditions, with a view to removing both the idea of a God who is the author of evil, and that of an evil Principle which is the enemy of the good God, and they never cease to preserve in man his prerogative of freedom. Similarly, when Père Teilhard says that his explanations provide an 'easy solution' to the problem of evil, or even that the problem 'disappears', he does not, of course, mean that in his view evil itself vanishes. It means no more than that he thinks he has been more successful than those for whom the world was 'ready-made' from the beginning, in accounting for the inevitability of suffering in a creation that is still developing, and also for the threat contained in the continual possibility of sin: for if 'there is nothing that brings greater bliss than the attainment of union', there is on the other hand 'nothing more laborious than the pursuit of union'[66]—and that accounts for the perpetual temptation to avoid it. Moreover, he emphasizes with equal force that evil itself, and moral evil in particular, is always, like freedom, a mystery. One cannot but wonder, then, whether some of the criticisms levelled against Père Teilhard would not, in fact, apply through him to the greatest doctors in Christian tradition—to St. Augustine,[67] to St. Thomas, to all those for whom, in the words of Mgr Charles Journet, the paradox of evil is that it *exists,* but has *no being*:[68] to all, in short, who refuse to attribute to evil, in Manichean fashion, ontological reality.[69]

It is difficult, again, to understand how the same critic, after reading the section in *Le Milieu Divin* we have been summarizing (whose position in the book and whose tone indicate the importance Père Teilhard attached to it), could have spoken of his 'vague and distant spirituality, bordering on pure symbolism'.[70] Equally unreasonable is the comment of a theologian, who after a rapid study confined to *The Phenomenon of Man* (in which he noted that the word 'sin' is never used) concluded that Père Teilhard's 'synthesis has no place for true sin';[71] we may say the same of another critic who, as though it were in contradiction to the teaching even of *Le Milieu Divin*, reminds us that 'the Prince of this world will draw into his domain all of this universe that is lost'.[72] It is indeed disturbing to see a theologian making this sort of criticism of Père Teilhard even on a point in connexion with which it would seem that, from his own point of view, he should rather be praising him. On more than one occasion, and for some time now, regrets have been expressed in the Church that many preachers, either in the pulpit or in their writings, are 'afraid to preach hell-fire'. This Père Teilhard, for his part, was not afraid to do, in the plainest and most vigorous terms. Ever since he first began to write, he had reflected on this 'formidable mystery'.[73] He was well aware that among all the mysteries that claim our faith 'there is not one that conflicts more sharply with our human ways of looking at things'. Père Teilhard, in fact, never wavered in his faith, and he could rightly say of himself that 'nobody, I imagine, has ever thought that I was lacking in faith'.[74] The nature of his writings was generally such, we should remember again, that it did not lend itself to a lengthy treatment of the essence of sin or to an analysis of the sinful state of mind; he may, too, have thought that a certain obsession with sin darkened and distorted the Christian synthesis. Moreover, in his religious meditation, he normally preferred to concentrate on the divine realities and the 'expectation of the Parousia'. Nevertheless, he reflected deeply on sin, even if he did not cover the whole of the problem. Following many other great spiritually minded thinkers, he pointed out its effect of causing disintegration; and in his evolutionary outlook he redisclosed an important dogmatic tradition whose echo had been lost: *Ubi peccata, ibi multitudo*.[75] At the same time he rediscosed the corresponding tradition, deriving principally from the Gospel of St. John and the Epistle to the Hebrews, of the work of gathering together and uniting accomplished by Christ. When, for example, we read that through his redemptive act Jesus 'saves guilty creation as it is about to return to dust', and that he 'comes to re-establish in the world the harmony of effort and the convergence of beings', or that, 'to reunite and bring together the vast flock that is scattering, there must be a mighty Shepherd',[76] we cannot fail to be reminded of what Scripture says about him who was to die in order 'to gather into one the children of God who are scattered abroad'[77] or who became 'the great shepherd of the sheep by the blood of the eternal covenant',[78] Our Lord Jesus Christ.

Even in writings that were principally 'scientific' in character, Père Teilhard more than once analysed the intrinsic nature of the sin that most fully expresses its evil will: the 'revolt' against God, whose forms may vary, and do in fact vary 'constantly', but whose essential temptation is always the same.[79] In dealing with original sin (*peccatum originans*) it may be true that, yielding to pressure from teachers who looked to him, in view of his knowledge of human origins, for the explanation they lacked, he occasionally offered explanations that were rightly judged to be unsatisfactory. These, moreover, varied, were given somewhat against his inclination, and were expressed in the modest form of 'mere pointers, to give a rough idea, and, in the form he gave them, certainly untenable'; or again they were 'thoughts offered for criticism by theologians', and he did not attach permanent importance to them.[80] The distinction he made, here again, between the 'cosmic basis' of sin and its 'realization in history'[81] justifies us in rejecting the most unfavourable interpretations of his thought. He regretted the too one-sided Augustinianism of theological tradition as established in the West, and liked to dwell on the views of Clement of Alexandria, for example, or even more St. Irenaeus. But here again, in this as in other connexions, we should not look to Père Teilhard for a complete course in theology. It is here, perhaps, that the fact that he was not a professional theologian is the most noticeable. At the same time his wholehearted adherence to the dogmas of faith was none the less complete. Far from shrinking from affirming the most awe-inspiring of them, he could explain that 'the existence of hell adds to the divine Milieu an accent, a gravity, a contrast, a depth which would not exist without it';[82] and if he had written nothing else about sin, such explanations of its consequences would presuppose without any possibility of doubt an extremely serious and extremely profound idea of the thing itself. A realization of this will bring out the full import of what was said in our third chapter, that Père Teilhard had the courage, now by no means common, to face our ultimate end and to judge everything in the light of it.

Chapter 11

NATURE AND GRACE

Final progress does not come automatically: but neither is there a final end that is obtained by the unaided action of man's will. The final end is divine, and however necessary and fine man's effort may be (whether individual or collective) it cannot by itself produce that end. It is 'of another order'. The result of man's effort can never by itself have any positively supernatural value. This is a point on which Père Teilhard is perfectly clear. He does not believe, as more than one mystical thinker is tempted to do, that man participates naturally in divine life. It is true that the empirical point of view he adopted often led him to counter the teaching of those who believed in fixed species and, even more often, materialist views based on the law of entropy, by demonstrating the ascent of life and of Spirit; but at the same time he was careful to make it clear (even though this may have been to anticipate more ultimate explanations) that that ascent should be attributed not so much to an impulse from below as to an attraction from above. After seeking to show that man has an 'urge to *Some Thing* ahead of him', he concludes that that urge 'cannot achieve its full fruition except by combining with another and still more fundamental aspiration, one from above, urging him towards *Some One*'.[1] He was never tempted to accept '(extreme) theories of immanence and autonomy', and was even surprised at their success: 'extrinsic forces are so much part of our experience and so excellent!'[2] In his spiritual writings, which have a solid basis of dogma and are addressed to believers, he can start from the assertion that 'far from light emerging gradually out of the womb of our darkness, it is the Light, existing before all else was made, which patiently, surely, eliminates our darkness', and again, 'fire, the source of being: we cling so tenaciously to the illusion that fire comes forth from the depths of the earth and that its flames grow progressively brighter as it pours along the radiant furrows of life's tillage. Lord, in your mercy you gave me to see that this idea is false, and that I must overthrow it if I were ever to have sight of you'.[3]

He does not confine himself, however, to recognizing the divine activity and divine initiative in general. Just as, in the domain of knowledge, he makes a clear distinction between on the one hand what he calls the 'natural branch' of his 'interior trajectory' and on the other hand the truths that he holds by his faith as a Catholic; and just as he knows that his 'love of the invisible' came to him as 'a zest given to him from Heaven', and that for 'the fire to blaze out' had called 'for a spark to fall on him from on high';[4] so on more than one occasion he draws an equally sharp line between the two 'orders' of nature and of grace or the supernatural. He points out, it is true, the correspondence or, to use his own word, 'coherence' between the two; he is fond of bringing out their analogies; he insists, as we shall see, on the development of the former as being indispensable for preparing a suitable field for the emergence and growth of the latter; he is fascinated by the way each is woven into the other, by their 'wonderful contrived interplay';[5] he marvels at their 'alliance'. Nevertheless, he is equally careful, when necessary, to emphasize the distinction, which only God's gift can eliminate, between the two. Thus, in a letter that describes a discussion on religion that he had prompted, he says:

'Even M. T. seemed to me to regard the search for a religion as a vast scientific enterprise, whereas the Absolute, it is only too clear, cannot be "*taken* by force", but must *be given* (made manifest) to minds that await it'.[6]

These two allied aspects of the relation between nature and grace come out very clearly in numerous passages dating from every period. In connexion with charity, we read in a letter of 1916:

'If we are to love our neighbour "other than do the heathen", we must learn to supernaturalize our sympathies: and this supernaturalizing will always be suspect or incomplete if it is not haloed by a love that extends to the wretched, to the least interesting and least attractive people. It is in this particular sphere that charity reigns supreme, detached from every outward human appearance (Even then, moreover, it is still a truly human feeling: the poor wretch who is helped and cared for in a Christian way, is truly loved for himself, clearly seen in his right place, as a member of Jesus Christ.).'[7]

Some months later, Père Teilhard wrote, under the title *Le Milieu Mystique*, a first outline of his spiritual teaching. In this he says: 'I can see that every, even natural, perfection is the necessary foundation of the final mystical organism that You are building up through the medium of all things. You do not, Lord, destroy the beings that you adopt, but transform them as you consummate all that centuries of creation have developed in them.' And a year later he writes again, in *Le Prêtre*', 'The whole world is concentrated, exalted, in expectation of union with God. And yet the world comes up against an impassable barrier. Nothing can reach Christ that Christ does not take and assume into himself.' In the first essay that was entitled *Mon Univers* (1916) he carefully distinguishes, in order to study their relationships, 'Omicron, the natural term of human and cosmic progress' from 'Omega, the supernatural term of the Kingdom of God' or 'Plenitude of Christ'. Later, he was to abandon this particular terminology, but he retained the distinction it expressed. In a letter (26 July 1917) to Père Victor Fontoynont, who had been his fellow-scholastic and was to remain a life-long friend, he wrote (underlining the final syllables of the last word in order to make his meaning perfectly clear): 'Natural evolution is without any doubt sancti*fiable*.' On 29 December, in a letter this time to their common friend, Père Auguste Valensin, he spoke of 'the great fissure of the supernatural', while remarking, too, that this fissure was preceded by 'other precipices'. In the same month, he writes to Père Valensin again: 'You should note the following point carefully: I do not attribute any definitive or absolute value to the varied constructions of nature. What I like about them is not their particular form, but their function, which is to build up mysteriously, first what can be divinized, and then, through the grace of Christ coming down upon our endeavour, what is divine.'[8] Again, in his second memorandum for Maurice Blondel, he says that 'in the end, all our work amounts to producing the victim upon which the divine fire is to descend'.[9] In *Le Milieu Divin* itself, he criticizes the error that consists in 'seeking divine love and the divine Kingdom *on the same level* as human affections and human progress', and adds that 'the true Christian supernatural, frequently defined by the Church, neither leaves the creature where he is, on his own plane, nor suppresses him: it "superanimates" him'.[10] An essay dating from 1938, but not published until 1945, in *Études* ('Social heredity and progress') distinguishes the two ways, direct and indirect, in which is effected the 'gradual incorporation of the World in the World Incarnate': first, through the preparation 'in a Mankind increasingly turned inward upon itself' of the subject of 'this high transformation', and later through the grace of Jesus Christ; and, the better to emphasize the infinite difference in value between the two orders, Père Teilhard adds, in the same essay: 'all human enrichment is but dross, except in as much as it becomes the most precious and incorruptible of all things by adding itself to an immortal centre of love'.[11]

The passage of time introduced no change into his teaching, and the fundamental distinction was always preserved. In 1942 a 'note on Christian perfection' shows that man's 'natural powers' represent so many powers that can be 'supernaturalized'. And somewhat later, on 20 August 1947, a short address on 'the priest and scientific research' contains a similar thesis: 'every fruit of research is by its nature Christifiable: *Christifiabilis* and *Christificandus*—it both can and must be Christified.' It is on that ground, and not because he confuses the role of priest and scientist or substitutes one for the other, that Père Teilhard justifies the priest's place in the laboratory: 'at the source from which every truth and every new force emerges, so that Christ may inform every new contribution that man makes to a Universe that cannot stand still'.[12] In 1948 he wrote an article for *L'Anthropologie* in which, since it was addressed to scientific readers, there was no need for him to enter into theological refinements. Nevertheless, in his conclusion, he was at pains to suggest, if not a coincidence, and still less an identity, at least a mysterious correspondence between 'Noospheric' unity and 'the mystical super-organism joined in Grace and charity' in which Christians believe. In those two, he says, we have two realities, one natural and one 'supernatural'. They tend, not to be fused into one, but 'to come together and harmonize in Christian thought—the critical point of maturation envisaged by science being no more than the physical *condition* and the experimental aspect of the critical point of Parousia postulated and awaited on the authority of Revelation'. For the Christian, he concludes, 'the whole process of hominization is simply a *preparation* of the final Parousia'. It is thus, in the light of those remarks, that, as a believer, he can 'illumine and *carry further* the genesis of the Universe around him in the form of a Christogenesis'.[13] Again in this same year, 1948, he explains (in *Comment je vois* and also in a lecture on 'The Directions and Conditions of the Future'), still from the same collective and evolutionary point of view, that 'the completion of hominization', in the form in which, he believes, he can see it taking shape, or 'the collective consummation of earthly Mankind', must be a preliminary condition—necessary but not in itself sufficient—of the 'divinization' of man and the establishment of the Kingdom of God. He asks us to recognize 'at the very heart of the social phenomenon', but distinct from it, the emergence of a 'sort of ultra-socialization' which is the supernatural formation of the Church. In 1949, he sees in the 'ultra-human' and the 'supernatural' not one and the same thing, but 'the two complementary terms on which is centred a single hope that embraces the whole universe'.[14]

When we turn to what Père Teilhard wrote during his very last years, we find the development of a tendency towards an extreme systematization and condensation of thought that could endanger the retention of these essential distinctions. Nevertheless, in 1950, when he was turning over in his mind his essay on *Le Cœur de la matière*, which was an opportunity to look back on the road along which his thoughts had travelled, he wrote to his cousin Marguerite Teillard-Chambon: 'My views, as you know, hardly change, but they simplify themselves and interlock with such an increase of intensity—in the interplay (so wonderfully contrived) of what I call the two lines of curvature (or convergence)—the cosmic ("natural") and the Christic ("super-natural").'[15] In this same year, 1950, he notes, in another private letter, how clearly the very title of a booklet in which he was attacked (*L'Évolution rédemptrice du Père Teilhard de Chardin*) showed that the author had not understood what he said: he implies that in my view the cosmic picture will have some sort of immanent, saving, virtue— whereas in everything I have written I have always insisted that the "redeeming" properties of evolution must flow from a Christic (personal and transcendent) centre'.[16] We should, moreover, note that the term 'redemptive' (which appears only in this particular context) was not used spontaneously by Père Teilhard, but was influenced by the title of the pamphlet. Finally, in 1955, the very year of his death, he repeats (in *Le Christique*) that the 'convergent Universe' he has attempted, rightly or wrongly, to describe, and whose stages he has sought to determine, as yet contains only 'spiritual potentialities': only Christ, therefore, 'through the two-fold virtue of his Cross and Resurrection' can 'amorize' and so bring to their term 'both the powers of growth and life and the powers of diminishment and death that lie at the heart of the Noogenesis in which we are involved'.

Although Père Teilhard approaches the subject of the supernatural from a number of different angles, and though he never set out to treat it, even summarily, for its own sake, the passages we have quoted show no variation in his teaching. The great Noogenesis in which the history of creation culminates, and its extension into human history, have a double reality, cosmic and necessary on one side, moral and free on the other; but they are, and necessarily must be, no more than a preparation for the end for which God made us, and which he willed to reveal to us in his Son.[17] Moreover, such a preparation is absolutely indispensable. 'If the fruit is to burst open, it must first be ripe.'[18] The natural elements of this world, 'which the supernatural re-fashions so that they are made *more* and *other*' are no less necessary 'to fuel the operation of salvation and provide it with suitable material; the supernatural plenitude of Christ rests on a natural plenitude of the world'.[19] Between the two 'there is neither separation nor discordance but coherent subordination'.[20] Thus salvation is 'linked with

the earth's fulfilment', and 'some natural human unity' is given
the task of preparing the 'higher unity *in Christo Jesu*'.[21] 'If
Christ is to be the Saviour and the life of souls in their supernatural development, he must first satisfy certain conditions
affecting the World, taken in its experiential and natural fulfilment.'[22] This, again, is forcibly suggested to us by a double
analogy, that of the appearance of mind upon earth at the
term of a vast biological evolution entirely directed towards
providing it with a suitable organism, and that of the first entry
of Christ into our humanity. Père Teilhard was fond of emphasizing the latter, the analogy between the first and second
coming:

'For Christ to appear on earth for the first time it was obviously necessary (as no one would question) that, following
the general process of evolution, the human type should be
anatomically developed, and socially advanced, up to a certain
degree of collective consciousness. That being so, why should
we not take a further step, and believe that in the case of his
second and final coming *too*, Christ is waiting to reappear until
the human collectivity has become capable (because fully realized in its natural *potentialities*) of receiving from him its
supernatural consummation? After all, if there are without any
doubt exact physical laws for the development of spirit within
history, why should there not be, *a fortiori*, laws for its further
expansion and ultimate culmination?'[23]

In other words, the Pauline concept of the 'fullness of time'
must hold good as much for the second coming as for the first
—without the gratuitousness of the work of salvation and its
supernatural character being impaired in either case. Père
Teilhard expresses this from another angle, and in more suc-
cinct terms: 'Christ needs to find a summit of the World for
his consummation, just as he had need to find a Woman for
his conception.'[24]

Père Wildiers, who quotes these last two passages, rightly
notes that this way of expressing the indispensable part played
by a natural fulfilment of mankind 'completely maintains the
gratuitousness both of salvation and of the Incarnation'.[25]

A condition is not a determining cause, and 'coherent subordination' is not identification. Père Olivier Rabut, again, has

noted the closeness of Père Teilhard's position to that of St. Thomas Aquinas, for whom 'sanctification fulfils and continues the creation'. If we accept that this creation 'develops by evolution' we shall have to interpret St. Thomas by saying, with Père Teilhard, that 'sanctification fulfils and continues the evolutionary ascent'. It is an explanation or, if you prefer, a legitimate application, of the maxim *Gratia perficit naturam*. 'Christian salvation is not thereby eliminated nor replaced. It is the grace of God that saves, and not the forces of evolution, although grace makes use of evolution. Divine salvation makes use of the natural instruments that *dispose* man to accept God's gifts and to make them bear more fruit. All we have to do is not to confuse the disposition to receive with the gift that is received.'[26] It is, in fact, very much in line with Thomist thought to hold that 'the Christian is not made by a mere denial of the world of which he is part, but by transcending it'.[27] We should be equally justified in seeing, in such a concept, a commentary in terms adapted to our own time but faithful to the perennial spirit of Christianity, on the thought that St. Irenaeus expressed as follows: 'Deus . . . temporalia fecit propter hominem, ut maturescens in eis, fructificet immortalitatem' ('God made temporal things for man, so that coming to maturity in them he may reap the fruit of immortality').[28] More exactly, too, and closely, it is the same thought as that expressed by Pope Pius XII in 1958, when he said, in words that were indisputably correct but could be similarly misrepresented: 'For the first time men are becoming conscious not only of their interdependence but also of their wonderful unity. And this means that mankind will become continually more correctly disposed for becoming the mystical body of Christ.'[29]

Two other words are used by Père Teilhard to describe the relation between nature and the supernatural: each sums up one of the two aspects in which the relation should be considered: 'integration' and 'transformation'. Both appear as early as 1918 in *La foi qui opère*:

'Christian faith is not fatal either to the rational method of conquering the world or to man's confidence in himself (on the contrary, it stimulates and inspires them). But, in conformity with the law of the integration of the natural in the supernatural, it is superimposed upon them both. It is erected on the laboriously maintained foundation of human endeavour, to preserve it, direct, organize and transform it.'

Père Teilhard, as we have already seen, is constantly using this word 'transformation', or 'transfiguration' with various shades of emphasis, and various degrees of intensity appropriate to cases that themselves varied but were still 'analogous' in the Scholastic sense. The notion soon came to hold an important place in his thought, associated with that of the 'critical point': 'a mysterious notion . . . that does not eliminate "critical points" but allows them still to retain their special significance—a notion that links super-nature to nature, as it does spirit to matter—that allows us to seek higher realities *through* the wretched husk of all physical appearance and physical conquest'.[30] Père Teilhard notes that 'passing from one level of existence to the other, living properties subsist only by being transformed or transposed' and these analogies lead him to the 'fundamental transformation' that must be effected in us and must continue throughout our lives.[31] In *Le Milieu Mystique*, he said, speaking to God, 'I shall have no rest, unless an active influence, coming forth from you, bears down upon me, to transform me'.[32] Again, in *La foi qui opère* he spoke of 'the creative energy' that 'is waiting for us, ready to transform us, beyond anything that man's eye has ever seen or his ear has heard'. Earlier, in 1916, in *La Maîtrise du Monde*, he had seen in 'the flame that lights up to greet the promise that the world holds' the natural element which, once it has been purified, transfigured and supernaturalized, is to become in us divine charity. In his second memorandum for Maurice Blondel, he argues that this other fire, the fire of divine grace, is both a devouring and a transfiguring fire: 'for grace, to consume and to transfigure are one and the same thing: of the fire that is to re-cast me it is equally true to say that it will consume me and that it will fulfil me'.[33] He believes that 'everything can be transformed and divinized in this Fire that surrounds us and seeks only to come down upon the soul of everything we do'.[34] Thus, when he considers the missionary problem, he naturally comes to the conclusion that in

order to Christianize the nations one could, 'instead of destroying everything, try to transform it'—ritual, beliefs, and above
all 'mystical attitudes'.[35] Later, at the end of *Le Milieu Divin*,
he wrote that if our hopes are to be realized, the 'supernatural'
must intervene to 'transform nature', acting on it like a 'ferment', and in the body of that book he refers on several occasions to the 'unitive transformation' which is the fruit of the
Holy Ghost. Later again, he hailed 'the remarkable transformation that the idea of a spiritual evolution of the universe
allows us to anticipate', provided we appreciate that 'the transcendent God and the Universe in evolution no longer form
two antagonistic centres of attraction, but are entering into a
hierarchically ordered combination'.[36] He explains that, by
virtue of the incarnate Christ, the Word of God 'is relaunching
and transfiguring' the evolution that man had already taken
over, and that Christianity is seen to be 'a doctrine and prospect of universal transformation'.[37] In *Le Cœur de la
Matière*, again, he was to describe his awareness of the 'progressive expansion, within every being and every event, of a
mysterious inner clarity that transfigured them', and included
a passage on 'the astonishing power' possessed by love of
'transforming everything'. Finally, in *Le Christique*, he was to
define the presence of Christ in the universe as 'a transforming
presence' which is the effect and the continuation into infinity
of the Eucharistic transubstantiation.

In thus asserting the 'transformation' undergone by nature
in its passage into the supernatural order, Père Teilhard was
suggesting in a particularly forceful way the transcendence of
the supernatural order, and at the same time using a highly
traditional term to express it. 'It is astonishing,' he says in *Le
Milieu Divin*, 'that so few minds should succeed in grasping
the notion of transformation. Sometimes the thing transformed
seems to them to be the thing unchanged; sometimes they see
in it only the entirely new.'[38] We have already noticed an
instance of this lack of understanding, in connexion with the
paradox of man, as presented in *The Phenomenon of Man*.[39]
But it is in the present context that the 'mysterious notion' of
transformation is outstandingly important; it is here that the
'great metamorphosis' is produced.[40] Created nature remains

itself, it is not absorbed nor annihilated, and nevertheless it is transposed into a completely different state; it is re-cast, 'meta-morphosed',[41] 'transfigured',[42]—and not simply made greater, prolonged, or completed in its own order—that is what calls for the effective reality of the divine principle to which classic theology has given the name of supernatural.[43] We may add that Christian tradition, as we know, has readily accepted the changing of water into wine at the marriage feast of Cana as a symbol both of the transition from the Old Testament to the New and of the divinization of our nature by Christ.[44]

Any writer who wishes to produce a true picture of Père Teilhard would be failing in his duty if he did not point out, unhesitatingly, any deficiencies in his language and even in his thought; but on this point Père Teilhard would seem to be safe from criticism. One cannot, it is true, expect to find in his writings all the theses and refinements of a complete treatise on 'the supernatural order'; at the same time they abundantly bring out all that is essential in the Catholic statement of the problem. He allows nothing to interfere with 'the fundamental dogma of the gratuitous character of the supernatural', nor with 'the vital principle of renunciation'; it is a twofold govern-ing principle, which he asserted in *Forma Christi* and never lost sight of. And if he then proceeded to re-establish connec-tive relationships, too often strained or broken, in order or-ganically to correlate the two worlds that form a single world in the divine plan, it would be very wrong to blame him for the attempt. It would be more true to say, with Père Jean Daniélou, that 'he restores the Catholic harmony between na-ture and grace'.[45] No one who has studied his work could possibly maintain, as has been done, that he confused the whole issue, failing to distinguish between nature and grace, 'the temporal and the spiritual', and 'the kingdoms of this world and the kingdom that is not of this world'. For such a judgement sheer ignorance would seem to be the only possible excuse. It is equally astonishing that anyone could imagine that his thought may be summarized by saying that in order to attain his end all man has to do is 'to put his trust in the resources of his will to power', as though it was there alone that his 'supreme hope' lay; or that his teaching could be boiled down into the statement that, 'Everything that rises up in nature is grace, the divine Milieu, the mystical body of Christ.'[46] In the *Revue Thomiste*, M. Jean Daujat wrote, more justly, that 'Teilhard de Chardin admirably demonstrates' one thing, namely, 'that every effort and every human progress is destined to be, and must be, conquered for Jesus Christ'.[47] A passage in 'The Mass on the World' (written shortly before *Le Milieu Divin*) forcibly emphasizes that no natural process is capable of realizing this conquest, and that the transformation to be achieved is the most radical of all transformations. Here we reach the heart of the profoundly supernatural spirituality of Père Teilhard:

'If your kingdom, my God, were of this world, I could possess you simply by surrendering myself to the forces which cause us, through suffering and dying, to grow visibly in stature —us or that which is dearer to us than ourselves. But because the term towards which the earth is moving lies not merely beyond each individual thing but beyond the totality of things; because the world travails, not to bring forth from within itself some supreme reality, but to find its consummation through a union with a pre-existent Being; it follows that man can never reach the blazing centre of the universe simply by living more and more for himself, nor even by spending his life in the service of some earthly cause, however great. The world can never be definitively united with you, Lord, save by a sort of reversal, a turning about, an *excentration*, which must involve the temporary collapse not merely of all individual achievements but even of everything that looks like an advancement for humanity. If my being is ever to be decisively attached to yours, there must first die in me not merely the monad ego but also the world: in other words I must first pass through an agonizing phase of diminution for which no tangible compensation will be given me.'[48]

Chapter 12

THE TRANSFIGURATION
OF THE COSMOS

Transformation, turning about, metamorphosis, transfiguration—these and some similar words such as excentration and reversal, express in Père Teilhard's vocabulary an analogical concept with a number of different applications, ranging from the elementary domain of physico-chemical reaction to that of the loftiest spiritual realities, that of 'evangelical transfiguration' and of 'the great Act of reversal' accomplished on the Cross.[1] This is a fact that some minds have had difficulty in grasping, just as they do with the corresponding notion of the 'critical point'.[2] It would be a mistake to conceive the latter simply on the lines of the change from water to steam, or on the analogy of the cone whose surface becomes a point. These, as Père Teilhard warns us, are no more than 'remote comparisons'.[3] In the present case, more emphatically than in any other, the critical point is a 'point of annihilation', a point of death. But, however Père Teilhard applied the concept of transformation, there are always two sides to it. Those who do not appreciate its full value are looking at only one side, or feel they cannot accept the contradiction in the simultaneous existence of the continuous and the discontinuous, stability and change, in other words, of the same and the other. At the same time it is equally certain that this concept has from the very beginning played an essential part in the expression of Christian thought. It is at the heart of the teaching of both the Old and the New Testaments, resting on the words of Christ, 'I am come not to abolish (the law and the prophets) but to fulfil them.'[4] It is this that enables it to accept simultaneously the two statements of St. Paul that an oversimple logic would regard as contradictory: 'The form ($\sigma\chi\tilde{\eta}\mu\alpha$) of this world is passing away', and 'the whole creation has been groaning in travail until now'.[5] The concept is indispensable to an exposi-

tion of the Christian mystery, whether in connexion with the
work accomplished by God in individuals or in the Whole,
with the movements of Matter or with those of Spirit, with
the life of the soul or the life of the Cosmos, with the divinization of human nature or the entry of temporal creation into
eternity. It applies, it is clear, to the change that occurred in
the risen Christ, when he passed from the state of 'kenosis' to
the 'state of glory', of whom the Fathers tell us that 'resurrexit
totus Deus',[6] 'he arose wholly God', and St. Bernard that he
ascended into heaven, 'non ut maneret in carne sed ut trans-
ferretur ad spiritum'[7] ('not to remain in the flesh but to be
transferred to the spirit') : and yet in all those statements there
is nothing that denies the permanence of the Saviour's human
nature or the reality of his body. The same concept applies
equally to the change that is to come about in us. Our body is
not destined, as a result of the resurrection we are promised,
to an endless re-beginning of its terrestrial and fleshly existence, more or less sublimated by miraculous properties. What
is promised for it is not some revival of life, but a complete
metamorphosis which will make of it, as St. Paul, again, says,
'a spiritual body'.[8] And this, moreover, is equally true of the
vast collective body that mankind, as it works and achieves
progress on earth, helps to build up from generation to generation. Its present form is 'temporary' and it will one day be
definitively 'left behind', just as in the course of time it is at
death by each one of us individually.[9] The Universe, too, is
destined, in the Holy Spirit, for the 'great metamorphosis'.[10]

Just as Père Teilhard reminds us of the fundamental affirmations of our faith represented by the distinction between
nature and the supernatural, or moral freedom, or the reality
of sin, hell and evil spirits, so here he rediscloses the 'significance of the cosmic component of salvation'—a significance
which the historian must recognize, with Henri-Irénée Marrou,
'has been progressively blurred and lost in western theology'.
He brings out again, what is still too seldom appreciated, the
full breadth and depth of the traditional idea of universal
resurrection in Christ. He expresses it, it is true, in the new
light of its preparation in evolution, but what he discloses is

basically what Christian antiquity and the middle ages still saw in it and based their life upon.

When we speak of the breadth of the tradition—all that it embraces—we mean that, in contrast with what some thirty years ago had recently become a common mental habit, he is primarily concerned with the destiny of the entire universe. His eschatological expectation is not individualistic. It is principally, like that of the ancients, an expectation of Christ's return in glory at the end of all time. His being, like his thought, reaches out towards the fulfilment of the mystical body, the perfect realization of the Pleroma or 'the consummation of the divine Milieu'. He knows that the present world, through the power of Christ and the faith of the Christian, is becoming 'the glorious living crucible in which everything melts away in order to be born anew';[11] but he generally looks at this prospect only as subordinate to one even vaster: it is the world itself that he sees disappearing, in order that it may be born again. He urges us to look with the eyes of hope on the picture whose expected realization inspired St. Ambrose, for example: 'Resurrexit in Eo mundus, resurrexit in Eo caelum, resurrexit in Eo terra'—'in him the world, in him the heavens, rose again, in him the earth'.[12] 'The form of this world passes away'—this 'wretched form'—but this world itself 'mutatus in formam meliorem', changed into a better form, is destined for eternity:

> *Mundus habebitur atque novabitur, ipse sed alter . . .*
> *Terra novabitur, et reparabitur orbis imago.*[13]

The *innovatio electorum* (making new of the elect) corresponds to this *commutatio elementorum* (transformation of the elements),[14] and God who created all things is also the one who will transform all things: 'faciens omnia atque transformans, renovans universa ac sublevans' (making and transforming all things, renewing and exalting all).[15] Thus we are all proceeding towards a 'new heaven and a new earth', but one whose newness will be not a substitution but a making anew: 'demutatione potius quam creatione', by transformation rather than by creation:[16] it will not, absolutely speaking, be a new heaven and a new earth, but heaven and earth become other, transfigured.[17]

It is the full depth, too, of this great traditional idea that Père Teilhard brings out afresh. This he is able to do through his concept of transfiguration, through turning-about, which echoes the ancient concepts of *conversio, commutatio, immutatio, innovatio, transformatio in gloriam.* He looks forward to a 're-casting of our earth'.[18] He writes that, 'ultimately, God can be attained only through possession of the world', and not, we may be sure, 'by a negation but by some sort of turning about of visible things'. And he adds that it is principally the notion of this turning about and the act that realizes it that have to be discovered, in the light of our desire for them and in prayer;[19] for in such a matter the abstract idea is not enough. This is a point that may well be missed by readers who do not appreciate how much he insists on the effective realization in practice of a spiritual principle. These last remarks date from the end of 1939. Two months later, he came back to the same question. Like all true thinkers, he was continually dissatisfied with the form in which he had expressed his thoughts, and on this occasion he wrote, in connexion with *Le Milieu Divin*: 'I think that I can see that in this first expression of what I felt I have not made sufficiently clear a fundamental point—that, at the term of our effort (which is both salutary and necessary) towards convergence on and with all things, God can finally be attained only by an act of turning about'.[20] In fact, *Le Milieu Divin* is already completely explicit on this point. It speaks not only of 're-casting' and 'transformation' or 'transfiguration', but also of 'excentration' and 'turning about into God'. Here, then, we have the supreme and most radical 'critical point' that must be traversed, with the 'miracle' following at the end.[21] We may simply note that the scrupulous anxiety for accuracy we find in his correspondence shows the cardinal importance Père Teilhard attached to this idea. It is apparent, too, that for him it was no mere speculative hypothesis, no parascientific or pseudo-scientific prediction, but a legitimate extension of the line of thought that emerged from his observation of nature; it was a spiritual development of thought based on faith and hope. It was a magnificent and eminently justified 'extrapolation' of the principle that he had, very early in his career, recognized as the governing principle behind the whole of existence.

In looking forward to the great final mystery, Père Teilhard's faith, again like that of the ancient writers, was never held in check by any timidity of concept. 'Shatter, my God, through the daring of your revelation, the childishly timid outlook . . .'[22], and this prayer, included in 'The Mass on the World', was answered. Nothing that he wrote is an obvious echo of apocalyptic imagery—even though he liked to contemplate the 'fine and curiously modern' prospects opened up by St. John in the last chapter of his Apocalypse;[23] and nothing, again, recalls certain other characteristics that derive from obsolete cosmologies, nor are they replaced by similar characteristics borrowed from more recent science. The very notion of transformation, in the radical form in which he conceived it, rules out any Concordist tendency. Similarly, he rejects as 'absurd' any prophesying about the future of the earth, any 'representational anticipation' that was by way of producing a 'Utopian picture';[24] still more emphatically did he exclude any attempt to represent anything whatsoever, even as a mere suggestion, that is impatient of representation. At the same time he did not refrain from indicating what one might call the essential mechanism that will enable our world to reach its end: and it was precisely the fact that he did so that made it possible for him to refuse in any way to satisfy those idle speculations that continually crop up. His view is as simple as it is bold. He first rejects the hypothesis of a 'cosmic or sidereal catastrophe' that is to destroy our planet. Such a catastrophe, no doubt, would 'correspond neatly enough to our individual deaths', and it is for that reason that it naturally suggests itself to us; but it would still, if we may put it so, leave in existence the fragments of the ruined machine. 'It would bring about the end of the Earth, rather than the end of the Cosmos—and it is the Cosmos that will have to disappear.' Moreover, although a catastrophe 'is perfectly conceivable if we look at the world from the material side (at the material end)', it seems quite out of the question, 'if we look at it from the spiritual end': 'unless the universe is to be impossible for the thought that was born in it, it must rest solidly upon the future'.[25] Finally, and this is an even more telling argument, to make the Parousia dependent upon an accident of this sort would be to believe 'that it could be effected without any precise relation to any determined state of humanity, and at no matter what moment in history'.[26] We may dismiss, too, the idea that our species may become extinct by dying from lack of food, or through old age, since such contingencies are purely imaginary. Even more untenable is the theory of our 'sidereal migration' by astronautics, which people fall back on who have been made to realize the inevitable end of their 'golden age' on earth.[27] These hypotheses either leave the Universe in its present wretched condition, or arbitrarily annihilate it. However, 'we need not rack our brains to find out how the material immensity of the universe can ever vanish: all that is needed is for spirit to reverse, to move into a different zone, and the form of the World is immediately changed'.[28]

In this we have a fine commentary on the saying of the Apostle. It is thus that 'the form of this world' will attain its definitive fulfilment. Such an explanation is seen to be the consequence 'of the essential fact that Noogenesis (which is what Anthropogenesis essentially amounts to) is a *convergent phenomenon*, that is to say a phenomenon directed by its very nature towards some conclusion and consummation *whose origin lies within it*'.[29] We may add that, in regard to the reality of matter, to the relationship between the world and spirit, and to the conditions of human knowledge, it calls for something more than empiricism or a crude realism. Without being idealistic, Père Teilhard's thought is that of a period that 'has been through idealism'. We may reasonably surmise that it was formed under the influence of his contacts with his friend Père Auguste Valensin, of his debt to whom, as we have said, he was very conscious.[30] We should realize too, and this is of prime importance, that the type of 'idealism' that was characteristic of him has ample warrant in spiritual tradition,[31] and that other evidence of it may be found in his writings—for example in this thought, itself equally in line with tradition, from *Le Milieu Divin*: 'The fires of hell and the fires of heaven are not two different forces, but contrary manifestations of the same energy.'[32] Both the Greek and the Latin Fathers tell us the same. A transformation of the angle of view is sufficient to effect a transformation of the world. Everything, accordingly, will perhaps end 'through a turning about, psychic rather than sidereal, which will have the appearance of a death but will be in fact a liberation from the material plane of history, and an Ecstasis in God'.[33] In the disappearance of what must perish, this will be 'the consummation of the divine Milieu'. The hidden reality will suddenly have been made manifest, while the outer husk will have disappeared. 'Like a flash of light from pole to pole, the presence of Christ, which has been silently accruing in things, will suddenly be revealed . . . Like lightning, like a conflagration, like a flood, the attraction exerted by the Son of Man will lay hold of all the whirling elements in the universe, so as to reunite them or subject them to his body.'[34]

In this we should note, in the first place, how well this view of the 'ultimate end', unlike gnostic systems and so many other human speculations, conforms to the logic of the Christian faith, according to which 'man's salvation is not an element in the drama of the cosmos'; rather 'is it the Universe, on the contrary, that follows man's destiny'?[35] According to St. Paul, in particular, 'man's salvation and the transfiguration of the world' are closely bound up with one another, but 'the procession is from man's salvation to the transformation of material creation' and not vice versa.[36] The same is true of Teilhard's view.

We should note, secondly, that the 'inversion of spirit', the 'psychic turning about', 'the turning about into accession to Omega', are not effected by themselves, that is to say by some force immanent in man or the cosmos; it is not like a ripe fruit dropping from the tree. The 'cosmic convergence', brought about through 'the critical point of co-reflexion', does not by itself entail 'the Christic emergence'.[37] Like so many 'grains of consciousness', men have become capable of 'falling, through what is most fundamental in them, into a new field of attraction that now acts not simply on the complexity of their structure but directly on their centre'.[38] It is still, however, necessary for this 'field of attraction' to become active in this way. In other words, certain natural conditions have come to maturity on earth, in man. It is to this 'point of human maturity' that will correspond the 'Parousia-point' which will be, for mankind, the 'point of emergence'.[39] However, a 'necessary preliminary condition' is not a determining cause, and not even, in fact, a 'sufficient' condition. The return of the Son of Man, his coming, as Scripture says, 'in power and majesty', is a supernatural fact, and it depends entirely on initiative from on high. It is this initiative alone that has governed the synchronism, as a result of which the Glory of the Son of Man will finally burst forth, universally unchallenged, at the moment when a creation 'has been taken to the paroxysmic peak of its capacity for union'. Then will take place 'the unique and supreme event, in which history (faith tells us) is to be fused into the transcendent'.[40] This, then, for the faithful who have risen again, will be the final 'ecstasis in God'. 'It would be vain, the Gospel tells us, to speculate about that hour or about the ways in which that awesome event will come about.' The divinization of the new world in Jesus Christ will necessarily be so radical that it escapes, as we have just said, our methods of investigation, both as it concerns the 'external world' and as it concerns our own nature. All we must do is *to await it*: await it with longing, as the true Israelites first awaited the Messiah.[41] Such an attitude will again be a victory of Faith which, unable to find support in any perceptible element and knowing them all to be impermanent, forces us into total detachment.

A recent article in the *Bulletin* of the Protestant study centre in Geneva agreed with Père Teilhard that 'Christ draws all things to him', that 'the *totus Christus* cannot exist without the world', but added the criticism that 'Christian eschatology envisages a rupture' and that 'the world will not be in Christ without a complete turning back'. The author of the article based his comment on *The Phenomenon of Man* alone, in which he had not been able to find a complete exposition of a Christian eschatology—no more, indeed, than he would have found a dogmatic exposition of the mystery of the Trinity in a

Catholic treatise on natural theology.[42] It is a pity that, apart from unpublished essays, many of which were no doubt unavailable to him, he did not widen his views of Père Teilhard's thought by studying *Le Milieu Divin*.[43] He would have found in this the answer to the apparent contradiction on which he commented. In fact, he would have found the very word 'turning about' (*retournement*) that he quotes against Père Teilhard.[44] He would not, it is true, have found a certain one-sided concept of 'rupture', characteristic of Protestant thought —but that is quite another matter.[45]

More surprising are the comments of Père Guérard des Lauriers who, on the other hand, has read *Le Milieu Divin*, but sees in it a 'pathetic affirmation of hope as regards the flesh, but without resurrection'. For Père Teilhard, he concludes, 'evolution is a sufficient answer to everything'.[46] To say that *Le Milieu Divin* makes no mention of death or the resurrection is, indeed, an extraordinary distortion of the facts, completely ignoring the evidence of the text.[47]

Père Olivier Rabut puts forward a much more balanced interpretation. In his view, 'Père Teilhard hopes that what our labours have achieved will in some way be eternalized, redeemed; he seems to suggest that an earth which has been sufficiently organized by man will be ready, as such, for resurrection'. Provided we emphasize and qualify exactly, in the light of Père Teilhard's own explanations, the words 'in some way', what he says is completely accurate; but the end of the sentence, I fear, contains a certain ambiguity in the words 'as such'. For while it is true that, for Père Teilhard, the earth must one day be 'ready, as such', in that form, it does not follow that it will one day be ready, as Père Rabut would seem to interpret it, 'to rise again as such in that form'. It is the exact contrary that is true. The transfiguration of the cosmos will change it completely. Père Rabut thinks, again, that *Le Milieu Divin* exaggerates when it speaks of the earth as 'the body of him who is and of him who comes', even though it adds that it is this body 'through what lies beyond it'. We believe, as Père Rabut does, that the elliptical form and the emphasis of some of Teilhard's expressions would seem to suggest a sort of natural identity of Christ and the Universe.

In this case, however, Père Rabut might well be less critical if he allowed full significance to the phrase 'through what lies beyond it'. He does, in fact, add 'the Universe may well disappear once its task has been accomplished, or some completely different Universe may serve to hold the risen. We should not attach too much importance to the present economy of things'.[48] No one, however, I believe, could be less liable than Père Teilhard to over-estimate 'the present economy of things', or to attribute to it a permanence that amounts to eternalizing it. This is made quite clear not only by the phrase whose full meaning Père Rabut does not seem to have appreciated—the very Teilhardian phrase 'what lies beyond'—but also by other more explicit passages. Perhaps, too, he has not appreciated the paradox in his suggestion of a resurrection in the same body but a different universe. Finally, he may have attributed too little weight to the firm doctrinal tradition, referred to earlier, which emphasizes the substantial identity of the glorified world with the world in which we now suffer, in spite of the radical change that is to transpose it from one state to the other. Is not St. Gregory the Great one of many who tell us: 'Terra et caelum . . . per eam quam nunc habent imaginem transeunt . . . Erit caelum novum et terra nova: quae quidem non alia credenda sunt, sed haec ipsa renovantur.' ('Heaven and earth pass away in the form they now have. There will be a new heaven and a new earth; and yet we must not hold that they are other: they are themselves made new.')[49]

Such criticism of Père Teilhard in this context, made with varying severity according to the circumstances, would seem to be accounted for, at least in part, by a certain failure to bear in mind the Church's tradition. With this is combined the difficulty of focusing attention on both aspects of the concept of *immutatio* simultaneously. It implies, in a way that allows no dissociation, both continuity and discontinuity. The concern we find to ensure discontinuity is, indeed, fully justified; but it is, rather, in other domains that it would now appear to be threatened. It must, in fact, be recognized that a certain number of contemporary theologians are carrying to an extreme a tendency that the Fathers of the Church and, later, the great

Scholastics, constantly fought, and are offering us a picture of the 'life to come', in its secondary beatitude, which maintains it in marked continuity with life here below.[50] They read in St. Paul that 'the form of this world passes away', but they believe that they can still maintain that the form of our body will remain—and this leads them to put forward too facile predictions with regard to material satisfactions and physical pleasure in eternity: as though the bliss of the elect was to consist partly in a sensual delight that is not transfigured but heightened.[51] Rightly holding that the glory of heaven cannot destroy anything, any more than grace can, but must on the contrary complete all things, they place very little emphasis on the character of renewal, of radical transformation that is effected by the completion. Often enough, this may be no more than carelessness or awkwardness of expression. At the same time, if we allow a too literal imagination to dominate eschatological description, and so stimulate a desire that is still of flesh and blood, we find that we have travelled a long way from Scripture:[52] a long way, too, from the thought of the Fathers, for whom 'when this body has put on immortality, it will be transformed in its entirety, like iron which, plunged into fire, becomes fire—or rather, transformed in some way known to the Lord who makes it to rise again'.[53] It is far, too, from coinciding with the thought of the mystics, when they tell us that 'there is no common measure to the present world and the world to come, for their objects could not be more utterly different'.[54] The most authoritative theological teaching, as represented in the West by that of St. Augustine and St. Thomas, tells us the same.[55] The latter unhesitatingly denies to the risen body all use 'of food and generation', since they are ordered in man 'ad statum vitae mortalis'—to the state of mortal life—nor does he accept that one may attribute the pleasures of food and drink to a being who has no need of nourishment. It would not be fitting, he says, thus to attribute to the elect what in men is now accounted a vice.[56]

Père Teilhard is infinitely closer to the sources and witnesses of our faith, and infinitely more faithful in following the impulse of Christian hope. He takes a much more serious and balanced view of 'the great and longed-for consummation that is to restore our body'.[57] At least in principle, he achieved a better balance between 'continuity' and 'discontinuity', or between the relation of 'heaven' and 'earth'.[58] He asked himself, as Maurice Blondel had done: 'What solidity and durability is there in the form of this world, and what do we take with us—what remains in eternity—so that our person, which is bound up with all the contingencies that enclose our moral and religious life, may subsist as a function of the elements that make up our present activity and our decisive option?' The answer Père Teilhard worked out is not the same as Blondel's, but it tries in the same way to satisfy the double requirement the latter so clearly formulated when he added, 'I would not like to exaggerate the reality of these outward appearances that are necessary to the building up of our personality, nor to arrive at a sort of ultimate acosmism.[59] Even if we cannot accept in their full literal sense the explanations he gives (which themselves varied slightly), and even if we feel we cannot integrate them, as he sometimes does, with what was most systematized in his views,[60] Père Teilhard's work can have the salutary effect of ridding our minds of the pointless dreams, and of the materialistic fog in which a decadent thought might otherwise have entrapped us. By helping us better to understand the definitive casting off of the old that death is to effect in us, it sweeps away the mirage of all the 'Judaic fables', as the ancient writers call them, or all the 'paradises of Mahomet'. Thereby it directly assists in freeing us from the *irrisioin fidelium*, 'the mockery of the unbelieved' so feared by St. Augustine,[61] and, following him, by St. Thomas.[62] It can, and must, teach Christians once more to give up the too-human hopes, fruits and sustenance of a petty individual will-to-live, by rejecting, in the hope of greater good, 'the contemptible husk of every physical form and every physical possession'.[63]

This does not mean that we are to conceive a heaven that has no relation with our earth. We continually come back to the two correlative and inseparable characteristics of the same concept. *Immutatio* is total transformation or transfiguration; it is continuity in discontinuity; it is not, accordingly, restoration to life but glorious resurrection. 'Αλλαγησόμεθα, says St.

Paul[64]—we shall be changed; it is what Origen expressed in his concept of μετασχημάτησις,[65] refusing, as Père Teilhard did, to imagine the unimaginable.[66]

It is an odd thing that Origen, in direct contrast with Teilhard, was accused by the predecessors of our own more materialistically minded theologians of denying any continuity between the earthly condition and condition in the beyond;[67] and yet on this point both Origen and Teilhard are in perfect agreement. Both are recognizably more faithful than their respective critics to the thought of St. Paul and to his very words; for it is in the Epistle to the Philippians, again, that we read, 'We await a Saviour, the Lord Jesus Christ, who will change our lowly body to be like his glorious body, by the power which enables him to subject even all things unto himself.'[68] Moreover, it is Our Lord Jesus Christ himself who tells us, at the end of the Apocalypse, 'Behold, I make all things new.'[69]

Chapter 13

PERSONALISM

Père Teilhard de Chardin spoke of a 'cosmic consciousness' involved in the very first manifestations of thought. He welcomed the 'awakening on earth of a certain "cosmic sense", by which each one of us tends to become habitually and in a practical way conscious of his ties with the evolving Universe'.[1] We should not conclude from this that he succumbed to any 'cosmic temptation' or that he gave himself up to 'earthly dreams':[2] on the contrary he diagnosed the danger of the one and pointed out the emptiness of the other. This is evident from what we have already seen. No misconception could more distort his thought than to interpret it as the mere development, neither 'completed' nor 'corrected', of this 'cosmic consciousness' or 'cosmic sense'. The concept reflects something very different; it is, as he tells us himself, 'a Christian cosmic feeling', whose exact shade may vary with times and individuals, and whose most authoritative representatives he saw in a St. Francis of Assisi or a St. John of the Cross.[3]

Nevertheless, according to one of his critics, Père Teilhard sought for 'the Universal', which is 'the spirit's dearest wish', in 'the sensible'. We are told that he wished 'through a veritable imperialism of matter' to realize 'unity at the sensible level that is directly explorable'.[4] It is true that in a very few passages the terminology Père Teilhard uses may have given a misleading impression. The whole effort of his thought is none the less based on an irresistible movement of 'concrete transcendence'[5] whose force bursts out in a number of significant expressions. The reader may remember what he says in *La grande Monade*: 'I felt heavy upon me the dead weight of a final and definitive isolation—the distress of those who have made the round of their prison and found no way out from it . . .' In this universe, if it represents the whole of being, we are 'immured'.[6] Nor should we see in this a passing crisis of melancholy, an outburst of romanticism, or some youthful notion later to be overcome. On 28 December 1943, in Peking, Père Teilhard gave a lecture on happiness. In this the same sentiment emerges as we find in his solitary meditation in the Flanders trenches in 1918: if man can see nothing beyond, then he can only turn away, or try desperately to turn away, 'in horror from the terrifying cosmic machine in which he is caught up'.[7] The passage of time seems not to have weakened but to have intensified this feeling: in 1950 Père Teilhard, in *Le Cœur de la Matière*, once again adopted for the sake of argument the hypothesis of unbelief, and again we find him emphasizing 'the agony of feeling oneself imprisoned, not so much spatially as ontologically, in the cosmic bubble'.

Distress, horror, agony: can these fairly be regarded as a series of synonyms for enthusiasm or intoxication? Can they, as has been suggested, express the spiritual state of a man who is discovering the unity he dreams of 'at the sensible level that is directly explorable'? To break the circle, burst the bubble, escape from space and duration, disentangle oneself from the mechanism, find a way out—that is our great concern, and there we have the great problem. It is not Plato nor Plotinus but Teilhard who compares our world to a prison and speaks of escaping from it.[8] 'Escape' was a word that he was not afraid of using, even though it is now frequently considered, without discrimination, as pejorative. He rejects 'escape' only when it seeks to be a certain 'individual anticipation (more or less fictitious) of consummated Progress',[9] which disguises a selfish refusal to accept one's duty. And yet 'it would be so stifling to feel oneself ineluctably confined to this superficial and experiential facet of our cosmos'.[10] Again, in 1924, when he is explaining the main themes of *Mon Univers*, he shows us 'the effort of souls desperately straining in their desire to escape from the Earth'.[11] In 1926, he says that he finds consolation for the 'constriction' of this earth in the thought that it is perhaps 'one of the conditions of our emergence or "exstasis" '.[12] Later, in *Le Milieu Divin*, he tells us how indispensable is 'the heart-rending escape from the zones of material experience';[13] and in *The Phenomenon of Man* he envisages, as a counter to the threat of 'relapse into the multiple', the prospect of 'an escape from entropy by turning back to Omega'.[14] In 1937, *L'Énergie humaine* speaks of the dream of 'the escape of our bodies from their determinisms and of our souls from their isolation'. 'Escape' is found again, in 1944, in *La Centrologie*, the 'escape from total death' whose possibility he wished to establish.[15] On 10 March 1945, in a lecture given in Peking on 'Life and the Planets', he develops again the precise idea we find in *La Grande Monade*, and once more defines the term towards which we are moving as 'an escape from the planet, not in space or outwardly, but spiritually and inwardly':[16] a definition that might make his position even more unacceptable to some of our contemporaries who have so intense a phobia of any sort of interiority. Once again, in *Le Cœur de la Matière*, he writes, 'the more, Lord, the years go by, the more I believe that I can recognize, in myself and in those around me, that the great and intimate concern of modern man is not at all so much to dispute the possession of the world as to find the means of escaping from it'.[17] Finally, in 1952, we are shown that the 'salvation of the species' does not lie in any dream of 'temporospatial consolidation' or 'expansion' but in a 'spiritual escape'.[18]

Such an escape, however, could be conceived as the flight from a superficial world in which being is lost and broken up into multiple individualities that can never succeed in coming together again; it would lead to a return to the true Being in which all would be an undifferentiated unity. Many mystics, in many countries, have so understood it. Père Teilhard thinks of it in a very different way. His view is the exact opposite. His transcendent Universe, the Universe on which his heart is set, the Universe that he contrasts with the 'Universe spread out in time and space',[19] is above all a 'personal Universe' and a 'personalizing Universe'. It is, to use another favourite expression of his, a Universe of 'souls'.[20]

'I really believe,' he wrote to a friend in 1917, 'that my vocation has never seemed to me so stark and clear: to personalize the world in God,' and to that vocation he always remained faithful. One could quote any number of passages, from any of his different types of writings, to show that that was so; for on this point there was no question in his thought of confining his aim exclusively to an exposition of Christian teaching or spirituality—it was to him a truth of the natural order which had to be brought out, at least in an embryonic form, by philosophical reflection. One of his essays, written in 1936, is in fact entitled *Esquisse d'un Univers personnel*—a sketch of a personal universe, or, we might say, a universe that is *person*—and the very title has a concentrated dogmatic content as illuminating as it is enigmatic. In 1917, when he was writing *Le Milieu mystique*, he divided it into five parts, each dealing with one 'circle' of reality, and the fifth, the 'supreme circle', is the 'circle of the Person'. In a later series of essays, he took as his aim not simply 'to vindicate the preservation of persons' or 'to maintain and safeguard the primacy of the Personal',[21] but, if we may so express it, to 'constitute' the person and establish its decisive and definitive value.[22] In September 1934, when, at the request of Mgr Bruno de Solages, he was engaged on the essay in apologetics that was to appear under the title *Comment je crois*, he told a correspondent that in it he wished to affirm his faith 'in the ever-growing personality of the world'.[23] 'The universe,' he wrote in a letter of 1935, 'is a vast thing, in which we would be lost if it did not converge upon the Person.'[24] In 1937, he ended his essay on *L'énergie humaine* with a section on 'the principle of conservation of Personality',[25] and sets out once again to establish that 'the universal and super-human towards which (evolution) is carrying us must be seen as at once *incorruptible and personal*'. He never tired of emphasizing that in the 'human rebound of evolution' there is 'an *irreversible* rise towards the *personal*'.[26] He denounced as an aberration and 'terrestrial neo-religion' that tries 'in a muddled way to picture the Godhead as a diffuse energy' or as 'a super-society with neither head nor face'. He severely criticized all systems of thought and action, all political theories and 'social groupings' which, at least in practice, regard 'the person as of secondary importance', and 'place the primacy of pure totality first in their programmes'.[27] No one has shown our age more clearly than Père Teilhard, and in language designed to be understood by it, how 'mankind is in danger of allowing all that has been stimulated in it by the progress life has made, to be swallowed up in the *materia secunda* of philosophical determinisms and social mechanisms, and how Christianity counters this by maintaining the primacy of reflective, that is to say personalized, thought'.[28]

He explained, very rightly, that if Christianity does in fact succeed in doing this 'in the most effective of all ways', it is not only by defending speculatively the idea of the single God, the centre of total convergence (which it does through its teaching, which is centred in itself and yet universal)—it is 'much more by passing on and developing through its mysticism the sense and in some way the direct intuition of that God'.[29] A personal God, a 'hyper-personal' God, a God who is 'the supreme pole of personalization', 'the ultra-personalizing centre':[30] that is the great Object he sees in all the lines followed by his quest, the term at which he strives to make man's great quest culminate. 'Love dies,' he tells us, 'in contact with the nameless and impersonal';[31] and man will find no rest until he has met 'what is supremely Personal and supremely Personalizing'. What is more, without the hope of meeting it, man will never have the heart to carry on with his task, for only such a being can make possible 'the astonishing process of personalization that is to make the whole of evolution an object of love'.[32]

Thus in 1936, when he was considering the state of our human world, he wrote: 'Society will inevitably become mechanical unless its successive aggrandisements are not gradually crowned by Some One.'[33] Again, on 18 October 1940, he wrote from Peking: 'on all sides the battle rages unchecked; but . . . if you get back to the source of the conflict, you realize that the root of the evil is not in the apparent conflicts but very far away from them, it seems, in the inner fact that men have despaired of God's personality.'[34] 'God is Person! God is Person!' He never tired of repeating that phrase, and insisting that 'we think of him as a Person: A God who was not personal would not be a God'.[35] In his old age we find his faith and his prayer giving their testimony to this same principle: 'At no moment in my life have I found the least difficulty in speaking to God as to a supreme Some One.'[36] He would be sad, he tells us, not to share this testimony with

many men, of every social and cultural background, who have
allowed themselves to be persuaded that such a faith is now
no longer possible. As he pointed out himself, 'God . . . is
almost inevitably conceived by the modern positivist as a
shoreless ocean', as a 'diffuse immensity'; 'unlike the primi-
tives who gave a face to every moving thing, or the early
Greeks, who defied all the aspects and forces of nature, modern man is obsessed by the need to depersonalize (or imper-
sonalize) all that he most admires'.[37] Men are ready enough
to accept a 'principle' or 'law' or 'mystery of nature', but seem
to be ashamed of believing in 'a God who is concerned with
men's destiny and what they do'.[38] 'Nine times out of ten'
even those who can rise sufficiently above appearances to
glimpse 'an ultimate Spirit of the universe', picture it to themselves as 'a vast impersonal power in which our personalities
will be submerged'.[39] Similarly, in his *Journal d'une mission
ouvrière*, Père Loew says that 'a certain number' of the many
workers he knows 'affirm or admit that there is something
higher than us', but they never say 'someone'. It is difficult to
say how that something should be defined. For many, it is, for
example, 'the mystery of nature', but if you want to call it God
they protest.[40] Like all men these, too, have within them a
nostalgia for unity, and it would do them infinite good to hear,
either directly or through some intermediary, the authoritative
words of a man who tells them that, 'the generative principle
of our unification is finally to be sought not in the sole contemplation of a single Truth, or in the sole desire for a single
Thing, but in the common attraction exercised by a single
Being'.[41]

To achieve this was, in fact, one of Père Teilhard's main
projects. 'On the whole, our world denies the Personal and
denies God because it believes in the Whole. It all comes back
to showing the world that it must, on the contrary, believe in
the Personal because it believes in the Whole.'[42] If it does
this, it will avoid the 'Charybdis of the world that is aimless
because dispersed' without falling prey to the 'Scylla of a collective and depersonalized existence'.[43] It was in this form
that Père Teilhard saw 'the great and unique problem, that of
the One and the Multiple', which is fundamental to all physics,

all philosophy, and all religion,[44] 'in the urgency and the difficulties' it presents to the 'real humanity' of our time,[45] 'and whose urgency and difficulties must be seen in terms of real men and women'. Although he conceived the essence of his project much earlier, it was not until about 1928 that he defined it more exactly, when he came to appreciate more clearly the new form assumed by the great problem. Initially, his reflections were mystical in character, and his language in this connexion was more questionable. In *La Lutte contre la Multitude*, for example, he had written that men must have the courage to shatter their own petty individuality and in some way depersonalize themselves, 'in order to become Christocentric'.[46] And again, in 1923, he was to say, in 'The Mass on the World', 'My God, I deliver myself up with absolute abandon to those fearful forces of dissolution which, I blindly believe, will this day cause my narrow ego to be replaced by your divine presence.'[47] He spoke, in imprecise terms, of 'burying oneself deep in God, recognized as the fundamental element that controls our movement and forms us'. Like all mystics, he used the words 'annihilation', 'extinction'. He liked to say the prayer, 'a little strong, but most beautiful, of one of our sixteenth-century fathers', to the heart of Christ, which ends as follows: '. . . ad puram annihilationem meam'—'for my cleansing extinction'.[48] It is true, of course, that he does not mean more than the stripping-off of the ego, that is to say getting rid of self-love, of egoism, of 'the spirit of ownership'; he meant a receptive attitude to 'passivities', the imitation by the Christian of the process by which the Word of God 'emptied himself'.[49] Such interior dispositions—which undoubtedly go much further than a mere attitude of spiritual edification—were not to be abandoned by Père Teilhard. He continued to accept that 'union with Christ essentially presupposes that we transfer to him the ultimate centre of our existence'.[50] Nevertheless, as he became more concerned with 'intellectual structures',[51] another prospect opened up for him. Thus, on 15 July 1929, he wrote: 'After the idea of the Spiritual, that of "Person" immediately assumes in my view of the world an extraordinarily increasing importance'.[52] In another letter of the same year, dated 16 September, he is turning over in his mind 'a sort of spiritual cosmogony—but not a metaphysic—of the person'; in the theory that is beginning to take shape, 'the immortality of the soul and of personality . . . ceases to appear as anthropomorphic or self-interested expressions of the truth; it takes on an essential significance in the structure of the world'.[53] Some days later, on the 29th, he writes again: 'My mind is now completely occupied in constructing for itself a world in which man will be the key and not an anomaly'; and four years later, in 1933, he notes 'the continually increasing value that the natural development of *his* thought is causing *him* to attribute to the Person in the structure' of the Universe.[54]

On countless later occasions, he combated the idea 'so prevalent in our day that the universal is opposed to the personal', an idea that is in reality 'no more than an impression' and 'cannot stand up to analysis'.[55] Père Teilhard developed the converse idea, showing that 'a Universe in process of psychic concentration is *identical* with a Universe that is acquiring a personality';[56] that 'cosmic evolution is carrying out in us a work that is by nature personal'; and, correspondingly, that 'the effort of personalization' results in the collecting of beings into a 'fascicle'.[57] On innumerable occasions he emphasized the great law that 'union differentiates': a law which, like the idea of the 'critical point', can accept a whole series of analogical applications at an increasingly profound level.[58] This emphasis is, indeed, so characteristic of Père Teilhard that the Abbé J. P. Blanchard has said, 'As the famous "I think, therefore I am" *is* Descartes, so "union differentiates" *is* Teilhard.'[59] In contrast with the 'agglomeration' which 'stifles and neutralizes the elements it encloses', organization 'produces the complexity on which its unity flowers'; union 'centrifies', and does so the more decisively the more there is a transition to a higher level. In the case of man, he tells us, union, 'at the level of the reflective', completes the process of personalizing;[60] it 'superpersonalizes'.[61] This 'structural law' is as much a law of action as a law of being; it becomes for us 'the law of moral perfection'.[62] It finds its supreme application, as we shall see in the next chapter, in union with God, in which 'the self-subsistent individual who is united to him grows only in so far as the union itself grows', so that perfect union is achieved only 'in and through the plurality of persons'.[63]

In working out this doctrine, Père Teilhard, we find, is careful to preserve the distinction between 'individuality and personality': a distinction that can easily be lost sight of, since the person does not initially present itself 'to our experience except linked with individuals'.[64] For Père Teilhard, they represent two 'partly independent' notions. We may understand individuality in a restricted sense, which is bound up with the present state of our world and defines it not simply by the distinction between beings but by their separateness: in that case, he says, individuality decreases, as being a now useless support, in proportion with the increase of personality:[65] the personality which, in the individuals that we now are, is no more than in embryo.[66] On the other hand, he is equally careful not to succumb to the phobia of anthropomorphism, just as in biology he was not afraid of appearing anthropocentric:[67] nor could we say that that made him any the worse philosopher. He did not allow himself to be frightened by Spinozism, that teaching 'so arrogantly hostile to all analogy drawn from the forms of our consciousness'; with Victor Delbos, what he saw in it was more a 'deficiency'.[68] He even is at pains to show that 'the widely accepted ideal that the All, even when expressed as Spirit, can only be impersonal' is the effect of a 'spatial illusion'.[69] If he proceeds to say that men are capable of raising themselves 'to the perception of their "molecular" nature' and that thereby they 'cease to be closed individuals and become parts'[70] we know in what sense we should understand him, and will find his assertion no more disconcerting than that of St. Thomas, when the latter tells us, with less qualification, that 'every part exists naturally for the Whole' and that 'each individual person is related to the whole community as the part is to the whole'.[71]

Moreover, in combating the dangers that at this moment threaten the 'existence of "souls"',[72] Père Teilhard is well aware that he is running counter to the general drift of his age; but he is not concerned to give way to what he has recognized as a prejudice, and a pernicious prejudice. He is thus far from being the prophet 'of a universe that destroys individual values', as some were saying around 1930[73]—unless, indeed, by individual values we mean what is still no more than sensible plurality—what, in fact, we have, in pain and hope, to cut ourselves off from—though not for the sake of a universe that is itself sensible. He is a long way from throwing human beings into 'the anonymity of the zoological group'; and 'the very structure of *his* scientific thought' places him straightway 'at the antipodes of a social totalitarianism which leads to the termitary'.[74] How far removed, indeed, is Père Teilhard from those minds which, from century to century, believe so readily that they are rising above facile thinking and a vulgarized Christianity, when in reality they are falling into a denial of personality that is characteristic of pre-Christian thought.

Many passages he wrote make it quite clear that in his Christian personalism there is nothing either facile or vulgar; that it knows how to apply 'corrections by analogy' and so allow their full place to the movement of transcendence and the strictest 'theological negatives'; and finally that it is not only compatible with the loftiest mysticism but, by a sort of circumincession, it culminates, after having been formed by mysticism, in engendering it. Of all the passages that make this clear, let me quote one, taken from his *Esquisse d'un Univers personnel*. I have chosen it, because it was written, reflected on, and lived, by a man whose Christianity was as demanding as his thought:

'What can we conceive that will suffice, in our present state of organization, to alleviate for mankind the agony of the evils that torment it? All that is needed is for its consciousness to become alive to the Object that is being born of its sufferings. It is this faith and this hope that is given to man by the idea of a personalization of the Universe. We must therefore look for our essential satisfaction in the thought that by our struggles we are serving, and leading to salvation, a personal Universe. We must consciously lose ourselves in the universal Being. If there really exists a natural centre of things, that Centre will react. *We shall not see it more distinctly than the age of the World allows.* But because we have turned towards it, its reality will make itself felt in the light and warmth that descend upon us.'

Chapter 14

GOD ALL IN ALL

Teilhard's philosophy of the Person and Totality is a philosophy 'at once pluralist and monist'.[1] It forms one with the philosophy of Evolution and Convergence, and with the passage of time it assumes its form to a more marked degree. It is based on an analysis that reveals a 'concentric structure' in reality. 'A universe whose stuff is personal' and a 'universe that follows a convergent curve come to the same thing'; and, for Père Teilhard, such a universe is 'the only milieu with a capacity both for the Christ we worship, so that we may receive him, and for the Man of whom we dream, so that it may be of value to him'.[2] On the other hand experience shows him also that those of his contemporaries who 'have been fundamentally cut off from the influence of Christianity' find great difficulty in accepting a personalist point of view. He sees Christianity as 'the only spiritual current capable of developing in souls' a sense of an Absolute that is at once universal and personal, 'in other words the true "mystical sense" '.[3] It is not that the mystical sense, in a first basic significance, is not congenital to man, but that it needs to be given something to nourish and illuminate it. In human nature there is 'a sense and a presentiment of the total and final unity of the world lying beyond its present, sensibly apprehended, multiplicity'; and 'this holds good as much for the Hindu and the Sufi as for the Christian. It is this that allows one to estimate the mystical "tenor" of a writing or of a life. But it is expressed with considerable difference in each particular case'.[4] Père Teilhard, as we might expect, boldly faced this grave problem of mysticism, and it was in Christian personalism that he found the solution. In this connexion again, his work is of great assistance to us. It contains an antidote to the illusory attraction of mystical systems that are increasingly appealing to western minds. Père Teilhard had for a long time been pointing out the error in

the 'false mysticisms', such as that of Schuré, and had shown
the danger in 'naturalist mysticisms' that look for 'mysteries
(and their solution) in the plane of our own experience and
of our own sensible universe, and not within a circle of the
universe that lies deeper than our world'.[5] Later, his travels
all over the world had made him conscious of an even more
far-reaching danger; he met many souls 'who were helpless
victims of the most pernicious fantasies'; he was familiar with
'the only too numerous reefs on which mystical attempts have
so often come to grief'; and the clarity of his analysis calls
on us to choose:

'An effort to escape spiritually, through universalization, into
the inexpressible: mystics of all religions and of all times are
in complete agreement about this general orientation of the
interior life in search of perfection. But this superficial uniformity disguises a serious opposition (or even a fundamental
incompatibility), which originates in a confusion between two
diametrically opposed ways of understanding and hence of
attaining the unity of Spirit.'[6]

He called these two 'antipodal' ways, and described them
concisely, as 'the road of the East' and 'the road of the West'.[7]
In one we find 'release of tension and expansion', in the other
'tension and centration'. In one, 'dissolution of individuals in a
diffuse immensity'; in the other, 'the paroxysm of what in each
element is most incommunicable'. It may well be that he expressed this too simply and on occasion forced the contrasts,
as was once pointed out to him in a letter by the Abbé Jules
Monchanin; the latter was deeply versed in Indian mystical
thought, and found in Père Teilhard's views a certain pragmatist emphasis and a too exclusively western presentation.[8]
Père Teilhard himself realized that he was only outlining a
schematic picture of the two; all he wished to do, he said, was
'to distinguish two possible essential types of mysticism' without claiming that either is ever to be found 'in the pure state'.[9]
With rigorous perspicacity he notes two things. First, the paradox that the most extreme western approach is today coinciding, in the 'slant' it is adopting, with the oldest forms of eastern
mysticism; this it does when it turns its back on authentic
'spiritual concentration' and accepts a 'diffuse energy' that

makes it 'forget the essential'.[10] And secondly, rigorous though his final verdict is, he can nevertheless continually discern in eastern mysticism certain values that are capable of conversion. He did not himself, it is true, make any methodical effort to include 'the eastern ascent towards the Unconditioned' in the Christian synthesis (as did Jules Monchanin or Jacques-Albert Cuttat), by drawing it 'into the orbit of the personal God'. He spoke of his disappointment at not having found in Asia 'the reservoir of thought and mysticism' which he had hoped at first 'would rejuvenate our West'. Nevertheless, he never entirely abandoned the plan of 'enriching our mind a little with the heavy current of vigour' still flowing through the East. It was thus that he was sympathetic in his examination of the ancient Buddhist propensity 'to establish the underlying rhythm of the world, to construct a perspective of its countless evolutions, to look forward to the supreme Buddha who is to redeem all things'.[11] A later study of the spiritual contribution of the Far East ('L'Apport spirituel de l'Extrême Orient,' 1947) showed, moreover, that he could analyse the problem from a number of different angles.[12] In any case, the passages, based as much on interior experience as on external observation and history,[13] in which he contrasts the mysticism of identification with the mysticism of union, are in no way 'arbitrary'.[14] They bring out the essential factors and forces much more clearly than do any number of more scholarly and subtle studies. With great objectivity they reject the superficial and deceptive view that all mysticism is one, by disclosing the contradictions that underlie 'expressions that are verbally almost identical'. They clearly demonstrate the congenital defects of 'eastern' mysticism (or, as others would put it, of all 'natural' or 'naturalist' mysticism), contained in its impersonalism, and show that under a number of different forms it is always, ultimately, a mysticism 'without love'.[15] This has been well appreciated by Père Olivier Rabut.[16] Another reader of *Le Milieu Divin*, who is particularly well informed on these problems, has said, in words that clarify one's judgement of the whole body of Teilhard's work: 'Unlike Yoga, which implies a cosmifying of consciousness and leads to a depersonalizing of man and of God, Teilhard's approach—the Pauline approach, the Christian approach, in short—proceeds from a God so radically personal that he personalizes the entire universe through man.'[17]

Nevertheless, the terms 'monism' and 'pantheism' have been used in connexion with Père Teilhard, as though he had deified 'a universe undergoing a perpetual evolution'.[18] His 'Christian monism', it has been said again, is in reality an 'absolute monism', including and fundamentally vindicating 'the elementary forms of monism on which it rests'.[19] He was not unaware that such accusations would be made against him. 'More than one of those who see me will shake their heads, and accuse me of worshipping nature', he wrote in 1917, in *Le Milieu mystique*; and this was when he was trying for the first time to distinguish the different possible lines that mysticism could follow—the 'natural force' which, he saw, was liable, as it developed, 'to be halted by obstacles, or to fall into perversions and deviations'. It can, he went on, 'evaporate in empty poetry, be lost in naturalist mysticism, sink into pagan pantheism'. We should note the adjective. When Père Teilhard rejects pantheism, it is seldom that he is not careful to specify it in some way, as some particular form of pantheism. Thus he condemns in turn 'ancient pantheism', 'common pantheism', 'the Hindu type of pantheism', 'the pantheisms of east and west', or 'humanitarian neo-pantheisms'.[20] What he emphatically rejects is 'the pantheism of effusion and dissolution'; it is the 'materialist illusion' that is characteristic of 'the majority of pantheisms'; it is the pantheism that 'in order to overcome the Plural' attempts to 'abolish it';[21] he will have nothing to do with 'heterodox forms of the pantheist impulse' such as 'Spinozism. Hegelianism or theosophy'.[22] These are 'pantheisms of the inanimate' which look for 'a formless energy' to which they may cling as to 'the great stability'.[23] There are, again, 'so many artistic or religious pantheisms for which access to the great All means communion, in dissolution, with nature'.[24] In fact, except in a very few passages, he is never prepared to condemn the word itself without any exact qualification; one result of this was that when, occasionally, he was writing with special 'candour', he did not guard himself against misinterpretation by those to whom words are a hypnotic. In 1918, in his first autobiographical essay, he wrote 'I believe that I was born with a "naturally pantheist" soul'; and in the same essay we find, 'the pantheist tendency is so universal and so persistent that it must have in it a soul of naturally Christian truth that we must baptize.'[25]

The baptism, however, of which he dreamed for this soul was no mere superficial operation. It was a profound 'transformation', which was to 'dominate, capture and assimilate it'; or, to put it even better, it was in very truth a mystical death and a resurrection.

'Far from running counter to my deep-seated pantheist tendencies, Christianity, properly understood, has always—*precisely because it preserves the Personal*—guided them, given them precision, and above all confirmed them by giving them an exact objective and a beginning that can be experientially verified . . .

'A perfect mutual transparency in a perfect mutual possession—such is the only pantheistic fusion that is logically conceivable in the divine ambience.'[26]

The Christian cannot compromise with doctrinal pantheism, for 'while claiming to unify beings it confuses them, in other words it in fact annihilates the mystery of union'. This, however, does not prevent it from being an 'immense temptation', since it is based both on a tendency that is deeply rooted in human nature—the 'preoccupation with the All'—and on the evident results of the progress of thought during these last centuries. How, then, when we oppose the pantheists, can we prevent their 'taking with them all that is most vital in this world that we claim to save and bring back to God?' How are we to see that 'the passion for the All' does not end in 'worship of the world'? It is more urgent than ever before that a Christian should 'wrest from the pantheist the fire with which he was threatening to set the Earth ablaze with an ardour that was not Christ's'.[27]

It was this Christian that Père Teilhard resolved to be. Very early in his career, he himself had felt like 'the atom that sees in the depths of itself the face of the universe'; it had made him feel a 'hallowed emotion' that was never to fade. He might well have drawn from it, in the system of thought he was

constructing, no more than a new version of the old idea of
'man the microcosm' and so quietly developed his 'pantheist
tendency', just as one quietly succumbs to a temptation. But
at the same time, as we pointed out again in the preceding
chapter, he realized that the Plenitude he sought, the Absolute,
'the one thing that is necessary', would always lie 'beyond'.
Later, the discovery of generalized evolution, with its law of
'increasing complexity', gradually led him to look for personalized Spirit, always lying 'ahead'. This again was to arouse a
new conflict and present a new temptation, for the problem
then would be to reconcile his new 'propulsive faith in the
Ultra-human' and his 'ascensional faith in God'. However,
between all these different elements—the direct feeling of presence, the passion for unity, the twofold awareness of the
'beyond' and the 'ahead', the triumphant faith in personal
Spirit—between all these a balance was being established, or
rather a fusion, a higher synthesis; and all these rays began to
converge on the God of his Christian faith.[28] 'My supreme
hopes, the very hopes that neither eastern nor western pantheisms could satisfy, are fulfilled by faith in Jesus.'[29]

Thus, against the 'pantheist solution', in the normal, un-
qualified sense of the word, he set the 'Christian solution'.[30]
He refused 'in following his innate taste for the universal, to
fall prey to pantheism'.[31] It is true, nevertheless, that on one
occasion he spoke of 'the pantheist aspect of Christianity',
though he was quick, at the same time, to make it clear that
he realized the paradoxical character of the expression. On
another occasion, he sent a friendly criticism to Père Auguste
Valensin, who had just contributed an important and 'illuminating' article on *Pantheism* to the *Dictionnaire apologétique
de la foi catholique*, for having dismissed too summarily
'living pantheism', the pantheism of the poets, which was, according to Père Teilhard, 'the mysticism of which Spinoza
and Hegel were the theologians'; he reproached him, again,
on the ground of having criticized all pantheism, in a way
that was not too radical, but too purely negative and for that
very reason less effective.[32] The expression of the criticism
shows us clearly what portion of the truth he believed the
word could contain. As a result of the Incarnation of the

Word, what is offered us in Christ, is, with no admixture, real participation in the divine life, so that all become, 'without losing themselves, one and the same person',[33] *Filii in Filio*, the theologians say. In other words, he is afraid lest we should allow the mystical realism of St. Paul and St. John to be weakened or watered down. He shared this fear with some of the best minds of his generation, and if we look back at the period we shall have to admit that it was not without justification. Père Teilhard is well aware, and recognizes explicitly, that a 'materialist or pantheist perversion threatens our thought when it tries to use the powerful but dangerous resources of organic analogies to express its mystical concepts'. He accordingly proceeds with caution, linking 'the urgency and irreversibility of the physical and biological relationships of the present universe' to 'the warm flexibility of social relations';[34] and he continually bore in mind that this linking of the two sorts of 'relationships' gave him only a 'sighting' and not an adequate concept of what remains a mystery. At the same time, he did not allow this caution to degenerate into 'timidity'.[35] It was in order to keep closer, even in verbal agreement, to the Pauline phrase ἐν πᾶσι πάντα θεός that, in the Epilogue to *The Phenomenon of Man*, he says of the ultimate end to which we are called: 'this is indeed a superior form of pantheism, without trace of the poison of adulteration or annihilation'; it is 'true pantheism', the very converse of those he rejected;[36] and it is with the consciousness of being a simple and faithful echo of Christian truth that he wrote, again: 'God becoming finally *all in all*, in an atmosphere of pure charity (*sola caritas*): in that magnificent definition of the Pantheism of differentiation is unmistakably expressed the very substance of Christ's message'.[37]

We see, then, that Père Teilhard varied between using and rejecting the word. He would have liked to retain it, subject to the necessary explanations, and in this he was exercising the right that every writer has, provided he makes his intentions clear, to construct his own vocabulary when he is not using words that traditional rules or long and well-attested usage confines to one particular meaning[38]—and we know that neither of those conditions applies to 'pantheism', which is a comparatively recent word',[39] even though it occurs incidentally in a decree of the Congregation of the Index, dated 15 June 1855.[40] At the same time, in his desire to retain the word, could Père Teilhard have avoided being misunderstood? However that may be, it is evident that there was no variation in his thought—if we take into account the personalist emphasis we have pointed out, and provided that we do not mistake for a theory that he professed what was no more than an indication of a mental bias or a 'temptation' at this or that particular moment of his life. Just as his 'Hymn to Matter' is addressed to a matter that is understood in the opposite sense to that which it bears in all materialist systems, so the definition of his 'Christian pantheism' (if we are going to retain the word) is the exact opposite of anything that is ordinarily meant by pantheism. Again, an essay written in 1950, with the significant title 'Two inverse forms of spirit' ('Deux formes inverses de l'esprit'), is expressly devoted to emphasizing unmistakably the fundamental opposition between pantheistic ideology on the one hand, and on the other the personalist mysticism of union as derived from Christian faith.

The synthesis on which Père Teilhard's personalism rests can give it a persuasive force that is not possessed to the same degree by other personalist systems, which may sometimes be more acute in their inner analysis or have a sounder metaphysical basis, but are less objective in their approach. It has the advantage of effecting 'a more explicit (and more artificial) reintegration of the Personal in the general picture of the world', since that picture shows us that the world 'is traversed and moved by a flux of centration'.[41] Such a synthesis sets its author in direct opposition to Spinoza, the supreme pantheist, who dreamt of 'absorption in the immense calm in which is swallowed up all personality'.[42] It does, however, entail certain difficulties that we shall shortly have to note. For the moment, we may confine ourselves to the central affirmation, which has great force and is brought out with great clarity. The 'All' is neither a 'heap' nor a 'bloc'. The unity of spirit in God and with God, which is the fruit of an 'amorization', must produce the opposite of a depersonalization. Love, which is 'the higher form of human energy', 'the higher and purified form of an inner universal attraction', love alone is capable of 'carrying the Personalization of the cosmos to its term'. If we look at it not simply in man but in its first source we shall understand it still better. 'The action of love in producing differentiation and communion', by which God is ultimately to be 'all in all', is the complete contrary of a process of absorption by which God—if we could continue so to call him—would become 'All'.[43] God-Love is not a Godhead that re-absorbs.

This view is eminently and profoundly traditional. St. Augustine was certainly no monist or pantheist, and it was Augustine who described our eternal end in the words *Haereamus uni, fruamur uno, permaneamus unum* ('let us cleave to one, let us enjoy one, let us remain for ever one').[44] And it is of Augustine that it has been said that his theology of the mystical body, in its radicalism 'which carries unity in being to its extreme consequences, would seem to come close to some sort of Christological pantheism'.[45] That great doctor, however, was primarily concerned to make Christians realize the wonders of their unity in Christ, and in comparison with his phraseology Père Teilhard's could be taken for a masterpiece of cautious qualification. Nor, again, was St. Gregory the Great any more a pantheist in saying, 'In illo qui ubique est, unum sumus' ('We are one in him who is everywhere').[46] We may say the same of the disciple of St. Gregory whose yearning, like his master's, reached out to the blessed city 'ubi est dies aeternus et unus omnium spiritus', 'where eternity dwells and there is one spirit of all';[47] and in the ninth century, in a less happy neoplatonic 'hierarchic' context—admittedly outdated—we find John Scotus Eriugena putting forward the analogy contained in Teilhard's law: 'Inferiora vero a superioribus naturaliter attrahuntur et absorbentur, non ut non sint, sed ut in eis plus sal\ventur, et subsistant, et unum sint.'—'It is the nature of lower things to be drawn to and absorbed in the higher, not in such a way that they cease to be, but so that they are more fully preserved in the higher, and they subsist, and are one.'[48] To turn to the twelfth century, no pantheism could be found in the admirable 'Golden Letter' of William of St. Thierry,[49] or in his friend St. Bernard, who, like William, so often defined our end, following St. Paul, as 'unity of spirit in God'.[50] To these we could add any number more, against whom the same charge was nevertheless brought by insufficiently perceptive thinkers or insufficiently observant historians.[51]

There is no question of the boldness of the thought that reconciles opposites without allowing one to be destroyed by the other, and that brings together extremes by pursuing both union and distinction to their limits. It calls for boldness to rediscover or even to maintain the fullness of the doctrine in the face of the softening and weakening that it too commonly experiences. There is no doubt that we are justified in questioning the roads by which Père Teilhard seeks to lead us to the concept of a 'theosphere' unified in love; but he cannot be criticized on the ground that he allowed himself to be deceived by what he himself called 'the pantheist mirage'. In his 'panchristism', as he again said, 'there is no pantheism'. The universal influence of Christ, as conceived by him, 'does not dissociate, but consolidates; it does not confuse, but differentiates; it does not allow the soul to stagnate in a vague, idle, union, but drives it continually higher along exact roads of activity'.[52] Again, in considering the boldness of his views on man's ultimate term, we should remember that if they are indeed bold, the same may be said of Scripture. It is the boldness we find in the Song of Songs, as constantly interpreted by Catholic tradition, in its glorification of the perfect marriage of human nature with God in Christ. It is the boldness that distinguished Christian mysticism both from merely platitudinous spiritual and moral systems and from the natural mysticism we constantly meet in history. *Unum estis in Christo Jesu* —you are one in Christ Jesus. 'Through the return to him of the Christ who bears the world, *God will be all in all.*'[53] It is the boldness of St. Paul, on whose words Père Teilhard continually meditated, and to whom he was continually referring. 'All the same,' he once exclaimed, 'we've a perfect right to speak as St. Paul did!'[54] And on the last page of his diary, three days before his death, on Maundy Thursday 1955, he again noted: 'St. Paul, the three verses': ἐν πᾶσι πάντα θεός'[55].

Can we say that such boldness leads us into a materialistic monism? Is it not rather pure Christianity?[56]

Chapter 15

A REVERSAL OF METHOD

In its underlying inspiration Père Teilhard's spirituality is one thing, in its presentation of doctrine quite another. The correctness of the former does not necessarily entail the complete success of the latter. There are occasions when distinct objections suggest themselves; and even when we accept what the author says our minds are still not completely at ease. Some of these objections and questionable points have already been touched upon, and we must now return to them and deal with them more fully. In this chapter we shall examine those that are raised by the method adopted in *The Phenomenon of Man* and similar writings.

Without embarking on any purely scientific discussion, and without criticizing *The Phenomenon of Man* for not being also a treatise on metaphysics, it is to be regretted that we do not find in it some more fully worked out investigations of the epistemological problems whose solution seems to dominate the undertaking. The Preface already tells the reader what it is essential for him to realize if he is to avoid gross misconceptions. This, we believe, we have already made quite clear. We may, however, wonder whether such brief statements, even when emphasized and expressed in more detail in other parts of the book, are sufficient to justify or even fully to explain Père Teilhard's method. It is a fact that numbers of scholars, including both natural scientists and physicists, have allowed themselves to be misled. There can, indeed, be no doubt but that the author himself reflected deeply on these preliminary questions and that he appreciated their very great, even decisive, importance. Even when he is entering on the most unfamiliar ground, it is with full reflection that he proceeds. We may, again, dismiss the criticisms of those who, looking no further, speak of 'transgression' because they do not recognize in these procedures the precise application of the concept of science as they have learnt it from their textbooks, or those who denounce a 'confusion of domains' without first having asked whether the value of a scientist might not in some cases consist in breaking down the divisions drawn by specialists before he entered the field.[1] All that such methods of judging the book amount to is to sanction prejudice. At the same time it must be admitted that Père Teilhard did little to guard against them. He did not, in fact, concern himself to arrange the results of his reflection and organize them into a whole, and so present them for discussion. Numerous and penetrating though his indications are, they are always more or less incidental. They have to be picked up here and there as they occur in his work, and to do so is made all the more difficult by the fact that they are spaced out over a number of years and that the language in which they are expressed varies from time to time.

Père Teilhard was well aware that there was bound to be resistance to his views. He fully realized that he was in fundamental opposition to some of the main tendencies in the scientific world of his time. After planning the first sketch, still very brief, to which he had given the significant title *The Phenomenon of Man*, this is what he said (the date is 31 July 1930):

'The *Revue des questions scientifiques* has asked me whether they may print a note on *The Phenomenon of Man*, in which I have managed to express quite a number of things that are important to me—some of them, moreover, not exactly classing me among the "advanced" scientists. My thesis, in fact, is that man is the key to the understanding of the universe (the latter becoming for all true science an *irreversible* advance towards spirit). Now, following the prophet Einstein, quite a number of physicists (or talkers) are beginning to assert the existence of a universe that is finite and reversible, in which duration will give way to space, the only definitive and fundamental reality, and so disappear. All this seems to me a delirium of geometrization in ultra-specialized minds (these ideas would radically wipe out all faith, all morality and even all appetite for research). Nevertheless they are very much in the air. And so now I am among the reactionaries.'[2]

'Reactionary'—elsewhere, and more seriously he speaks of himself, still from the scientific point of view, as a 'revolutionary', even though, of course, one can find a certain number of thinkers who anticipated him.[3] There are thus two ways in which one may regard his break with the habits of thought prevalent in the scientific circles in which he moved. In 1940, when he was on the point of finishing the final draft of *The Phenomenon of Man*, he wrote: 'I shall have the pure scientists against me as well as the experts in pure metaphysics';[4] later still, at the end of 1952, when he had just finished an essay on 'Hominization and Speciation', he foresaw that, 'it will probably upset a good many biologists and anthropologists if it ever appears'.[5] And yet he said again and again, with complete conviction, that in the 'long series of essays' written at intervals throughout his scientific career, parallel with his field and laboratory work, he had always tried 'not to philosophize in the absolute but, as a naturalist or physicist', to discover the significance of the facts of every order that he had been able to observe.[6] He admits, indeed, that 'appearances and a certain overlapping due to the vastness of the subject' may sometimes give the reader a contrary impression; for when they approach 'the whole, physics, metaphysics and religion'. He none the less maintains, even in cases where he is dealing most boldly with the future of man and the conditions of his activity, that he never 'goes beyond the field of scientific observation'; all he wishes to do is to provide 'an extension of our biological perspectives—no more and no less'.[7]

'No more and no less' recalls the similar double qualification we found in the foreword to *The Phenomenon of Man*. In determining the relation of that book to *Le Milieu Divin* we examined chiefly the implications of 'no more'. Here it is the 'no less' that we should consider. Père Teilhard was a specialist in natural science, and he works by analysis in accordance with procedures that are proper to his special discipline. He knows that analysis is indispensable; he always carries it out cautiously and meticulously, even charily,[8] but he refuses to be limited to it. In a passage that for all its brevity is of capital importance, he says: '*Analysis*, that marvellous instrument of scientific research, to which we owe all our advances, but which, breaking down synthesis after synthesis, allows one soul after another to escape, leaving us confronted with a pile of dismantled machinery and evanescent particles.'[9] It builds up the edifice of science—this little edifice, as the young Renan said, 'which is continually growing taller';[10] but it does so only by pulling down the great edifice of reality. To say this is not to condemn analysis, but simply to admit that it is not everything. It is only one of the operations of the mind. It is the most fruitful of them from the point of view of our action on the elements, because it is the basis of all our technique, but it is not the only one, nor the most important if we wish to advance our understanding of the universe. Analysis, by dissecting so to speak to infinity what Père Teilhard once called 'the strictly experiential skin'[11] enables us to know it more and more fully; but beyond a certain point the game is not worth the candle. If we continue to persist in following up in detail the action of infinitesimal causes, in a sector that itself is confined, no true advance is made. We then have to 'adopt a more profound and synthetic approach to things'; we have to envisage a wider object and take it as a whole in which we shall try to distinguish new specific properties.[12] The scientist who is not only content to use the 'marvellous instrument' of analysis but has no desire to know anything that analysis does not tell him, thinks that he is being rigorous, but in reality he is slipping into one of those tendencies of the human intelligence which is to 'break nature up into pieces'.[13] He is then liable, through a sort of inside-out metaphysics or mysticism, to accept a materialist or nihilist dogma: materialist, if he falls into the illusion of 'regarding the elements of the analysis as more real than the terms of the synthesis':[14] nihilist, if he sees the universe disintegrating and eluding him even as his analysis proceeds, just as others see it disintegrate and elude them when subject to 'our fallings off and in the process of its own perdurance'.[15]

Such, according to Père Teilhard, was the mistake or the inevitable fate of nineteenth-century science; 'instead of attaching the progress of things to a higher pole of spirit', it 'conceived it as held up and confined by the elementary forces of the multiple. It projected the centre of the world downwards.

Its mysticism was lost in the cult of matter'. The reason for this was that the temptation was too strong:

'Let us go back in mind . . . to the first moment when animate and living bodies yielded . . . to the scientific pressure of analysis . . . In all domains simultaneously, the real, however spiritual and simple it might appear to be, was seen to be patient, both spatially and temporally, of decomposition, or of reduction to more simple elements. It was the period when transformism had only just appeared, and transformists believed that they could follow out a continuous chain of forms linking man to monocellular beings. It was the period, again, when chemistry was building a bridge between the organic and the inorganic: the age, finally, when physics was hoping to reduce the forms and energies contained in the universe to calculable movements of invariable masses. From these initial successes was to emerge—and indeed was directly born—the illusion that if man was to put his hand on the ultimate motive force in nature, all he had to do was continually to carry further his rational investigation of measurable antecedents. The secret of the universe lay hidden in the shadows of the past and in the depths of the atom. Analysis would disclose it. And when the laws of nature were known, man would complete himself, artificially, by his own powers.'[16]

In this illusion there was 'something both simple and intoxicating'; and in spite of many disappointments the spirit which produced it has by no means disappeared. In biology, in particular, 'it still leads scientists to refuse to consider man as an object of scientific scrutiny except through his body', and, 'while accepting the undeniable fact of the general evolution of life in the course of time, many biologists still maintain that these changes take place without following any defined course, in any direction, and at random'.[17] In short, as a correspondent wrote to Père Teilhard, ' "positive" science, after working to remove man from the position in which orthodoxy had enthroned him and putting him back in his place "with the other animals", never, in this field, went beyond the purely material, anatomical, plane'. The paradoxical conclusion drawn from that narrow view—a conclusion that was eminently non-scientific—is that everything else that is human 'remains therefore *sui generis*, which makes things easier, of course, for juridico-literary, anthropology, even if unbelieving'.[18]

The time had come, Père Teilhard concluded, boldly to reverse the perspective or 'the direction of advance'; to over-throw this false principle 'that the secret of things lies in their elements, so that to understand the world all we have to do is to arrive at the most simple of the terms from which it emerged'; to show that if we start from such a principle, which is in no way scientific, we can do no more than 'reach the extreme lower limits of the real' and obtain 'the unity of im-poverishment in homogeneity'.[19] The time has come, not, in the first place, to set 'mysticism' against 'mysticism', but to set a true science, more comprehensive in its object and more positive in its results, against a negatory illusion that has be-come a parasite on a stunted science. 'The time has come to realize that an interpretation of the universe—even a positivist one—remains unsatisfying unless it covers the within as well as the exterior of things—mind as well as matter. The true physics is that which will one day achieve the inclusion of man, in his wholeness, in a coherent picture of the world.'[20] In order to do this, we do not have to abandon the idea of the Phenomenon, but we must break through 'the magic circle of phenomenalism'.[21] We have to realize that 'human reflec-tion is not an epiphenomenon of the organic world, but the central phenomenon of vitalization'.[22] The progress already achieved in the scientific study of evolution commits us to this approach:

'For pragmatic and methodological reasons that are per-fectly legitimate, physics has been primarily concerned to fol-low phenomena in the direction in which they break down—or disintegrate into atoms. The fact of evolution intervenes to remind us that the chief movement of the Real is a synthesis, in the course of which the plural appears in progressively more complex and more highly organized forms, each further step in unification being accompanied by an increase in interior consciousness and freedom.'[23]

If we thus make up our minds to take the whole of the phenomenon as the object of science, we shall finally succeed in discovering the 'natural centre of total coherence of things';

we shall see that 'Man, the centre of perspective, is at the same time *the centre of construction* of the Universe'.[24] 'In the spirit of man, as though in some unique, peerless fruit, is gathered together all the sublimated life—that is to say, all the cosmic value—of the Earth.'[25]

The reversal that Père Teilhard wishes to effect is thus completed. 'The spirit which I think I can discern,' he wrote in 1929, 'is loaded with the spoils of matter. I now see all the grandeur, all the physical and historical attributes, with which science has been loading matter for the last hundred and fifty years—I see all these transferred to one characteristic stuff inherent in all things. Entropy has been replaced for me by "the highest consciousness" as the essential physical function of the universe. The world seems to me to "tumble", if I can so put it, forward and upward upon the spiritual.' This is indeed a 'inversion of cosmogony',[26] and to effect it, and dethrone 'the majestic and inflexible entropy'[27] of the materialist world calls, in fact, for nothing less than a 'conversion' of science.[28] Père Teilhard constructs a new science of evolution, which is summed up in the law of 'growth in the human "trajectory"'.[29] His world, he says on another occasion, 'is the world of modern science completely in reverse'.[30] It is hardly surprising that there was not a general readiness to effect such an inversion. The more fundamental it evidently was, the more desirable it was that it should be accompanied by a profound critical investigation of the very idea of positive science and its various stages, by a methodical examination of the operations of science (including their respective presuppositions) and by an attempt to distinguish as closely as possible the nature of the objects of each operation and the type of knowledge that could be expected from them.

To achieve this was all the more important in that Père Teilhard is constantly obliged to introduce new notions for which positive science, in the strictest sense in which the word is normally used, is unable to find room. He speaks of the 'internal aspect' or of the 'within' of things, in terms that recall those used by Maurice Blondel in *L'Action*, but with the further difficulty that he sees this 'within' everywhere, starting even at the lowest level of organized matter.[31] In other

words, rejecting the initial convention (often implicit and unnoticed) accepted by every scientist as he enters the laboratory,
he claims to operate on what is real being and not on what are
abstract relationships. He frequently practices what Père
Christian d'Armagnac has called 'extension of concepts'[32]
and Père Dubarle 'a distortion' of common usage.[33] This
applies to the concepts of orthogenesis, energy, and consciousness. For example he brings together, in contrasting
them with one another as two species of the same genus,
'physical energy' and 'psychic energy'. The latter is not the
physicists' 'tangential' energy; it is a 'spiritual' energy or an
'energy of centration', completely 'different in its behaviour',
'manifested phenomenally in ways that are completely irreducible', and not patient of measurement. In 'hominized' energy
he distinguishes three parts, according to whether it is 'incorporated', 'directed', or 'spiritualized', and in the third type
he sees 'the flower of cosmic energy'.[34] Conversely, he
does what a number of by no means incautious philosophers
have done before him (Ravaisson, for example, and Lachelier,[35] and Bergson—not to go as far back as Leibnitz)—he so
extends the notion of consciousness, which is related for him to
that of 'centred complexity', as to apply it to every sort of
psychism, even rudimentary and ephemeral,[36] and even to
more elementary syntheses which common sense regards as
lacking any psychic glimmer. While his language in this
connexion may be questionable, it is nevertheless the sign of
an essential movement of thought, and the accusation that he
includes different things in the same name would not hold
good; for it is only after making many explanations and
corrections and distinctions in the words he uses, that 'consciousness' thus becomes 'a universal molecular property'; it
is then, he says, no more than a 'germ', a 'segment of consciousness'; a 'partial interiority' at an 'infinitesimal degree',
because this interiority still lacks any subjectivity. It is not
specifically 'consciousness of self'; the 'within of things' becomes consciousness in the full meaning of the word only
when complexity, which makes itself increasingly felt as a
counter-current to entropy, 'is carried to extremely high
values'.[37] Or again, Père Teilhard distinguishes, with even

greater care, three essential sorts of 'centreity'—fragmentary
centreity, phyletic centreity, and eu-centrism, to which three
essentially different sorts of consciousness correspond.[38] Thus
the analogy works out perfectly, and the philosophers may
take comfort. At the same time, it is in fact precisely the
analogical character of the concept that raises difficulties for
the scientists.

Père Teilhard, again, sets out to determine 'the qualitative
laws of growth',[39] and this is a formal heresy in the eyes of a
science that claims to be based on the measurement of
quantity. At times it even seems as if he wishes to establish
a 'hierarchy of values'—although he disclaims such a wish by
explaining that all he seeks to do is to record a succession in
duration, using the 'exact parameter' he has found in the 'rise
of the reflective'[40] without having to introduce 'the notion of
the absolute best'.[41] Finally, he puts forward the view that in
the phenomenal 'without' can be distinguished a 'transphe-
nomenal' element which is something 'invisible',[42] and which
nevertheless science cannot entirely leave out of account; he
goes so far, too, as to postulate the reality of 'souls'.

These views evidently contain much that scientific minds
find shocking and that upsets those who, in spite of what
Bergson has to say about biology and the social sciences of
man,[43] can conceive no scientific ideal other than reduction
to mathematical terms; but what is more, they are, to say the
least, disconcerting to unadventurous or purely academic
minds. Père Teilhard himself is not content simply to emphasize the general movement that tends, as he points out, to
unite 'the various departments of empirical science'.[44] He
goes much further. He believes in fact that it is 'inadmissible'
and 'dangerous that there should be a zone of chaos between
our science and our knowledge of man and the natural
sciences'.[45] He re-adopts an idea that originated a century
ago, but among philosophers rather than scientists, in particular in Ravaisson's celebrated report on nineteenth-century
French philosophy (*Rapport sur la philosophie en France au
XIX*e *siecle*),[46] develops it more deeply, and resolutely puts
it into practice. At the same time he refuses to put the blame
for the dissociation he wishes to remedy exclusively on

philosophy, as is generally done today, and tries to fill the
'chaotic' gap he notes by broadening the modern idea of
science and making it more flexible.

This he hopes to succeed in doing by introducing his 'third
abyss', the abyss of complexity. This in fact revolutionizes
classic concepts, since the third abyss is not simply an addition
to the two first, with a corresponding complication in our
representation of the real, but is different in nature. While the
first two, Pascal's completely abstract and mathematical
abysses of the infinite and of nothingness, are 'infinities of dispersion', the third is 'the abyss of synthesis'.[47] By this concept Père Teilhard gets rid of the idea of 'a space that expands
or contracts while retaining the same character', and thereby
re-introduces into nature a relation between Quantity and
Quality. 'The stuff of the Universe'[48] is thus seen to be
changed. Moreover, as we have already seen, Père Teilhard
finds that he has to admit that his own 'physics', which covers
a wider field than ordinary physics, resembles that of the
ancient Greeks much more than it does that of the present
day, and that it is 'a kind of phenomenology or generalized
physic'.[49] There is no reason, I think to take exception to the
word 'phenomenology', which Père Teilhard uses in quite a
different sense from Husserl and philosophers who have developed Husserl's concept on their own lines.[50] It is more important to keep in mind the expression 'generalized physics' or
'hyper-physics' and 'ultra-physics'. Occasionally at least, Père
Teilhard goes further: he does not entirely disclaim an intention to speak in metaphysical terms, except in so far as metaphysics is a sort of 'geometry' which seeks to deduce the universe from certain *a priori* principles.[51] Or again, as he said
in 1948 in *Comment je vois*', what he is attempting is 'a
biology with *n* new dimensions', a 'non-Euclidean' science.

His method and his teaching have been defined, in more
normal terms, as 'an inductive philosophy of nature', which
gives evidence, both by what it leaves out and by its positive
contribution, of the need that is today so widely felt for a
mental synthesis 'in which anthropology and cosmology are
united, are mutually involved and rely upon one another'.[52]
This is very close to what Mme M. Barthélemy-Madaule notes

when she says that 'Teilhard is not a scientist who, as some maintain, gradually allowed somewhat hazardous generalizations to emerge in his mind' but 'a man in whom, from start to finish, science and philosophy were brought face to face and confronted one another'.[53] It is for this reason that some writers have suggested (with justification and fruitfully) a kinship with Aristotle[54] or with Scholasticism.[55] Père Teilhard himself noted the resemblance between his own and the Aristotelian concept of nature. He sought to instil new life into the old theory of matter and form by adding to it a further dimension, that of duration,[56] though without feeling obliged to retain the actual words; and we know that he felt the same about St. Thomas Aquinas. He was much more anxious than many Thomists of the strict school to carry further St. Thomas's effort, and he welcomed its continuation by Père Sertillanges. 'Let us be glad,' he wrote, to strengthen our minds by contact with this great thought.'[57] Equally instructive is the comparison with Blondel's thought suggested by Père d'Armagnac, which, as we shall see later, lends itself readily to further development.

Such comparisons are effective in bringing out the significance of Père Teilhard's thought, but those who recognize conclusive force only in an analytical science will be confirmed in their hesitation to accept it. I believe that so 'revolutionary' a scientific undertaking as Père Teilhard's would have profited by showing, more fully and methodically, why it is essential to widen the narrow outlook of such minds and how that can legitimately be done without prejudice to analysis. He would thereby have cut the ground from under the charge of anthropomorphism or anthropocentrism: that, as we have seen, was a charge that he was justified in meeting, since it presupposes a complete misunderstanding of what was original in his thought and was often inspired by a dogmatism whose arbitrary character he demonstrated. At the same time it was a charge which, if ever it could be justified, could ruin his work. It would, further, have been advantageous perhaps to analyse and establish more fully the idea of the 'Phenomenon of Man'—the central idea, at once so new and so fruitful but apparently so paradoxical, that 'only man can be of use to man in deciphering the world', that man is 'the key to the whole science of nature' and 'the solution of everything that we can know'.[58] What is more, had he done so, he might perhaps have reassured the theologians more completely: theologians who are disturbed either by some of his conclusions that they think go too far (since pure science cannot prove God, and any confusion of orders is highly undesirable), or, more often and for the contrary reason, by what he omitted to say (because, they think, an attempt to produce a concrete synthesis cannot afford to leave out the great truths of metaphysics or even completely to ignore the great dogmas of faith concerning man and his destiny). He would have anticipated more effectively the confused or contradictory impressions that cause some, even sympathetic and admiring, readers to feel that his work contains two conflicting strands.

We must, however, be fair. If Teilhard's point of view is in some way really new, it is only natural that on first acquaintance it should be disconcerting. Even the most lengthy explanations could not prevent this, for it takes time to become accustomed to anything unfamiliar. What is more, if it is really new, it would be quite contrary to the laws that govern the progress of human research to expect from the author a perfectly clear considered vindication. In such cases, the factors that vindicate the work are to be found in the work itself; like the method used, they are part and parcel of it, and it is for others to study it patiently and attentively and so disclose them.[59]

In point of fact, there can be no doubt about the fundamental novelty of the point of view.[60] If Teilhard's 'phenomenology' attaches considerable importance to 'extrapolations', these are much more than mere guesses; they do not constitute some vague 'cosmogonic poem', they spring from profound scientific experience, from long familiarity with biological realities, and from a penetrating understanding of life.[61] And we may undoubtedly say much more than this. Père Teilhard has his own way of looking at the real; and one of the consequences of this, as we have already seen, is that he has his own individual way of distinguishing and combining mental disciplines. Whatever the difficulties or shortcomings of this original manner, it is in no way purely arbitrary. It has the power of shedding a real light on one of the facets of the real, and of bringing out one of the aspects of truth. Some remarks of Nicholas Berdiaev, himself a philosopher, provide a good statement of the problem and may help us to understand it:

'All the attempts,' he writes, 'to grasp the world of experience from outside without first looking into the abyss of man have done no more than penetrate the surface of things. We cannot penetrate deeply into the universe if we dissociate it from the problem of man, for the meaning of everything lies precisely in man. Positivism may be recognized as the extreme expression of the tendency that not only seeks to attain the universe from outside, as far as possible from the interiority of man, but also includes man himself among the objects of this exterior world.'[62]

What Père Teilhard sought was in fact the meeting-point between the two problems, or the two fields of observation, noted by Berdiaev. He was looking for the transition from one to the other, and the illumination of one by the other. Just as he did not deny in principle the legitimacy of metaphysics (or reflective analysis), so he obviously did not deny that of scientific analysis. What he did do was to point out a duality between the two which had, in fact, widened to become an abyss. In those who practised the latter he noted a habitual prejudice that made them exclude the former. Metaphysics appeared to him ineffective so long as it had no roots in science; and scientific analysis, both in its often extravagant claims and in its too departmentalized and too cautious specialization, was unable to offer any fundamental explanation.[63] He recognized very early that 'it never sees beyond the crust of things'; that what is called the 'physico-chemical' matter which it takes as its object 'is an abstraction (in the strictest sense of the word) obtained by isolating the elements of the cosmos from everything that at a certain level represents a higher form of unification; as such, it does not exist in the nature of things'; that true matter, 'original matter, is something more than the particulate swarming so marvellously analysed by our physicists'.[64] Thus his central affirmation coincides with Berdiaev's, but he sets out as it were to force science itself to confirm it. Using methodical positivism to make a flank attack upon and so destroy the doctrinal positivism which Berdiaev criticizes, he seeks to oblige that science to become, rationally, both more ambitious and less exclusive. 'Let us,' he says, 'as true positivists see whether the Universe coheres, in its elements and in its mass, when we try to extend it along its line of increasing personalization, in the direction indicated by its spearhead which is man.'[65] In the course of that inquiry the being who had hitherto been only the subject or the artificer of science will become its 'principal object'. 'Human science' will become essentially the 'science of Man'. In moving on to an extension of its own concepts, and making room for synthesis while still seeking to understand, it will become accustomed to considering the refraction of human subjectivity in the objectivity of matter—or traces of Spirit in matter.[66] It will then realize more and more clearly that materialism is only 'a crude way of looking at things', and will find itself gradually obliged to postulate the essential realities without which the problem of man cannot be solved, in as much as these are 'simply the general conditions that the totality of our experience must satisfy'. Science will show that 'all consistence comes from Spirit'. It will establish 'objectively the primacy of Spirit'.[67] And some day, perhaps, we shall be able to say that, through this approach, Teilhard's work has been one of the most effective factors in bringing our age back to an understanding of being.[68]

In any case, 'one of the most interesting and valuable things in this work is that in it we can see a philosophy in search of itself'.[69]

Chapter 16

FAITH AND INTELLIGIBILITY

For Père Teilhard 'the general conditions that the totality of our experience must satisfy' may be reduced to two, of which the second is itself a condition of the first. These are the irreversibility of Spirit, and evolutionary personalization; and both ultimately presuppose a further, supreme condition which ensures in advance the solidity of the whole. To this Père Teilhard gives the name of Omega Point. These conditions, which are introduced by the operation of a law of recurrence, must be regarded, again, as belonging to the 'physical' and not the 'metaphysical' order.

In this connexion, Père Teilhard's language sometimes becomes, if not more tentative, at least more qualified. We should in the first place note one obvious point: when he writes of Omega Point he does not always mean the same thing, or we may say, more exactly, the reality to which he applies the word emerges in its fullness only by stages. As Père Roger Leys has pointed out, the choice of the expression, which some have found strange, derives, no doubt, partly from 'the custom of using the Greek alphabet to designate points in a geometric diagram' and partly 'from the words of the Apocalypse'.[1] In it, accordingly, we have a term that is at once scientific and scriptural, a symbol of the twofold character of the teaching summed up in it. Omega, 'the higher pole of evolution' is in the first place, as the word indicates, a point of arrival; it is the term that marks the maturity of a world that has at last become centred: it is the realization of unity, the completion of convergence, in the highest complexity of consciousness. It is a 'thing that is as yet without a name', a thing that is 'supra-physical, not infra-physical'.[2] In other words, 'genetically speaking', it is the centre defined by the final concentration of the Noosphere upon itself.'[3] But it is also, or rather it is in consequence, 'the meeting point between the Universe that has reached the limit of centration and another, even deeper, centre', recognized as the necessary condition and guarantee of this irreversible completion of the Universe. And finally it is the Centre itself, the 'supremely autonomous focus-point of union', 'the self-subsistent and absolutely ultimate Principle': it is 'the only true Omega' which, if it is to fill that role, must 'already in itself be one', and which in consequence is, as Scripture says, at once Alpha and Omega.[4]

Thus there comes about the inevitable intrusion into biology of the problem of God, and we see how science must find room for it.[5] This does not mean any science, of no matter what type, but science in the wider sense, which, as we saw in the preceding chapter, Teilhard was anxious to establish. It means the science which, from the very first steps in its inquiry, envisages 'the within of things', in other words the science that is not satisfied with handling abstractions, relationships or laws, but fastens on the real—even though it may not grasp the real except in its objective manifestations. It is principally here that, for a formal analogy that is not broken down by the extreme diversity of the structural categories of thought and of its content, our minds must turn back to Aristotle. Just as in Aristotle the demonstration of the prime mover, itself unmoved, is introduced in the eighth book of the *Physics*, so in Teilhard a sort of 'physical' demonstration of the existence of God, 'Omega Point', endowed with the attributes of autonomy, presentness, irreversibility, and finally therefore of transcendence, is introduced to crown 'the science of evolution'.[6]

Some readers, as we have already said, find the result inconsiderable. What, they ask, is this God who is not unmistakably recognized as creator and is glimpsed only in his role as the final centre of the Universe? This, I believe, is to forget that every proof depends upon the point from which it starts and, if it is to remain rigorous, must necessarily be confined to one aspect of the real. There has never, for example, been any question of objecting to the proof by final purpose, or by the degrees of being, on the ground that it is not at the same time a proof by efficient causality or by movement. It is universally recognized, again, that the celebrated 'ways' of St. Thomas Aquinas complete one another not in the range of their development but rather in the determination of their object. All that we must admit, therefore, is that Père Teilhard's scientific proof cannot by itself give the whole sum of truths at which natural reason, in the totality of its impulse, can arrive; that it does not constitute a complete system of thought; and that there can be no question of simply substituting it for classical metaphysics. *Non omnia possumus omnes.* This proof—assuming it to be valid—nevertheless takes us a very long way; and Père Teilhard himself, after establishing that God must have 'a personality higher than that which he stimulates', envisaged the day when 'a more profound analysis' of the conditions of the evolving Universe would lead to 'recognizing in the God of Evolution an exact equivalent of the attributes accorded by medieval philosophy to the *Ens a se*'.[7] Starting exclusively from scientific observation, it was difficult for him to reach a strict conclusion that involved creation, and it is here that the limits he imposed upon his undertaking make themselves most sharply felt. On the other hand, this did not prevent him from expressing, in some fine passages, 'the notion of creation', in terms that come very close to those used by St. Thomas.[8] Further, to hold it against Père Teilhard that his God is envisaged exclusively in his role as Omega, that is to say as the final centre of the universe or as the God of evolution, is to forget the fundamental axiom of Thomist philosophy that by natural reason we attain not God 'in himself' but only 'the relationship that all things bear to him'.[9] 'No one but the centre himself can penetrate within the centre.'[10] Nevertheless, with an effort towards a total systematization, and a meticulousness of method, each of which serves (since each might be carried too far) to modify the other, Père Teilhard arrives at 'the *primordial* influx of the transcendent nucleus of Omega', of the Omega which is 'the last term of the series and is also *outside all series*'.[11] It is seen to be 'the higher term that directs the progress of hominization', which 'radiates' as the force that both *provides the impulse* behind and totalizes Centrogenesis.[12]

On the other hand, there are some who think that the author of *The Phenomenon of Man* goes too far, and this may well be because they have not formed an accurate idea of his intention. Père Teilhard himself is well aware that the line of argument he is putting forward has hardly the same compulsive force as the establishment, for example, of a physico-chemical law or a mathematical demonstration.[13] We should note carefully his exact words. The problem of God, he tells us, 'is inserted', at a certain point, in the science of evolution; and again, 'if biology is extrapolated to its extreme point, it leads us to an analogous hypothesis: the hypothesis of universal focus . . . of psychic interiorization'.[14] This implies that every final solution that is personally given to the problem of existence calls for the intervention of a personal decision; still more, however, every solution that is positive in character is seen by Teilhard as an act of synthesis that allows access to a new level of being and therefore involves an element of what in his language will be called 'faith'.

In *Comment je crois* Père Teilhard explains what he means in this context by faith, not, as yet, in the sense of supernatural faith but in the widest sense which is capable of analogical application at different levels:

'On the strictly "psychological" plane I mean by *faith* every adherence of our intelligence to a general view of the Universe. One may try to define this adherence by certain aspects of freedom ("option") or affectivity ("appeal") that accompany it, but those seem to me derived or secondary characteristics. In my view, the essential note of the act of psychological faith is to perceive as possible, and accept as more probable, a conclusion which, in spatial width and temporal extension, cannot be contained in any analytical premisses. *To believe is to effect an intellectual synthesis.*'

Since the unity of the world is a unity that is synthetic in order, adherence to it and to the conditions it presupposes must also necessarily be synthetic in order. It will be 'an intellectual synthesis', in other words a faith. Such an act will be the complete opposite of an irrational act, since it is by it, and only by it, that I shall be able to account to myself for the totality of experience'.[15] Père Teilhard proceeds to explain how this is done.

Schematically, various hypotheses can be envisaged, from the moment we arrive at the postulate of Omega Point—still understood in its first meaning, as simply 'the peak of hominization', as the completion of 'human co-reflection', as the definitive success of cosmic evolution culminating in the triumph of Spirit.

In a first hypothesis this Omega Point may be regarded as too conjectural. We shall then have to abandon the view that Spirit can finally overcome the forces of Matter, give up all idea of final purpose and irreversibility, and fall back on the old materialist concept, refashioned in the form of the idea of Entropy or in some similar form. Père Teilhard recognizes that if in fact a carefully conducted examination shows that life, taken as a whole, does not regress, and if it suggests that the conquests of Spirit are indestructible, this is still only a demonstration 'of the empirical order' and applies 'to only a limited area and phase of the Universe'. He none the less rejects a hypothesis which after all is only a mental attitude and offers a solution of despair. This he does for reasons that he calls 'bio-energetic',[16] by which he hopes to be able 'directly to connect "immortality" with some essential property of cosmic evolution'.[17] 'If evolution . . . is to continue to progress in a hominized setting, Man, by physical necessity, must *believe*, as forcefully as possible, in the absolute value of the movement which it is his duty to forward.'[18] 'Man', in fact, represents, 'combined with the freedom to accept or reject his task, the formidable faculty of appraising or criticizing life'. If, therefore, the Spirit whose promise he bears were doomed to perish, a day would inevitably come when he would realize this and would himself be paralysed. He would 'no longer consent to labour like a Sisyphus'.[19] He would have to give up all activity. The instinct to live would no longer be sufficient—at least when intellectual consciousness had, in our species, reached its full maturity, when 'evolution' had become more highly 'reflective' than it now is in the majority of men:[20] for it must be admitted that 'the more mankind becomes organized and technically centred on itself, the more (in spite of certain appearances) does its upward force—the thirst for discovery, for knowledge and for creation—tend to predominate over the elementary needs to establish his position and to survive':[21] but the more necessary, too, does it become for this force to justify itself in its operation and the more vulnerable it therefore becomes. This is a point that we must carefully bear in mind, if we are not to misunderstand the 'real crux of the problem of man' and so lay ourselves open to an easy refutation: if man were to come to realize that Spirit had in the end failed, what would be inhibited in him would not, we may be sure, be 'his concern to work productively for more well-being', a concern that is still animal, but his 'passion for discovery with a view to fuller-being';[22] what he would lose would be 'his passion for growing greater'.[23] In other words, it would be creative action, disinterested action, 'true action' that would suffer:

'In the case of *true action* (by which I mean action into which one puts something of one's own life), I cannot undertake it unless I have the underlying intention of making "a work of abiding value" . . . A sort of essential instinct makes me in some way feel that the only joy worth experiencing is to collaborate, as one individual atom, in the definitive construction of a World: *nothing else can ultimately seem worth while to me*, except to release some infinitesimal quantity of the absolute—to liberate a little being, for ever. The rest is just intolerable vanity.'[24]

We may thus assume, or rather we can predict, that should Mankind have evidence of the coming total reverse and be faced with the prospect of universal death, then one day the whole of it, by a radical use of the first form of freedom (which is freedom of action), would, in its essential act, come to a halt.[25] It would mean an absolute withdrawal of effort, a strike. No longer 'drawn towards more being' and unable to consent to a reversion to animal life, this wretched, paradoxical species 'would infallibly and rapidly become extinct: even astronomical piles of calories placed in its hand would not save it'. 'Reflective action and the anticipation of total disappearance are *cosmically incompatible*.'[26]

This introduction of 'the problem of action' should not be misinterpreted. Père Teilhard, who notes in this connexion his initial debt to Maurice Blondel,[27] is not appealing, in some sort of emotional empiricism, to man's desires and to his possible sense of disappointment. He is not simply saying that if man is to retain his zest for action he must believe in the definitive value of his action and that he must therefore postulate that definitive value.[28] His line of argument proceeds in fact from the desire to avoid empiricism. He recognizes that he has introduced 'a postulate; it is that the universe, by structural necessity, cannot disappoint the consciousness it produces';[29] but he is at pains to show that it would be contrary to reason to reject the postulate. The 'absolute strike' he refers to would not result from an emotional disappointment but from an offence to the intelligence. Man would not recoil from something that horrified his senses but from the absurdity of absolute death. 'Unless we are prepared to admit that the cosmos is an intrinsically absurd thing, we must hold that the growth of Spirit is irreversible.'[30] In this rejection of a universe that is seen to be 'incapable of maintaining the life it has produced, once that life has become capable of reflection and criticism', in 'this obstinate insistence that our being displays of refusing to build up in itself anything that is not immortal',[31] we should essentially recognize a 'respect for the value of being'.[32] In other words, it is a profound intellectual requirement, of which man is called upon to become increasingly conscious;[33] but while the reasoning based upon this requirement is not a mere emotional reaction, neither is it a speculation of the purely logical or metaphysical order. 'If we are not to regard the world as having become suddenly meaningless and contradictory, we are entitled to attribute the value of experimental and physical reality to everything, within us and around us, which shows itself to be a *necessary* condition of the preservation and heightening in Man of his powers of invention and purposive thinking.'[34] He puts it, again, in another way: 'The fundamental choice for being, without which the world, in becoming a thinking world, would logically return to dust, necessarily entails faith in some final consummation of all that surrounds us.' That is why, Père Teilhard concludes, 'the idea of a Spirit of the Earth' is no Utopia.[35]

In such reasoning there may be more philosophy, and even

metaphysics, than Père Teilhard would have admitted. There is no need, however, to dwell on what might be no more than a verbal dispute. What cannot be said, in any case, is that the reasoning is 'pragmatist' in order, in the narrow or 'bad' sense in which Père Teilhard rejected pragmatism.[36] It is no more so, for example, than the famous argument of St. Thomas Aquinas (the precise way in which its import is understood is immaterial) which is based on the 'natural desire' of the mind. Like the angelic doctor, Père Teilhard has a lofty concept of the intelligence;[37] for all his mysticism, he is careful not to bring mysticism into conflict with intelligence; he is determined to maintain the pure notion of truth 'intact', even against the best-intentioned apologists.[38]

At the same time he does not exaggerate the practical effectiveness of his argument. He has worked it out, he says, 'for *his own* personal use'. In fact it is his own experience that goes into it; and while he tries to give it scientific rigour, he realizes at the same time that so long as reflective consciousness is still in process of development men have countless spontaneous ways of deluding themselves. 'The demand for the absolute' is present in each one of them, but it is sometimes 'no easy matter to bring it to the surface'. If I cannot convince you, he says, 'it is because you do not look as deeply as you could into your hearts and your minds'[39]—from which it is clear that he realized in advance that he would only be able to convince a few. When we face the problem on the scale of the Whole and in relation to a future that seems to us lost in the far distance, it is always possible for us to accept absurdity as the ultimate solution, without realizing that we thereby oblige ourselves to accept a contradiction. We may, on the one hand, surrender ourselves, more or less deliberately, to an abstraction that claims to be scientific, and so postpone our decision indefinitely. On the other hand, however cogent the reasoning, immediate experience is always at hand, apparently contradicting it, and it is sometimes difficult to overcome the 'vertigo of fragility and instability'.[40]

That explains why, although the intelligence insists on the intelligibility of the world, it nevertheless remains, in practice, the object of choice. For the same reason, it is not fully affirmed, in present conditions, except in an act that deserves to be called, in the 'psychological' sense referred to earlier, an act of faith. The refusal, however, to make this act, the refusal to believe in 'some irreversible perfection' that gives meaning to the universe, would in this case be just as much a claim to think an absurdity, or a refusal to think at all.[41]

Once it has been decided that the world is intelligible and that if it is to be so, then Spirit must one day be victorious—in other words once man 'has attained the level of faith in a spiritual evolution of the world'[42]—two hypotheses, again, call for examination. Man arrives at a new cross-roads, and has the opportunity to effect a new synthesis in the ascending series, which will introduce him to a new level. The 'fundamental structure' of Omega may be appreciated in two ways. We may look upon it either as a point that is still ideal and potential, or as one that is already real and actual. We may see in it either a unity of pure convergence, to be realized in its entirety in the future, or as a Being who is already drawing us to him, so that we may be gathered up and united in him. In other words, once we have taken the first step of postulating 'this point of total interiorization and irreversibility', we may either be satisfied with that and go no further, or we may consider whether we must not necessarily push on still further and so arrive at its supreme condition of intelligibility. Père Teilhard seeks to show that this further step is indispensable; and this he does from the angle of 'bio-genetic purposes', reasons of 'evolutionary excitation' or 'spiritual activation'. What man needs, in fact, is not only to be 'saved from disgust' but to be given 'the zest to work to the maximum'.[43] In order to satisfy these 'supreme requirements of our action'—which are also, we have seen, requirements of our intelligence— Omega must be independent of the forces that make up evolution: if not, the Omega centre would itself in turn disintegrate. What is more, it must be 'Some One': if not, the impulse that carries us to it would in reality achieve no more than 'to plunge us back again into super-matter'.[44] It must be a Force that dominates time and chance . . . a 'transcendent Reality'.[45]

This, in a new context, is the eternal dilemma of immanence and transcendence. If Omega is regarded as a purely immanent point, the triumph of Spirit is only apparent, since it is not definitive, or is realized, at any rate, only in unification, which means that it is realized in a check to personalization. One cannot, therefore, dispense with a supreme Centre, real, actual, and independent, 'which finds its own consistence in itself'; we must have a Being who is 'not only at the head of all the series but is also in some way outside all series'—in short, a transcendent Being. 'In him, everything rises up as though towards a focus-point of immanence, but from him, too, everything comes down as though from a peak of transcendence.'[46] Only such a Being can 'give a cosmic consistence to the centres of consciousness, to the monads'; only he can 'make the personal treasure, the centre within every soul, imperishable', only he can definitively ensure their 'escape from Entropy'; only he, what is more, 'the lovable and loving Centre', henceforth has the strength to draw them towards him in order to give them eternal life—not in 'unification', for that would destroy them—but in 'union', which makes them be with the fullness of being. This is the realization of the 'theosphere'.[47]

Once, therefore, we have accepted the reality at least in the future of Omega Point regarded as the completion of convergent evolution, we are justified in concluding ('quite apart from any reference to or reliance upon Revelation') 'that the tide of consciousness of which we form a part is not due simply to some impulse that comes from ourselves, but is made to rise by a Star upon which we all, individually and as one whole, gradually realize our interiorization in union'. 'The multiple rises up, drawn and embraced by something that is "already one": that is the secret, and the guarantee, of the irreversibility of life.'[48] This 'already one' or this 'star' is—to put it as St. Thomas does in the question of the *Summa theologiae* which expounds the 'five ways'—'what men call God'.[49] It is 'God, reflecting himself personally on the organized sum total of thinking monads, in order to guarantee them an assured issue and to determine exact laws for their hesitant activity—God, leaning over the mirror of the thinking earth, now become intelligent, there to imprint the first traces of his beauty'.[50]

'And it is thus, in the end, that above the rediscovered greatness of man, above the revealed greatness of humanity, not
violating but preserving the integrity of science, the face of
God reappears in our universe.'[51]

Such, then, are the stages in the 'gradual discovery'—by
those who know how to use their eyes—not only of Something
but of *Some One*, at the summit produced by the convergence
upon itself of the evolving universe.[52] And yet, however imperative the demand for intelligible illumination which logically raises this latter hypothesis to the level of certainty, we
cannot say that the certainty rests on 'tangible evidence'. Without it, we have nothing but absurdity, but the intelligence
accepts total absurdity more readily than a partial, strictly
limited absurdity. Science itself is impotent to provide the
only solution that preserves the integrity of science. Here
again, therefore, man, as a concrete being, cannot in the end
refrain from making up his mind by a 'fundamental option'—
because in the end he must consent to change from one plane
to another, to 'hoist himself', we might say, up to the sphere of
transcendence: and the necessity of such an option will again
bring into question the result of his first step, the intermediate
hypothesis he might be tempted to adopt. That hypothesis is
essentially precarious, for if we do not press on into what lies
beyond we inevitably fall back into what lies behind. 'Once it
is admitted that being is better than its opposite, it is difficult
to stop short of God; if it is not admitted, discussion ceases to
be possible.'[53] In that sentence Père Teilhard closely links the
principle of intelligibility to the principles of being and of
value. It is in this complex sense that it is correct to say that
science, as understood by him, does not decline to understand.
And it is in this sense again that in his view (as he said in a
lecture he gave to students of the *Ecole normale supérieure* in
1932–3) there are in the life of the spirit 'only more and more
elevated acts of faith'.[54] Such a view undoubtedly broadens
the concept of science, and this is supremely so in this development. Père Teilhard does not, however, 'make the mistake of confusing the truths of faith and of science'. When he
shows which of the two terms in the various alternatives that
appear in succession 'has the weight of logic on its side', his

science does not force personal assent: all it does is constantly to offer 'rational invitations to an act of faith', and in the final act in that series, it 'emerges' itself into 'worship'.[55]

The act of supernatural faith that entails adherence to the Christian mystery is of another order again, and up to this point this has not had to be considered. We may nevertheless say that it has been objectively prepared. 'Once the personality of God has been admitted, the possibility, and even the theoretical probability, of a *revelation*, that is to say a reflection of God upon our consciousness, not only present no difficulty but are eminently in conformity with the nature of things.'[56] This supernatural revelation, which will shed a new light for us on the intimate Being of God and on his modes of operation, will also give us 'an important and even essential confirmation of his actual existence': 'first in religious terms, to strengthen our worship, but in intellectual terms, too, to give us confidence in our reason'.[57] In these we meet the propositions of classic apologetics. When Père Teilhard does not take his initial stand, as he does in *Le Milieu Divin*, within the Christian faith, he is careful not to encroach on the data of the mystery. He believes that the complete study of the phenomenon of man can reinforce revealed truth by providing certain 'findings or suggestions', but he believes also that these findings must always be vague and fugitive, 'always ambiguous beyond a certain point'.[58] Thus he tries to confine himself to speaking only of what is 'capable of being Christianized'.

Whether the whole of this latter has always the power completely to convince reason, is quite another matter, which each individual's reason has to decide for itself. Towards the end of an article on *The Phenomenon of Man* in the *Heythrop Journal*, Fr. J. L. Russell has rightly distinguished the two. His own opinion is that while Père Teilhard's final conclusions are reasonable and are important and suggestive both for theologians and philosophers, nevertheless he puts them forward with an appearance of inevitable necessity that the evidence does not warrant. At the same time Fr. Russell adds that he cannot see anything in the book than can rightly be called 'unorthodox'.[59] Père Teilhard could no doubt have accepted this verdict. His method did not perhaps remain throughout

as 'safe and modest' as he intended,[60] but this was inevitable
as soon as he attacked the great ultimate problems. He himself recognized that a certain amount of reasoning 'imbued
with mysticism and metaphysics' had in fact made its way into
a vision of the future that he intended to base exclusively on
scientific considerations.[61] A concept of the world such as
his, he says elsewhere, 'demands only a minimum of metaphysics, and is supported by the greatest number of arguments
from experience'.[62] As M. Albert Vandel has said, there may
well be, in the general development of his approach, at least
a certain element of 'didactic presentation',[63] which makes it
into something more than and other than pure scientific inquiry. In spite of the assured tone noted by Fr. Russell, it
must be frankly admitted that the ideas Père Teilhard puts forward, even though 'based on arduous investigation and
sustained-reflection', are still 'largely tentative and personal';
for, 'while this aura of subjective interpretation may remain
imperceptible where the field of observation is limited, it is
bound to become practically dominant as soon as the field of
vision extends to the Whole'.[64] In a hidden way, his faith in
Christ, based on reasons that formed no part of his system,
maintained his own effort, even though he did not introduce
it into the premises from which he reasoned and even though
the conclusions at which he arrived remained independent of
it.[65] So long, however, as that faith is not at hand to shed its
full light for him, his universe has still to remain only 'half-
personalized', 'half-amorized'.[66] Père Teilhard came to recognize this more and more clearly. So long as it is not identified
with the Christ of Revelation, Omega Point, which is arrived
at only by 'extrapolation', remains by nature conjectural and
postulated; and even if we attain certainty of its existence 'it
answers our expectation only in vague and misty outlines in
which the Collective and the Potential are dangerously confused with the Personal and the Real'.[67] That sentence from
Le Christique echoes and reinforces what he said in one of
his earliest essays, *L'union créatrice*, in which he already recognized that 'without the knowledge of Christ the whole ontological system' he had just been presenting 'would remain
very precarious and hypothetical'. If we are to overcome the

indecision that makes man continually wonder 'whether there really is in the world the issue of which we dream, or whether we are not life's dupes', it is of the utmost importance that 'a tangible element' should intervene to show him the influx of the 'real term' his mind guesses at, and thereby guarantee its existence for him.[68] Again, the very carefully worked-out essay of 1948, *Comment je vois*, in the section dealing with mysticism, passes directly from the recognition of the insufficiency of the idea of a 'dynamic and progressive neo-humanism', or 'a common faith in a future for the Earth', to the fullness of 'Christic faith'. 'If we are to maintain and animate the evolutionary effort of hominization, completely and unfailingly, *something more* is essential: the final centre of biological involution must be plainly seen and must come into the picture in unmistakable terms: and it is at this point, I believe, that Christic faith comes in', presenting us with 'the mysterious figure of the risen Christ of the Parousia'.[69]

Whatever the imperfections in Père Teilhard's work these statements give us a just principle on which to base our criticism of them and, if excuse were needed, we should hardly need to look further.

Chapter 17

NEOLOGISMS AND ANALOGIES

Père Teilhard attacked problems of the utmost difficulty 'confidently and almost naïvely'. Père Olivier Rabut makes this comment towards the end of the book we have already had occasion more than once to quote. To such problems, he adds, there is no perfect solution. 'Any discussion,' he says again, 'of Teilhard's shortcomings can hardly fail to be useless. Others can fill in more exactly the detail he omits. He is big enough for us to forgive him for not having seen everything. He opens up for us horizons of which we had never dreamt. We should reflect on the truth that he first brought to light, and then gradually determine more accurately its theological significance'.[1]

Père Teilhard himself once said very much the same, at a time when he was feeling, unwilling though he was to be in the least what is called an innovator, that he had perhaps at any rate given an impression of excessive innovation. 'I am convinced,' he wrote to a friend, 'that a more traditional expression of my views is possible—for my paradoxes may serve to make felt with a more immediate impact points on which classical philosophy calls for qualifications in wider and more flexible terms.' On another occasion, speaking of an essay that he had written very rapidly, he said, 'it is entirely "an inquiry", that is to say *sub*-orthodox, not yet fully worked out', and he was resolved to improve it.[2] Thus his boldness was basically much less revolutionary than might appear; in any case, it was, in intention, the boldness of a 'creative fidelity'. Often, even, it brought him back, to a degree that he himself did not realize, to a rediscovery of a number of major themes in a tradition that the theology he learnt in his youth had somewhat neglected. On several occasions the plain facts have obliged us to recognize this, and at the same time to defend him against unwarranted criticisms. A study of many of his confidential writings has enabled us, we believe, to understand him better; for, while the intentions a philosopher discloses in private can have little influence on our judgement of his reasoning, it is different with a religious thinker; in his case, much can be learnt about the general orientation of his thought by getting right back to the source of its first expression, and by seeing how its author integrated it into his life.

Of the correctness of his orientation, as we have seen, there can be no doubt. Nevertheless we have noted incidentally a number of points that present, or seem to present, some difficulty, and to these we shall add some more in this chapter. They all relate to ways of expressing things which are also, in varying degrees according to the context, ways of thinking.

In the first place we must recognize that Père Teilhard sometimes seems unnecessarily to exaggerate the originality of his teaching in the field of religion or morality. In his enthusiasm for the new prospects opened up by generalized evolution, he over-emphasizes, in a way that can even be annoying, the contrast between 'yesterday' and 'tomorrow'. He is all the more inclined to do this in that his knowledge of Christian thought throughout the centuries was never (as is true of many, even better theologians than he) more than elementary. In his anxiety, accordingly, to produce a more effective apologetics, he felt himself more obliged than he should have done to 'modernize' Christianity, in order, as he put it, that he might make it 'get off to a completely new start'.[3] It is this that is responsible for those black and white contrasts that crudely schematize or even distort traditional views, offering in their place what he claims to be a new view, but which is, because of his procedure, excessively hard and fast. Had he been more familiar with the great apologists or had he even simply read the appropriate article on the matter by one of his own teachers,[4] he would never have written, so peremptorily, 'In early apologetics, the choice of a religion was principally dictated by miracle.'[5] In so far as it has any foundation, the charge of 'juridicism' which he brings against certain propositions cannot, as he sometimes seems to think, be brought against the main stream of theological tradition. Had he been more widely read in the great spiritual writers of the Christian past, and had he compared them carefully with representatives of other mystical systems, he would never have drawn this over-simplified picture: 'In his efforts to unite himself with the divine, Man has hitherto tried only two ways: either to withdraw from the world into the "beyond", or, on the contrary, to submerge himself in things.'[6] A similar misconception leads him to find 'a great difference between the results arrived at by *his* analysis of a personal universe and the laws accepted by ancient moral systems'.[7] This would be completely true only if we had to believe, as he does, that for the ancient moralists 'perfection' was always synonymous with 'privation', 'purity' synonymous with 'dissociation of the sexes', and the 'charity' they urged consisted in no more than 'binding up wounds' or 'merely pouring an oil of loving-kindness over the world's suffering'.[8] But he confuses, or seems to confuse, somewhat too hastily, 'Charity as it is preached to us'—as it is sometimes preached to us would be more fair—'a static charity that is all resignation', with the charity of the Gospels.[9] In fact, what he is referring to, and what indeed merits his criticism, is, as he says elsewhere, the mentality of a certain sort of 'average Christian', not indeed of an earlier age but modern, whose anaemic religion has completely 'whittled down' the teaching of Christian revelation.[10] It is religion, accordingly, as seen by a certain type of unbeliever, into whose mouth he puts the words; he does not, it is true, accept them completely himself, but neither does he apply to them the correction we should expect: 'We have no use for a religion of conformity: our dreams are of a religion of conquest.'[11] On such occasions, one would like to be able to say to him, 'Why do you make it seem as though you wanted to be an innovator, whereas all you are really trying to do is to be rejuvenator? Why are you ready to accept, without any distinctions, an image of the Christian past that is derived from a present that often suffers from sclerosis?' Père Teilhard, it is true, might answer, 'I obtained this image from recognized theologians. They seemed quite satisfied with it. Is it my fault that I accepted it?' The same man cannot do every job, and it is doubtful whether Père Teilhard would have given us the best of his work if he had had to spend his time searching into the depths of a vast tradition which he found insufficiently studied by his contemporaries and not always sufficiently followed up in life.

Some of his extreme ways of expressing things can be explained by a stylistic manner due to the literary genre he adopted. To emphasize a contrast is one way of bringing out an idea. Nevertheless, we find a certain amount of clumsiness in his work. It occurs sometimes in his very earliest writings: in these the mystical outpouring is given free rein in language that is at times somewhat loose, soon to be corrected or given greater precision by a more carefully worked out teaching. 'Supra-real Unity', for example, is on one occasion said to be 'diffused throughout the immensity of the World'.[12] This is language that he did not use again and indeed explicitly criticized. On the other hand some shortcomings became more pronounced with the passage of time. We have already referred to those superlatives that make their way in series into the writings of his last period. We are asked to envisage a 'super-evolutionism', to attain 'super-life' ourselves, to tend towards a 'super-reflection', to allow ourselves to be 'super-personalized', to achieve a 'super-communion' in a 'super-love', etc.[13] The precedent of the pseudo-Denis and his disciples or imitators is not sufficient to sanction a procedure that reflects, it is true, a care for exactness and is not used imperceptively, but which we have to admit is sometimes irritating or tedious; and we should remember, at the same time, that our now classic vocabulary of 'the supernatural' was formed in the same way. We may well have doubts, again, about the appropriateness of some other expressions such as, for example, 'Christianity cannot maintain its position except by becoming ultra-Christian'.[14] If these are to be correctly understood, by which I mean both in an acceptable sense and in the sense the author intended, it must be noted that, in Père Teilhard's vocabulary, 'ultra' is the strongest superlative he uses but never indicates a real transcendence. As for similar words in which 'super' or 'ultra' are replaced by 'neo' ('neo-time', 'neo-milieu' into which we would be introduced by a 'neo-Christianity' that answered the summons of a 'neo-humanism', 'neo-spirituality', 'neo-energy', 'neo-sense of the species')—although one would not deny that some are apt, at least one of them, I believe, is

quite unacceptable, since it is liable to produce a serious misunderstanding in the reader's mind, just as at times it had the
effect of aggravating in the author the tendency it reveals.[15]
One might perhaps say the same of the expression a 're-born'
Christianity which occurs in *Le Christique*: the adjective, like
the prefix, could in fact allow the reader to understand something like the 'new Christianity' of the Saint-Simonians. And
yet it means something completely and utterly different. It is
still precisely the same Christianity, the Christianity of Christ,
for we are told that it is 'as certain to triumph tomorrow as it
was in the first days'; even though, in the course of centuries
and more particularly in our own time, something in it is
transformed or grows greater or is 're-born' in the minds of
believers, it none the less remains, in substance, 'continually
homogeneous with itself'.[16]

There are other cases where one has to be still more wary
of criticizing too hastily a vocabulary that appears peculiar,
but which Père Teilhard had to coin in order to meet the demands of strict technical accuracy. Had he carried out his
plan, formed about 1951, of 'compiling a dictionary of *his own*
terms (notions)', the truth of that comment would, no doubt,
be even more obvious. On the other hand, when, in his *Note
sur le Phénomène chrétien* (1950), he speaks of the 'ultra-
monotheism' of 'the religion of Christ', his language seems
completely apt. Similarly, when *Le Milieu Divin* refers to 'the
foundational attraction' exercised by the Eucharist which 'mystically transforms the myriad of rational creatures into a sort
of monad in Jesus Christ',[17] the language seems no more
daring than that of St. Paul on which it is modelled; one could
even maintain that it is less daring than Paul's. In fact, while
the latter speaks simply of a single body in Christ, a single
body of Christ, Père Teilhard qualifies his words with a twofold emphasis: the single monad in Christ is 'a sort of monad',
and his words are to be understood 'mystically'. One could find
any number of similar precedents in the most fully-attested
tradition. It would be equally a mistake, I believe, to detect a
materialist or pantheistic tendency in the lyrical language he
uses in this passage from the 'Hymn to Matter': 'Universal
matter, immeasurable time, boundless ether, triple abyss of

stars and atoms and generations; you who by overflowing and dissolving our narrow standards of measurement reveal to us the dimensions of God.'[18] The man who writes that passage obviously does not believe that the 'dimensions of God' are dimensions in space and time, any more than he takes the stars, and atoms, and generations for the three Persons of the Trinity. Like many mystics, it is in the most material reality, that is to say in what is most external to and distant from the reality of God, that he reveals a striking symbol.[19] He had no need to be familiar with his predecessors in order spontaneously to use a paradoxical way of attaining knowledge and expressing it, or to disclose the basis that underlies 'this curious property of being that consists in having at each extreme attributes that are quasi-symmetrical', to so marked a degree that 'nothing more imitates God, his immensity, his eternity, his simplicity, than matter'.[20]

We now come to a charge that is not infrequently levelled against Père Teilhard. It goes much further than his language and affects the whole body of his work. He conceived the progress of human social groups on the model of the evolution of life in general, and he spoke of spiritual, and even of supernatural, realities as 'biological' realities. One could, if one wished, attribute this to an inevitable 'professional distortion'; but one would have at least to agree that in so doing he brought out some illuminating analogies. Thus, in *The Phenomenon of Man*, we have the analogy between 'the development of a phylum' and that of 'a human invention'.[21] It will be noted, moreover, that it is often biological reality that is illuminated, and even more markedly, by spiritual reality: does he not, in point of fact, speak, in connexion with the evolution of life, of 'instinctive invention'?[22] We should perhaps be grateful that a natural scientist should remind us, by telling us about the 'biological value of the social',[23] that if we take a large-scale view of our human history, we will find that it has some of the features that characterize the great universal history of nature. It is healthy at times to see mankind not only 'as seen from Sirius', but also 'as seen by a geologist and palaeontologist'.[24] Père Teilhard was undoubtedly quite right in saying that what he wanted was 'the scientific study of an

Anthropogenesis' taken out of the hands of 'teams of literary men', humanists, jurists and metaphysicians, not to mention doctors, and 'at last treated as an extension of biogenesis'.[25] Moreover, he expressed this point with a precise emphasis, as is indicated by the words he underlined in this passage from a letter quoted by Claude Cuénot: 'Man can be understood only by ascending from physics, chemistry, biology and geology: in other words, he is *first of all* a cosmic problem.'[26] Such a view of man is necessarily very incomplete. It can only serve as a first introduction to the study of man, and any critic would be justified in pointing this out. It is impossible, however, to believe that Père Teilhard was not fully aware of this. It was simply that this was his point of view, the point of view dictated by his specialized knowledge; it represented a basic truth which he saw too often misunderstood, and he had something new and important to say about it. More than other writers, he was in a position to disclose in 'the cultural evolution of man' the characteristics by which it can be recognized as 'an intensified prolongation of natural animal evolution',[27] one, moreover, in which he also disclosed a 'transformation'.[28] Had he decided to go further and give proper weight to the historical or psychological point of view, he would have been going outside his own field, and even if he had had anything pertinent to say it is doubtful whether his contribution would have carried us very much further. It is only at the cost of a certain narrowness of scope, which may sometimes even distort the picture, that any fruitful point of view can be given expression.

Here, again, as in other cases, Père Teilhard's real position is not so oversimplified and one-sided as might be imagined. He does not reduce the social fact to a biology whose theory is fully worked out in advance. He is well aware, for example, that, 'however suggestive and useful the analogy, it would not be strictly accurate to compare the progress of man's social consciousness to the formation of a collective brain'. He thinks that it would be 'absurd to identify a society with a group of cells'. The *generalized biology* he conceives would borrow some of its perspectives from sociology, just as it would contribute some of its own to the latter—and when he begins to work out the links between the two disciplines, he continually makes use of 'analogy'. We would not, I believe, be far wrong in saying that the place held in classical philosophy by this notion of analogy, is held in Père Teilhard's dynamic cosmology by the notion, itself analogous, of transformation. He had a fundamental intuition of that notion, which is expressed as early as 1916 in an essay entitled *La maîtrise du monde et le règne de Dieu* ('Mastery of the world, and the Kingdom of God'): 'In conformity with the particular order of our world', he says there, 'everything takes place through the transfiguration of a pre-existing analogue'.[29] Later, he explained that 'for the Universe, the fact that it is indisputably in a state of cosmogenesis . . . does not mean that throughout the whole range of things there is only a single type of birth and transformation.'[30] If, therefore, he refuses to separate 'biological' and 'spiritual', and before that 'biological' and 'social', it is not by any means because he wishes to reduce the spiritual or even the social to the biological, or unilaterally to conceive the first two of those terms as expressions of the third. If he brought out the relationship between them more emphatically than the contrasts, it was not only because he wished to react against popular misconceptions or the shortcomings of a spiritual philosophy that has no roots in fact; there was a more precise reason—he wished to counter the denials of the sociological school of Durkheim and Tarde which dominated thought at the time when his own was becoming active, and in whose 'self-styled definitive criticisms' he pointed out 'what was true, but, still more, what was wrong.'[31] To say that he wished to establish a 'sort of panbiology, which would extend to all the sciences the categories proper to one of them' is therefore a gross exaggeration, to say the least; and Claude Cuénot is right in protesting against such an assertion.[32]

That being so, there is no reason, it would seem, to take exception to Père Teilhard's language, when he speaks, for example, of the 'psychic temperature' that would be produced by the Noosphere 'at the planetary scale', or of the 'Megaman' who would represent a certain magnitude 'as biological as a gigantic molecule of protein', 'as real in the evolutionary process', or, again, of 'human mega-molecules', and even 'grains of thought', and so on.[33] All the reader may do, according to his mood, is to smile at language that sometimes verges on the comic, or to appreciate its ingenuity, which is always directed towards making more objective the 'phenomenon of man'. Sometimes, again, he will admire its vigour and beauty when it develops into striking imagery. We find this, for example, when Père Teilhard expresses the original character assumed by evolution at the stage of man as 'this prodigious anatomy of a vast phylum whose branches instead of, as normally, diverging, continue ceaselessly—like some huge efflorescence—to fold back more closely upon one another—like an enormous flower, I repeat, closing in on itself'.[34]

There is no great difficulty in accepting the extension of such language even to the things of religion. 'The Catholic point of view', Père Teilhard says in all innocence, 'is a realistic and biological point of view.' In the redemptive Incarnation he tries to make us see 'a prodigious biological operation'. In connexion with the 'great schism' that will have marked the end of all time, of the 'grand option' that will have separated the chosen from the damned, he says that it will be 'ramification once again'.[35] Christianity is for him a 'phylum of love in nature'. Similarly, he proclaims his faith in the reality of the Church-phylum and he describes this 'living Church' as 'the seed of supervitalization implanted in the Noosphere by the appearance of Christ Jesus'. 'I was born,' he says, 'right into the Catholic phylum.' Defending papal infallibility against the objections of non-believers, he says that it is a dogma 'completely in conformity with the great law of "cephalization" that governs the whole of biological evolution', etc.[36] Writing from Rome to a friend, he describes as follows the emotion he felt as he stood in the Vatican basilica: 'In St. Peter's, I really felt the tremendous character of the "Christian phenomenon": What I mean is the clear and unshakable assurance, unique in this world, of being in direct contact with a personal Centre of the universe. From the "planetary" and "biological" point of view that, I repeat, is a phenomenon of the first order: it is unique.'[37]

We should note, too, the fine saying that dates from the last month of his life: 'Nothing can stand up against an ever-

growing love of "the Christic Phylum".[38] In this, it is
abundantly apparent, there is nothing resembling irreverence,
any more than there is when, in explaining the 'segregation'
of the man who chooses his own damnation, he borrows the
word from the vocabulary of geology.[39] We would be quite
justified, no doubt, in finding this terminology 'unusual and
confusing', perhaps, even, 'regrettable'. For some readers, in
fact, it may have made 'an otherwise outstanding testimony
less intelligible and less convincing'.[40] We may, however, attribute equal weight to opinions that express quite the opposite
view, and believe that, for all the disadvantages of the particular bias we have noted, Père Teilhard's language acquires a
special forcefulness from the coherence of a thought that in
every order remains faithful to its governing structures. It
would in any case be a mistake to take his habitual expressions
and concepts in a popular or over-material sense: they are, he
tells us, 'archetypes' that allow him to express his thought and
through which he can communicate his vision of things.[41]

Another thing we must not lose sight of (as we noted before) is that, however far he may have taken the analogy with
biology, he constantly emphasized the *alteration*, the *metamorphosis*, the *inversion* which is produced in the evolutionary process with the appearance of man, in other words with
reflective consciousness. At the level of man, 'it is biological
evolution itself that seems to take on a new form in its general mechanism'.[42] While, for example, he states that man
must be understood in accordance with 'the general conditions of development and functioning that hold good for pre-
human forms', he immediately adds, 'but we must always remember at the same time that these conditions occur in him
only in the humanized state'. While he admits that hominization was indeed 'a typical case of mutation', this is true, he
makes clear, 'but only if we add "a mutation *unique of its
sort*"', one which causes the emergence of a series of completely unique new properties.[43] Until man, the tree of life un-
folded like a fan, multiplying and differentiating species, like
a 'spread of radiations diverging more and more'.[44] As the
metaphor we quoted earlier suggests, what happens then is that,
in virtue of 'the extraordinarily agglutinative property of

thought', the astonishing species represented by man folds in upon itself; and, among other consequences, this 'phyletic intertwining' produces a new form of heredity—'social heredity'—transmitted by 'phyletic recording of human experience'. In this we have 'a new law instituted by nature'. Formerly, then, divergence was found everywhere; now, it is convergence. The layers of the human wave fold back on the Centre of their 'implosion'. A web of hitherto unknown relationships is formed; and so the Noosphere is created, which differs 'profoundly' from the Biosphere 'in its structure and in the value of life it produces'.[45] Thought carries life further only by introducing a contradiction into it.[46]

We see, then, that in order properly to understand Père Teilhard's 'biologism' (if we wish to retain the word), we must introduce the classic notion of analogy, in its aspects both of difference and of resemblance. In so doing we are not correcting his view but defining it. And in more than one instance, too, we may note that he is very careful in the analogies he uses not to emphasize one of the two aspects without the other to balance it. This is the case with the Kingdom of God conceived under the appearance of 'a human association'. This analogy, he points out, 'is true, since union *in Christo* is effected between persons; but it is incomplete. To arrive at the truth, we have to correct it by analogies taken from realities that are strictly real and physical'.[47] The same may be said of the paradox he ventures when he speaks of a 'complexity' of the divine Being, in which 'resides the perfection of his Unity'. 'We should not be frightened of the word'; he is at pains to make clear 'it is perfectly sound, but only provided that we correct it in a way that profoundly modifies its force.'[48] In the 'complexity' he means there is nothing numerical, and we saw earlier, in fact, that he certainly means to retain 'simplicity' as one of the divine attributes.

The various examples we have looked at lead us to the conclusion that Père Teilhard's language is normally very carefully weighed, and is designed to express a thought that is more careful to maintain correct emphasis and balance than at first appeared. If it sometimes appears to us too extreme we should not take exception to it until we are sure that it is only because of what we have been used to—as happens so often in the history of human thought, including the history of theology. Finally, we should remember that those who have no experience to describe, no new seed of thought to bring to fruition, know nothing of the difficulties, the hesitancies, the approximations, the awkwardnesses, that accompany the attempt to express one's ideas adequately. They have little to contribute to mankind: they may be excellent teachers, which is indeed a great and indispensable merit in them, but one of a very different order.

Chapter 18

CREATION, COSMOGENESIS, CHRISTOGENESIS

When we come to Père Teilhard's treatment of the creation of
the world and its consummation in Christ, we leave verbal
problems behind and enter the field of doctrines, and even, up
to a certain point, of metaphysics.

If not in *The Phenomenon of Man*, at least in a number of
other essays, both earlier and later, Père Teilhard seems, in
fact, to have entered that field deliberately: and for this reason,
that he wished to deal with creation. We have to consider
whether the explanations he put forward are completely acceptable from the point of view of Catholic teaching. Some
critics have gone so far as to say that in Teilhard 'the mystery
of creation *ex nihilo*' is 'radically excluded',[1] and to see this
exclusion as an indication of 'veritable metaphysical
monism'.[2] So expressed, the accusation has no foundation. But
even supposing that it rested on the evidence of some unmistakable expressions, these would still have to be regarded as
isolated aberrations, for they could not outweigh any number
of perfectly clear passages which form one coherent whole.
In the course of a long life a writer may quite well contradict
himself occasionally. His thought may lose its grip for a moment, or he may fail immediately to realize the consequences
of a statement whose terms he has not weighed with sufficient
care. Père Teilhard, one need hardly say, believed in God—
but he believed also, and affirmed, that, transcending the
world, 'God could dispense with the world', that he was self-
sufficing;[3] that the inevitability that we see in the world is only
'a consequence upon the free will of the Creator'.[4] That in
itself is enough to dismiss the accusation.

It is true, however, that the mode in which creation is
effected often occupied his mind. He tried to account for the

creation of any given being by a mechanism of union. *Deus creat uniendo—creari est uniri—plus esse est plus, a pluribus, uniri*—God creates by uniting; to be created is to be united; to be more is for more to be united by more—such axioms appealed to him and they led him to dream of constructing a metaphysics, his own metaphysics, which would be a 'metaphysics of union'. Should we not, then, conclude that he did not grasp in its full rigour the idea of creation *ex nihilo*? That he postulated some element, as debased and diffuse as you care to imagine, that pre-exists the creative act; in short, that, as so many other systems have done, he postulated a Matter co-eternal with God? This, again, would be a misconception. In Père Teilhard's mind it is not the notion of non-being that has to be replaced by that of the multiple or the unifiable: it is the notion of the pure unifiable or the pure multiple that has to be identified with that of nothingness. This is for him an ultimate concept which he calls 'physical nothingness' or true 'nothingness' or again 'creatable nothingness'; it is a notion that corresponds to that of a possible world, a 'physically possible' world. We may put it another way: it is factual nothingness, as opposed to a pseudo-idea of (physically) contradictory nothingness. Pure multiple, then, nothingness without any sort of existence is 'that on which all possible worlds converge axially'.[5]

Père Teilhard notes in the first place that 'where consciousness takes a step or a leap forward . . . this advance is always linked with an increase of union'. He sees each particular being, as it appears in the course of the world's evolution—that is to say in the course of the creation that continues unceasingly throughout duration—as resulting from the union of a number of elements which, in relation to that being, are a sort of relative nothingness, since they are still unconcentrated, unorganized, un-unified multitude. Or rather, as he puts it more exactly, this new being, in the newness of the synthesis that brings it into being, results not from those elements but from the act that produces it from them.[6] In Père Teilhard's language, then, every 'multitude' will be defined as 'the non-being of something more simple than itself'—he could equally well say, expressing the same idea from another angle 'more complex', 'something higher than itself, which can be born, and seeks to be born, from its cohesion'. This antecedent multitude, however, already exists only because it is not itself 'pure multiple'; it consists already in a certain number of centres with a more or less rudimentary organization. The 'pure multiple', as such, has no sort of even evanescent existence. One cannot assimilate it to any sort of Matter at all: 'at the beginning of things we should not conceive some ὑλή', no matter how 'formless' we care to imagine it. 'Where there is complete disunity of the cosmic stuff (at an infinite distance from Omega) there is *nothing*.'[7]

If we look at the creative act from our point of view at each moment in duration, in the light of cosmogenesis, we see that it is a 'process of arrangement and unification'; but we should not conclude from this that it is still so when we look at it at its initial moment or in its totality. If 'to create is to unite' the converse is equally true: ultimately, to unite is specifically to create. The world, taken as a whole, is therefore created *ex nihilo subjecti* in the strictest meaning of the phrase. 'Before' the creative act we cannot even say that there is something intangible, some sort of vague outline or shadow of being; for 'such an outline or shadow already has some positive significance', and nothing is positive that has not already experienced an initial influence of union. Before there is any unification we can speak only of the negative. Pure multiple must be thought of more as a pure 'potentiality of dispersion' and creation would consist in 'reversing' this. 'Before' the world was, 'God' (if we may put it so, again in Père Teilhard's words) 'stood alone'.[8] It would, accordingly, be a gross distortion to compare Teilhard's view of the creation (in spite of some distant verbal resemblances) with the struggle between divinity and chaos in ancient mythologies, or with the gnostic concepts readopted by Jacob Boehme or Milton,[9] or by modern idealism.

Père Teilhard himself said that he had no difficulty in accepting the notion of creation *ex nihilo subjecti*. It was, he said, 'a metaphysical notion', and because the word 'metaphysical' was liable to be understood by some as synonymous with abstract or simply with logical, he added: 'It would be better to say meta-experiential, which is an ugly word but avoids any ambiguity.' If we leave aside revelation, which adds a temporal connotation to the notion, it expresses the essential relationship, one that the universe *in globo* bears to God, who, of his own free choice, makes it to be. But—and this is the point—it holds good, in its full rigour, only 'for the whole', for the universe considered 'in its total formation throughout all ages'.[10] It is evident that it cannot, without qualification, be applied 'historically and experientially' since history and experience presuppose an already existing world, within which they are wholly contained: they are *de mundo, ab intra*.[11] To quote Père Teilhard again (he is developing his thought and expressing it more exactly in an attempt to explain the genesis, by union, of successive beings): 'my aim has not been precisely to find a metaphysical solution of the universe, but rather to disclose an *historical and practical form* assumed by the development of creation'. What he finds there, accordingly, is simply 'an apparent, empirical law', in accordance with which 'a progressive unification of things accompanies, and serves as a measure of, their ontological growth'. In short, the more complex the synthesis a being represents and the stronger the unity (necessitating a correspondingly strong creative influence) the higher it is seen to stand in the hierarchy of beings. 'That,' Père Teilhard concludes, 'is all I claim.'[12]

Within our world, accordingly, beings appear in succession as so many new syntheses in which earlier elements are at once united and transformed. It is a question of a 'creative union', and the term holds good both for each new individual that appears in the unfolding of the world, and for the unfolding itself—though the latter is, in fact, primarily a 'convergence'. 'Creative union' does not claim to represent a metaphysical doctrine but 'much more a sort of empirical and pragmatic explanation of the Universe'. In choosing the title of *L'Union Créatrice* for the essay he wrote during the winter of 1917–18, Père Teilhard had in mind the title of Bergson's *Creative Evolution*, and if the essay is to be properly understood we must see it, as Père Teilhard himself did, in relation to Bergson's book:

'While, in Bergson's *Creative Evolution*, the cosmos is seen as a radiation that spreads out in different directions from a centre of emission, the picture of the universe presented by "creative union" is one of reduction, of convergence, of centripetal confluence that starts from an infinitely distended sphere. Though both theories are equally evolutionary, each is the converse of the other.'

While the intervention of the first cause is expressed in a union, and by the fact of that union, it is at the same time expressed in a transformation. 'Creative transformation' is the title of another of Père Teilhard's notes dating from approximately the same period. This union and this transformation are a truly creative act, which nevertheless rests on a 'subject'. In itself the act is 'coextensive with the whole duration of the universe' in growth, even though one must, of course, 'all along the curve followed by being in its growths, distinguish individual levels or points'. The newer and higher the synthesis to be effected has to be, the more profound the 'creative transformation'.[13] Its operation is continuous, since the universe is continually growing ('cosmogenesis'), but a certain number of strongly marked phases can be distinguished when it is more fully in action. The supreme instance of this will be the creation of man. We cannot say, *simpliciter*, that man, in as much as he is a particular being born into his indicated place in the universe, is created in his entirety *ex nihilo*, because (both according to the letter of Genesis and according to the doctrine of evolution) the matter of his body is provided for him by pre-existing elements. His soul—spiritual, 'perfectly centred' and relatively independent of the body it animates—does not by itself alone constitute a being: as the principle of unity of the human being, it cannot appear except in the 'operating of an act of union', that is to say in acting on a subject of action commensurate with itself, this action consisting in 'unifying around itself a universe that, without it, would sink back into plurality'.[14] This is what Père Joseph Maréchal was expressing when he said, 'the spiritual soul is created only *in corpore* and cannot operate without the assistance of nature'; 'such a concept', he concluded, 'is certainly acceptable' not only to orthodox Catholicism in general but 'to Thomist philosophy'.[15]

All this sometimes rather laboured thought of Père Teilhard's in connexion with the idea of creation dates, for the greater part, from the years 1916 to 1920. In the course of the following years he carried it further in some directions, with a certain amount of hesitation; but as he came to conceive the idea of a strictly scientific, 'phenomenological' synthesis, he treated the subject with more reserve. Nevertheless, on two later occasions, he attempted to preserve his 'metaphysics of union' by seeking, not to reduce *esse* to *unire* or *uniri*, or to identify the two notions, but rather to see them as 'forming a natural couple'. He could then widen his field of observation again and vindicate the classic teaching on God who, subsisting in himself, is self-sufficing, by a first sense in which the equation affirmed between *esse* and *unire* can be read. To be is in the first place in some way to unite oneself, without there being any question in this case of a reduction of the multiple to unity. Such is the being of God, considered in the unity of the three Persons.[16] We have here a hint of a consideration of the 'mystery of the absolute co-esse' as developed by the Abbé Jules Monchanin, of the 'triune co-esse' in which the 'Christic co-esse' is rooted and in the likeness of which it is to be achieved.[17] Returning, then, to the problem of creation, Père Teilhard will point out that while the creative act can be conceived as an act of union, this is only subject to an express condition: if it is to be so conceived, 'we must reject the time-honoured evidence of common sense concerning the real distinction between the mobile and the movement, and cease to imagine that the act of union cannot operate except upon a pre-existing substratum'.[18] If we are correctly to interpret these passages, we must take into account this explanation, which reinforces his previous explanations and should completely reassure theologians, I believe, on the essential point. We may indeed, if we wish, hold that he is wrong here in 'rejecting the evidence of common sense', or in assimilating the case of the 'mobile-movement' couple to that of the 'unified-multiple' couple; but, granted that, since he so explicitly rejects any idea of a 'pre-existing substratum', we cannot say that he rejects or compromises creation *ex nihilo*, even in this last form of his speculation on the matter. We

must, nevertheless, admit that he did not achieve a perfectly
clear and coherent formulation of his thought. It may be—in
fact there can be no doubt about it—that he started by trying
to unite everything in a synthesis that was too simplified and
too what one might call physically attainable. It is quite possible, as his successive 'second thoughts' would seem to indicate, that he realized this; and that may explain why he did
not try to develop this theory in his major works. He put it
forward first in 1918, but only 'on a provisional basis', wondering modestly whether it might not be a 'mixture of truth and
error'; in it, he says, things are put in a way that 'needs to be
carefully weighed if they are not to be misunderstood'. On
another occasion he had written, 'I am perfectly ready to
recognize that the theory of "creative union"—if not in what
is central to it, at least in its extension to the initial creation
and to the formation of the human soul—calls for corrections.'
Shortly afterwards, on 13 January 1919, he made a note for
his own use: 'My definition of creative union needs to be
corrected and explained', and: 'If the expression is found more
orthodox, instead of "union creates" (creation = a sort of union) we could say "creation unites" (*Deus creat uniendo*).' He
continued to feel his way towards a better definition. Again in
1948, after fresh efforts at precision, he said that 'he could not
of course shut his eyes to the precarious and provisional element in such a metaphysics':[19] and while recognizing the
value and indeed the indispensability of the line of thought he
suggests, we may well endorse that judgement.

We may end this chapter with a number of critical observa-
tions, already briefly presented on several occasions in earlier
chapters, which will take us to the heart of Teilhard's spirituality.

The first concerns the relation between the evolution of man
and the Kingdom of God, or supernatural salvation. Natural
progress, moral involvement, and religious act are not only
three distinct things; they are heterogeneous in nature. In
spite of some abrupt short-cuts, which the context generally
makes clear,[20] Père Teilhard, as we have seen, was generally
alive to this complexity. What we need to know is whether
that meant that he had completely unravelled the tangle in

which they are involved. There can be no doubt that he was more concerned to demonstrate the closeness of their connexions than their distinctions. Did he always succeed in finding an adequate way of expressing 'the radical incorporation' which he tells the Christian he must effect 'of terrestrial values in the most fundamental concepts of his Faith, those of Divine Omnipotence, of withdrawal and charity'?[21] Does not the emphasis on 'incorporation' somewhat obscure the necessity above all to maintain the eternal values contained in those fundamental values? Or was Père Teilhard too ready to believe that some explanations could be cut short, thinking that everybody could, as he did, obtain a balanced view of the vital solution?

At a time when his thought was beginnning to be fully developed, he prayed in the ardour of his faith to the 'Lord Jesus' finally 'to show himself, to those who love him . . . as the physical centre of creation'.[22] Here is an occasion when we must realize that it is in fact *in faith* that he is formulating his prayer. He is not affirming a completely natural immanence of Christ in the world, a naturalist immanence that he would regard as a contradiction in terms, since it would be a denial of all that faith teaches him about the personal being of Jesus Christ, about his divine and human reality. The adjective 'physical', to which he was always to remain attached, is chosen primarily to indicate the realism derived from his faith. It is not used in contrast with 'spiritual' or 'personal' or 'supernatural', it is designed to exclude what may be called a 'moral' sense, that is to say the vague, metaphorical and more or less unreal sense, the 'superficial' and 'everyday' sense, the 'somewhat nominalist sense' that 'physical' was given in the narrow theology commonly taught in his youth. That theology seemed to Père Teilhard—with some justification, we may agree—to have allowed the mystical realism of Scripture to disappear.[23] He, at any rate, was anxious 'to give, with complete orthodoxy, a great unity and a great "physicalness" to the sanctification of souls and bodies *in Christo*'.[24] Similarly, when towards the end of his life, he was once again meditating on the Heart of Jesus and contemplating it as a 'fire that can penetrate all things and that is gradually spreading through all',[25] the very form of the sentence shows clearly that he is not speaking of a fire which, by virtue of its nature and cosmic function, is already present everywhere. Père Teilhard himself pointed out the confusion in another writer. The writer in question, he says, 'naively confuses the planes of the Real and makes his Christ a physical agent *of the same order* as organic life or the ether.' We should not, therefore, even if it is only to see a certain naïvete in it, attribute to him an idea that he accounted 'both reprehensible and laughable'. He recognized the justice of Maurice Blondel's remark that 'a purely physical supernaturalism is a contradiction in terms', and regretted having given occasion for it through the 'naturist' tone of some of his earlier essays.[26] It would, however, be going too far if we said that he was later completely immune from that charge.

Both his apostolic zeal, in fact, and to no less a degree his need to systematize, more than once caused him, almost as though in spite of himself, to abandon the caution he sought, successfully, to maintain in such books as *The Phenomenon of Man* and *Man's Place in Nature*. That need to systematize, however, was not accompanied by a corresponding skill in marshalling his thought. This is apparent as early as 1919, in his exchange of views with Maurice Blondel.[27] An all-embracing view should mark the difference of planes, a difference which stems not, indeed, from a lack of unity in the real but from the make-up of our being and the functioning of our intelligence. We have to ask whether he succeeded in bringing out in his universe, as fully as he should, that differentiation of planes. Was the distinction between the orders always sufficiently marked? Had he a sufficiently strong feeling of the revolution introduced by the revelation of the mystery of the supernatural, 'this paradoxical mystery' as St. Clement of Alexandria calls it?[28] Or, if he felt it strongly enough himself, did he succeed always in transmitting his feeling to his reader? His constant aim was to bring together in our humanity of today (to use his own words) the movement towards the Above and the movement towards the Ahead. Did he not sometimes, and more markedly towards the end, appear somewhat to sacrifice the former to the latter?[29] He tried to show in Our Lord Jesus Christ 'the synthesis of the created Universe and its Creator':[30] did he not sometimes seem to establish this synthesis at a too accessible level and thus, in spite of the qualifications and corrections we have noted, and against his unmistakable intention, to some degree naturalize Christ? In some over-hasty expositions, did he not appear, as though *a priori*, to fuse together Christogenesis and Cosmogenesis? Again, he sought to bring out the wonder of the universal 'diaphany' of him who in the first place had effected, at one particular point in time and space, his 'epiphany'; though unambiguously affirming the causal link, did he not sometimes seem in practice to overlook it, and so tend to drown the unique datum of Faith in the ocean of a natural mysticism?[31]

It will be noted that our questions relate principally to what he *appeared* to do: and in more than one instance even the appearance vanishes as soon as one looks more closely. Père Teilhard's faith was as complete as it was ardent and firm. If he seemed to go beyond some positions generally adopted in the Church, he would never have been willing to lag behind any one of them. It was simply that it fell to him to explore truths which, without being new, stretched out like continents untrodden by man. 'St. Paul and the Greek Fathers speak of a cosmic function of Christ: the exact content of that phrase has never perhaps been brought out.'[32] That was precisely what he would have liked to find in the theology of his time—more light on 'the organic and cosmic splendours contained in the Pauline doctrine of Christ gathering up all things.'[33] The least, then, we can do is to recognize that he will have done more than any other man of our time to open up a vast field of inquiry for theologians, and that they must make it their business to apply themselves to it. It is hardly to be wondered at that we can find some indecision in his writings, or things that are awkwardly expressed, or some lack of precision in his thought, or some verbal inconsistencies. He raised problems of great importance that urgently needed to be attacked but that he could not by himself solve completely. He opened up some wide avenues of research. He brought out a capital idea, the analysis of which he could not by himself carry further. It was Newman who, himself thereby expressing a very

Teilhardian idea, warned us that by reason of the nature of the human mind it takes time to master a new idea.[34]

Finally, we should remember that, throughout his whole life, Père Teilhard had to struggle to define a spiritual attitude for which there was no adequate model in past centuries. This was because it had for the first time, without distorting the perennial Christian ideal, to make that ideal accept the responsibility towards a developing world or, as he put it, towards Cosmogenesis, that man had newly come to feel. Even if he succeeded in doing this for himself, he may not perhaps, in his fine candour and his fine confidence in man, always have realized the misinterpretations to which his message could be liable when it reached minds that lacked at least one of the two experiences that were so intimately combined in himself. It was thus that, strong in his Christian faith and judging others by himself, he did not foresee sufficiently clearly that every unbeliever would not conceive the progress of the earth in exactly the same way as he did. What was more, he sometimes seemed to believe that if one devoted serious effort to the construction of the world, that would in itself be sufficient to ensure at the requisite moment the discovery and the recognition of the demands of the Cross. Nevertheless, the disadvantages of such dangers or misconceptions are a long way from outweighing the positive good of which they are the counterpart or inevitable shadow. In his beautiful 'Hymn to Matter'—which is equally a hymn to spirit—he wrote, 'Raise me up, then, matter, to those heights, through struggle and separation and death; raise me up until, at long last, it becomes possible for me in perfect chastity to embrace the universe.'[35] In those words he clearly emphasized the arduous conditions that allow entry into the new world, but it is not everybody that can understand them. He appealed to men: 'Who will at last be the ideal Christian, the Christian at once new and old, who will solve in his soul the problem of life's balance by allowing all the life-sap of the world to flow into his effort towards the divine Trinity?'[36] That appeal was made in 1916, and was constantly repeated later; some of those who heard it may have been tempted to answer in a way that did not fully respect 'the balance of life' as he defined it; others may have been more concerned to 'concentrate all the life-sap of the world' then to direct it 'towards the divine Trinity' on high. Or again, they may have tried to carry out in two separate stages the programme that Père Teilhard insisted must always be realized in one single process of 'attaining Heaven through fulfilment of earth'.[37] He was not always sufficiently careful, as we said before, to guard against such distortions of his meaning. At the same time, we should recognize how mistaken is the suspicion, expressed on more than one occasion, that he himself fell into the same error. Such things are no more than the unavoidable accidents that are always bound to happen. No real thinker is absolutely 'fool-proof'. Nevertheless, if we take an over-all view of his audacity we shall find that it was the 'gay audacity' of faith.[38] At the very moment 'when mankind was becoming conscious of its collective destiny and could conceive it only as terrestrial or alternatively as transcendent',[39] he was at hand to stand at the cross-roads and point out the only safe road. Allowing, it is true, for the inevitable imperfections of human nature, our ever-fruitful Mother the Catholic Church, to whom it would be putting it much too low to say that he was always and in all circumstances to remain unshakeably faithful, can herself recognize with joy that in Pierre Teilhard de Chardin she gave birth to the authentic witness to Jesus Christ whom our age so sorely needed.

Chapter 19

THE LEGITIMACY OF TEILHARD'S EXTRAPOLATION

If we look at Père Teilhard's work in its final and most systematized form, we shall, I believe, meet a further and central difficulty.

As we know, he continued more and more to develop views about the future that he regarded as essential. They were for him 'the great discovery of his life: to cut out from his work these considerations of the future or to reject them as of minor importance, would be seriously to mutilate his concept of the world'.[1] They were, no less than his reflections as a palaeontologist on the human or pre-human past, the fruit of his 'reflections on the present crisis' in our history. They were already beginning to crystallize during the years before the Second World War, the shock of which hastened the process. Just as the First World War had been for Père Teilhard the incubation period for the idea of *Le Milieu Divin*, so the Second World War served the same purpose for the idea of 'human convergence' or 'planetization', and the rest of his life was occupied chiefly in 'clarifying the elements of this new anthropology'.[2] The first idea had been thought out earlier on the Ypres front, in Champagne or before Verdun, serving with his regiment of Zouaves and Tirailleurs; the second during his enforced leisure in the Peking 'concession'. But neither were for him a mere 'matter for speculation'. Although the second did not to the same degree as the first touch the depths of the interior life, it made no less an appeal to his apostolic zeal and seemed to him to have a more immediate significance for the whole body of non-Christian humanity. 'The upheaval,' he wrote, 'that is going on at this very moment raises the question of the future of man on earth.' It grieved him to see that 'nothing was being published to give a constructive, dynamically Christian interpretation of what is happening', and he thought that by carrying further the effort he had put into his reflection on hominization and the Noosphere, he would be able to supply the interpretation that the Church and the whole world so sadly needed.[3]

From the scientific point of view, he regarded this as a new development of capital importance. 'The concept of human convergence on itself seems to me as revolutionary a step (for all human thought and activity) as ever was that of a "revolving" earth or of biological evolution.'[4] One can well imagine that his patience must have been sorely tried when he saw, particularly in Catholic circles, that his contemporaries were still wasting further time in arguing about the evolution of species, just as happened of old, in the same circles, and with such unfortunate results, with continued arguments about heliocentrism.

'Through the narrow crack that Darwinism opened in zoology a century ago, the sense of duration has so fully, and now so permanently, entered the whole field of our experience that it now requires an effort, for example, to cast our minds back to the time—not so long ago (about 1900)—when the formation of species was so bitterly argued, without anyone suspecting that fifty years later the whole economy of mankind would be based on the birth of the atom.'[5]

Nevertheless, he could see how 'obstinately', among his opponents, 'the truly infantile idea persisted that the word "evolution" disguised what was no more than a "local" dispute between biologists', and that even in that restricted sense the theory of evolution might be simply a passing fashion—whereas, in his view, transformism had become 'the form of thought outside which no scientific explanation is possible'. The contrast became more marked when, after his years at Ore Place, he developed the irresistible feeling of a 'deep, total, ontological drift in the universe'. It left him with a sensation of 'amazement'.[6] Both the opponents, moreover, and the defenders of transformism seemed to him equally irrelevant in their line of argument.[7] 'Let us have done with it once and for all,' he wrote in 1950, in a passage in which one can detect a certain amount of exasperation.[8] In 1929 he was already saying that he 'had had more than enough of this dispute', and a year later he said that he was 'tired to death of having continually to kick his heels on the doorstep of threadbare and otiose arguments about the principle of some sort of evolution'. 'It is only the ship itself,' he adds, 'by which I mean the World whose future prospects are so wide, that interests me, and that has been true for a long time.'[9] His eyes were now more firmly directed ahead, to a new 'battle-front', the only one that now seemed to him worth considering.[10] Does this mean that in embarking on this new campaign, which brought him to grips with a new cycle of problems, he fully succeeded in capturing and consolidating his objectives? We shall try in this chapter to show that this can hardly be admitted.

It is commonly thought today that anthropogenesis has come to a complete halt. With man as we know him in ourselves, we are told, evolution has produced her final fruit and nothing more that is essentially new can be expected. This Père Teilhard regarded as an illusion, and a pernicious illusion. Towards the very end of his life, he tells us that 'with the full force of *his* interior conviction, he has taken up a decisive attitude on this crucial question'. In his view, 'zoologically and psychologically speaking, Man, who, in his trajectory, is at last seen to be integral with the cosmos, has as yet reached only an embryonic stage, beyond which we can distinguish a wide fringe of the ultra-human'. Man 'has not yet said his last word'.[11] Hominization is not like a harbour at which evolution was to disembark, but has launched us 'on the ocean of an immense future on which there can be no possible halt until the appearance of a unique Centre of the Noosphere'.[12] A 'super-evolution' of mankind is in progress.[13] It would, no doubt, be useless to try to foresee the concrete forms it will take, but we can nevertheless indicate 'in what direction, and along what axes the metamorphosis of man will be effected'.[14] What is happening, in fact, is that, though the movement of convergence that we have seen is characteristic of it, our species is tending to constitute itself in a 'closed system', a true 'superconsciousness', in which 'the plurality of individual reflections' is grouped together, and acquires new strength, 'in the act of a single unanimous reflection'. We have no ground for doubting that this tendency will be successfully realized. After hominization, which was still an 'elementary phenomenon', we are advancing towards a 'second critical point of reflection', in this case 'collective and higher': 'the critical point of socialization' or 'co-reflection', which will ultimately bring with it full 'humanization'.[15]

We should not attach too much importance to what we are told about this 'super-organism', that it will be made up of all human individuals just as the biological individual is made up of cells. Here again, there is no more in this biological language than an analogy, whose shortcomings were recognized by Père Teilhard himself. The individuals that enter into the composition of such a super-organism are not conceived as ceasing to be so many reflective, personal, centres. It is made quite clear that that is certainly not the case. They are thinking cells—just as for Pascal the members of the human genus were thinking members—just, again, as in Scripture and the hymn in the liturgy the walls of the heavenly Jerusalem are built of 'living stones'. Here, however, we meet a question that cannot be evaded: is it possible to conceive a 'critical point' of collective reflection, which possesses so extraordinary a property and nevertheless allows the whole effect of the first 'critical point' to remain operative? Looking at it from the converse angle, is not the 'critical threshold of reflection' by which man was constituted,[16] necessarily unique? In other words: must we not say this about the super-organism envisaged in our future, that it must inevitably be a superhumanity of such a nature that our present humanity, in spite of the avowed intention of preserving it, will not be advanced further but destroyed? Or, again from the converse angle, however capable of astonishing progress our present humanity has shown itself to be in the course of the thousands of years since its appearance, would it not be chimerical to imagine that still further and as yet unsuspected advances could bring it to a new 'critical point' which would introduce it to a true 'change of state'— that change, remember, being effected within the duration of time? Can anyone who doubts that be fairly accused of an 'immobilist prejudice'?[17] We do not have to go back to the idea that human civilization is no more than a 'monotonous series of reversible oscillations', nor to refuse to see beneath those surface oscillations 'some underlying drift';[18] nor do we have in consequence to close beforehand the road to vast and as yet unspecifiable advances, but these are questions that we would seem to be perfectly justified in asking. We may wonder whether, to express the envisaged 'planetization of man', such expressions as 'second critical point' or 'second hominization', if taken in the literal sense that Père Teilhard sometimes seems to give them, are not too strong, or whether they are not even self-contradictory.[19] We have his own statement that the 'threshold of reflection bears in itself something definitive';[20] he asks, too, 'what advance could there be upon thought?' These represent views that he never retracted. But did he, we may ask, in his explanations, get to the bottom of the truth he expressed in those terms? As we shall see, our first answer will have to be somewhat hesitant.

With this goes a corresponding difficulty, in that Père Teilhard did not perhaps fully realize all the implications of what from day to day he was trying to conceive more clearly. We can be quite certain that he did not envisage the coming of a species of 'supermen' for whom our mankind would be no more than a preparation, in the way that certain animal species have prepared the way for the human body. He had no intention of reducing us to this purely transitional role. What he had in mind was not a disappearance—or a state of subjection—but an advance. 'To dream of a superman is still an evasion, if the dream means that we forget or underestimate the man we might be'; it is today and in each one of us that 'the transcendence of man' must be effective. He would certainly have endorsed those remarks of Maurice Zundel.[21] His thought has nothing in common with Nietzsche's myth, which he expressly rejected. In his view, while Nietzsche was right in observing that 'the individual, faced by himself alone, cannot fulfil himself', he 'put the wrong construction' on the fact.[22] Nor was there anything in common with the fantasies of a Paracelsus or a Renan, as revived in his own way by M. Jean Rostand, who wonders why 'through the operation of the same causes that brought us into being' we might not some day produce 'a new animal, *Homo sapientior* or *Metanthropus*, or whether we might not succeed in bringing out a man-made superman, either through an improvement in controlled mutations, or by the perfecting of a chemical synthesis, or by increasing the cerebral mass of a given individual, or by working on some particular area of the organ of thought'.[23] Père Teilhard was not thinking of any transformation that is physiological in basis, nor of the appearance of a new type of individual. The word 'super-humanity' had no such meaning for him, any more than did 'ultra-human', which he began to use freely after a certain date, or 'super-human', again, which he did not hesitate to use on at least one occasion.[24] What he envisaged all the time was 'the terrestrial future of humanity', of our humanity, that is; it was 'the future of the human species'.[25] This great 'single-minded' being towards whom he wished to believe we were progressing, this 'still nameless thing', this 'Reality constituted by the living union of reflective particles' to which, he thought, each one of the crises we pass through brought us closer, was for him a being still endowed with the same essential attributes, subject to the same conditions, and capable of the same perfections, as each one of our individual beings: the only difference would be an increase in intensity. And, correspondingly, the cells of which this being was made up would still, in their 'incommunicable singularity', be so many personal beings, with a more strongly developed personality.[26]

The point, however, is this: if these things were carried to their limit would they still be compatible? What could be meant by an 'ultra-reflection' that was specifically a 'consciousness raised to the power of two'?[27] Is it not, to say the least, ambiguous, to speak of 'a vast grain of thought, on the sidereal scale', or of a 'particular type of conscious synthesis that emerges', for mankind, 'from its laborious and industrious concentration'?[28] Is it really consistent, in the same sentence, to define an 'evolutionary neo-humanism' as 'dominated by the conviction that there is an ultra-human', and as being simply 'a humanism of fully evolved man'?[29] From the fact that man is 'destined to synthesis' can one conclude that 'something greater, more complex, more centred than man is taking shape before our eyes, beyond the Spirit of the Earth'?[30] Some expressions of this type might have reflected their author's deliberate intention. But does not Père Teilhard betray the indecision of his thought or its lack of accuracy, when, in language that contrasts with his normal assurance, he speaks of 'a harmonized collectivity of consciousnesses *equivalent to a sort of* super-consciousness', 'a sort of common personality',[31] or again when he says that he is coming to see that 'under the influence of co-reflection' the multiple 'reflective centres' represented by human individuals will be totalized in a 'still nameless something', in which every difference will vanish at the boundary between universe and person? Although he adds, with fine intrepidity, 'this is what the law of complexity—consciousness, pushed to its limit, demands', this extremist logic does not make his concept any more clear, nor does the argument from analogy by which he tries to confirm it make it any more certain.[32] 'Some hundreds of thousands of years ago,' he says, 'upon the first emergence of reflective consciousness, the Universe was surely and beyond question transformed in the very laws of its internal development. Why, then, should we suppose that nothing new will appear under the sun of tomorrow, when the rebounding of Evolution is in full flood?'[33] Surely one could equally well, and even with more truth, reverse the argument and say that if with reflection something completely new was produced by a turning back, then it becomes difficult to imagine on earth, within human history, a second turning back modelled on the first; what one can expect is a new step forward, an advance along the new road that now lies open once and for all; not a mutation, properly so called in the full sense of the word, but a more profound development.

Père Teilhard said very rightly, in *L'énergie humaine*, that it is a delusion to believe that we can in some way look into this universe 'from outside, as though we were gods': we are 'embodied' in it, but at the same time we are not completely 'immersed' in it. As he says in the same passage, there is in us an active power of 'dissociation' and reflection; and it is even by this power that man is defined. In virtue of that power, Man, though in no way external to the world, is in some way transcendent of it; and it is because of this that all human progress in the world, throughout the course of history, can be registered only within this fundamental relation Man bears to the world. Although Père Teilhard does not completely overlook this aspect of the real, since he states all the premises on which it rests, he habitually tends to obscure it.

On this point he may perhaps be unduly influenced by a too empirical and too purely temporal picture of the things of the spirit. There is evidence, I believe, for this in the fact that he is too inclined to speak of such things in terms of 'psychism'—even though he does not simply confuse psychism and reflection.[34] 'Thought,' he writes elsewhere, 'has never yet been studied in the same way as the immensities of matter, as a reality of cosmic and evolutionary nature. Let us take the step.'[35] Père Teilhard took that step, and, as I have already tried to show, his bold approach proved extremely fruitful. When, however, he said that the nature of thought was 'cosmic and evolutionary' what he did was to include in that nature practically the whole nature, the whole reality (at least so far as we know it at present) of human thought: or, if that is going too far, we may at least say that he confined himself to a consideration of the 'cosmic and evolutionary' aspect of a thought that would not be thought if it included only that aspect. After telling us that he proposed to study Spirit exclusively as a phenomenon, in its objective manifestations that are patient of scientific observation, he later proceeds to say, not so happily, that 'Spirit is not a meta- nor an epi-phenomenon, but the phenomenon'.[36] In short, the 'phenomenon of man' would appear to him to have embraced, at least in man's eyes, the whole of the 'human paradox'.[37] In other words, he may not have been sufficiently on his guard against the trap laid for him by his phenomenological point of view. That point of view, which in principle should have been adopted simply as a matter of method, would seem to have ended by becoming exclusive—at least in some stages of the systematic construction Père Teilhard attempted. That is why it would not be possible fully to recognize in that construction the originality of the paradoxal reality represented by human thought, or reflective consciousness: a reality that is born in time, grows in time, is conditioned in countless ways by time, and yet, as soon as it appears, by its very being, dominates time. *Quasi in horizonte existens aeternitatis et temporis.*[38]

Is Père Teilhard much more successful when, in order to establish his concept or to make it more probable, he has recourse to a factual argument? He has, it is true, good ground for rejecting the trite objection that 'we have not outdistanced Plato' and that therefore mankind 'will never produce anything superior to Plato—or Beethoven'. To this he can reply that our experience is too short to be conclusive. Even if it is admitted that 'in each human element the individual power to feel and think reached its ceiling . . . thirty or forty thousand years ago', that still proves nothing against Père Teilhard's thesis. However, he continues, taking the offensive:

'To say that in its essence (that is to say in the concentration upon itself of the whole of the earth's psychism), Hominization has now finally and for ever come to a halt, is, in my view, formally to contradict the fantastic spectacle that stares us in the face, of a collective Reflection that is rapidly increasing in step with a progressively more unitary organization.'[39] Here we find the observation of a fact and its interpretation curiously run together. One could retort that the spectacle 'staring us in the face' still covers so slight a section of duration that it cannot justify any certain conclusion. Moreover, to be too hasty in taking it as a pointer would involve one in anticipating for a not too far distant future a complete realization that we are told elsewhere will certainly not come about for millions and millions of years.[40] More conclusively, we may point out that even if the accelerated progress of unitary organization does in fact offer a 'fantastic spectacle' —foreseen by Père Teilhard at a time when it was still hardly perceptible—yet the intelligence of human beings does not by any means appear to be advancing 'in step with it'. We can perfectly well note 'the growing impossibility for the individual of being economically and even intellectually self-sufficient', and we may recognize in that a social phenomenon of great importance, without identifying it out of hand with a 'process that is generating terrestrial thought', with a 'movement of cerebration'; nor is it evident that as the Noosphere

'tightens its network' there is a proportionate 'rise in its psychism'.[41] Even if it were perfectly clear that a certain sort of
'collective reflection' were rapidly rising, would that necessarily mean that it was paving the way to and heralding the
coming of this new Being which, in virtue of its passage to the
limit of development, is to be *the* collective reflection of a
super-humanity? Would it mean that we are travelling through
an 'ultra-evolution' towards the 'return' of a 'new critical
point' beyond which the 'ultra-human' would come into its
own?[42]

Finally, we might well wonder whether Père Teilhard himself did not find that he was obliged to introduce, or rather
to retain, a loophole in his system when it was considered in
the new and over-rigid form it was tending to assume? To put
it more fairly, did he not himself, fortunately, limit its apparent scope? On the one hand, as an effect of 'folding-back'
and 'co-reflection' he saw the formation in the future of the
'closed system' referred to earlier, 'in which each element sees,
feels, desires and suffers for itself the same things as all the
others at the same time'.[43] But on the other hand he still envisaged, in line with what was constantly in his mind, this
future mankind as made up of free persons, each responsible
for his final decision. He saw it, in each one of its members,
drawn—just as the mankind we know today—towards 'two
antagonistic poles', and he then realized that it might well, by
an 'internal schism of consciousness', split into two: when the
time came for the great and definitive option, one of the two
branches might choose to be 'excentrated' on Omega Point
recognized in its transcendence and in the appeal of its love,
while the other, by rejecting it, might become permanently
set in a direction from which there was no issue.[44] One
could not, it is true, say that there is necessarily a contradiction between these two series of considerations, but that is
true only if we also admit that the unity achieved by 'co-
reflection', real and important though it may be, will fully
affect only the still sensible part of being, that part, as Père
Teilhard rightly says in this context, which 'sees, feels, desires
and suffers', that part of himself by which man is a microcosm. The 'single vast mirror', the human mirror in which,

in Père Teilhard's grand metaphor, the face of the universe
will finally be seen, would in fact be simply no more than a
mirror, allowing the deep-rooted, higher zone of each personal consciousness to retain its autonomy.

If Père Teilhard really meant to say more than this, while
still remaining within the confines of this world, it would
then be impossible entirely to reject the conclusion that on
this point he allowed himself, as Père Olivier Rabut says, to
be drawn into a 'rash extrapolation',[45] or, as he said himself
of other scientists, that he did not escape the temptation unduly 'to extrapolate ahead the curve of hominization'.[46] While
Père Teilhard was more successful than they were in refusing
to 'picture' the future to himself, he did not, perhaps, weigh
his words with sufficient care, and he does not seem completely to have mastered his forward-looking views. The governing idea is sound enough: it is the idea that men are called
one day to become, without being lost in it, 'one and the same
someone',[47] and this because they are called to become members of one and the same Christ. In this we have a supernatural mystery, which is effected in conditions completely
different from those that govern our human experience, which
is to attain its fulfilment only in a transfigured universe, and
which presupposes a pre-existing personal centre. In contrast
with a super-humanity that lies entirely in the future, God is,
as Père Teilhard says, a 'transcendent super-ego'; he is an
'ultra-centre of convergence, not only potential but eminently
actual'.[48] We may, therefore, and indeed we must, hold that
the union of each individual man with God and the union of
all men with one another in God—in Christ—'personalizes'
them to the full. We owe a great debt to Père Teilhard for
having persevered in reminding us of this, and even more for
having tried to demonstrate it, in so far as such realities are
demonstrable. We are in agreement with him again when he
points out 'the dominating and unifying influence of a focus of
personal energies and attractions'.[49] On the other hand, it is
impossible to see how the mere fact, on earth, of the socialization of individuals could be capable of producing the same
effect or even of truly establishing its conditions. Between the

two processes of personalization there are, to say the least, profound differences in modes and in power.

This is not to suggest that Père Teilhard confuses the two. He does not do so, any more than he confuses the prospects of its future on earth offered to the human species with the prospect opened out in the beyond for each one of us by his own transcendent and super-natural destiny. Père Teilhard is anxious to bring out their reciprocal relationship and, for a didactical purpose we might say, he first adopts a point of view that looks at it from this side: in some passages, then, he gives the impression, though it is no more than an impression, of developing a philosophy—one might almost call it a mythology—that is questionable, whereas in reality the inspiration behind him is already the indisputable truths of his faith. Such a procedure is justifiable, because it is natural that while a line of thought is being worked out its balance should be still uncertain, and that a solution that is only glimpsed should not immediately disclose its full coherence. We may add that Père Teilhard expresses in human, or 'ultra-human', terms what, in his concern to proceed in easy stages, he holds back until later, to present it then as the 'trans-human' reality in the light of Revelation. To express it in such terms is again legitimate, and the more so in that we are concerned here with two distinct aspects of the same reality, the ultra-human being for Père Teilhard the still terrestrial aspect of what, at the same moment, becomes, under the influence of a 'vivifying transformation',[50] the trans-human. From this arises the initial inevitable ambiguity of the concept of 'super-humanity', which can, according to the point of view, cover either one of the two concepts of ultra-human and trans-human, but which must initially seem to be more or less confined to the first. And from this again arise the questions that are prompted by such an ambiguity; these will not be raised in the form of objections as such, but rather as a way of clarifying the position.

Even while he retains his terrestrial outlook, Père Teilhard nevertheless makes it quite clear that all the progress he anticipates in man's future is ultimately the work of God.[51] He does not even believe that socialization, at whatever point in our history we look at it, can produce its effect of personalizing, without God being acknowledged by men as the great personal centre in which they are to be gathered together in a common adoration. On the contrary, in his view, 'pure collectivity' is something 'monstrous'. It can 'stifle us in its numberless arms'; but it cannot 'affect us, or bring us closer together, in the marrow of our being'. Similarly, he says that 'Mankind, so exalted for the last two centuries, now that it is halted at the collective, is a terrifying Moloch'.[52] He believes that it is pure Utopia to believe in the power of a technique 'of social arrangement' to unite men, in the absence of the only worth-while union that is achieved by love—'by itself, the compression of the human mass' is not enough 'to warm the human heart'—and that it is equally Utopian to believe that men will ever be able to love one another, unless they love another in God.[53] It is, he says again, 'an organic heresy' to see 'the totalized Reflective' as 'forming a single soul' in terms of duration. What he envisages is something quite different: it is 'a soul which superanimates all the assembled souls'.[54] Such statements take us a long way beyond any social or cosmic naturalism. Finally, 'the point of human ultra-reflection' or 'critical point of planetary reflection', must not be 'a mere spark in the night' nor the establishment on earth of some 'ultra-human' light: it is the 'critical *and final* point',[55] the concentrated phase of maximum tension, the term of the 'human trajectory',[56] and it represents our passage, by translation or dematerialization, to another 'sphere of the Universe', as explained in an earlier chapter (Chapter 12) on 'the transfiguration of the cosmos'. As the point of 'ultra-hominization', it will mark, as we have just seen, the moment without extension that is to follow immediately upon our access to the trans-human.[57] This will be the final condition and instantaneous sign of the Parousia. The whole of this teaching, for reasons we have already explained, does not, and could not, come out as clearly as this in all Père Teilhard's writings;[58] but if we allow that to weigh with us, the scope of our criticism will be greatly reduced. All we must bear in mind is that the notion of the converging universe, which is central to Père Teilhard's thought, needs something more to fill it out.

Père Teilhard was without doubt right in thinking that in this world we are advancing towards a certain unity of culture, and that this advance, which in its totality is irreversible, represents on the whole a progress for spirit. He was right in denouncing the 'intellectual myopia' of those who continually believe they can detect the 'approach of a human breakdown', and in trying to restore our courage by urging us to see the great crises of our history as crises of birth.[59] He envisages with confidence the great fact of 'socialization whose hour seems to have struck for mankind'; he looks beyond the improper, clumsy or hateful forms it has assumed and is the first to condemn them.[60] He wishes to teach us to distinguish between mob-thinking and a certain ideal of community of thought. He assures us that the current of life has not become 'fixed' in man, and that the creation that 'is still being continued in us' must lead us to a goal, even an earthly goal, more 'exalted and distant' than we imagine. He shows us, opening out before us, 'a new and limitless field of evolutionary developments, the domain of collective creations, associations, representations and emotions'.[61]

The essential core of these views we may, I believe, reasonably accept. It is even perhaps only a timidity of mind, the fruit of an instinctive clinging to habit, that prevents us fully from sharing Père Teilhard's point of view when he goes on to say: 'If mankind indeed continues, through socialization, to advance towards the fullest consciousness, to what distances (at the present rate of acceleration) will we not have been carried after some hundreds of thousands of years?'[62] In itself (and here again Père Teilhard was right) the fact of socialization does not in any way mean the end of 'the era of the person'. But, when he hailed it as a 'beginning' of that era,[63] he was perhaps rather forgetting that he saw it at the same time as 'the rise of civilization'—and civilization, surely, began (in his own words) at least 'from the moment when *Homo sapiens*, having achieved (principally by way of agriculture) stable groupings in considerable clusters, really began to establish a permanent network of thinking centres on earth'.[64] If the phenomenon of man is a 'social phenomenon', if man in isolation can neither think nor progress,[65] we are justified in concluding that all reflection is already co-reflection: in other words, that 'socialization' began with the awakening of human reflection, that it is correlative to it, and that it constitutes the very life of humanity throughout time. Socialization can, therefore, become more pronounced without our necessarily having to imagine in our terrestrial future some mysterious 'critical point' from which would date the appearance of some no less mysterious 'superorganism'.[66] In point of fact, for all the impression given by certain passages, even in his last years he did not normally imagine anything quite like that. He may well on occasion have dreamed of 'another humanity'—relatively other—that would arise at the critical point and take over from our own in a universe that had not yet arrived at its temporal term; and he may have attributed to this 'other humanity' a 'universal love' that would spontaneously introduce on earth the sovereignty of charity.[67] But this chimerical element seldom enters into his thought. The thought itself is completely independent of it—even though he did not always, maybe, warn the reader against a chimerical interpretation. His 'final extrapolation'[68]—which in any case he only puts forward as 'probable'—is quite a different matter. It concerns, as we have noted before, entry into eternity. The supreme 'point of maturing', which is to bring access at last to 'the higher limit of cosmic infolding', will mark what will be the supreme major mutation: it will be 'a certain critical state of metamorphosis . . . beyond which we can no longer distinguish anything in the future—precisely because what will come about will be an unmistakable "critical point" of emergence, or we might say of emersion (in the astronomical sense) from the temporospatial matrix of the universe'.[69]

Even though we may not have to follow him quite so far as that, we can nevertheless accept the essence of Père Teilhard's thesis as it emerges from the main body of his work. Thus Père Rabut summarizes it, with approval, as 'the universe rises up to fuller unity and consciousness', and we may add with him, as with Père Teilhard himself, 'through that

movement God makes ready the Kingdom and salvation'.[70]
There is a certain relation, even if we cannot completely succeed in determining it, between the natural, collective and
terrestrial future of humanity and its supernatural and eternal
end. 'The concrete evolution of mankind and its institutions,
science, the State, work, culture, art, civilizations, have a significance in God's design' in addition to the moral use which
each one of us has to make of them, whatever the period in
which he lives, in the course of his individual life. The whole
'human adventure' must be related to the 'final realities of
which the Gospel tells us'.[71] Whether in the particular form
in which Père Teilhard expressed it, or in some other form,
this idea, thanks more to him than to any other writer, has
become generally accepted. It has ample support in the earliest tradition.[72] It now seems an essential element in the
Church's consciousness, if one can judge not only from a
number of writings that indicate Catholic opinion, but from
many highly authoritative declarations, directives and corresponding practical activities. Moreover it is not being accompanied by the confusions of mind that some seem to fear and
that others are not always successful in avoiding. 'Teilhard
himself,' however, as Père Charles Duquoc notes, 'is very
studied in his expression of it': 'he shows very clearly that
even if human evolution in its successive forms is directed
towards the establishment of personal relationships between
men, it does not effect them automatically: history's final relation to the Kingdom always remains open.'[73]

Everyone speaks in the light of his own experience. Père
Teilhard conceived the ideal of the humanity that was to
come on the lines of his own experience of working in a scientific research team. He was 'greatly struck by the absolutely
complete union that research in common can establish between the most dissimilar enthnological elements'.[74] In the
evening of his life he gave a generous welcome to the an-
nouncement of the international geophysical year planned for
1956–7, hailing it as 'Year One of the Noosphere'. Once men
gave themselves all to the same effort directed towards the
same quest they would have 'a common soul'. 'A magnificent
brotherhood in the good fight' would be supreme among them.

This would be 'the triumph of Spirit'. Scientific progress achieved in common would at the same time be a corresponding progress of consciousness.[75] For Teilhard, the notions of research, of urgency, of the future, gradually widen their scope, and would appear to an outside observer to be relegating to the background the notions of actuality, of communion, of presence. Nevertheless, as Père Teilhard never ceased to realize, if man is correctly to balance his activity he must henceforth clearly discern 'the already recognizable face' of him towards whom, through all things, he is moving. The mystical attitude of *Le Milieu Divin* still makes itself felt. And the more the years go by, the more the man who seeks the truth recollects and looks into himself, questions himself about the Presence, studies the Presence more deeply, advances further into the 'Sacred Presence'.[76]

Chapter 20

TEILHARD'S PICTURE OF THE CHRISTIAN

In contrast with the type of man whom he calls 'pantheist' or 'neo-pagan', or again 'neo-humanist'[1]—or 'terrenist', a passage in *Le Milieu Divin* gives a picture of the perennial Christian as seen by Père Teilhard in the situation of today. While the former 'loves the earth in order to enjoy it', the latter, who loves it equally well, does so 'in order to make it purer and draw from it the strength to escape from it'. The former 'adheres to the world', the latter 'pre-adheres to God' and thereby triumphs over the world. The former 'holds that man divinizes himself by closing in upon himself'; for the latter 'the culmination of life is death in union'.[2] Again, while the former does not lack a certain mystical sense, he cannot get away from a dream of 'fusion' or 'unconsciousness'; and in this he is just like those who follow the ancient eastern spiritual systems, which can still seduce the human mind. The true Christian, on the other hand, sees that beings attain the height of personalization to the extent that they 'converge in Christ Jesus'.[3]

This fundamental attitude governs the whole of the Christian's practical behaviour. Purity, faith, fidelity, charity, loving-kindness, hope: this is the noble band of the principal virtues whose role it is to introduce us into the divine Milieu and ensure for us its growth. They must accompany even the most worldly of our actions. They develop in contemplation which, under an appearance of withdrawal into immobility, is in fact the highest and most intense form of life. In extolling the contemplative life, Père Teilhard, using language whose freshness is very reminiscent of that of Paul Claudel,[4] speaks in tones that are worthy of St. Gregory long ago:

'The inward tension of the mind towards God may seem negligible to those who try to calculate the quantity of energy accumulated in the mass of humanity. And yet, if we could see "the light invisible" as we can see clouds or lightning or the rays of the sun, a pure soul would seem as active in this world, by virtue of its sheer purity, as the snowy summits whose impassive peaks breathe in continually for us the roving powers of the high atmosphere.'[5]

We are shown the perfect symbol of the sovereign efficacy of this silent purity, this pure contemplation of God, in the Virgin of Nazareth:

'Have we ever thought of the meaning of the mystery of the Annunciation? When the time had come when God resolved to realize his incarnation before our eyes, he had first of all to raise up in the world a virtue capable of drawing him as far as ourselves. He needed a mother who would engender him in the human sphere. What did he do? He created the Virgin Mary, that is to say he called forth on earth a purity so great that, within this transparency, he could concentrate himself to the point of appearing as a child.'[6]

When Père Teilhard wrote those words, during his exile in Tientsin, on a subject that had long been dear to him,[7] he probably had no idea that he was reproducing almost literally an ancient traditional theme, that of the *Verbum abbreviatum* which is used in some Churches precisely for the liturgy of the Annunciation, and which was specially loved by St. Bernard and the Cistercian school.[8] However that may be, he certainly knew that he was echoing every Catholic when he said again in connexion with the same mystery, 'the Church adds, addressing the Virgin Mary, *Beata quae credidisti*. It is in faith that purity finds the fulfilment of its fruitfulness'.[9] Even if we do not attach much importance to these coincidences, we cannot fail to recognize, in the correctness of the emphasis Père Teilhard uses, the great voice of tradition. We see it still living, neither slavishly repeated nor altered, but its own self, continually new, with nothing lost of its original freshness. It is the voice that is ever raised in contemplation of the same reality, stimulated by the same Spirit.[10] And it is specially profitable for us to hear it in this new echo now, at a time when many, in the Church itself, bowing to the prejudices of our age, are wondering whether the contemplative vocation has any permanent value.[11]

With his roots in the surest tradition, the Christian of today and of all time, whose picture we find in *Le Milieu Divin*, is much more than an ideal concept. Even if one were unacquainted with any of his more intimate writings, autobiographical notes and correspondence, one would feel this in every line. In the inspiration that so deeply influences his life, this Christian is the writer himself. It would not be possible to explain the immensely salutary influence of this little book, generally in a hidden way, in spite of its shortcomings, if we could not see in it the reflection of a personal experience. Neither the vivid awareness of a problem that is crucial to our time, nor the ardour of its zeal, and even less the literary skill, would be sufficient to account for it. You do not have to be a disciple of Père Teilhard, nor even be able to appreciate his philosophy of science, nor have any opinion one way or the other about what this 'pilgrim of the future'[12] looks forward to, in order to reap the benefit of its salutary influence. We feel that the divine Milieu we are invited to enter is no figment of the imagination, nor the dream of an idealist, nor an inaccessible country—because we feel that it is one of the dwellers in that country who is telling us about it.[13] By the faith of the Gospels, the faith 'that moves mountains', continually nourished in prayer, he could discern the adorable presence of a Goodness beneath this 'vast horrible thing', 'this grim enormity', this 'menacing Reality', this 'universal horror', that the Universe inevitably appears to be to the natural intelligence of any one who is not 'either a simpleton or a child'. For Père Teilhard 'the agonizing immensity of the World is transfigured into a centre of loving energy'.[14] Spurred on by the vigour of the impulse towards righteousness found in purity—this 'divine virtue' that has such power 'to transform souls'—his desire reached out beyond all earthly nourishment 'to lead him face to face with and to the heart of the unique grandeur of God'.[15] 'Christian love—something that can never be understood by those who have not tasted it'—the love that realizes 'within the community of souls what purity effects in the individual',[16] had made him understand 'in a flash of joy' that it 'is a love that builds up the universe' and that God's omnipresent action never ceases to weave 'the network of forces that produce the organism of the total Christ'.[17] It was the sweetness of this love that gave him his apostolic zeal, and it was through this 'first source of strength'[18] that he gained souls for Jesus Christ in all parts of the world. Finally, it was because of his fidelity, the 'jealously guarded fidelity',[19] tempered in the fire of trial[20] that at every moment gave him access to God's good will and pleasure, that God was always for him 'eternal discovery and eternal growth'.[21] He never faltered in his hope of the return of the Son of Man and the 'consummation of the divine Milieu'. It was thus that he could, without danger of losing his head, 'allow the very heart of the earth to beat within him' that he might so Christianize it.[22] Secure against idolatry, he could contemplate the Risen Christ, the conqueror of death, and the conqueror of the World, 'clothed in the glory of the World'.[23]

In some of its characteristics, Père Teilhard's spiritual teaching is both so individual and so lofty that it is not surprising that it is not always fully understood. After twenty centuries the spirit of adventure is being born again in the history of Christianity. When his teaching is not, in all innocence, distorted, it often remains apparently unnoticed. Some are inclined to see in it only a subjectively complicated approach which may be disregarded in forming an estimate of Père Teilhard's work. Such misunderstanding, indifference or neglect is still frequently to be seen. It is not everyone that is really familiar with the realities of the 'interior life'—even though no one can afford to be entirely ignorant of them—and it is not always the 'philosophers and the scholars'—('the wise and the prudent')—who are best qualified to appreciate them. But what is more sad is this: there are in the Church, we fear, among those who have been concerned to criticize Père Teilhard's work, some who go too far and, without meaning to, are playing the part of Bossuet in his worst period —when, in order once and for all to finish off the opponent he had sworn to overthrow, he exposed these realities and problems to the unintelligent mockery of the wordly-minded. Differing though it does from the situation that prevailed at the court of Louis XIV, the situation today nevertheless lends itself equally well to a similar success. Other critics have done no more than show that, just as a good literary historian is not necessarily a good literary critic, so one can be a master of the history of spirituality without thereby having the skill to give a spiritual estimate of one's contemporaries. As must be clear, I am far from accepting without critical examination all the views expressed by Père Teilhard, nor would I hold that his spiritual way, even if a true way, is more than one among many. *Nec totum Evangelium omnis implet Christianus.*[24] Although God wishes to lead us all to the same end, he began by making us different; and thus a Catholic pluralism is something necessary and hallowed. At the same time it is worth making an effort to understand a teaching that does indeed seem to answer a profound need of our age, but in which it would be dangerous to isolate its most original characteristics from their great basis in tradition.

Père Teilhard's work, moreover, is deeply marked by his temperament. In the first published text in which this temperament is apparent, the article on 'La nostalgie du Front', which appeared in *Études* during the 1914 war, he sees in himself 'the I of adventure and quest, the man who is always wanting to go to the furthest ends of the earth', and as if that was not enough, in the middle of the night, as he stares at the front line which is soon to be the starting-line for the attack, 'In the light of the flares, the trenches gradually merged in *his* mind into a vast line running across the continents and leading to some infinitely distant place . . . somewhere beyond all things.'[25] In 'the great wind of war',[26] far from the abstractions, the attenuations, the wordiness, of social life', he could breathe freely. The symbolic character, the new Elias, in which he pictured himself, takes pity on 'those who take fright at the span of a century or whose love is bounded by the frontiers of a nation'.[27] Nevertheless, this feeling of the universal that he was to retain in all circumstances was not the most profound feeling he experienced. Like the Elias of the Bible, Père Teilhard calls down *fire*: the fire of heaven, 'the fire which was in the beginning', the substantial fire, 'fundamental and personal', the fire 'that can penetrate all things'.[28] It is as to 'an energy', 'a fire', that his ardent devotion appeals to the Sacred Heart: 'Lord, it is as a fire that I desire you.'[29] 'Pray that whatever happens I may never allow myself to desire anything but *the fire*.'[30] When his field of action became that of the geologist—but one who still had a battle to fight—he very soon realized that, for all his passionate attachment to geology, his real interest now lay elsewhere. 'It is the Other that I now seek, the Thing across the gap, the Thing on the other side.'[31] 'The world holds no interest' for him 'unless he looks forward'.[32] In spite of the impression that might be given by certain passages, we should note that this 'ahead' is not a mere future; nor is the movement that continually carries him further an exotic feeling of either duration or space.[33] He is anxious to lose no opportunity for experiment and research,[34] but throughout every sort of expedition and exploration what he is essentially looking for is an issue, *the issue*, from space and duration: it is to migrate to 'another sphere'.[35] This is the fundamental attitude that, transposed, was increasingly to characterize his spiritual life. He was to 'keep pressing on, in an ever-increasing faith'.[36] His whole life—not simply his life as a traveller, but his 'intimate existence' was to be a 'great and splendid adventure',[37] and his life of research, too: since 'one cannot stop short in one's thinking . . . we must press on boldly and in a filial spirit, ever further ahead. The waters will hold us up, if we are making our way towards the Lord'.[38] Everything, therefore, was to cast him upon the 'ocean of the "Unique Necessary",'[39] of the 'unique essence'.[40] Detachment from 'the surface of things' or 'from the earth's crust' was soon to become detachment from his own self, 'as though', he said in a moment of confidence, 'some great force had driven me away from myself'.[41] In other words, an 'impassioned indifference' will be found even in his work. 'All the pettiness of things will almost tangibly vanish for *him* in infinitely greater perspectives', as though he were breathing in 'some sort of unbounded freedom'.[42]

'I experience a sort of peace and sense of plentitude at feeling myself advancing into the unknown, or, more correctly, into what cannot be determined by our own means. . . . I have an almost physical sensation of God catching me up and clasping me more closely as if—with the road ahead disappearing, and men, beside us, fading away . . . only God were *ahead* and *around*, *thickening* (if I may use the word), as we advance.'[43]

He has difficulty in expressing his meaning, because his experience is so vivid and so individual that it cannot readily be put into words. But since it is always an experience in faith, and since 'what lies beyond all things', 'the fire come down into the heart of the world', has for the Christian that he was a name and a face, Père Teilhard could express the heart of his spirituality in the words of the Apostle Paul which head part three of *Le Milieu Divin*: 'Nemo sibi vivit, aut sibi moritur . . . Sive vivimus, sive morimur, Christi sumus.' 'No man lives or dies to himself. But whether through our life or through our death, we belong to Christ.'[44]

As we know, his life was one of very great activity. Much the greater part was devoted to scientific work, and in that sense it was close to the common vocation of all men which is to be occupied in 'secular' tasks, and was not the life of the contemplative. This does not mean that *passivity* played only a subordinate part in it. The two aspects of the spiritual life, the active life and the passive life, are not essentially in contrast with one another as two externally distinct types of life, or as two stages that succeed one another in time. Just as, correctly understood, faith in man in no way impairs faith in God but, on the contrary, nourishes it and is nourished by it, so even in the exercise of the most active of his powers man is called on to undergo, freely to 'suffer', deep in his being, the divine action that is to transform him. It nevertheless remains true that until death, which is the universal law, intervenes, the hindrances to activity presented by suffering and physical infirmity can be the specially favoured aids to this unitive passivity. They are part of the 'essential significant act—the gesture'.[45] It was with this in mind that, recalling the memory of his sister Marguerite-Marie who died in 1936 after many years of sickness, Père Teilhard wrote:

'O Marguerite, my sister, while I, given soul and body to the positive forces of the universe, was wandering over continents and oceans, my whole being passionately taken up in watching the intensification of all the earth's tints and shades, you were lying motionless, stretched out on your bed of sickness, silently, deep within yourself, transforming into light the world's most grievous shadows. In the eyes of the Creator, which of us, tell me, which of us will have had the better part?'[46]

Chiefly in the form of spiritual trial, the summons to passivity was addressed as much to Père Teilhard himself as to his sister. There is no need to emphasize the difficulties he encountered from the beginning of his scientific career, and which were to remain a continual trial until his dying day. They presented him with difficult and sometimes tragic problems of conscience, which he always sought to solve by looking for the highest perfection—the 'most perfect', the desire for which had made, and kept, him a Jesuit.[47] On each occasion, diffident of his own powers, he begged for light from others: 'With Our Lord's help, I shall not weaken; but the terrible difficulty of life is not so much to do what is best, but to see the best. What I long for is to have the strength, and also the deep joy, that comes from the *certainty* that one is doing *the best.*' His only fear then was 'of being unfaithful to true courage and true detachment'.[48] At the same time he understood that 'the greater the body, and the more it leads us to a higher form of spiritualization, the more it must at times weigh us down and make us suffer', and all his examinations of conscience and all his discussions led him always to the same conclusion: 'What is asked of me is, while following my own individual line, always to be more fundamentally "Jesuit".' Then, once he had turned the corner he would enter into a 'vast tranquillity'.[49] Like a true son of St. Ignatius, he practised 'indifference', and rejoiced when the situation he was in made its practice easier.[50] Cheerfully giving up 'opportunities of external action', he told himself that 'the best way of ensuring that an attitude will prove successful, is to live it as faithfully as possible'.[51] 'I discovered,' he once wrote, referring to fresh obstacles, 'that there could be a deep satisfaction in working in obscurity—like a leaven, or a microbe. In some way, it seems to me, you become more (more intimately) a part of the world'[52]—a characteristically Teilhardian commentary on the counsel in the *Imitation of Christ*, *Ama nesciri*. When he was setting out for Rome in 1948, he said to his Superior, 'I am going to tell them down there everything that is in my mind—not what is on my mind because, you see, there is nothing on my mind.' When, with the passage of time, it becomes possible without indiscretion to publish some of his most intimate letters, readers will better understand the beauty of the witness his life gave both of obedience as a religious and of fidelity as a Catholic.

There is no need to wonder to what extent, in the conflicts that were continually being renewed, Père Teilhard was in the right or in the wrong. On more than one occasion he was deeply distressed not to meet, in those on whom he depended, with the same trust as he always gave to them: to feel, and perhaps sometimes to believe, that he was to some extent treated as undesirable or suspect; not to find in an authority that was dear to him the strength that encourages even when it does not fully approve. 'It is distressing,' he once wrote, 'that in Rome they don't try to see what is constructive and preservative in my work.' Someone who knew him very intimately once had occasion to write to one of Père Teilhard's superiors: 'He is the soul of uprightness and sincerity; he is all ardour and courage; and he has the feeling that, in virtue of his studies, his connections, and his qualifications, too, he has a sort of scientifico-religious mission *in partibus infidelium*'; he deserves 'gratitude at least for his intentions', and he should not be allowed to have the 'impression that he was fighting a lone battle'. Père Teilhard nevertheless did all he could to remain, from every point of view, on normal and cordial terms with the Church in whose divine mission he believed with his whole heart. If he wished that he could publish his *Le Milieu Divin*, the really important reason was that he would thus receive 'some sort of approval from the Church' for *his* effort.[53] He was by no means resigned to appearing as 'a spiritual adventurer'. At the same time, 'it is possible', he said, 'that it may be my destiny to live until the end marginally to official ideas and attitudes; but, on my side, I would do anything to put an end to that situation'.[54]

On the other hand we have to accept the fact that a distant authority is hardly in a position to read individual minds. Père Teilhard was a religious, and his thought was developing along lines that gave some ground for disquiet. When problems are obscure and the solutions proposed seem to many to be unreliable, and when the opinion of those who are held to be competent in such matters is unfavourable, it is only reasonable to take a line of prudent reserve. The safest course is obviously at least to postpone a final judgement. Père Teilhard was told that before a verdict could be given, the matter must be studied and weighed; meanwhile he must have patience. Even in the most favourable circumstances prudence will not allow authority to rush its fences by too great a show of encouragement. There is even more reason, when a situation appears complex and confused, to leave it to time to do its work. Even the most sympathetic authority cannot remove every obstacle. Consider, for example—the mere fact of not denying every form of transformism in relation to the origin of the human body was for a long time, in the judgement of accepted theologians, sufficient reason for suspicion, and even more than suspicion. In this case, however, there is more to be said. Père Teilhard's personal interior experience was too authentic and too deep, it was (to use his word) too *innate*, for it ever to be possible to be left out of account in his formed thought and his teachings. It had been 'developed', 'extended', 'transformed', into knowledge and love of God. Even so, in spite of his persistent efforts, he was not always able to find ways of expressing it which, without doing violence to it— 'without distorting and *weakening* it',[55] would both clarify it for him and harmonize it with the most sensitive demands of faith. Père Teilhard attacked this problem with patience and loyalty, but he always kept his eyes fixed firmly on his vision.[56] 'And yet, in truth (without, I think, the least touch of conceit) I do believe that I can see something, and I would like that something to be seen.'[57] For that, indeed, we have no ground for reproaching him. Far from it, for, as

Marcel Légaut said very rightly, in the tribute he paid to Père Teilhard in 1955, 'Spiritual unity is not produced by forcing minds into compartments, by the retrenchments, the timidity and cowardice that assume an air of submission. It is arrived at after an effort to achieve lucidity, an effort that calls for courage, that is directed by faith, made fruitful by grace and purified by trial and the passage of time.'[58] It is, however, a fruit that never becomes fully ripe in this world, and that is why, at least for those who are not thoroughly familiar with Père Teilhard, the ambiguity in some of his expressions still persists. 'To help in bringing to birth a new soul from what already exists', was indeed a noble task, to which he felt called and which he thought he could not decline without proving a failure; but to the outside observer it could be a disturbing project. As Père Teilhard himself made clear, 'this was the really delicate point in relation to obedience'. 'It is practically impossible to be in any way myself without *ipso facto* making myself a centre of influence in directions that cause anxiety'; 'what some have interpreted in my attitude as obstinacy or indiscretion is simply the effect of my absolute inability to prevent my sense of wonder from bursting out'.[59] Some of the criticisms that were levelled against him were, no doubt, often unjust in their immediate application; nevertheless we can see in them a fear, not so much for Père Teilhard himself as for others, that could not always be unfounded. Often again, as history shows clearly enough, men cause one another suffering without either side being to blame; and for obvious reasons nowhere is that more true than within the Church, where the spiritual interests at stake are so important and so complex.

Crippling though they were, the difficulties Père Teilhard encountered were themselves only the symbolic exteriorization of another conflict, more universal and more profound. It was a conflict that of all conflicts was the most dramatic, and he lived it in the very depth of his being, as though in a chosen centre of convergence and resonance. It was the conflict between the 'two great forces' which he had long seen locked in struggle and to reconcile and unite which was his whole aim.

It was not that he felt that it was inevitable and could have
no 'issue' or that he normally experienced it himself as a
temptation. He utterly rejected the belief that the 'schism'
could ever be complete between the supernatural truth of
salvation preserved by the Church, and the growing body of
human truths that emerges from the work of mankind: 'that
can never happen'.[60] Nevertheless, 'two worlds' lived side by
side in him, 'two domains of life that are generally regarded as
antagonistic'. He had not erected 'any water-tight bulkhead
between them'. With complete confidence, he allowed them
'full freedom to react upon one another', so much so that he
could write, 'after thirty years devoted to the pursuit of interior unity, I have the feeling that a synthesis is being effected
naturally between the two currents that claim my allegiance'.
In him, 'by pure chance', 'the two essential components of the
ultra-human', the natural and the supernatural, faith in the
world and love of God, were combined in the correct proportion, and so their 'fusion' was effected. Was not that, he
asked, 'on the scale of the individual, the particular solution, at
least in outline, of the great spiritual problem that at the
present moment confronts mankind as it presses forwards'?[61]
Moreover, he himself felt no sense of constriction within
Christianity.[62] Even when his zeal made him the most impatient, to the point of later regretting it, he never dreamed of
any 'illegitimate development of dogma'; he refused to allow
it to be 'rationalized'—which would be equivalent, he said, 'to
impoverishing and vulgarizing it'.[63] But neither the firm
assurance of his faith, nor the clarity of the solution 'at least
in outline', could prevent an apostolic anguish from wringing
his heart when he looked at the great cleavage he witnessed in
the world around him.

It is here that we see the link between his spirituality and his
apostolate. He knew from daily experience that others needed
his help and he had always a very lively sense of his priestly
responsibilities. While it may be true that, as has been said,
Père Teilhard's writings do not derive 'in their principal
order, from apologetical motives' but were initially prompted
by 'the desire to illuminate his own mind' (in which, indeed,
they resemble all serious apologetics), nevertheless the apos-

tolic aim of the whole of his work is equally certain. It informs the method, it explains the slowness and caution of certain lines of approach, the temporary imprecision of some concepts, and the 'irreducible element of indetermination' in his views about the future.[64] He was not one of those defeatist Catholics, eaten up, without admitting it, by an inferiority complex, whose worst fear is to be caught red-handed in apologetics, and who can accept the word itself only in a bad sense. Teilhard is not ashamed to insist on the 'Christian's duty as an apologist'.[65] Among his numerous essays, there is a whole series with an immediately and directly apologetic character, whether addressed to the unbeliever or explaining to religious authorities the present spiritual situation and intellectual requirements. Their very titles reflect this character. Even so, this remains an artificial distinction. Speaking of the whole body of his work, completed or projected, in its two parts, *ad usum Christianorum* and *ad usum Gentilium*, Père Teilhard wrote, 'All together, in short, they constitute my Apologetics.'[66] 'It is not given to every one,' he thought, 'immediately to arrive at supernatural views of the Incarnation', and that thought determined his method. In *L'esprit de la terre* he wished, he tells us, 'to present an essay almost scientific in nature, in which, following a line that the majority of unbelievers can understand, the values of spirit, of God, and of personality are vindicated'.[67] We could say something very much the same about many of his other essays. Following lines that differ somewhat but always converge, they seek tirelessly to turn the reader's attention, his efforts and his hopes, 'towards some divine centre', to lead him up to 'the expectation of some revelation',[68] to communicate to him 'the burning vision of the universe that is not impersonal and closed but opens out, beyond the future, on to a divine centre'.[69]

It is true that Père Teilhard refused to 'try to formulate the theory of a general apologetics'. His aim was more modest. He purposely confined himself to setting out simply 'the personal way of understanding the world that *he* found himself progressively led to adopt'; to describing 'the developments of a personal experience',[70] in the belief that this procedure would be more convincing, seeing that he knew without possibility of

mistake that 'he had discerned in the depths of *himself* certain
essentially human characteristics: characteristics, therefore,
that had universal value'.[71] Just as, in his philosophical reflections, he refused to consider man independently of the Cosmos,
so he never dissociated his own interior life from his apologetical interest; or rather, his apologetical interest, aroused by
his knowledge of contemporary man, is shaped by the demands and developments of his own interior life;[72] as early
as 1919, in a note on the teaching of the Gospel in a new age
('Note pour servir à l'évangélisation des temps nouveaux'),
he wrote: 'Because I am conscious of feeling very intensely
the aspirations, as others feel the pitifulness, that make up the
soul of my age, I regard it as a duty to bear witness to my
brothers in the apostolate, of this, the fruit of a prolonged
personal experience.'

One of his major objectives was to overthrow the 'barrier
that for the last four centuries has continually been rising up
between reason and faith', to close the 'breach', continually widening since the Renaissance, between the 'naturalism'
that cuts off the world from the Church and 'the Church that
anathematizes the world'.[73] It was an unhappy situation, and
all the more paradoxical in that both science and religion
seemed unable to 'subsist except in the movement that brought
them together'.[74]

On the other hand Père Teilhard was well aware that this
was no mere misunderstanding; he realized that 'Christ will
always be *signum qui contradicetur*'—the sign that will be rejected, and that we shall never be able to reconcile this evil
'world' with Him. At the same time he is anxious to show the
men of his time that in order to enter the great home of
Christianity they do not have 'to leave outside the door all
that is greatest and most precious in what the latest efforts of
the human mind have won'. He refuses to stand aside and
watch 'faith in an Ultra-human' being usurped and monopo-
lized by unbelievers, whose very unbelief makes it impossible
for them to direct mankind towards its goal. He will never
accept that 'anyone should be able to say that if he moves away
from God it is in order to become more sincerely human'.[75]
Thus, with a constant generosity of mind, he looks for support

in every positive element, every 'plenum' he can find around him. He says, for example, 'However worthy of condemnation many of the forms assumed by "faith in the world" may be, they derive from an undeniable effort to be loyal to life (that is to say to God's creative action) that we must respect.' And, turning to Christians, he urges them never to give 'the impression of fearing what has the power to give new life to and to broaden our ideas about man and the Universe'. 'The world,' he tells them, 'will never be vast enough, nor Mankind strong enough, to be worthy of Him who created them and made Himself incarnate in them.'[76]

His project, however, is even wider in its scope and at the same time more positive. What he wishes to work for is the 're-awakening' and 'emancipation of Catholic thought'.[77] More precisely, his programme may be summed in two pregnant words, to 'Christify evolution'. Nor, again, will he accept the restrictions of any one particular point of view. In the Catholicism of the first half of the twentieth century, Père Teilhard was one of the rare thinkers to be deeply and vitally interested in the great spiritual systems that divide the world between them. In this we can no doubt see something of the influence of Père Léonce de Grandmaison, but it is even more due to reflection on his own mystical sense, sharpened by his contacts with the East. He hoped for a universal confrontation of such clarity that it would illuminate for the minds of all men in all parts of the world the 'essence of Christianity'.[78] Like every great apologist, he fights against any mean and narrow interpretation that seeks to present the object of Christian faith as 'a sort of alien proliferation'—adding, in his own language, 'without analogy or roots in the Phenomenon'.[79] To the 'integrism' that he sees is narrowing dogma and the Christian ideal, he opposes the 'integralism' which is less simple and less 'convenient' but which calls on 'the totality of the resources contained in Christian truth to channel off towards the Kingdom of God all the "potentialities" that are in ferment everywhere around' us in the world.[80] The whole essence of his argument comes back to showing that in Catholicism we have the only organism of thought and life that can 'give a total meaning to the world that is being re-

vealed around us', in as much as 'under the influence of Catholicism and in the light it sheds, the world in its entirety
takes on a maximum of coherence for our intelligence, and a
maximum of appeal to our zest for action'.[81] A parallel and
contrast has not unnaturally been suggested with his fellow-
countryman from Auvergne, Blaise Pascal:[82]

'The marvellous cadences,' writes M. Jacques Mettra, 'in
which Pascal so musically expressed man's anxiety, are far
from losing their appeal. It is nevertheless true that Pascal's
dialectic may well be losing its grip on minds that are so
strongly imbued with the passion for science and the human
ambition it expresses; minds, again, in which has been aroused
the sense of man's condition as in the first place a collective
adventure. It is here that *The Phenomenon of Man* is at hand
to take over from the *Pensées*, and that is no small praise.'[83]

When Père Teilhard was engaged on *The Phenomenon of
Man*, he wrote: 'I hope that the Lord will help me, since it is
entirely as an attempt to make his countenance seen and loved
that I am taking such pains.'[84] *Le Milieu Divin* itself, which
establishes us from the start in the heart of Christian life and
faith, does not even so abandon the aim of helping to find a
solution to the 'difficulties of religious thought'; it is addressed
more particularly to those 'who hesitate on the threshold of
the Church, or turn away from it', to those who 'fear that they
may be false to themselves or diminish themselves if they
simply follow the Gospel path'; he wished to 'prove to them by
a sort of tangible confirmation that this fear is unfounded',
and that 'Christ, who is ever the same and ever new, has not
ceased to be "the first" within mankind'.[85] In both cases, he
was writing in answer to the special summons that he had
heard deep in his own being and which had taken the practical
form of his vocation to the priesthood and the religious life.
He had expressed this in one of his meditations dating from the
time of the First World War, to which in fact he gave the
title *Le Prêtre*:

'There are countless shades of tone, my God, in your summons, and there is an essential diversity in vocations. Countries
and nations and social categories each have their apostles. For
my part, Lord, for my most humble part, I would seek to be

the apostle and (if I dare say such a thing) the evangelist of your Christ in the universe.'

In the address he gave in Paris, in the Church of the Rue de Sèvres, some days after the death of Père Teilhard, to whom he had been closely bound by long years of brotherly intimacy, Père René d'Ouince compared him to the great missionaries who were the glory of the Society of Jesus, to such men as Matteo Ricci, Robert de Nobili, and Alexandre de Rhodes.[86] Just as they wanted to win distant civilizations for Christ, so he wanted to win this new continent, the modern world of science. The analogy could be extended to the methods used in either case. Both called equally for depth of faith and emancipation of mind, the latter being the fruit of the former. But while the earlier missionaries had addressed themselves to people who, until their coming, had hardly heard the Gospel tidings, Père Teilhard was speaking to a world that was turning away from them. 'There,' he exclaimed, 'there lie the Indies that call me more loudly than the Indies of St. Francis Xavier! But what a vast problem to be solved, no longer of ritual but of ideas, before one can really convert them.'[87] What he had to undertake, accordingly, was a reconquest, and in many respects it was a double conversion that he had to effect; for he saw 'the devotees of earth bestirring themselves' and aroused for the first time under the influence of the great idea of evolution 'to a true form of religion, charged with limitless hope, striving and renunciation':[88] but at the same time he saw them doomed to failure by their rejection of Him who alone could ensure success for their efforts and give consistency to their dream by transfiguring it. Looking on the other side, again, and examining his own spiritual environment, he saw to his sorrow that 'we have lost our contagious influence';[89] 'for a reason that is not clear, something in our time no longer "clicks" between Man and God, as God is presented to him today'.[90] He deplored 'the terrifying inertia' of a considerable part of Christian thought, 'the constricted and timid atmosphere' in which it was enclosed—an attitude so contrary to the spirit of the Gospel—and the too abstract way in which theologians worked in a domain 'into which neither the aspirations nor the life-blood of the Earth penetrated'. He deplored everything that prevented believers from showing themselves more fully 'Catholic', all that made Christianity appear to the outsider 'a closed and established whole', rather as a 'system' than, as he would have liked to see it, 'an axis of progression and assimilation'.[91] Was he right in so interpreting what he saw? Did he not sometimes exaggerate? Was there a really sound basis for what he himself wanted? In his conviction that, if our faith today lacks contagious force, it is because believers lacked the vital impulses of modern man, was he not paying too little attention to one of the sides of the truth?[92] In refusing to accept the Church simply as a 'refuge' he was undoubtedly right; but when he wished to see her operating as 'a motive principle for mankind' we may wonder whether he had a sufficiently complete and correct idea of what that 'motor' should be.[93] In any case, what is really admirable is that, saddened though he was by such reflections and torn though he was by the antagonism, his faith remained as firm as a rock. His interior life was familiar with 'conflicts',[94] but the anguish he suffered in his apostolate never made him lose his own bearings.

When, on another occasion, he said, 'A religion that is judged to be inferior to our human ideal is a doomed religion', that was in no way a cry of despair; it was a warning. Even when appearances give a contrary impression, he never doubted the 'axis' that carries the promises of God. The Abbé Paul Grenet has well noted that his soul was not 'cut in two', it was only 'haunted by two worlds that believe one another to be contradictory but which Teilhard for his part felt were complementary'.[95] It was not on his own behalf, but on behalf of others, of 'a whole people of the spiritually homeless', dramatically multiplied in our day, that a confidential memorandum addressed to his superiors begged them to allow 'the possibility of believing *at the same time* and *fundamentally*— believing each through the other—in God and in the world'.[96] The 'faltering' of Christian consciousness caused some to say (and they tried to convince Père Teilhard of this) that the 'season for the flowering of the Gospel was past' and that the time had come 'for some other stock instead to take root and grow in the field of religion', but he himself never faltered.

He became only the more resolved to clear the way he thought was needed 'towards a Christian renewal', and he offered himself for the task—the 'combat'—in the belief that he 'was perhaps better prepared for it than others'.[97] 'The Church,' he insisted, 'is still as living as ever, you only have to leave her to grow.'[98] Each new crisis that intervened in his life had the effect of making him understand more clearly that we cannot attain Jesus Christ, even 'making our way through the fog', except by 'becoming more and more fully one with the Church', and, by ourselves exalting her above all 'petty interests', making her to be more loved.[99] He was rapt in admiration of her 'splendid stability'.[100] He was not checked by what has proved a stumbling-block to so many others, for he had been quick to understand that 'the Catholic is the man who is sure of the existence of Jesus Christ . . . in spite of many stumbling-blocks'.[101] His attitude morally obliged opponents of the Church to speak of and about her only with the greatest respect. 'I am putting my trust,' he said in his worst hours, 'in him for whom alone all that I do is done.'[102] Again, he would beg his brother-Jesuits to pray for him, that the Lord, he told them, 'may help me, during this difficult time, to act in conformity with the faith (the most precious of all my possessions) he has given me in his omniaction and omnipresence, for those who love him, in all the forces of this world'. Eager though he was to communicate a vision that seemed to him salvific, he was equally concerned to take no risk 'by pressing on too fast' of 'ruining or damaging anything in others'.[103]

In 1918, affirming his 'faith in the Plenitude, the Beauty and the Kingship of Christ', he added, 'I have no words to express the continually replenished treasure-house of strength, of light and of peace into which the fundamental vision of Christ in all things is unceasingly transformed for me. In very truth, *venerunt mihi omnia bona cum ipsa*—with that vision all good things have been given to me.'[104] Thirty years later he could still write: 'I have never felt myself more completely and utterly dependent, soul and mind, on Christ Jesus. I have a bitter-sweet feeling that I am absolutely powerless without him.'[105]

In his continually renewed efforts to explain his position, he was unable (as is true of any mortal man) to cover the whole of reality, and of this he was well aware. Like every worker who marks out a new line of search, as he pursued 'that instinctive persistent attempt of the human mind to reduce the world to unity',[106] he was conscious of penetrating deeper into reality as his ideas gained in precision, and at the same time, by that very fact, of leaving more and more regions unexplored. The very newness of his vision, in so far as it had an element of augury and, so to speak, of the inevitable, was to make it more one-sided in many respects. Most of the criticisms we have looked at may be reduced to that acknowledgement. Now that we have come to the end of this study we must do something more than remember what we said, as Père Teilhard did himself, about the limitations inherent in every intellectual system. If we are to appreciate his spiritual teaching and the religious thought that gives it a solid foundation in his own mind, we should re-read two passages that seem to give an excellent picture of that mind. The first is from the second of the two memoranda he drew up for Maurice Blondel, written on 29 December 1919. In this he says: 'I am absolutely convinced that there is infinitely more truth in the empirical and complex attitude of the Church than in all our simplifying philosophies. The practice of the saints, even though difficult to rationalize, is the reality that must be accepted, that is "imposed", the concrete truth. It is that, accordingly, that must mould our attempts at systematizing, and it will never be possible for it to be fully contained in them.'[107] Later, much thought and work and prayer was crystallized in these few words, at once confident and humble: 'Jesus, help me to complete the perception and the expression of my vision—of my vision of your hidden and universal essence, O Golden Flower! Help me to make the gesture, to find the word, to give the example that will best reveal you—without shocking or antagonizing—through convergence.'[108]

Much earlier, he had written to his eldest sister Françoise, who was undergoing a distressing interior conflict before she decided to enter the Little Sisters of the Poor:[109] 'You are looking at your crucifix from the wrong side. It is not only the

Cross we should see, but Jesus Christ upon the Cross.'[110] Père Teilhard never ceased to see the Cross and feel its significance, little though he may have allowed the majority of those he moved among to suspect it. He contemplated the Crucified Christ, and his faith was so strong that in the Crucified he always at the same time saw the Risen Christ. His own death on Easter Sunday makes us hope that the dearest wish of his life will have been granted.[111]

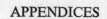

APPENDICES

Appendix 1

LETTERS FROM PÈRE TEILHARD TO
PÈRE VICTOR FONTOYNONT[1]

15 March 1916

Alas, no! I'm not at Verdun. In fact I'm a long way from it, since
a couple of hundred yards from my billet the sea washes the infinite monotony of the Belgian strand—the grey sea in which the sly
mines are bobbing up and down, tossed about by the waves like
huge evil sea-shells. While the fighting goes on in the East, I'm
living here practically in peace. This makes it even more inexcus-

---

[1] Père Victor Fontoynont, s.j. (1880–1958), who is known to the general public only through his masterly *Vocabulaire grec*, was a classical
scholar, a philosopher, a theologian and a notable Hebrew scholar. No
one could say how far and wide his activity reached, since he was too
self-effacing to impress his individuality upon it in any obvious way. In
his religious Province no one could stimulate, encourage and advise as
he did, and, if need be, criticize and correct, whether in the order of
intellectual work or of apostolic undertakings. He was behind the two
great series of 'Théologie' and 'Sources Chrétiennes'. 'Few men,' it has
been said, 'gave so marked an impression of having reached the core of
the essential human and religious problems.' Pierre Teilhard and Victor
Fontoynont both came from Auvergne; they first knew one another at
the novitiate in Aix-en-Provence, in 1897, and met again later during
their philosophical and theological studies. In 1929, after teaching philosophy at the colleges of Bollengo and Mongré, Père Fontoynont
was appointed Prefect of Studies at the theological scholasticate of
Fourvière, where he remained until his death. Whenever Père Teilhard
passed through Lyons he would have a long and friendly interview with
him. Cf. Donatien Mollat, *Le Père Victor Fontoynont* in *Le Messager
du Coeur de Jésus* (1959), pp. 399–409. Other details may be found in
Auguste Valensin, textes et documents (1961), in particular pp. 66–7
and 335.

In 1950, at the age of seventy, deeply moved by some distressing
events, Père Fontoynont wrote this short poem, under the title 'Visita-
tion 1950', as an answer to Baudelaire's well-known verse 'O Mort,
Vieux Capitaine', symbolizing the reaction of the natural man:

> *'Mais il est un appel et plus humble et plus tendre:*
> *Courez à ma vieilesse, ô ma divine Soeur.*
> *Quelque chose en mon sein brûle de vous entendre:*
> *Une enfance endormie tressaille dans mon coeur.*
> Vous viendrez cette fois par l'hiver et les ronces:

able in me not to have answered your card from Toulon, the one in which you tell me your epic story about the Vardar. Fortunately your line of the 10th, received yesterday, came to break the spell that was paraylsing me; and I send you double thanks for it, because not only does it give me news of you, but it makes me resume a correspondence that means a lot to me. Aren't you one of the few—and they keep getting fewer—with whom I have a real understanding, to whom I can say anything and be sure of being understood?

But first of all, I must congratulate you on your expedition to the East and on the cross you won in those distant parts. I was almost jealous of you, you know, when I heard you were sailing. I really would have enjoyed that great adventure overseas and the free air of the Serbian mountains filling a soul swollen with all the fullness of war!—Get back soon to Salonika—indeed I very much hope you will: but don't despise the leisure God is arranging for you deep in the heaths of Morbihan. In the lull of these last three months, you can't imagine with what freshness of soul I've renewed contact with God and the ideas that are so dear to me.— Externally, my life since September has been as follows: after the bloody offensive of the 25th, carried out south of Arras, we moved to the Lens area to take over trenches recently captured by the English. It was a bad sector, in mining country (not far from the Lorette ridge) but I was glad to have been in it, because it gave me some idea of the awful trench life in the Artois. The shelling and the mud were made up for by the great number of industrial centres, rich in brave hearts and commercial resources, that are still functioning quite close to the lines. We stayed three months in that area—sombre, but not without charm. On New Year's Day (for the third time since April 1915) we were in Belgium: and there we've stayed. As I told you at the beginning of this letter, we're having a pretty quiet time. Three times a month, on an average, we have a spell that takes us, over a famous river and near a completely ruined city, into sand-bagged trenches that

---

La montagne a perdu sa parure de fleurs.
Mais vous m'apporterez votre divine Annonce.'

'But there is a cry more humble and more tender:
Hasten, my divine Sister, to comfort my age.
Something in my breast is on fire to hear you:
A slumbering childhood trembles in my heart.
This time you will come when winter is here, and the briars:
The mountain has lost its array of flowers.
But you will bring me your divine tidings.'

run in an irregular line across a network of canals and causeways. Communications are sometimes difficult, but the sight of sheets of fresh water glittering under the pallid sky in the setting of the dunes is full of a piercing charm that is made even more intense, when the guns and mortars are quiet, by the great silence of two armies keeping watch on one another. Against this background of smiling poetry and of generally stilled conflict, I have been occupying myself again, both because I feel the need and because I think I should, in thought and prayer, stimulated now and again by reading one of those books (the only sort that should be written) in which a life is laid bare, Newman's *Apologia*[2] or the *Voyage du centurion*. Would you believe it, that Auguste Valensin was astonished that at the front I've not dropped philosophy?—as though to philosophize couldn't be the most absorbing and intimate of prayers, as though the best attitude of the servant who is waiting for the Master were not devotion to the first of his human obligations—to see things clearly in himself and around himself. I feel that the war has made me quite indifferent to my own personal future, but has given me a greater passion than ever for Ideas, Causes, Action. What about you?

So, I have got down to thinking out and to jotting down in an exercise book some notes on a subject that has always been for me the real problem of my interior life—rather as the question of Rome was for Newman or the sense of the demands of the soul for Psichari—I mean the problem of reconciling progress and Christian detachment—of reconciling a passionate and legitimate love of all that is greatest in Earth, and the unique quest for the Kingdom of Heaven. How can one be more Christian than any man and yet be more man than any? It is an excellent thing to study the sciences or philosophy or sociology, in order to please God, and to carry out a task that has been given us. But that is not saying enough: so long as, in my studies or my work, I cannot see any possibility of loving my task; so long as I do not see that I must devote myself to it so that, precisely by means of what I win by it (and not only because of the moral value of my efforts)

[2] Cf. Letters of 2 February 1916 (*MM*, pp. 93–4); 22 July 1916 (ibid., p. 114); many of the great Cardinal's ideas 'have entered my mind as though returning to a home they had lived in for a long time'; 9 January 1917 (p. 167). Teilhard, like Newman, 'bitterly experienced, without being scandalized, the bitter temptation of being born before the due hour or season for his thought' (22 July 1916, p. 114). He well understood, too, what Newman meant by 'Myself and my Creator', echoing it later in one of his retreat notes (1945): 'However many people and friends surround us, each one of us is Alone before God.'

I may advance and become an organic being in an Absolute; so long as the World appears to me only an opportunity to acquire merit, and not some κτῆμα ἐξ ἀεί to be built up and embellished—so long as such things can be said, I shall be no more than a half-hearted laggard among men, and they will look on me as being (and blame my religion for it) something less than a full man, and a turncoat. And would anyone feel justified in saying that they are completely wrong? I am concerned, therefore, in order to satisfy myself and to 'systematize' my interior life, to find out what there may well be (of divine in)—what may be predestined beneath the very matter of our cosmos, of our humanity, of our progress. And I feel drawn to the study of the currents, the links, all the things 'in nobis sine nobis' which carry us along, and which we direct into channels, which we instinctively worship and against which we fight—the sum total of which makes up 'our (life), our cosmic organism'. For it is there that God must lie hidden. I believe that every man who has any awareness experiences this cosmic life with very great force. It drives some to isolation and the return to the fundamental oneness of original matter; that is pagan pantheism, the motionless slumber in the arms of great Nature whose task it is to operate and to guide all things. For others, it is a summons to master the universe, to examine all its secrets, to become one with all men in a higher community in which conscious minds will be illuminated by convergence, in which consciousness will have freed or penetrated all matter.—The capacity to love cannot with impunity be dissociated from its object: if you try, mistakenly, to cut off our affectivity from love of the universe, are you not in danger of destroying it? An initial justification of the Christian attitude is to emphasize, with St. Paul and St. John, the 'cosmic' wonders of the heavenly Jerusalem—the union of souls in a wonderful organism, the body of Christ—the living current of grace drawing with it, penetrating, and transforming God's chosen monads—and this is the fundamental answer: our deep-seated 'cosmic' aspirations are transposed to a new universe that satisfies them 'eminenter'. But it is not enough to make use of these urges. Here again, cannot *the object, the actual matter* of our human passions be transfigured, transformed into the Absolute, the definitive, the divine?—I believe it can. I shall put the intoxication of pagan pantheism to a Christian use, by recognizing the creative and formative action of God in every caress and every blow, in every inevitable and irreducible passivity—I shall direct upon its natural objects the noble passion to fight for knowledge, for mastery, for organizing; but behind that will lie the ultimate aim of carrying on God's creative work begun, for example, in the unconscious development of the human brain, but destined to produce souls of a more refined spiritual tone or of a new and subtly different character—and that, moreover, precisely *as a result of* the influences and organs of a higher civilization; I shall divinize the ingenuous or inquisitive love of nature, by considering that something of this mysterious whole represented by Matter, must through Resurrection, pass into the World of heaven—my efforts to forward human progress being even (?? perhaps) the necessary condition for the development of the new Earth.—And so, with no break, carried along by the natural graduated advance of the material, the living, the social, I find at the term of my desires the 'cosmic Christ' (if I may use the phrase), he who gathers together at the conscious Centre of his Person and his Heart, every movement of atoms, cells, souls . . .

That is what I can vaguely see, and am trying to bring out, still lacking proper form, in what I'm writing, just as though I were standing at your door in Ore Place, talking with you. I would like to be able to love Christ passionately (*by loving*) *in the very act* of loving the universe. Is it a wild dream or a blasphemy? Besides communion with God and communion with the Earth, is there communion with God through the Earth—the Earth becoming like a great Host in which God would be contained for us? . . . I would like that to be true (for my own sake and for that of many others, and so that the strongest pretext the world has for looking on us as abnormal[3] may be removed)—In any case I enjoy noting down my ideas in this direction—subject to having, if need be, to add at the end, 'and that was all a dream'.

I'm a little ashamed at having told you all this. Perhaps I'd do better, instead of speculating so much, to look for more opportunities for ministry. But apart from the material to be sanctified not being easy to find, and calling for a more roundabout way of cultivation (made up primarily of comradeship, example, and devotion . . . Pray for that) my innate, and very pronounced, inclination to be, as Newman says, 'unobtrusive and uncontroversial', throws me back upon myself. I have no influence on my Saracens, except

[3] Cf. Pius XII, Christmas broadcast, 1957: 'The Christian should even consider it a disgrace to allow himself to be surpassed by the enemies of God in eagerness to work, spirit of enterprise, and even sacrifice.' (*Acta Apostolicae Sedis*, 50, 1958; *Docum. Catholique*, vol. 55, 1958, col. 14.) The Christian vocation contains a summons to 'an unremitting activity, austere, and directed to every part and every aspect of life', and we should reject 'the subtle pretexts invented as an excuse for the inertia of some Christians'.

what comes from a certain sympathy. On the French, it is
sporadic, and at the moment made difficult either by too frequent
changes or by a trench routine that makes it impossible for me to
live as I used to do in the front-line dugouts and keeps me tied to
an isolated ruin a little to the rear.—You see that I've told you
'heaps of things', and even too much. Write to me.

Very fraternally in Christo Jesu

TEILHARD

P.S. My brothers are well. The eldest (of my younger brothers),
who was married in November, is an observer in a 'sausage
balloon' in the middle of the Vosges: the other is an artillery lieu-
tenant in the Oise;—the second youngest of the brothers, after being
a bombardier in a battery near Soissons, is now an officer-cadet at
Fontainebleau.—At the end of November I was on leave and met
three of my four brothers together! I found the rue Pascal *exactly*
as it was when I left it in horizon-blue (I felt I'd only been away
a day), with *Citoyen* Bellut just the same as ever.—Only, in the
streets, wearing my tarboosh, I looked down my nose at the shy
and pale-faced auxiliaries in their tan uniforms . . .

II

22 July 1916

I received your card of the 17th this morning and I hasten to answer it. I do hope that this reminder of my continuous even if too
silent affection may bring you some consolation! Earlier, I had had
an envelope addressed by you, sent from sector 509 on the 14th
May (?) but with no letter inside, which was a great disappointment to me and made me wonder what on earth had happened to
you.—So you're back on the coast for a second time, without the
glory of any bloodshed. 'Ama nesciri . . .' I know, from experience, that it's very galling to have to do without one's little bit of
glory, and to be taken away from the tilling of ground that you
have chosen and loved. But, then, we have to make up our minds
sometime, don't we, in practice to set above every joy and every
interest the austere charm of adhering to the divine Will, and to
delight in it just for God's own good pleasure.—I pray, you may be
sure, for your battalion and for your own future . . .

I am writing to you from a charming village in the Meuse, right
in a 'refreshment zone' (that's the official term) after coming back,
for the second time, from the Hill 304 area; our sector was between Avocourt Wood and Hill 304—places with great and sad

memories, where we neither did nor suffered anything very heroic. The time of big attacks was over, on this side of the river, when we arrived there. The shelling, particularly in the rear area, was still pretty heavy, and the appearance of the lines was absolutely volcanic. But in spite of everything it was already pretty quiet, and it's only by favour that we can be reckoned among the glorious defenders of Verdun. Many S.J.'s in these parts, Neyrand for one. I only ran across Père Rameau, brown, tanned, mellowed (if I may say so) both physically and morally by camp life; and I've regretted this loneliness, since the month of June has coincided, for me, with a certain spiritual depression that came from an almost complete lack of opportunity to do anything useful or remarkable, just at the time when I was hoping that my activity in the regiment would reach its peak.—Now I feel I'm coming back to life, and the zest for life and thought is returning.—Since my February letter, I've set out in a little piece called 'La Vie Cosmique' (!!), which I'll certainly let you see if we ever get out of this war, the ideas I was telling you about then. Provisionally, it was in a way my intellectual testament that I drew up there, in the calm of Nieuport . . . In it, I quite shamelessly salute 'sacred evolution' and emphasize the fact that since the Cosmos is hallowed and renewed by the Incarnation in the very roots of its development, it is a fundamental part of the Christian's duty to cooperate in the maturing, even the natural maturing, of everything (retaining, of course, a proper hierarchy of values). Natural progress is, in a sense, the axis (or one of the axes) of the Kingdom of God; and the new Earth must emerge from the fulfilment of the old.—I am coming more and more to feel that there is a legitimate—and how fundamental!—reconciliation to be made between those who worship Christ and those who worship the world (by the latter, I mean those who are possessed by a strong and disinterested passion to make Life grow greater). In the burning questions of liberalism, of emancipation, etc., of 'secularization', of the immanence of our destinies, there lie hidden, beneath fanaticism and sectarianism, legitimate postulates, and the perception of an unanswerable logic that leads inevitably to new situations and new points of view.—To co-operate in releasing these new currents, in stripping from them their mask of atheism and showing that they are Christian, that is a great hope which, I assure you, supports me like a vocation. It seems to me that tomorrow, if we can get together, a certain number of us—each in his own branch and using his own ideas—should be able to do a great deal, each backing up the other, to bring about a salutary mediation between the followers of heaven and the fol-

lowers of Earth. Alas! that Rousselot[4] is not here! . . . I can foresee that the study I mentioned above will need a good deal to complement it: it needs something on 'the meaning of the Cross', on
the 'counsel of virginity', on everything that has the appearance
of a cleavage between Christianity and natural progress. I don't
know whether I'll find the time to write these between now and the
end of the war, and I hope not.—From the immediately apostolic
point of view, I'm not doing much: and I'm feeling rather worn
down. I'm beginning to think that only two jobs are worth having:
chaplain or fighting man. The medical service is no use to me—less
and less so.

Goodbye, we'll pray to the Lord for one another. Get well
quickly.

P. TEILHARD

III

26 July 1917

Yesterday, with immense pleasure, I received your two cards of
July 4. I rather envy you all your work and all your adventures.
Things here are much more static. Last year, we were shuttling
between Bar-le-Duc and Verdun. This spring we've hardly moved
from the Chemin des Dames. We don't yet know what autumn has
in store for us. At the moment, we're going to a training camp.

. . . You're perfectly right. 'One single soul' is the true reality
that emerges from the Cosmos. But the point is that this soul has,
in the vast physical armature (which is perhaps only a totality of
souls), its roots, its extensions, or, if you so prefer it, a great part
of itself that is not yet 'segregated' nor spiritualized . . . Spirit is
still *in process of creation* 'de limo totius naturae', if not as regards
the spirituality of individual souls, at least as regards their as yet
unprecedented types or characteristics and as regards their social
synthesis. That is why natural evolution, *which is still going on*,
seems to be without any doubt capable of sanctification *ab intra*,
precisely as the souls which it is continuing to produce and dif-
ferentiate.—It is very important to note that Faith, which might
appear to be able to be so static and serene, can continue to shine
in the world only in so far as believers take part in the 'fight for

---

[4] Père Pierre Rousselot, their fellow-theological student for a year at
Ore Place, a Professor in the faculty of Theology at the Institut Catholique in Paris, and the author of the well-known thesis on *The Intellectualism of St Thomas*, was killed at Éparges in the spring of 1915.

the light' which is a development of natural reason. There is a hallow *opus humanum*, I am more and more convinced.—And then, attractive and easy though it is to believe in a total spiritualization of the Cosmos, it is still a fact that the flesh rises again, and that the new Earth (which we may call the body of Christ) will form a *physically* linked Whole.—That may serve a little to put our universe in correct perspective—still pretty chaotic and mixed up, but in the *totality* of which the creative action, with our conscious help, is developing the form of perfected humanity.

I have a lot to say to you about this subject, and about other related ones . . . these thirty months of solitary thinking, in an atmosphere of great events, has formed me, I think, in the way a long retreat does. I am becoming at the same time very realist and very mystical: you know what I mean?—I wish we could meet.

What would you say about an association of people sufficiently mature and congenial (in our order, or close to it) whose aim would be to formulate, draw attention to, and suggest in a *provisional* and initiatory way, solutions for the problems of the religious order that have now to be faced?—I am struck by the fact that the Church almost entirely lacks an *organ of research* (in contrast with everything that lives and progresses around her). Yet she will never keep the faith luminous for her children and for those outside her, except by *seeking*, in a search that is felt to be a matter of life or death . . . There you have a fact that may astonish the smug theologians, but it's a fact of everyday hard and salutary experience. There must, then, be organized under the direction of the *Ecclesia docens*, an *Ecclesia quaerens*. In these days there are crying problems that nobody, outside a few private conversations, expresses clearly or faces directly. There are ideas, still rudimentary and partially erroneous, but liberating, which germinate and die in the mind of individuals . . . We should have, I'm sure, an organ (sure, obedient, esoteric) to collect, centralize, and sift all that; I would almost call it a 'laboratory', set aside for such work. I'm not shutting my eyes to the immense difficulties and the suspicion setting up such a 'factory' would meet with! But the question is above all to decide whether the institution is not practically essential or at least a timely device, if we are to be in time to prevent a schism between natural human life and the Church. What do you think? Goodbye. Pray for me.

                                                        TEILHARD

Appendix 2

EXTRACTS FROM 'LE MILIEU MYSTIQUE'[1]

Lord, it is you who, through the imperceptible goadings of sense-beauty, penetrated my heart in order to make its life flow out into yourself. You came down into me by means of a tiny scrap of created reality; and then, suddenly, you unfurled your immensity before my eyes and displayed yourself to me as Universal Being. Lord, in that first figure, so near and so concrete, let me savour You at length, in all that penetrates, and in all that envelops—in sweet odour and light—both Love and Space.

I have thought to hear it said, Lord, that among your servants there are some that feared to see a heart feel too much (just as they fear to see a spirit think too much) . . . But I cannot believe that they were right. For indeed, Lord, if a man close his soul to the summons of the immanent Divine, with what substance will he nourish the means by which he hopes to sustain his prayer?

Just as there is but one created Matter to carry the successive increases of consciousness in the Cosmos, so there is but *one fundamental feeling* underlying all forms of mysticism: and that is *an innate love of the human Person, extended to the whole universe.*

This passion, like every natural force, can be subject, as it develops, to checks, to perversions, to deviations . . . It can be dissipated in empty poetry, it can be lost in naturalist mysticism, it can sink into pagan pantheism.—But it is still true that it is this one

---

[1] 'Le Milieu Mystique' was written in the Forest of Compiègne, at Beaulieu-les-Fontaines (Oise). The manuscript, completed on 13 August 1917, was sent by Père Teilhard to his sister Marguerite-Marie. He intended then to submit it to 'one of the Fathers in Lyons . . . in whom I have complete confidence'. He probably meant Père Vulliez-Sermet, who was at that time novice master in the Lyons Province. Cf. *MM*, pp. 200, 209. At the end of the work, Père Teilhard points out that he has not tried to describe the mystical life itself: 'All I have tried to do is to bring out its natural and cosmic roots.' In it he describes in turn: the circle of Presence, the circle of Consistence, the circle of Energy, the circle of Spirit, the circle of the Person. The three extracts we give are taken from the first, the third, and the fourth circles.

single passion that springs up in, that is primordial in, the heart of man.

If, then, a man wishes to erect in himself, for God, the structure of a sublime love, the first thing he must do is to sharpen his sensibilities;—he must, by prudent and unremitting familiarity with the most moving realities, foster in himself the feeling of, the taste for, the Omnipresence which haloes all things in Nature. Under this tangible stuff, it is you, Lord, who appear to us, You who fill us with delight, You who reveal to us, little by little, the wonders of your existence among us.

The multitude of beings is a terrible affliction.—The vision of the Presence has released me from it.

Through contact with an Object so specially loved, something entered, like a ray of light, into the dark cloud.—A crystal drop spread through the powdery opacity.—And everything became not only warm and diaphanous but radiantly transparent. Everything was transformed into a single limpid whole, in which the separateness of things could no longer be seen. Brightness reigned throughout.

And at the same time that transparence reached me in my turn. It penetrated me. It made its way down into the very depths of my being—to where I thought nothing could still be found. Passing through me, it washed away in its mysterious waters the plurality and the dark places of my being. And I knew an unbelievable solace in feeling that there was indeed an Other; and that through that Other I was one with all things.

I feel now that what I am existing in is my intangible homogeneity, made up of countless inter-fused presences. I know the variety of each one of these presences and I feel the different appeals they make. But I see them now only as shifting tints of one and the same light or as areas of sweet perfume ranged throughout one and the same atmosphere. I pass through them without ever emerging from that which makes them one. Beneath that inessential medley and those surface beauties, the Presence that fills all things is the only source that sheds light for me, and the only air that I can ever breathe.

God's creative power does not in fact fashion us as though out of soft clay: it is a fire that kindles life in whatever it touches, a quickening spirit. Therefore it is *during our lifetime* that we must decisively adapt ourselves to it, model ourselves upon it, identify ourselves with it. The mystic is given at times a keen, obsessive insight into this situation.

In the ambience of higher Energy in which beings move, he then sees human liberties as independent, *unabsorbed* nuclei, that are able partially to isolate themselves from the divine exhalations that envelop them and seek to enter into them. These nuclei can, if they wish, armour themselves against the radiance that seeks to penetrate them and guide them. They can also, if they have received the light, resist its transforming action, or, again, in self-centred exclusiveness, cast a shadow behind them.

And anyone who has this insight, and who loves, will feel within himself a fever of active dependence and of arduous purity seizing upon him and driving him on to an absolute integrity and the complete utilization of all his powers. Such a man, in virtue of his inner vision, is sworn to a work that is never ended of self-correction and development; and this governs his whole life with a delectable tyranny. How could he ever rest, so long as the least discord still remains between the vibration of his soul and that of the divine ambience? And how conceive that this ideal concord can ever be realized?

In order to become perfectly resonant to the pulsations of the basic rhythm of reality the mystic makes himself docile to the least hint of human obligation, the most unobtrusive demands of grace.

To win for himself a little more of the creative energy, he tirelessly develops his thought, dilates his heart, intensifies his external activity. For created beings must work if they would be yet further created.

And finally, that no blemish may separate him, by so much as a single atom of himself, from the essential limpidity, he labours unceasingly to purify his affections and to remove even the very faintest opacities which might cloud or impede the light.

Not, indeed, in order to arrive at a self-annihilation that would cause its own personal being to disappear, but in order to achieve an identification that will complete its nature, the soul must no longer make any distinction, in any part of itself, either in its texture or in its processes, between itself and the clear, vibrant, ambiance into which it casts itself.

. . . The vanishing is not yet complete . . . the contours can still be guessed at . . . a little eddy shows that the union is still imperfect . . . More obedience is called for, the heart must open still wider, purity must be more intense!

There are no limits to this communion of an activity that seeks to equate itself with its first Principle: no limits to the rectification of attitude, nor to the flexibility of the will, nor to the transparency of heart and mind.

The mystic experiences a joy that no words can express in feeling that by this active obedience (which is very different from the passive acceptance which at first satisfied him) he is adhering *indefinitely more closely* to the encompassing Godhead. As he becomes a more perfect *instrument*, so, indefinitely, he *becomes* more *one* with the creative power. Just a little more, he feels, and God himself, finding no resistance as he imposes conformity to the divine plans, will no longer distinguish between the tool he holds and his own almighty Hand.

One day, I remember, I could find no words in which to express the testimony in which my whole life sought to be embodied. The wind, and indifference, carried away half of what I could say; and the rest was not understood . . .

And it was then I felt that all of us, so long as we exist, crushed to suffocation on the surface of the Earth, are living, on this side of things, in miserable estrangement from one another. The network of actions, writings, sounds, that knits together is inert and crude. It can mould us only in a rough and ready way, and it can neither transmit nor faithfully preserve our image. Nature is a bungler. When frost and hail have destroyed the finest shoots and the largest heads of grain in the field in which spirit ripens, she still, after the corn has been brought in, leaves trailing on the ground a harvest of energy and good will.

It was then that I cursed Progress. And, in my disappointment, I dreamed of a common Centre into which all things would drive the most vital roots of their sensibility and energy—of a universal Centre, living and benevolent, which would itself be at hand to help our desires to do what is right, when we do not know either how to express them, or how to retain them, or how to realize them.

—No being in the world would be able to ignore or reject the words that this infinitely sentient Focus sought to receive and transmit; for they would echo in the depths of every creature's being, mingling with the irresistibly imperative demands that Life gives voice to.

—No untoward accident could destroy the seed that this infinitely preserving Centre had resolved to keep and use. In its due time and place, it would germinate, and bring joy to the mind that conceived it.

—Such was the dream that solaced my disappointed activity.

It was then, Lord, that you offered my aspirations and my endeavours the inner shelter of your divine Essence, so mysteriously one with our universe, and that you said to me, 'Look, it is I.

'It is I, at the common heart of your being and of all things, to welcome the wildest of your longings, and to assure you that not the smallest fragment of them will be lost to the Good.

'It is I, immutable beneath the generations, ready to save for those who are to come the treasure which might be lost today but which the future will inherit:—one day I shall pass on to another, whose name I know, the thought that is in your mind. And when that man speaks and is heard, it is you who will be heard. Do you yourself know from whom came the idea that moves you and which you cherish as though it were your own?

'It is I, the true bond of the World. Without me, even though beings may seem to touch one another, they are divided by an abyss. In me they come together, for all the chaos of endless time and space.

'It is I, to sustain, and make fruitful, and give peace to, your endeavour.

'It is I, above all, to continue it and consummate it . . .

'You have fought long enough that the World might be divinized. It is now for me to force the gates of Spirit.

'Let me pass!'

II

EXTRACT FROM FORMA CHRISTI[1]

. . . To the soul of the believer, centred vitally upon Christ, every activity of things (natural in their basis, supernatural in their extensions) brings a contact with Christ; he touches Christ through them.—And the more firmly that soul believes in his omnidependence in relation to Christ, the more the omni-action he undergoes

---

[1] 'Forma Christi' was written during the first three weeks of December 1918, in the Seminary at Strasbourg, where the Superior had given Père Teilhard the use of a room during the daytime (*MM*, pp. 263, 267). He wrote it after meditating in the Cathedral close by: 'Faithfully, each time, I pay a long visit to the Cathedral and beneath its dim vaults, I try to introduce a little more order into the world of aspirations—still, in spite of everything, very confused—I feel within myself. I try to do something to harmonize them with that intensely powerful current of practical and mystical life from which emerged the pillars and ogives and stained glass that surround me like a miniature universe' (2 December 1918, *MM*, p. 261).

becomes concrete, dominant and certain: *Credenti, omnia convertuntur in Christum.*[2]

In order to answer this universal demand that envelops it on all sides and fashions it, the soul, by a natural impulse, tries in its turn to make its way, actively and positively, towards Christ. After believing in the Action that is his, it devotes to him the work that is its own. To Faith it adds *right intention*. Here we have the beginning of the second phase of Christ's invasion of his universe.

Already, in virtue of the fundamental unity of our being and the world, we may say of every man of good will, that everything he does on this earth is related, more or less directly, to the spiritualization of the universe. The virtue proper to good will is to harness this work for God, that is to say to make *all* progress (even natural and even in its *opus materiale*) which we achieve in the development of Spirit, serve the interests of the mystical body. *By its intention*, which integrates us, as living members, with Jesus Christ, each one of our efforts, in its entirety, extends much further than ourselves: it reaches, and serves, the Christ who lives in the depths of our being . . .

Thus, through the combined power of Faith and Intention, a new world, without changing the characteristics of the old, is constituted for the Christian within things. A deep and simple zone, co-extensive with all created beings, is revealed to him at the heart of the universe: a zone in which

> Quidquid patimur, Christum patimur.
> Quidquid agimus, Christum agimus.

—Whatever is done to us, it is Christ who does it: whatever we do, it is to Christ we do it.

Once we become conscious of this universal mystical atmosphere, we feel the vast fullness of the Incarnation being realized around us . . .

[2] Cf. letter of 2 December 1915: 'It is St. Paul who says that for those who love God, everything works together for the greatest good of the soul' (*MM*, p. 82). Letter of 27 May 1923: 'It seems to me that the only solution is blind and absolute faith in the meaning assumed by all things, even diminishments, for the man who believes in God's universal animation of everything that happens.' See similar passages in Appendix 5, and Chapter 3 above.

Appendix 3

PÈRE TEILHARD'S LETTERS ON THE DEATH OF HIS SISTER FRANÇOISE[1]

(TO HIS PARENTS)   *Ore Place, Hastings.*
                                                    7 June 1911.

This morning I had a telegram direct from Shanghai (by the kindness of one of our Fathers, I think) telling me that Françoise had just gone to join Albéric. You had given your loved daughter to God, and now he has accepted her for ever. He alone is the Term of all things, so that for God, on his side, to take someone to himself is not to separate but to reunite that person. May his will be done. I know that you will often have been saying that during the last three days, though it will not have prevented you from suffering cruelly; and I would give a great deal to be with you both just now, and to be able to talk to you for a while. Our best consolation, surely, is that it is difficult to imagine a holier and more lovely end. Françoise has indeed found the death she longed for more than anything—she told you that again in her last letter—in China and for the sake of China.[2] For us, it is true, it was a joy that she could still from time to time talk with us—but wouldn't we be rather selfish to mourn too much, at seeing her reach a goal she longed for as a distant ideal for which she gave every day of her life? How many times has she spoken to me of her desire to see God as soon as possible . . . Our Lord is giving her her reward even before its time: we have no right to regret the good she might have done had she lived longer. The fine life is the life that fulfils the plans of God. Now, in Françoise you have moulded and given to God a saint: you could not dream of a more beautiful future for your child.—Here, we shall pray very much for her and for you both. I have sent a message to Canterbury, too, where there will be many mass intentions. But I think few prayers will so affect God as those of the old folk whom Françoise has led to Paradise, those of the

[1] See below, pp. 367–8.
[2] She had written to Pierre, at the beginning of 1911: 'Don't forget, what I really want you to ask Our Lord at your first Mass is to let me have and keep China completely until my last day' (*Soeur Marie Albéric du Sacré-Coeur, Petite Soeur des Pauvres*, p. 77).

Chinese most of all. Be of good heart, my poor father and my dear mother: the times of suffering pass by and they bring us closer to God: it is then that we have something to offer to God, and gain something that enables us to stand before him with confidence. Remember that the children you still have love you all the more for it, and would give a great deal to comfort you. I kiss you both . . .

PIERRE

(TO HIS FATHER)   *2 July 1911*

I have just written to mother for her feast-day, but I can't refrain from adding a line for you, if only to tell you once again that I am very specially with you in heart in these days when the memory of Françoise must be so much more intense for you. Since my last letter we have had news from Shanghai and in spite of all the consolation it holds I fear that it must have brought you some sadness too: it brings back so many memories; it makes the fact of separation living and concrete; and then, when you read the news, you feel so sharply the impotence of words to express what could be learnt from just one look, one moment of conversation, one treasured word . . . At least we know she died happily: she went where her fondest wishes were taking her. Isn't that the great thing? It is true that God has asked you for a very hard sacrifice, my poor little *papa*, and one that makes no sense except for a man who believes in our crucified Lord, in the value of suffering, and in the extreme disproportion between the joys and sorrow of here and now and those that await us. He has judged you worthy of your daughter . . .

PIERRE

Appendix 4

LETTER FROM PÈRE JOSEPH MARÉCHAL

Louvain-Eegenhoven
26 November 1931

From the philosophical standpoint adopted by Père Teilhard, his thesis can be defended: to the origins of natural evolution, he attributes latent potentialities, sorts of 'rationes seminales',[1] which already partake of the nature of 'thought' or of 'freedom', but it is thought in embryo, and freedom that is still under constraint. Various metaphysical interpretations of this 'reason' that is immanent in things, either as action or even as essence, can be put forward: some correct or tenable, others unacceptable from the Christian point of view. I do not know whether Père Teilhard has published his own; but I know him well enough to be sure that it is intelligent and orthodox.

In spite of its interiority and spontaneity, consciousness in man is still linked, by a natural connexion, with organized matter: our consciousness is not the consciousness of pure spirits. Since man is in continuity with the rest of matter (even though not in complete dependence on it) he thus holds, by right, a place in the chronological series and theoretical concatenations of natural History: there is a 'phenomenon of Man', and we cannot conceive a total discontinuity between phenomena. What Père Teilhard sought to do was to construct an empirical theory of man, considered in his continuity with the rest of nature but without claiming to explain the 'whole' of man by that continuity; conversely, to interpret nature itself, in its ascending movement towards man, by analogies suggested by the immediate and wholly interior perception of our conscious life; to bring out in all its fullness the correlation in man of the interior world of con-

---

[1] Cf. 'Basis and foundations' (1926): The birth of beings 'is preceded, in reality, by a gestation without assignable origin. By something in itself (is not this what St. Augustine called *ratio seminalis*?) everything is extended into some other preliminary reality, prolonged by something else, everything is found linked in its individual preparation and development (that is to say, in its own duration) with a general evolution in which cosmic duration records itself (*VP*, p. 129).

sciousness and the exterior world of matter—that is primarily what he sought to do. Obviously, however, this 'man', the object of a natural History enlarged to the scale of the 'Noosphere', is still not equivalent to the 'man' disclosed to us by our interior life, by which I mean the man whose spiritual initiatives and unquenchable thirst for perfection leave behind all correlation with matter.[2]

[2] Shortly afterwards (24 August 1924) Père Teilhard wrote to Père Auguste Valensin about some further comments that Père Teilhard had, at his own request, received from Père Maréchal: 'They are full of illumination, sympathy and the real charity that I knew I should find.' In 1929, Père Maréchal had approved (after suggesting 'judiciously' some corrections in detail) the article on 'The Basis and Foundations of the Idea of Evolution', written in 1926, which Père Dorp had wished to publish in the *Revue des Questions scientifiques*: but the article was 'stopped relentlessly by the diocesan censorship of Malines. Some suspicious canon had riddled it with question and exclamation marks . . . I took the matter philosophically. All the same, this obstinate and persistent obstruction is infinitely wearying' (to Père Valensin, 29 September and 30 December 1929). On 10 February 1930, Père Maréchal wrote to Père Teilhard telling him how extremely sorry he was that this had happened.

In the article already quoted from *Bijdragen* (vol. 21, 1960), 'Evolutieleer en Toekomstverwachting bij Teilhard de Chardin', *Theologische Bezinning*, Père Smulders expresses a judgement similar to Père Maréchal's: 'This concept, which lays strong emphasis on man's affinity with the material world, at the same time seems sufficiently to respect the dogmas of the spirituality and creation of the human soul. Dissatisfied with the general definition, which defines the spiritual in a negative way, as non-material, he characterizes the human soul as a degree of interiorization which is precisely the Thomist *reditio completa ad seipsum*. And in stressing the unique and absolute value as being of every individual man, the Teilhardian concept not only leaves room for the doctrine of the creation of the soul, but entails it. In producing man, evolution produced a being which is one more link in the chain of evolution, but which in virtue of its absolute value stands in an immediate relationship to its Creator, (pp. 277–8). Cf. *La Réflexion de l'énergie* (*QS*, 1952, p. 483): 'Something intervened in the general process of the vitalizing of matter: something so subtle that at first its entry did not appear to disturb anything. And yet it was something fundamentally so violently active that after some hundreds of thousands of years it has completely transformed the face of the earth.'

Appendix 5

PÈRE TEILHARD AND THE MORALITY OF INTENTION

In *Le Milieu Divin*, as we have seen, Père Teilhard starts by examining a thesis according to which man's action 'has *no* value *except* in virtue of the intention that directs it'.[1] Whatever one may think of the way in which he formulates an idea that is often more lived than postulated in theory, and whatever one may think, similarly, of the views he later puts forward to correct the idea, it is difficult not to admit that he was right. What he rejects is a doctrine that insists exclusively on intention: a subjectivist doctrine, that would imply, if its internal logic were fully appreciated, a scepticism or a contempt directed at the action itself, considered in its proper finality and its objective result. He holds that the true Christian should not be included among those 'who contribute to the human task (as they will, unwisely, have been told to do—I quote:) "only with the tips of their fingers".' (p. 52). But in defining his own position, Père Teilhard is careful not to go to the opposite extreme. The thesis he is denying, he admits, 'contains a very great deal of truth: it rightly emphasizes the role of intention as the necessary start and foundation of all else: it is the golden key which unlocks our inward personal world to God's presence (p. 55). The only criticism he has to make is that it is "an incomplete solution" ' (p. 53).

One has only to go on reading *Le Milieu Divin* to realize that intention holds a leading place in it—one could almost say that it monopolizes the foreground. Far from denying or passing in silence over its indispensable role, Père Teilhard is at pains to clarify intention, to direct it, to purify it. He recognizes its 'value'. He wishes it to be continually more perfect. Without this concern, moreover, the book would be meaningless.

The search for truth is not an authentic search if it stops short at itself in order to be its own satisfaction, instead of being entirely at the service of the truth that is sought. One can say the same

[1] *MD*, p. 53 (our italics). What follows should be read in conjunction with Chapters 3, 10, and 11, above.

about a sincerity that turns back to itself as though to its proper end. Similarly, Père Teilhard believes that the intention put into the *operatio* is not sufficient, and may well be corrupted, if it attaches no importance to the *opus* that should normally be its fruit.—He nevertheless insists on 'purity of intention' (p. 133), as essential, as he had done in earlier writings.[2] 'There is no limit,' he says again, '*in respect of the intention*,[3] which animates our endeavour to act or to accept, because we can always go further in the inward perfecting of our conformity. There can always be greater detachment and greater love' (pp. 138–9). In this, if it is properly understood, we have one of the fundamental teachings of *Le Milieu Divin*, which tells us to see and look for God in all things, through all things, in what we do and in what we have to undergo.

However, in two successive articles in the Fribourg review *Nova et Vetera*, Mgr Charles Journet severely criticized Père Teilhard's teaching on the ground of misunderstanding the necessity both of moral intention and of supernatural grace.

In the first article,[4] Mgr Journet seems to believe that in Père Teilhard's view there is no distinction, provided the object of the activity be good in itself, between the action of the saint, or the 'Christian', and the action of the sinner, or 'atheist'. Every objectively well-adapted temporal action, every effective action in the order of external utility or progress would, in Mgr Journet's version of Père Teilhard's teaching, tend 'of itself and by itself', without qualification, to build up the body of Christ. This would quite certainly undermine Christian morality, and at the same time would equally certainly, he tells us, represent Teilhard's teaching, since in *Le Milieu Divin* we find, in set terms, 'All endeavour co-operates to complete the world *in Christo Jesu*' (p. 56).

Mgr Journet then introduces a contrast with Pascal's 'three orders'. Does he wish us to understand that we cannot retain the specific value of moral and supernatural intention except by denying all value to the endeavour, considered objectively? Would he hold that we cannot affirm the transcendence of 'the order of charity' except by denying that any sort of co-operation, even subordinate, and even extrinsic, is provided by the two lower orders in which this purely human effort is exercised? In particular, so

---

[2] 'Le Prêtre': 'through the pure intent of my will, the divine must flood into the universe' (*HU*, p. 135).

[3] Père Teilhard's italics.

[4] *Nova et Vetera*, July–September 1958, pp. 223–8. Note on *Le Milieu Divin*.

that there may be no confusion on this point, should everything
that belongs to the order of spirit be *excluded* from the order of
charity instead of being *assumed* by it? This is a criticism that a
number of commentators have in fact, and perhaps not without
reason, levelled against Pascal's teaching, at least in so far as it is
an implicit consequence of it. In that well-known and admirable
passage Pascal magnificently expressed the 'infinitely infinite distance' that prevents the lower order from raising itself up to the
level of the higher order, but he failed to bring out the transformation that the higher order can effect in the lower in order to
associate it with itself. In emphasizing the distinction between the
orders and their incommensurability, he did not sufficiently guard
against the interpretation that keeps them permanently separated.
Père Teilhard, for his part, in no way accepts such an erroneous
view; or we may say, if that seems too strong, that he does not
show any inclination to favour that tendency. But, simply because
he refuses to keep the orders perpetually separate, or to deny any
sort of co-operation between them, we have no right to accuse him
of failing to distinguish them. He was well aware, as we have seen,
of the distinction between the objective value of the work and the
moral intention of the act, as he was equally aware of that between
nature and grace.

To return to what we read in *Le Milieu Divin*: the purpose of
the book, he tells us, is to bring out the traditional doctrine of
'sanctification through fulfilling the duties of our station' (p. 65).
Whenever he explains his view (and this he does frequently) we
can see that he retains the 'co-operation' of our natural activity in
building up the body of Christ in its correct place and within its
proper limits, with complete accuracy. He never maintains that that
activity has value 'in itself' in the order of the Kingdom of God,
or that it can be sufficient to introduce us into it. No doubt, he is
well aware that 'the children of the world', that is to say the
'agnostics and irreligious', also 'unconsciously or involuntarily co-
operate in the Kingdom of God and in the fulfilment of the
elect', in the sense that 'their efforts, going beyond or correcting
their incomplete or bad intentions, are gathered in by him whose
Energy subjects all things to itself' (p. 67). In short, he knows
that, unwittingly and unintentionally the 'Roman legions' of old
marched for Christ:[5] but he hastens to add, 'that is no more than
a second-best, a temporary phase in the organization of human

[5] On preparations of the Messiah in history, see 'Mon Univers'
(1924), in *HU*, pp. 76–7.

activity' (ibid.). There is nothing reprehensible in this view; it is, in fact, what every Christian must necessarily hold, even though he may prefer to express it differently. No doubt, again, Père Teilhard believes that 'it is a matter of life or death that the Earth should flourish to the uttermost of its natural powers' (p. 69); this conviction derives from the whole of his evolutionary teaching with regard to the supernatural destiny of the universe, and anyone is perfectly entitled not to share it so fully. Nevertheless we cannot say that it is not in conformity with the design of the Creator who gave the earth to man. In any case, it is because of this doctrine that, for Père Teilhard even more than for other thinkers, an 'intention' that systematically dissociates itself from the work to be accomplished or its successful conclusion cannot suffice for the Christian; but it does not follow that the Earth's natural success is sufficient to secure for us our divine end. A condition is not a cause.[6] Père Teilhard never fails to emphasize the gulf between one order and another. He speaks, for example, of the necessity for the intervention of 'charity' (p. 142) or for the 'sanctification of human endeavour' (p. 65), or, again, of the 'metamorphosis' that must be effected by grace (p. 64), etc. Jesus alone, he concludes, is 'the Saviour of human activity' (p. 146).

Two years later, Mgr Journet returned to the attack, this time basing it on an over-all interpretation.[7] In support, he quotes another expression, again taken from Le Milieu Divin (p. 62): 'We bring part of the being which he desires back to God in whatever we do.'

It is only too easy to distort a writer's meaning by quoting it, as that sentence is quoted, out of context: a method that theologians might well leave to the less reputable type of journalist. In this case the words, as such, may be taken in a number of senses, and Mgr Journet has not hesitated to interpret them in a sense that is unacceptable. It would appear that, in his view, what Père Teilhard meant was: 'Whatever we do—be it wrong, that is, or be it right—whether we act with a good intention or from purely worldly motives—whether our behaviour be Christian or godless'—with consequences that can well be imagined. Teilhard's doctrine would be even more erroneous, more immoral and anti-Christian than it would be if Mgr Journet's earlier criticism were justified. We

[6] To the passages already quoted we may add 'Trois Choses que je vois' (1948), p. 8: 'the point of human maturing' is a 'condition (not a sufficient condition, of course, but a necessary condition) of the point of Christic Parousia'.

[7] Nova et Vetera, 1960, pp. 236–7, 311–13.

have, in fact, only to restore the sentence to its context to see through this sort of subterfuge.

In the first part of *Le Milieu Divin*, it will be remembered, Père Teilhard deals with what he calls 'the divinization of our activities', by which he means the way in which we can move towards God and sanctify ourselves in our actual daily activities. He addresses himself in the first place to those who already believe, to Christians, who wish to advance along the road of perfection. It is assumed that they already possess good will: they want to know how, in carrying out their mundane tasks, they can act in a Christian and godly way. It is in the course of explaining this to them that Père Teilhard says 'in whatever we do', etc., and he quite obviously means 'whether what we are doing is what is known as an act of piety, or whether it is simply a secular occupation'. This extremely simple meaning is the only one that could possibly be entertained by a reader who takes the passage at its face value. It is unmistakable not only from the general theme of the book and the position occupied in it by the sentence, but also from the immediate context. We have only to read on a little to find: 'Whatever our role as men may be, whether we are artists, working men or scholars, we can, *if we are Christians*,[8] speed towards the object of our work as though towards an opening on to the supreme fulfilment of our being.' Or again, a little later: 'God . . . is in some way in the tip of my pen, in the point of my pick, of my brush, my needle, in my heart and in my mind.' The Christian's activity, even when it is secular in its object or is applied to what is secular (which is necessarily the case for the vast majority of men), even when it is at its most humble and material level —that activity, provided it be 'super-animated' by divine grace (which presupposes that it is carried out in a Christian spirit) leads him to God. 'In whatever we do', again means not only in illustri-

[8] Our italics. There is a similar thought in 'Mon Univers' (1924): '*If we believe*, the force in which we meet so painful an obstruction suddenly ceases to be a blind or evil energy. Hostile Matter vanishes. And in its place we find the divine Master of the world who "under the species or appearances" of events, whatever they be, moulds us, empties us of our self-love and penetrates into us.' Moreover, the very title of the section, 'the divinization of our activities' would be meaningless if every human activity, no matter what, were already divine. And the 'divinization of our passivities' would indeed be an enterprise to be despaired of, if the objective efficacy of the work accomplished alone had value for the Kingdom of God. Mgr Journet's interpretation conflicts with Père Teilhard's most explicit statements, and constantly does violence to his thought. It reduces the book to nonsense and makes its whole plan a contradiction in terms.

ous enterprises but equally in 'the humblest work of our hands' (p. 62). Moreover, as Père Teilhard once again makes clear, this cannot be effected unless the 'human endeavour' of the Christian undergoes a veritable 'metamorphosis' (ibid.) at the hands of God. We find this repeated a little later in another form: *'For those who seek God,*[9] everything does not become good immediately, but everything is capable of becoming good: *omnia convertuntur in bonum.'*[10]

Mgr Journet, unfortunately, overlooks 'if we are Christians', 'if we believe', 'for those who seek God', and many other similar phrases. Many readers of *Le Milieu Divin*, with less complicated minds, would hardly have needed to read those qualifications in order correctly to interpret the book from which they have drawn the courage to seek God in their daily work.

Moreover, Père Teilhard's objectivism was not so pronounced that he could not write: 'Our own soul is the first of the tasks we

[9] Our italics again. Cf. 'Forma Christi': 'for the Christian', 'to the soul of the believer', etc. (See above, Appendix 2.)

[10] Romans 8. 28. He is speaking here of passivities. Père Teilhard then considers 'by what process and through what stages God effects this wonderful transformation of our deaths into a better life'. Cf. 'Introduction' (1944), p. 11: 'Under the influence of God, the determinisms and chances of the cosmos become flexible, are given a final purpose, and become animate around us, in proportion to our union with God and our prayer.' Earlier, in 'Note sur les modes de l'action divine dans l'Univers' (January 1920): 'For the believer, each thing, externally and individually, remains what it is for everybody: and yet the power of God solicitously adapts the whole to the believer's use. In some way it re-creates the Universe at every moment expressly for the man who prays. *Credenti, omnia convertuntur in bonum.'*
To L. Zanta, 20 May 1924: 'Let us simply ask the Lord to help us to maintain this attitude without bitterness, by showing us that his action can be incarnate even in the most disagreeable schemes of certain stupid or pharisaical minds. My whole interior life is more and more gaining purpose and strength in the union with God to be found in all the "internal and external forces of this world". But, if that attitude is to be effective, it must exclude *none* of those forces, neither death nor "persecution" in the intellectual field. If we believe, everything can be transformed into Our Lord. I may perhaps have told you before that I found the best general summing up of the Christian life in the phrase: "to be in communion, through fidelity, with the world hallowed by faith". I believe that puts it exhaustively and irreproachably.' Again, on 10 January 1927: 'I am delighted . . . that God in his Providence has made you feel that with a little faith one can always let oneself be carried along by the events which he animates "for those who love".'
Cf. Fénelon, *Instructions et Avis*, 24: 'All things, even the most terrible evils, are, as St. Paul says, converted into good for those who love God' (*Oeuvres*, Paris ed., vol. VI, p. 147).

are assigned.'[11] This is a remark well worth noting. He defined, again, the ideal of existence as 'fidelity to the divine Will'.[12] The most important thing, he said, was not to do great things but to do 'the smallest things in a great way'[13] and in that, at least, he was in agreement with Pascal. The 'divine ambience' of which he tried to give us at least a foretaste is not disclosed and does not progress through outstanding actions nor through the progress of civilization: its 'progress in individuals' is effected (and again this is what Teilhard teaches) only through 'purity, faith, and fidelity'; its 'collective progress' through the 'communion of the saints and charity'.[14] Here again Mgr Journet has overlooked the really important words, even though they are not tucked away; they appear as headings to sections, and occur on the very first page, in the table of contents, of *Le Milieu Divin*. Each phrase heads an elaboration of the idea it contains, and of these the very least one can say is that they certainly do not teach any form of moral or religious indifferentism.

It is true that Père Teilhard always maintained his criticism, in *Le Milieu Divin*, of the 'incomplete solution' of the problem of action. Earlier, in a letter of 21 December 1919, he had expressed his teaching on this point, with the freedom of expression, the touch of humour and paradox, the summary approximations, that are appropriate in a confidential letter to a friend: 'I sometimes think to myself,' he wrote, 'that the Church, after having believed in the immediate coming of the Parousia to the point of practically dropping the whole mechanical aspect of man—after having (as she saw the time running on) put her hand again to the handle of the terrestrial plough without any great conviction and protesting that the whole of that labour has not the value of a single *Ave Maria* (which is true enough, but not in the sense it is often understood)—will end, in a third phase, by seeing that her appeal to the transcendent does not dispense her from—indeed lays her

---

[11] To Max Bégouën, 8 April 1930 (*Cahiers*, 2, p. 26). Père Teilhard would have endorsed Keats's definition of the Earth as 'the vale of soul-making' (letter of 14 February 1918, ed. M. Buxton Forman, vol. 2, letter 114). Cf. *PM*, p. 261: 'But what, in the interest even of life in general, is the work of human works, if not to establish, in and by each one of us, an absolutely original centre in which the universe reflects itself in a unique and inimitable way? And those centres are our very selves and personalities.' Quoting that passage, I realize that it, too, could be given a reprehensible twist.

[12] *CM* (1950).

[13] Réflexions sur le Bonheur' (1934), *Cahiers*, 2, p. 68.

[14] *MD*, Contents (p. 12), and pp. 132–49.

under a special obligation of—working more effectively than others for the fulfilment of man's natural consciousness.'[15] Earlier still, in 1918, he had said in his meditation, 'Le Prêtre', 'It is the whole of my being, Lord Jesus, that you would have me give you, tree and fruit alike, the finished work as well as the harnessed power, the *opus* together with the *operatio*.'[16] After *Le Milieu Divin*, he was to continue to say the same. But that does not mean that he professed the thesis—one-sided, objectivist, naturalist, amoralist—attributed to him so insistently by Mgr Journet. The practical teaching of *Le Milieu Divin* is that if I act in a Christian spirit I can, trusting to the grace of God, begin to make my way to God through all my human tasks, by taking a fundamental interest in them, and not only in pious, sacred, or denominational activities. I can do so, and I must do so. The quest for God must be pursued in all things, and it does not deflect me from human duties and human ends. 'God is inexhaustibly attainable in the *totality* of our action' (p. 63): attainable, indeed, but not automatically attained by no matter what action. It is a wise and balanced doctrine, and Père Teilhard wishes to see it prevail against the distortions, the narrowness of interpretation, the scrupulosities, the withdrawals, which are perhaps less frequent today—they may, indeed, have given way to views with contrary shades of over-emphasis—but at the time when he was turning the book over in his mind, they were a very real danger, to be found in many religious circles. It is a practical doctrine, and to a large degree independent of views that were most individually personal to Père Teilhard, even though it is linked with his thought[17] and finds confirmation in it. It is a doctrine, after all, that is in complete conformity with the moral tradition which refuses to confine itself to a pure 'morality of intention', as it is with the Catholic tradition that affirms the consistence and value of the natural order, and with the spiritual tradition that can specially look for confirmation to Saint Ignatius Loyola and St. Francis of Sales. Père Teilhard's aim in this little book was, as he says himself, to make more 'manifest the validity of the thesis (so dear to Christianity) of sanctification through

---

[15] To Père Auguste Valensin, 21 December 1919.

[16] *HU*, p. 134.

[17] We have already pointed out (above, Chapter 18) that this connexion raises new problems, which Père Teilhard did not completely solve nor even always appreciate sufficiently clearly. That, however, is the law that governs all living thought. Christian thought is thus 'relaunched' from one century to another.

fulfilling the duties of our station' (p. 65).[18] And in that aim he was largely successful. I know—and if Mgr Journet comes to know it, I am sure he will be ready to welcome it—that many humble Christians, of very different cultural and social categories, engaged in tasks themselves equally different, have found in this doctrine the surest orientation of their spiritual life. If we look for pernicious illusions and deviations, it is not among those that we shall find them.[19]

[18] Cf. letter of 8 December 1918: 'Everything must be sacrificed to the clear duty in which God manifests himself' (*MM*, p. 263).

[19] Mgr Journet has further objections to Père Teilhard's doctrine. Cf. *Nova et Vetera*, 1960, pp. 330–33, and *Divinitas*, 1959, pp. 330–44. The most important of these have been touched on in earlier chapters. It was, I fear, a distasteful task; but I do not doubt that I may say of Mgr Journet, as of Père Teilhard, 'magis amica veritas'.

Appendix 6

ADDRESS GIVEN BY PÈRE RENÉ D'OUINCE, SJ, AT THE SERVICE FOR THE REPOSE OF THE SOUL OF PÈRE PIERRE TEILHARD DE CHARDIN, IN THE CHAPEL OF THE RUE DE SÈVRES, 27 APRIL 1955

Men of science and philosophers have already paid tribute to the scientist and thinker we knew in Père Teilhard de Chardin. In this gathering of prayer, after Mass celebrated by the Reverend Father Provincial, one who was for many long years Père Teilhard's friend and superior may be allowed to speak of the religious he knew and loved, and whom he revered with affectionate respect.

I know well, moreover, how arbitrary is that distinction in this case; for while we can conceive a religious leading his religious life side by side with his working life, conscientiously pursuing his scientific work as the duty attached to his station in life, just as a Carthusian tills his garden in his leisure hours, or as a Trappist cultivates the soil in between the hours of office, what we find in Père Teilhard is something quite different.

His religious faith was the soul of his scientific effort and of his intellectual quest. Few priestly lives, I imagine, have been so completely a single, integral life.

He entered the Society of Jesus at an early age, and adopted its apostolic and missionary ideal in a way that was at once so resolute and so individual, that we his companions, ordinary Jesuits as we are, were both amazed and abashed.

I can only give you the picture I see. Père Teilhard was of the blood of the great missionaries: a de Nobili, a Ricci setting out for unknown continents, eager to win the earth for Jesus Christ; of the blood of the seventeenth-century educationists who aimed to bring up the whole of Europe's youth in faith in Jesus Christ: he emulated the founders of the Paraguayan Reductions whose ingenuous dream it was to realize upon earth our image of the Kingdom of heaven.

Père Teilhard had the boundless, extravagant, ingenuous ambition to give the modern world to Jesus Christ; for he had an experience that he felt was an exemplar, and he did not believe that he had any right to keep that experience to himself.

At a time when a gulf seemed to be widening between the most living elements in the modern world and the Church, when those men whose passion for scientific research or for the advancement of man was most intense were turning away from the Catholic faith, Père Teilhard had met with an experience that was directly contrary.

Few men in his generation have shared so deeply and with such passion in the hopes, the efforts, the boundless ambitions of his time. There was no field of thought or action in which he found himself a stranger. But while the appreciation of earthly values was turning so many others away from the religion of their childhood, Père Teilhard's faith, with its roots deep in the past of a Christian family, and humbly maintained in strict loyalty to the observances of his Order, was confirmed by that same appreciation. The modern world, as a vital experience had shown him, had need of Jesus Christ, and could be saved only by Jesus Christ.

Such was Père Teilhard's message, as old as Christianity, but lived with such intensity that it was as though he had himself discovered it. In 1955, some weeks before his death, he wrote to one of his superiors in a memorandum that we might perhaps regard as his final testament, 'In me,' he wrote, 'by pure chance the proportions being favourable, the fusion was effected spontaneously.' The experiment had been made 'on too small a scale to spread explosively, but at the same time it is sufficient to establish that such an explosion is possible, and that sooner or later the chain-reaction will get under way . . . For the truth has only to appear once in one single mind to ensure that nothing can ever prevent it from spreading to everything and setting everything ablaze'.

He burned with ardour to communicate this message to all, in season and out of season, careless of risk and caution. In the first place he communicated it by the influence that radiated from his life. All those who came close to him, were it only on a single occasion, are unanimous: a fascinating power of attraction emanated from his person. It was not simply the charm of an unrivalled intelligence, an almost universal culture, a most rare gift for personal relations—it was much more the contagious force of a faith, the all-powerful attraction of a conqueror.

To Nietzsche's reproach that Christians did not behave as though they had been saved, Père Teilhard's mere existence was sufficient answer. He gave witness to the victory of Jesus Christ, and in unmistakable fashion it was manifest that he had been saved.

Few men have had so many friends, so diverse and so faithful. To all, believers and unbelievers alike, he appeared as a witness to Jesus Christ.

Père Teilhard exercised perfect discretion in his personal relationships, and not many of us realized how fruitful was his work as a spiritual director. Today, letters are coming not only from France, but from the Far East, from Central Africa, from America, expressing sorrow and recording gratitude. Some confess that it was to Père Teilhard that they owed their awakening or return to the faith; others acknowledge that a conversation or a retreat orientated their whole life.

When someone consulted him on a matter of faith, or explained his anxiety or doubts, Père Teilhard would never evade the question. Either in conversation or in correspondence, he would answer boldly and frankly; for he was incapable of mistrusting men or believing in their ill-will, nor could he adjust himself to the slowness that is inevitable if a formulation is to be progressively elaborated. He had little care for precision in expression, so that sometimes he gave an impression of rashness or irreverence, whereas in fact his boldness derived from an ingenuous filial freedom within a faith that had been his since his childhood, and he was completely possessed by an intrepid confidence in the victory of Jesus Christ.

The order to which he belonged watched over him with vigilant care, and called upon him for some severe sacrifices. He accepted this with complete loyalty, for he was incapable of resentment and incapable, too, of that human prudence that consists in leaving open one's line of retreat and sheltering from blows by only half committing oneself to the battle.

All in all, the lasting characteristic of Père Teilhard's personality seems to me to be his unvarying kindness. Himself, like all great workers, so thrifty with his time, he was ready to give hours to those who came to consult him, whether it was a student, or a Young Catholic Worker, or an old lady to whose questions there was no end. More than once I have reproached him for not protecting himself against the importunate. All he answered was simply, 'Can we ever be sure? In a conversation, in a word sometimes . . . there may just be something that will do good.'

He despaired of no one. He had a passionate faith in man, in whom he saw, as through a transparency, the active presence of Jesus Christ.

This faith in man, this unrepentant optimism, may sometimes have given a false impression. Did Père Teilhard, some asked, allow the mystery of evil and suffering its due place? Had he the sense of sin, of death, and of the Cross?

Let me, in conclusion, dispel any such doubts by reading one of the most telling passages he wrote: a prayer he composed some thirty years ago, in which he considers the supreme moment when his hour will have come.

'Now that I have found,' he wrote, 'the joy of utilizing all forms of growth to make you, or to let you, grow in me, grant that I may willingly consent to this last phase of communion in the course of which I shall possess you by diminishing in you . . .

'Grant, *when my hour comes*, that I may recognize you under the appearance of each alien or hostile force that seems bent upon destroying or uprooting me. When the signs of age begin to mark my body (and still more when they touch my mind); when the ill that is to diminish me or carry me off strikes from without or is born within me; when the painful moment comes in which I suddenly awaken to the fact that I am ill or growing old; and above all at that last moment when I feel I am losing hold of myself and am absolutely passive within the hands of the great unknown forces that have formed me; in all those dark moments, O God, grant that I may understand that it is you (provided only my faith be strong enough) who are painfully parting the fibres of my being in order to penetrate to the very marrow of my substance and bear me away within Yourself.

'The more deeply and incurably the evil is encrusted in my flesh, the more it will be You that I am harbouring—You as a loving, active principle of purification and detachment. The more the future opens before me like some dizzy abyss or dark tunnel, the more confident I may be—if I venture forward on the strength of Your word—of losing myself and surrendering myself in You, of being assimilated by your body, Jesus.

'You are the irresistible and vivifying force, O Lord, and because Yours is the energy, because, of the two of us, You are infinitely the stronger, it is on You that falls the part of consuming me in the union that should weld us together. Vouchsafe, therefore, something more precious still than the grace for which all the faithful pray. It is not enough that I should die while communicating. Teach me to treat my death as an act of communion.'[1]

It was thus that Père Teilhard prayed in Tientsin, in 1926. And now, thirty years later, his Lord has answered him. This year, in New York, in the evening of Easter Sunday, Père Teilhard sank into God.

[1] *MD*, pp. 89–90.

NOTES

ABBREVIATIONS

AM   *The Appearance of Man* (London & New York, Collins & Harper, 1965)

FM   *The Future of Man* (London & New York, Collins & Harper, 1964)

HU   *Hymn of the Universe* (London & New York, Collins & Harper, 1965)

LT   *Letters from a Traveller* (London & New York, Collins & Harper, 1962)

MD   *Le Milieu Divin* (London, Fontana Edition, 1964)

DM   *The Divine Milieu* (New York, Harper, 1960)

MM   *The Making of a Mind, Letters from a Soldier-Priest* (London & New York, Collins & Harper, 1965)

MPN   *Man's Place in Nature* (London & New York, Collins & Harper, 1966)

PM   *The Phenomenon of Man* (London & New York, Collins & Harper, 1959; revised edition 1965)

VP   *The Vision of the Past* (London & New York, Collins & Harper, 1966)

CM   *Le Coeur de la Matière* (1950, unpublished)

Énergie   *L'Énergie humaine* (1937 in *L'Énergie humaine*, Paris, Seuil, 1962)

Esquisse   Esquisse d'un univers personnel (1936 in *L'Énergie humaine*)

Introduction   Introduction à la vie chrétienne (1944, unpublished)

Écrits   Écrits du temps de la guerre (Paris, Goueset, 1965)

Multitude   'La lutte contre la multitude' (1917), in *Écrits du temps de la guerre* (1965)

AAS   Acta Apostolicae Sedis

Archives   Archives de Philosophie, 1961

Cahiers   Cahiers Pierre Teilhard de Chardin, 2, 1960

Cuénot   *Teilhard de Chardin, A Biographical Study* (London & Baltimore, Burns & Oates and Helicon Press, 1965). This is an abridged version of *Piere Teilhard de Chardin: Les Grands étages de son évolution*, by Claude Cuénot (Paris, Plon, 1958)

PG   *Patrologia Graeca* (ed. J. P. Migne)

PL   *Patrologia Latina* (ed. J. P. Migne)

QS   *Revue des Questions Scientifiques* (Louvain)

NOTE: page references to unpublished writings (duplicated or typewritten) are sometimes approximate.

NOTES

Chapter 1: The Essential Core

1 R. M. Grant, *The Letter and the Spirit* (London, 1957).

2 'Turmoil or Genesis?' in *FM*, pp. 222–3. Dr. Paul Chauchard has rightly pointed out that 'to confine oneself to *The Phenomenon of Man* and to overlook *Le Milieu Divin* would be seriously to mutilate Teilhard's thought', *L'Être selon Teilhard de Chardin* (1959), p. 19.

3 *La Pensée théologique de Teilhard de Chardin* (1961), pp. 47–8, 54, 97.

4 Roger Garaudy, *Perspectives de l'Homme* (1959), pp. 189–96.

5 'La Foi qui opère' (1918); *CM* (1950).

6 To the Abbé Henri Breuil, 9 September 1923, in *LT*, p. 87. Letter of 13 December 1918 in *MM*, p. 268.

7 To L. Zanta, 15 October 1926.

8 Quoted by Claude Aragonnès in *LT*, p. 153. To the Abbé Gaudefroy, 27 February 1927: 'For me, scientific research and "mystical" effort are but one single complex force that irresistibly insists on extending its influence.' In a lecture on 'Life and the Planets' (Peking, 10 March 1945), he commented with pleasure on 'the growing importance which leading thinkers of all denominations are beginning to attach to the phenomenon of mysticism' (*FM*, p. 123).

9 'Science et Christ (ou Analyse et Synthèse)', lecture given on 27 February 1921.

10 8 December 1939, 9 May 1950 (Cuénot, p. 288). As early as 23 April 1910 he was writing to his parents from Ore Place, 'Theology gives you a great deal to think about, and I am beginning to feel that there are so many other questions, less entertaining perhaps, but more vital than the sciences, that I am wondering whether some day I will not change my line.'

11 26 May 1925.

12 To L. Zanta, 3 October 1923.

13 18 January 1936.

14 21 January 1936 in *LT*, p. 219. 27 February 1927, to the Abbé Gaudefroy: 'I feel that I have a message to give, in an attempt

to make men realize the true magnitude and the true nature of the realities, to which, drugged by conventional ideas, their eyes are closed.'

15 August 1936. Cf. 'Le Phénomène spirituel' (1937): 'The definitive discovery of the spiritual phenomenon is tied up with the analysis (which science will undoubtedly undertake some day) of the "mystical phenomenon", in other words of the love of God.'

16 26 August 1923, in *LT*, p. 86. 'I let myself get caught up in the game when I geologize. But the moment I stop to reflect I am vividly aware that this occupation (though vital for me in so far as it is a part of the "total gesture" of my life) is by itself of no ultimate interest.'

17 7 October, 1948, in *LT*, p. 299. Letter of 16 August 1951.

18 *Énergie* (1937), *Introduction* (1944).

19 Letter of 25 January 1955 (Cuénot, p. 367).

20 Cf. Abbé Paul Grenet, *Teilhard de Chardin* (1961), p. 52. *Le Coeur du Problème* (8 September 1949): 'Addressing myself to those who, better placed than I am, have the task of directly or indirectly guiding the Church, I am trying candidly . . . to make them see where, exactly, lies the cause of the distress we are suffering from.'

21 Cuénot, p. 272. It is equally mistaken to speak of clandestine or semi-clandestine writings. They were always carefully signed and dated.

22 In either case they bore the reference: 'conscience'. Some papers were written expressly to ask those 'who have the right to guide *him*' to fulfil their duty of criticism and correction. He tries 'to make it easier for them' ('Mon Univers', 1918). 'This,' he says on another occasion, 'is the point on which I particularly want approval or correction.' With the intention of stirring up scandal, a periodical published extracts from a document that was in fact simply a memorandum addressed by Père Teilhard in 1936 to Mgr Constantini, at that time Apostolic Delegate in China. 'I had written it at the direct request of the ecclesiastical authority (to which in fact I sent it) in order to formulate more exactly, for the use of the Propaganda, certain ideas expressed in conversation at the Apostolic Delegation in Peking' (December 1936; Cf. letter to the Abbé Gaudefroy, 11 October 1936).

23 11 April 1951.

24 Typical of this is his exchange of views with Maurice Blondel in December 1919 (*Archives*, pp. 125–56).

25 Letter of 20 October 1924 (Clermont-Ferrand).

26 Letter of 26 February 1933. Cf. letters of 22 January and 18 June 1916 in *MM*, pp. 91, 100–1.

27 28 December 1933: 'All I ask is to be given advice.' 25 July 1935 (Cuénot, p. 164): he expresses the hope that 'by mutual control or correction on so wide a basis, it will be possible for us to extract the really orthodox elements and formulatas from the rather dazzling complex'. To a younger friend (22 November 1936) he communicates his thoughts 'in the hope that you will help me to see things clearly, and will pick out the elements that can be integrated into the *summa* that professionals will some day have to find a way of constructing.'

28 Letter of 13 July 1925. Père Louis Barjon has noted 'the profound humility and diffidence that are combined in Père Teilhard with an unshakeable certainty of the legitimacy not so much of what he says as of what he is working for. He is ready himself to endorse such criticisms as could be levelled against him. There is no self-conceit in him'.

29 He realizes that a particular essay has not 'quite come off'; but, he explains, 'I have had no hesitation in following the gospel precept', of not separating too soon the wheat from the tares, 'which governs all search for the truth and all scientific progress': 'l'Union Créatrice' (1917). Of another paper he said, a little later, that he regretted its 'bitter flavour'.

30 Letter of 1 February 1919; Cf. letter of 11 October 1918, in *MM*, pp. 281, 247.

31 'L'Étoffe de l'Univers' (14 July 1953).

32 M. Teilhard-Chambon, Introduction to *MM*, p. 36.

33 'Comment je vois' (1948), preface.

34 *Esquisse* (1936), Letter of 2 February 1920. Cf. letter of 5 August 1917: 'It's disappointing to realize how impoverished and reduced your ideas become when you try to fit them into a common plan' (*MM*, p. 199).

35 É. Boné, s.j., *Pierre Teilhard de Chardin*, *QS*, 20 January 1956. Cf. letter of 18 September 1916: 'We must pray . . . that Our Lord may keep us both humble and fearless' (*MM*, p. 128).

36 Letter of 8 October 1933. Cf. letter of 13 July 1925: He wishes to combine 'with sovereign respect for what is the truth revealed to his own mind, a sort of loving obedience to the truth that lies 'outside each one of us in the whole body of the Church'.

37 Letter of 18 September 1916, in *MM*, p. 128.

Chapter 2: Le Milieu Divin

1 21 June 1921.

2 To Père Victor Fontoynont, 15 March 1916.

3 In the spring of 1925 (Cuénot, pp. 81–2). These are referred to also in the tributes from Etienne Borne, Henri-Irénée Marrou, and Marcel Légaut, written at the time of Père Teilhard's death. He gave another retreat to *normaliens* at Gentilly, at Shrovetide, 1928: letter of 14 February 1928.

4 Letter of 25 September 1917 (*MM*, p. 204).

5 *LT*, p. 133. Cf. below, Chapter 20, p. 265.

6 Letter (Cuénot, p. 70). Cf. George Vass, s.j., 'Teilhard de Chardin and the Inward Vision' in the *Heythrop Journal*, 2 (1961), pp. 237–49: 'A reading of *Le Milieu Divin* brings the inescapable conviction that it was written straight out of personal prayer by the author.'

7 On 29 June 1928, Père Charles was very definitely in favour of publication, although he noted 'several points that need to be elucidated'. A year later, he wrote that the book was going to be printed (letter of 16 September 1929, in *LT*, p. 159). On 29 September 1929, Père Teilhard wrote to Père Valensin, 'Charles tells me that *Le Milieu Divin* is going to the printers at any moment now (*Lessianum*). I hardly dare to believe it yet. But what I do know is that all the official reports have been favourable.' Again, on 9 February 1931, he writes from New York, 'I saw Charles before I left, and he gave me the latest report on *Le Milieu Divin*. Some revisions are asked for (I shall try to get them done this year), subject to which it has been accepted.' Père Charles turned out to be over-optimistic. Cf. letters to the Abbé Gaudefroy, 7 October 1929, 14 December 1929, 22 August 1930, 20 March 1932, 22 May 1932.

8 At Christmas 1932, he wrote from Paris: 'Saw Père Levie here, who gave me the two final reports on *Le Milieu Divin*, both very favourable, except (in one of them) a request for a more accurate explanation of 'the meaning of the Cross', which I could easily meet. A shame that it should be stopped by Rome's intervention. Still, perhaps it is better . . .'

9 For example, Père Benoît Émonet (letter of 14 February 1928).

10 *Archives de Philosophie* (1961).

11 Cuénot, (French edition) p. 95, to the Abbé Gaudefroy, 31 December 1926.

12 Cf. letter of 29 June 1916 on the Heart of Jesus, 'Master of the interior life' (*MM*, p. 107), etc.; *MD*, p. 43 (*DM*, p. 11), 'this essay on life or on inward vision'. Even when his thought is most directed towards theory, what it aims at is 'the correct balance of *his* interior life', 'Mon Univers', p. 2.

13 From start to finish *Le Milieu Divin* is more 'practical' than 'theoretical'. Exhortation plays a part even in Père Teilhard's writings of a more scientific character. Cf. *Esquisse*: 'Instead of standing on the shore and convincing ourselves that the ocean cannot hold us up, we should set out boldly on its waters . . . It seems impossible to us that a human life can find its joy in deliberately losing itself in universal Being. Let us hazard this gesture, etc.' We shall see later, in Chapter 16, how this practical character fits in with theory. Cf. 'La foi qui opère', quoted in *HU*, p. 131. 'L'union créatrice', p. 15.

14 'The Grand Option' (1939), in *FM*, p. 59. 'The New Spirit' (1942), in *FM*, p. 83: 'To understand the spiritual events which are so convulsing the age we live in we need to be constantly looking back (I shall repeat this) to their common origin—the discovery of Time.'

15 Letter of October 1952: he regrets that, in apologetics, some writers have over-emphasized the theory of the expanding universe: 'supposing', he adds, 'the theory should soon collapse'.

16 'Mon Univers' (1924), 'Le Milieu Mystique'. Address at the wedding of Jean Teilhard d'Eyry and Odette Bacot, 1928: 'Creation never stops.' There are allusions to the theory of 'the general expansion of the Universe' and to the vision of 'an exploding Universe' in 'La Convergence de l'Univers' (1951), p. 1, and in 'Comment je vois' (1918), n. 3.

17 'The New Spirit', in *FM*, p. 83, 'Comment je crois' (1934), pp. 6, 11. 'Le Christianisme dans le Monde' (1933). 'Time and space', says P. Couderc in *L'Expansion de l'Univers* (1950), have become for us 'actors in the drama of the Universe'.

18 'L'Incroyance moderne, cause profonde et remède' (in *La Vie intellectuelle*, 25 October 1923). 'Foundations' (1926) in *VP*, pp. 127–8.

19 Letter of 28 September 1950 (Cuénot, p. 291–2); 'La Montée de l'Autre' (Peking, 20 January 1942), p. 13.

20 'The New Spirit', in *FM*, p. 84–85, 'La Mystique de la Science', 2, 'La Découverte du Temps' (*Études*, March 1939, vol. 238, pp. 730–2).

21 Cf. Louis Armand and Michel Drancourt, *Plaidoyer pour l'avenir* (1961), pp. 9–23. Mgr de Solages, 'La Mutation pré-

sente de la civilisation et l'adaptation de l'homme' (*Documentation Cath.*, 7 January 1962).

22 *Énergie*, 'Man's Place in Nature', in *VP*, p. 176.

23 'La Crise présente' (*Études*, 20 October 1937, p. 163). 'Mon Univers' (1918).

24 Cf. Fr. Russo, *Technique et Conscience religieuse* (1961), p. 25: 'Thus technical evolution is seen to take over from and continue, in a new way, biological evolution.'

25 'Le Christianisme dans le Monde' (1933).

26 Later, in 'Some reflections on the spiritual repercussion of the atom bomb' (*Études*, September 1946), Père Teilhard was to repeat this even more emphatically. When 'the first artificers of the atom bomb . . . got to their feet after the explosion was over, it was Mankind who stood up with them, instilled with a *new* sense of power . . . capable of development to *an indefinite extent*' (*FM*, pp. 141, 143).

27 'Faith in Man', address to the French section of the World Congress of Faiths, 8 March 1947 (*FM*, pp. 186–7). Cf. 'La Vie Cosmique', p. 2: 'The crisis, that always comes with new ideas'. 'Trois Choses que je vois' (1948), p. 2: 'the spiritual storm that has overtaken us'.

28 'Foundations', in *VP*, pp. 140–1. 'L'incroyance moderne'. 'La Crise présente'.

29 'Monde moderne, Monde chrétien', written in answer to a questionnaire in *Esprit*, 1946 (no. 125, p. 254) *MD*, p. 45 (*DM*, p. 13). 'Mon Univers' (1918): 'To judge from myself, the great temptation of our age is (and will continue increasingly to be) the belief that the World of Life and of human endeavour is greater, more immediate, more mysterious and more living than the God of Scripture.'

30 *MD*, pp. 47, 154. (*DM*, pp. 15, 137). See Chapter 6, pp. 72–8.

31 *MD*, pp. 43, 46. (*DM*, pp. 11, 15).

32 Cf. Louis Bouyer, *Introduction to Spirituality* (New York, 1961), pp. 21–3. Albert Valensin, s.j., 'L'object propre de la théologie spirituelle', *Nouvélle revue théologique*, 54 (1927), pp. 161–91. This does not rule out any distinction in method: cf. Père Maurice Guiliani, in *Christus*, 31, pp. 408–10.

33 Ephesians 4. 4–6.

34 'Le Prêtre' (1918), quoted in *HU*, p. 152.

35 Letter of 8 December 1918, in *MM*, p. 263.

36 To L. Zanta, 12 December 1923.

37 E. Boné, s.j., 'Pierre Teilhard de Chardin', *QS*, 20 January 1956.

38 'La Maîtrise de Monde et le Règne de Dieu.' 'Le Prêtre.' Cf. letter of 8 September 1916 in *MM*, p. 122.

39 'The Formation of the Noosphere', in *FM*, p. 173.

40 'La Mystique de la Science' (*Études*, 20 March 1939). Jesuit congress at Versailles, August 1947.

41 'L'Esprit de la Terre' (1931).

42 *Énergie* (1937).

43 *LT*, p. 363. Cf. Pope Pius XII, Allocution of 28 September 1958: 'The scientist's research generally culminates in adoration.' (Acta of H. H. Pius XII, 20, 1958, p. 427.)

44 'Réflexions sur le bonheur' (28 December 1943), *Cahiers*, p. 69.

45 *CM* (1950).

46 Letter of 7 November 1926: 'What I intend to do is to confine myself to the realm of a moral attitude, vigorously presented but still incontestably Christian' (*LT*, p. 134).

47 Letter to M. Teillard-Chambon, 29 January 1955 (*LT*, p. 361). Similarly, *Le Coeur de la Matière* might have been called a third version of 'Mon Univers'.

48 'Le Christique' (1955), introduction. He wished this last time to present it 'in its mature form', though he admitted that 'the expression had less freshness and exuberance than when the vision first came to him'. Even so, he wished to share it 'with the same passion'.

49 Letter of 13 October 1933.

50 Letter to Mgr Bruno de Solages. Cf. George Vass s.j., loc. cit., p. 249: 'the popularity of his writings would seem to suggest that such a "new devotion" can be the faithful expression at least of a modern spiritual desire: to be enchanted and carried away by the very discovery of Christ in whom we all subsist (cf. Col. 1. 17) and with whom we shall be one (cf. John 17. 21). Teilhard's attempt represented by *Le Milieu Divin* was worth while. It is the testimony of a great inward Christian experience.'

The Dutch hierarchy's pastoral letter on the meaning of the Council expresses clearly the problem envisaged by Père Teilhard: 'Technical discoveries are opening up a new dimension for our life on earth and are confronting us with the problem of discovering how secular work, which is a particular form of the Catholic vocation, fits into the perspective of "the one thing that is necessary", without committing ourselves to purely worldly attitudes.'

Chapter 3: Three Main Lines of Force

1 This procedure, I believe, will enable us to enter into the spirit in which Père Teilhard wrote; for him 'the important thing in life is not to circumscribe the Real . . . but to determine, within that Real, certain sure lines of progress and arrangement' (Letter of 17 November 1947).

2 *Ermites du Saccidananda* (1956), p. 22. Cf. Hans Urs von Balthasar, *Science, Religion and Christianity* (tr. Hilda Graef). Robert Guelluy, *Vie de foi et tâches terrestres* (1960), p. 40: 'the Universe . . . was created for the Church'. See also J. Maritain, *Raison et raisons* (1948), pp. 281–2. Jean Lacroix, *Historie et Mystère* (1962), p. 7, with its warning against a common form of humanism that would appear to hold that man's destiny is exhausted in his historical development.

3 'Mass on the World' (1923), in *HU*, p. 31: 'We must . . . come little by little to feel that the individual shapes of all we have laid hold on are melting away in our hands, until finally we are at grips with the *single essence* of all subsistencies and all unions.' (Ibid., p. 70.)

4 The epilogue to *Le Milieu Divin* bears this title (p. 130) (*DM*, p. 133). Later, in 'Man's Place in the universe' (1942) in *VP*, p. 216, he says that 'the importance of spiritual forces of expectation and hope must continually be recognized more explicitly'.

5 'La Vie cosmique' (1916), quoted in *HU*, p. 133.

6 *MD*, p. 151. (*DM* pp. 134–5) 'Trois choses que je vois' (1948): 'The Parousia (or Christ's return in glory) has a central place in the heaven of the Christian world, even though, as the centuries of expectation roll by, it is easily forgotten.' Letter of 13 October 1933: 'Do you believe that Heaven and the Kingdom of God should be seen not as a final term of the *Historic* but rather as a way of entering the domain of the Metaphysical?'

7 Letter of 17 November 1947.

8 St. Augustine, *City of God*, Bk. 22, c. 30, n. 5.

9 To his parents, 8 October 1911. During the war, in 1916, he read or re-read the *Apologia*: 'One of those books (the only sort that should be written), in which a life is laid bare', he wrote to Père Fontoynont, on 15 March. See above. Appendix 1, p. 243.

10 Letter to a friend, 13 October 1933. 'It is an essay,' he says,

'that I have been turning over in my mind (or, more exactly, have been praying) for a long time.' The phrase 'Sacrament of the World' had already occurred in 'Mass on the World' (*HU*, p. 26).

11 *MD*, p. 64. (*DM*, p. 33) 'Le Milieu mystique' (1917): 'Everything concentrates upon one single point, on one Person: and that Person, Jesus, is yours . . . Every presence makes me feel that you are close to me; every contact is that of your hand; every compulsion transmits to me a vibration of your will . . .' Letter of 20 September 1915. 'Don't we know that the real worth of our existence will ultimately be judged by the *degree of faithfulness* and obedience we have shown in submission to the divine will, *no matter what*, apart from that, may have been the brilliant or lowly function we have served?' (*MM*, p. 70).

12 Letter of 22 October 1925: 'And, after all, only one thing matters, surely, "to see" God wherever one looks?' A Protestant writer, Pastor Georges Crespy, with more insight than a number of Catholic critics, has observed that 'it is not difficult to recognize the Ignatian inspiration of the *Milieu Divin*'. 'Le Christ du Père Teilhard de Chardin'. *Revue de Théologie et de Philosophie*, 1958, p. 297. On the Ignatian phrase, see E. Iserloh, 'Gott finden in allen Dingen' in *Trier. Theolog. Zeitschrift*, 66 (1957), pp. 65–9. Cf. letter of 12 February 1919: 'He who, when seen by the eyes of faith, animates the whole complex of exterior events and interior experiences' (*MM*, p. 282).

13 *MD*, p. 73. (*DM*, p. 42) Letter of 12 September 1925: 'We come to recognize that nothing there is contact with is the true consistence we are looking for, and that it is impossible for us to make contact with what we now see to be the true consistence of the world: *Beati qui non viderunt et crediderunt*.'

14 When Père Teilhard was finishing *Le Milieu Divin* it was thus that he defined its object: letter of 31 December 1926. Cf. St. John of the Cross, *Spiritual Canticle*, st. 23.

15 Cf. *Multitude* (1917), quoted in *HU*, pp. 124–5.

16 Letter of 15 April 1923, in *LT*, p. 66. *CM* introduction: 'the progressive expansion, within every being and every event, of a mysterious inner clarity that transfigures them'.

17 *MD*, p. 49 note. (*DM*, p. 17, n.) In 1917 he defined the *milieu mystique* as 'the universal milieu, higher than that in which the ordinary life of appearance wanders restlessly'.

18 Letter of 13 December 1918, in connexion with Schuré (*MM*, p. 268). To L. Zanta, 10 January 1927.

19 *CM*, p. 2.

20 Earlier, 8 May 1911, Père Teilhard had written to his father: 'God is not sparing you losses and cares; but from all this, I think, it is still He who will emerge even greater for us, imposing himself on us the more as the rest disappears, the only one who can take the place of everything and reconstruct everything.'

21 This expression, doubtless derived from reading Blondel, had appeared earlier in 'The Spiritual Power of Matter' (8 August 1919, in *HU*, p. 65). Letter of 27 August 1931 (*LT*, p. 183). To the Abbé Gaudefroy, 31 December 1923. To L. Zanta, 24 January 1929. Letter of 14 August, 1918: 'As it says in the Gospel for the feast, we shall try . . . to attach ourselves ever more firmly to the possession of, and, in a way, the indwelling of the *Unum Necessarium*'; we find it again on 14 August, 1918, 1 January 1919, and 14 April 1919 (*MM*, pp. 226, 269, 292).

22 *MD*, 120. (*DM*, p. 98). Here there is complete agreement with Pascal, with whom Teilhard is at one in saying, 'Nothing that is not God can answer my expectation.'

23 To Max Bégouën, 27 April 1929 (*Cahiers*, p. 21). To the Abbé Gaudefroy, 12 November 1926. 'La Vie cosmique' (1916): 'Incapable of being mingled or confounded with the participating being whom He sustains, inspires and links with Himself, God is at the birth, the growth, and the ultimate end of all things.' (Quoted in *FM*, p. 304.)

24 Letter of 14 April 1919 (*MM*, pp. 291–2). Cf. Retreat (1941): 'the exercise of the omnipresence of transfiguration'.

25 Cf. 'Le Christianisme dans le Monde' (1933). Letter of 29 March 1917 (*MM*, p. 190).

26 *MD*, p. 73. (*DM*, p. 42) To Père Auguste Valensin. 15 July 1929: 'I feel that I have reached the state of being just a force —that presses on, without really knowing where, without taking pleasure in anything—but with supreme faith in the Spirit—and in Unity.' *Multitude:* 'to be pure of heart means to love God above all things and at the same time, to see him everywhere in all things'. (Quoted in *HU*, p. 124.)

27 To L. Zanta, 14 December 1929 (*MD*, p. 114 *DM*, p. 91).

28 Cf. *MD*, p. 100 n. (*DM*, p. 75 n.): 'the basic problem of the use of creatures'.

29 *MD*, p. 155. (*DM*, p. 138)

30 *MD*, p. 103 (*DM*, p. 78) (Teilhard's italics). 'The Pyx' (1916): 'God . . . is the heart of everything' (*HU*, p. 54). 'Le Prêtre': 'My God, you who are so much more remote in your

immensity and so much deeper in the intimacy of your indwelling than all things else.' (Quoted in *HU*, p. 135.) Similarly, in *CM*. Père Teilhard sought for what would be at once a 'way out' and a 'focus' for the universe. 'L'Union créatrice' (on the influence of the Incarnate Word): 'At the heart that is common to all things, it shines like a centre that is infinitely intimate and at the same time infinitely remote.'

31 'Christ in the World of Matter' (Douaumont, October 1916), 'The Pyx', in *HU*, pp. 54–5. Père Teilhard included this as an appendix to *Le Coeur de la Matière*.

32 *MD*, pp. 64–7 (*DM*, pp. 33–40), 'The Christian perfection of human endeavour'.

33 *MD*, p. 49 n. (*DM*, p. 17): a timely warning against 'the least admixture of what may be called Pelagianism'.

34 *MD*, p. 71. (*DM*, p. 40)

35 'Le Milieu mystique.' Letter of 7 November 1915 on 'abandonment without reserve to the divine will' (*MM*, p. 79). Letter of 13 October 1916: 'The only essential thing, surely, is to cling to the divine action, ever present, and the more to be adored the more our destiny outruns our anticipation and control' (*MM*, p. 132).

36 *MD*, p. 73. (*DM*, p. 46) 'L'Union créatrice', p. 13: in the spiritual man 'the need to act and assert himself changes imperceptibly into a yearning to submit and surrender'.

37 Returning to what has always been the symbolic life-blood of living faith, Père Teilhard saw each of these sets of forces symbolized in the two species of the Eucharist. Letter of 26 August 1923: 'the bread symbolizing appropriately what creation succeeds in producing, the wine (blood) what creation causes to be lost in exhaustion and suffering in the course of its effort' (*LT*, p. 86). 'Mass on the World' 'Receive, O Lord, this all-embracing host which your whole creation, moved by your magnetism, offers you at the dawn of this new day. This bread, our toil, is of itself, I know, but an immense fragmentation; this wine, our pain, is no more, I know, than a draught that dissolves. Yet in the very depths of this formless mass you have implanted—and this I am sure of, for I sense it—a desire, irresistible, hallowing, which makes us cry out, believer and unbeliever alike, "Lord, make us *one*" ' (in *HU*, p. 20).

38 *MD*, p. 115. (*DM*, p. 92, see also p. 114). See also p. 134. Letter of 6 January 1917 on 'the pain of isolation' (*MM*, p. 163).

39 Letter of 28 August 1918 (*MM*, p. 230).

40 *MD*, p. 115. cf. p. 142. (*DM*, pp. 92–3. cf. p. 123). Letter of
7 March 1954: 'Patience! Even so I ought to be able to manage
to establish myself a little better in the divine Milieu' (Cuénot,
p. 309).

41 *MD*, p. 79. (*DM*, p. 50) To Max and Simone Bégouën, 29 December 1947: '. . . The Christian principle that nothing in the
world is really of value except what happens in the end, after
we have done our best' (*LT*, p. 296).

42 Père Teilhard was fond of this remark, originally Léon Bloy's,
which he heard from Pierre Termier. It held for him the essence of his doctrine of passivities. To Joseph Teilhard de
Chardin, from Peking, 13 November 1943: 'These are just the
years on which I was counting so much, and I see them slip
by while I get practically nothing done. "Everything that happens is adorable", Termier was fond of saying. Properly understood, that idea sums up my whole religion.' To the Abbé
Breuil, from Saint-Germain-en-Laye, where he was convalesc-
ing after a serious illness, 23 September 1947: ' "Everything
that happens is adorable", Termier was always saying: but
that necessitates giving to "Christic energy" its real meaning
and its full reality in the Universe' (*LT*, pp. 288, 294).

43 Letter of 29 June 1916 (*MM*, p. 107). Cf. John 21. No principle is more rooted in tradition than this, nor more necessary
to bear in mind today. Cf. Isaac de l'Étoile, Sermon 47: 'The
voice of the Word determines every event' (*PL*, 194, 1181C).

44 Letter of 11 January 1919, in *MM*, p. 275.

45 *MD*, p. 71. 'La signification et la valeur constructrice de la
souffrance', in *Trait d'Union*, the periodical of the Catholic
Union of the Sick, 1 April 1933.

46 *MD*, pp. 82, 89. (*DM*, pp. 54, 61). To M. Teilhard-Chambon,
13 November 1916: 'Death surrenders us totally to God; it
makes us enter into him; we must, in return, surrender ourselves to death with absolute love and self-abandonment—since,
when death comes, all we can do is to surrender ourselves completely to the domination and guidance of God' (*MM*, p. 145).
The original 'source' of *Le Milieu Divin* is without doubt St.
Paul's words in Acts 17.28, 'in him we live and move and have
our being'.

Chapter 4: Christian Optimism

1 'Mise en valeur du Père Teilhard de Chardin', in *Le Figaro littéraire*, 27 December 1958, p. 2. Similarly, Jacques Mettra, in *Travaux et Jours* (Beirut, 1961), p. 23.

2 Claude Cuénot has rightly noted Père Teilhard's 'refusal to see human evil, baseness and hypocrisy': *L'Éducation nationale*, 12 (May 1955, p. 12). His refusal, however, to see these things, that is to say to attribute them to any particular person, had nothing in common with ignorance of them and the misconceptions it gives rise to.

3 *Trois Vertus-Clefs* (1960) pp. 73–4.

4 *MD*, pp. 107–10. (*DM*, pp. 82–7) Étienne Borne put his finger on the ultimate basis of his optimism when he said that 'he lived in the Parousia': 'Ce que je dois au Père Teilhard', in *Cahiers*, 2, p. 160. Cf. G. Crespy, op. cit., Chapter VI.

5 Letter of 22 August 1915 (*MM*, p. 68). Only a draft was written, and this has not survived.

6 *MD*, p. 81. (*DM*, p. 53). *HU*, p. 31.

7 'Multitude.' Cf. letter of 13 February 1917: 'I didn't know, I'm ashamed to say, that Schopenhauer had already spoken of the pain of individuation.'

8 Letter of 24 March 1917 (*MM*, p. 189).

9 On the meaning of *Dukkha*, the first of the 'four noble truths', see Walpola Rahula, *L'Enséignement du Bouddha* (1961), pp. 37–42.

10 *Esquisse* (1936), *PM*, pp. 226, 313. Cf. M. Barthélemy-Madaule, *Introduction à la méthode chez Bergson et Teilhard de Chardin*: For Teilhard, the individual 'taken in isolation, is the dwelling-place of anguish . . . The descent into self of *Le Milieu Divin* is characterized, indeed, by dizziness and darkness'. In *Bergson et nous* (1959), pp. 215–16.

11 Preface to *l'Énergie spirituelle de la souffrance*, by Marguerite-Marie Teilhard de Chardin (1951), p. 9.

12 Letter of 6 August 1944 (Cuénot, p. 246).

13 Letter of 12 September 1923 (*LT*, p. 88).

14 He was quoting the Lama in Kipling's *Kim*. 'It was civilisation that overawed the Lama. In my case, on the contrary, it is the immense mass of undisciplined human powers that overwhelms me' (*LT*, p. 70).

15 'Mass on the World': 'in our heritage of sorrow and hope,

passed down to us through the ages, there is no yearning more desolate than that which makes us weep with vexation and desire as we stand in the midst of the Presence which hovers about nameless and impalpable and is indwelling in all things. *Si forte attrectent eum,* if *haply they might feel after him and find him'.* Acts 17.27 (*HU*, pp. 24–5).

16 Cf.–the evidence of Père Pierre Leroy, s.j., in *Père Teilhard de Chardin tel que je l'ai connu* (1958).

17 Albert Schweitzer, *My Life and Thought,* (London, 1964), p. 279.

18 *The Satin Slipper.* Cf. 'Man's Place in the Universe' (Peking, 15 November 1942) in *VP,* p. 233, end: 'The characteristics of the crisis we are going through are not those of a break-up, but of a birth. Let us not be frightened therefore of what at first sight might look like a final and universal discord. What we are suffering is only the price, the annunciation, the preliminary phase of our unanimity.' Such a view, however, is possible only 'in the light of a general science of the world that allows their due place, in a third infinite (the infinite of complexity), to spiritual energies'. *FM,* p. 90. 'La Convergence de l'Univers' (1951), pp. 5–6.

19 Letter of 6 August 1915 (*MM,* p. 62).

20 *Multitude.*

21 To the Abbé Gaudefroy, 1 March 1924. To the Abbé Breuil, 26 May 1924: 'If truth is to advance, those who love it must suffer. This has ever been so.'

22 *PM,* appendix, p. 313. On the cosmic dimensions of Père Teilhard's sense of anguish, one should read Madame Barthélemy-Madaule, *Teilhard de Chardin, Marxism, Existentialism*; 'A Confrontation', in the *International Philosophical Quarterly* 1 (1961), pp. 657–66: 'Teilhard's whole construction is thought out in function of the anxiety of our day' (p. 658).

23 'Réflexions sur le bonheur' (1942), *Cahiers,* 2, p. 69.

24 'Un phénomène de contre-évolution en biologie, ou la peur de l'existence' (1940). Letter to Mme C. M. Haardt.

25 'A Note on Progress' (1920), in *FM,* p. 11. He reacted against the illusion of those minds that 'are inclined to slide gently into the belief that there never was in the past or will be in the future anything new under the sun' (*PM,* p. 98).

26 Letters of 4 July 1920 and 8 October 1933. To M. and S. Bégouën, 11 January 1941 (*LT,* p. 276).

27 Included in *The Appearance of Man,* pp. 208–73. Letter of 4

May 1931 (*LT*, p. 176) and 5 January 1954 (*LT*, p. 349). To the Abbé Gaudefroy, 22 May 1932. N. M. Wildiers, introduction to *L'Avenir de l'Homme*, p. 17.

28 *Esquisse.*

29 To the Abbé Breuil, 27 November 1923. Letters of 29 August 1916 and 5 September 1919 (*MM*, pp. 122, 306). 'Transformation . . . en l'Homme du mécanisme de l'évolution' (19 November 1954).

30 Ibid. One could even show that his extraordinary gift of sympathy and kindness to all were very largely acquired qualities. On one occasion he went so far as to say, in a significant outburst, 'instinctively, I would much rather have an earth full of animals than one inhabited by men' (*MM*, p. 202).

31 To M. Teillard-Chambon, 22 November 1952 (*LT*, p. 334), commenting on the film *Life begins tomorrow*. Cf. *HU*, pp. 109–10. 'The End of the Species' (1952) in *FM*, pp. 302–3.

32 To Père François Russo, 21 November 1952.

33 To the same, 21 November 1952.

34 'Le Christique', p. 10.

35 'Mon Univers' (1924). *FM*, p. 308. To Marcel Brion (*Les Nonvelles littéraires*, 11 January 1951). To the Abbé Breuil, 18 March 1934 (*LT*, p. 202). Hence the expression 'dramatic optimism' applied to Père Teilhard by M. Barthélemy–Madaule, *International Philosophical Quarterly*, 1, pp. 648–67. See Chapter 10 for a more detailed treatment.

36 *PM* appendix, pp. 311–13. 'La Convergence de l'Univers' (1951), p. 5.

37 *MD*, p. 78. (*DM*, p. 49).

38 Letter of 12 July 1918 (*MM*, p. 213).

39 Cf. letter of 6 January 1917 (*MM*, p. 163).

40 To M. and S. Bégouën, 10 April 1934 (*LT*, p. 202).

41 Jaques Madaule, too, saw this clearly: in 'Qu-est-ce que la vie?', *Semaine des intellectuels catholiques* (1957), p. 206.

42 Letter of 11 May 1923 (*LT*, p. 70). The italicizing of *issue* in this quotation is ours. So closely did Père Teilhard feel that he was a prisoner in this world, that he was obsessed by the quest for an issue, a transition or emergence, answer, or way out. H. Mondor has pointed out Claudel's obsession with the notion of *flight*: *Claudel plus intime* (1960), p. 54.

43 'The Grand Option', in *FM*, p. 50. *MD*, p. 151 (*DM*, p. 134): 'Expectation, anxious, collective and operative expectation of an end of the world, that is to say of an issue for the world', that is 'the supreme Christian function'. *PM*, p. 233. See *Man*,

p. 120, on 'the approach of a way out through which all that is most precious in what we have worked for may escape for ever from the threats of a total death lying ahead of us.'

44 'L'Atomisme de l'Esprit' (Peking, 13 September 1941), p. 25.

45 *NPN*, p. 120. *PM*, p. 254. 'L'Esprit de la Terre'. 'Comment je crois': 'The more man is man, the more can he give himself only to what he loves: and ultimately he loves only what is indestructible.' See Chapter 16.

46 'Le sens de l'Espèce chez l'Homme' (31 May 1949).

47 'The Formation of the Noosphere', in *FM*, p. 180. 'The Grand Option', ibid., p. 62, etc.

48 'The Grand Option', 2, 'The possible paths': 'Is the Universe utterly pointless, or are we to accept that it has a meaning, a future, an issue?' . . . 'On this fundamental question Mankind is already virtually divided into two camps' (*FM*, p. 42).

49 Letter of 27 May 1923 (Cuénot, p. 45). Leroy, p. 27. We shall see later, in Chapter 16, the different meanings he gives to the word 'faith'.

50 'Foundations' (1929) in *VP*, pp. 116–62, 'The 'conic' transposition of action' (1942), in *FM*, p. 89. See Chapter 13.

51 Preface to *l'Énergie spirituelle de la souffrance* (1951). 'Mass on the World' in *HU*, p. 31. 'La Foi qui opère' (1918).

52 *MD*, p. 78. (*DM*, p. 50) Cf. Letter of 23 August 1916, written from the Verdun sector: 'I don't know what sort of monument the country will later put up on Froideterre Hill to commemorate the great battle. There's only one that would be appropriate: a great figure of Christ. Only the image of the Crucified can sum up, express and relieve all the horror, and beauty, all the hope and deep mystery, in such an avalanche of conflict and sorrows'. (*MM*, p. 119).

53 *Esquisse.*

54 'La Foi qui opère', quoted in *HU*, p. 138.

55 *MD*, To Joseph Teilhard de Chardin, 5 September 1936: 'The only way of making life bearable again is to love and adore that which, beneath everything, animates and directs it' (*LT*, p. 227).

56 'Le Milieu mystique.' Cf. Yves de Montcheuil, s.j., *Mélanges théologiques*, p. 361: 'Every soul has a cup to drain. If it delays putting it to its lips, by so much it delays the time when it will begin to love better. To go to meet sorrow, is to go to meet life. It is to plunge into the only cleansing furnace that can make us holy. Suffering is not a second best, an annoying

accident that interferes to complicate things and add a further burden. It is *the road*.'

57 *Esquisse*.

58 'L'Union créatrice' (December 1917), no. 6. Letter of 23 November 1916 (*MM*, p. 147). Letter of 28 December 1916: 'I very much like Blondel's lines on sorrow . . . because through every word shone the creative, formative action of God, whose influence alone has the power to take us out of ourselves "in order to put in us something that is not of us"' (*MM*, p. 158).

59 *PM*, p. 233.

60 'Le Christ évoluteur' (Peking, 8 October 1942). Letter to Père Raymond Jouve, 6 July 1934.

61 'La Parole attendue' (Peking, 31 October 1940).

62 Letter of October 1934 (*LT*, p. 206.) He is walking 'in the shadows of faith' ('Comment je crois', end).

63 Letter of 8 September 1916 (*MM*, p. 123).

64 Letter of 16 August 1951 (Cuénot, p. 367).

65 Letter of 13 March 1932.

66 To Solange Lemaître, 2 March 1955 (*Cahiers*, 2, p. 157). Much earlier, on 28 May 1915, he had written: 'More than ever I believe that life is beautiful, even in the grimmest circumstances —when you look around God is always there' (*MM*, p. 56).

67 *MD*, pp. 75–6, 137. (*DM*, pp. 46, 118). Letter of 9 April 1916: he speaks of 'this triumphant joy' based on a faith 'in the transcendence of God' and in the fulfilment of his will through all misfortunes (*MM*, p. 98). See Chapter 20, p. 260.

68 Cf. 'La Foi que opère': 'When we are faced by the uncertainty, in practical terms, of the morrow, we must have surrendered ourselves to Providence, making it truly our sole interior support (and seeing Providence as being just as real, physically, as the things about which we are distressed); in the suffering that comes from the evil we have met with, in remorse for the fault we have been guilty of, in our annoyance at the missed opportunity, we must have forced ourselves to believe *without hesitation* that God is strong enough to convert *this* evil into good; we must, in spite of certain appearances to the contrary, have acted unreservedly as though chastity and humility and loving-kindness were the only lines along which our being could advance. In the twilight of death, we must have forced ourselves not to turn our eyes back towards the past but to look, even where the night is darkest, for the dawn of God. If we wish to obtain an idea of the operative virtue and achievement

of faith, we must have given long and patient attention to this effort.'

Chapter 5: Meditation on Death

1 Père Guérard des Lauriers, o.p. art. cit. *Divinitas* (1959), p. 241.

2 'La Foi qui opère', 1, 'la peur de l'avenir'.

3 *CM* (1950).

4 *Cahiers*, pp. 39–48.

5 *CM*, p. 14.

6 The analogy between this touch and Dostoievsky's dream in *The Raw Youth* will be noted. See de Lubac, *The Drama of Atheist Humanism* (London, 1949) pp. 202–4.

7 'If Man remains Man,' M. Jean Rostand has said, 'he will be able to hold out against everything, until the end of all things.' (*Le Figaro littéraire*, 18 March 1961, 'Que deviendra l'Homme sur la Terre?'). That may well be true—but one thing at least is certain, that man's end will come with the end of 'all things'.— There is considerable similarity between Teilhard's ironic reflections on the Moon and the 'irony of the nebulae' in André Malraux, *The Voices of Silence*, pp. 641–642.

8 Cf. 'Life and the Planets' (Peking, 10 March 1945) in *FM*, p. 123.

9 Cf. G. Weigel, s.j., in *The World of Chardin* (1961), p. 160: 'Long before Sputnik went into space he saw the high probability of man's early voyage into space.'

10 *Cahiers*, p. 48.

11 Ibid.

12 The same key words reappear, at a much later date, in a context where Père Teilhard expresses himself in a very different style: 'Something exists beyond the circle which restricts our view, something into which we shall eventually emerge. It is enough to ensure that we no longer feel imprisoned.' ('The Human Rebound of Evolution', 1948 in *FM*, p. 210.) See also Chapters 13 and 16.

13 Paul Claudel, *Tête d'or*, end. This play 'swarms with allusion to the prison in which man is enclosed'. François Varillon, s.j., in *Cahiers Paul Claudel*, 1, p. 187.

14 Both phrases come from Karl Marx. Cf. Gaston Fessard, s.j., 'La vie religieuse, cime et unité de la vie biologique et de la

vie culturelle de l'homme', in *Qu'est-ce que la vie?* (1957), in particular pp. 227–9. Cf. p. 221.

15 'L'Esprit de la Terre.' *Énergie*, Cf. Gaston Fessard, loc. cit., p. 229: 'Man as an individual has always been conscious of the contradiction introduced into both aspects of life, the biological and the cultural, by the prospect of death. The time has now come when he is forced to accept it as a social being.'

16 'Singularities of the Human Species' (1954), introduction, in *AM*, pp. 208–9. The whole of Père Teilhard's scientific work was devoted to breaking the circle in which a too narrow view of science, continued in an unwarranted extrapolation from its conclusions, imprisons us. He sought to show that there 'is an issue into the irreversible' (ibid., p. 209), and so to preserve the transition that faith can effect. See Chapters 8, 15 and 16.

17 'La Nostalgie du Front', *Études* (20 November 1917), p. 459.

18 To the Abbé Gaudefroy, from Tientsin, 12 October 1926. Cf. *Barrière de la Mort et Co-reflexion*, 4 (The sense of the irreversible): 'Tomorrow . . . Mankind will be seized by a sort of panic-stricken claustrophobia at the bare thought that it may find itself hermetically sealed within a closed universe' (New York, 5 January 1955). 'Réflexions sur la compression humaine' (1953): '1. The affliction of our century: a world that is being stifled; 2. at the root of evil: a Universe that is closing in'; a 'favourable issue' must be found. On the 'effects of planetary expansion' that astronautical science is preparing for us, see 'Trois choses que je vois' (1948), p. 5.

19 'La Foi qui opère', 3, 'La foi Chrétienne'. Cf. Paul Claudel, *Cinq Grandes Odes* (1931), 'La Muse que est la Grâce': 'To sing the great epic of man's release from chance', . . . 'The great triumphal road through reconciled Earth, that man, released from chance, may advance upon it.'

20 'L'Atomisme de l'Esprit' (Peking, 13 September 1941), p. 27. To the Abbé Gaudefroy, 16 June 1929: 'Never have I been more sincerely convinced that there is no possible issue for the Noosphere outside the Christian *axis*.'

21 'Un phénomène de contre-évolution en biologie humaine, on la peur de l'existence' (Paris, 26 January 1949).

22 Cf. *MD* (above, Chapter 3).

23 'Le Milieu Mystique', in *HU*, p. 117, Letter of 13 November 1916, in *MM*, p. 145.

24 'Energy of my Saviour', pp. 88–9. This prayer has brought comfort and strength to more than one death-bed.

25 *HU*, p. 29. Cf. 'Trois choses que je vois' (1948), p. 11: 'With-

out Christianity, the World becomes in a twofold way impossible to breathe in. In the first place, because it is, to our despair, closed ahead, with total death facing it; and secondly, because there is no longer any living warmth in it to give life to its terrifying mechanism.'

26 Last page of Père Teilhard's journal, Maundy Thursday, 7 April 1955 (*FM*, p. 309). Cf. To M. Teillard-Chambon, 4 September 1948: 'Death sets the seal upon life. On that point we must have absolute trust in God, for the "good end" depends on him alone' (*LT*, p. 298). 'L'Union créatrice': 'If it is to be transformed into a means to union, death must be accepted with humility, love, and above all immense trust'; by his death on the Cross, 'Christ operated this reversal of our anticipations and fears. He conquered death'. On death, 'which is the supreme force embracing every man in the world', which is neglected in too many intellectual systems, which was conquered and at the same time illuminated by Christ, see Père Gustave Martelet's 'Victoire sur la Mort, Éléments d'anthropologie chrétienne' (Lyons and Paris, *Chronique sociale de France*, 1962).

Chapter 6: The Basis in Tradition

1 For other reasons, this order was not completely retained when the two notions were treated, earlier, in Chapter 3.

2 'Mass on the World' (1923), in *HU*, p. 36.

3 'Le Prêtre' (1918) To describe this as 'trusting to the resources of one's will to power' is surely a gross misconception (*Divinitas*, 1959, p. 344). Similarly it was completely beside the point to recall (ibid.) that mankind's 'supreme hope comes not from itself but from its God'.

4 Letter to Père Auguste Valensin.

5 Louis Cognet. *Le Père Teilhard de Chardin et la pensée contemporaine* (1952), p. 118. Similarly, there is no justification for the author's further statement that Père Teilhard 'seems to run together suffering and sin in one and the same formula'.

6 *MD*, p. 64. (*DM*, p. 33) Letter of 13 November 1916 (*MM*, p. 145). 'Le Prêtre'.

7 First memorandum for M. Blondel (*Archives*, pp. 140–1).

8 Letter of 28 December 1916 (*MM*, p. 159).

9 It is only some effects of sin that enter into passivities, those

that prompt one to say (when one thinks, for example, of St. Augustine's repentance), *felix culpa* (*MD*, p. 87, *DM*, p. 59).

10 The notion of the divine Milieu reappeared, in 1955, in 'Le Christique'. It constitutes 'a dynamic reality in which every opposition between the Universal and the Personal progressively disappears (though the two are never confused)'; it is precisely the "Christic centre" of the Universe, to which the believer has continually more complete access through progress in the spiritual life. There is a similarity here with Origen, who united Christ and the Kingdom in his concept of αὐτοβασιλεία, *In Matthaeum*, t. 14, n. 7 (ed. E. Klostermann, p. 289). Cf. Henri de Lubac, *Aspects du Bouddhisme*, vol. 2, *Amida* (1955), pp. 265–7.

11 'Le Milieu mystique' (1918).

12 'La Foi qui opère (1918). Here again we are reminded of St. John of the Cross, *Spiritual Canticle*, st. 12: the world becoming finally 'a fluid and transparent mirror', and this phenomenal universe reflecting 'the image of love'. G. Morel, *Le sens de l'existence selon saint Jean de la Croix*, vol. 3 (1961), pp. 55–6.

13 To L. Zanta, 10 January 1927.

14 Cf. to Père Fontoynont, 22 July 1916, to whom he was describing the main lines of an essay on 'the cosmic life': 'one day we shall really have to make up our minds to set above every joy and interest the austerity of adhering to the divine Will, and of finding our own satisfaction in it, for God's good pleasure'.

15 Yves de Montcheuil, s.j., *Le Royaume et ses exigences* (1958), p. 33. This suggests the words that Dostoievsky attributes to the brother of Zosimus in *The Brothers Karamazov*: 'We are all in Paradise, only we refuse to recognize that we are; if we did, the whole world would become Paradise overnight.' Similar passages will be found in Henri de Lubac, *Amida*, Chapter 12, pp. 286–91. Cf. Georges Bernanos, *Dernier Agenda*, in Albert Béguin, *Bernanos par lui-même*, p. 147. There is a similarity in all mystical temperaments, although there are differences of quality, and contradictions, in their respective mystical systems. For Père Teilhard's, see Chapters 8 and 14.

16 *MD*, pp. 104, 113. (*DM*, pp. 79, 90) *Multitude* (1917): 'When man has made up his mind, with generosity of heart, to practise love of God and his neighbour, he sees that in correcting his own interior unity by accepting loss and isolation in a generous spirit, he has yet achieved nothing; that unity, in turn, has to

suffer an apparently annihilating eclipse before it can be re-born in Christ. Those, in fact, will be saved who boldly shift the centre of their being outside themselves and have the courage to love Another more than self, who in some way become that Other; and that means they pass through death in order to find life. *Si quis vult animam suam salvam facere, perdet eam*'.

17 'Mass on the World', in *HU*, p. 27.

18 Père Pierre Charles quoted the opinion of a professor at the theological college at Louvain, who said of *Le Milieu Divin*, as early as 29 July 1928, 'It seems to me in the highest degree original and new, and yet nothing could be more traditional.'

19 Good Friday (20 April) 1919, in *MM*, p. 293.

20 *MD*, p. 104. (*DM*, p. 79) Letter of 23 November 1916: 'I've come to think that the only, the supreme prayer we can offer up during these hours when the road before us is shrouded in darkness, is that of our Master on the Cross, *In manus tuas commendo spiritum meum*' (*MM*, p. 147).

21 'La Foi qui opère' (1918), in *HU*, p. 131.

22 *MD*, p. 142. (*DM*, p. 123).

23 This is already apparent in *CM* (1950). In the introduction to 'Le Christique' (1955) his own experience is described (and thereby even slightly altered) in terms that are too specifically Teilhardian, in line with the system presented in that essay.

24 Letter of 9 February 1931.

25 Letter of 10 June 1917, in *MM*, 195. Letter of 25 February 1929. 'Forma Christi'.

26 Louis Cognet, op. cit., pp. 141, 153.

27 *MD*, pp. 103. (*MD*, pp. 77–8).

28 'Quelques réflexions sur la conversion du monde' (Peking, 9 October 1936).

29 'Mon Univers' (1924), p. 18. 'Social heredity and progress' (1938), in *FM*, p. 35.

30 *Esquisse* (*FM*, p. 35).

31 Letter of 1 January 1917 (*MM*, p. 159).

32 *Introduction* (1944). There would have been no need to quote so simple a testimony, had not a critic given the impression that Père Teilhard did not believe in the divinity of the child of Bethlehem.

33 Letter of 8 September 1916 (*MM*, p. 123).

34 Letter of 11 October 1918 (*MM*, p. 247).

35 *Introduction* (1944): Every Christian has 'faith in the divinity of the historic Christ, not only as prophet and perfect man but

also as an object of love and adoration'. Cf. 'Le sens humain' (1929).

36 Letter (from Peking) of 21 September 1929.

37 'Esquisse d'une dialectique de l'esprit.'

38 'Le Christique' (New York, March 1955).

39 1 Cor. 1. 23–4; 2. 5.

40 To L. Zanta, 10 January 1927: 'I pray that you may be given the heart-warming vision of the mysterious Diaphany . . . by which the universal Christ illuminates the inner core of things —unique and already at a higher level—to act upon us through them and to draw us to their common peak.'

41 2 Cor. 5. 17. Cf. St. Bernard, *In Cantica Sermo* 75, m 8; '. . . Quia etsi cognoverat eum Ecclesia secundum carnem, id est secundum carnis infirmitatem, sed nunc non novit . . .' (*PL*, 183, 1148 bc).

42 In his annual retreats, Père Teilhard liked to meditate on the first and last visions in the Apocalypse, and also on a number of different gospel scenes, in particular the calming of the storm and Christ walking on the waters.

43 *In Matthaeum*, bk. xi. c. 24: 'Stultum valde est, eum in parvo loco vel in absondito quaerere, qui omnia complet et tunc universa commovebit et perlustrabit singula' (*PL*, 120, 814 bc).

44 *Peri Archon*, bk. ii. c. 11, n. 6 (ed. Koetschau, pp. 190–1; Migne, PG, II, 246).

45 For example, in 'Mass on the World': 'As long as I could see— or dared see—in you, Lord Jesus, only the man who lived two thousand years ago, the sublime moral teacher, the Friend, the Brother . . .' 'Can man ever give himself utterly to a nature which is purely human? . . . But now, today, when through the manifestation of those superhuman powers with which your resurrection endowed you . . .' (*HU*, p. 33).

46 Letter of 23 November 1916 (*MM*, p. 147).

47 *MD*, p. 117. (*DM*, p. 95) Cf. 1 John 1. 1–3.

48 *MD*, p. 117. (*DM*, p. 95) Cf. Père Auguste Valensin, February 1933: 'The Jesus whom I love, to whom I have given myself, whom I set above all things, is indeed the Jesus of the Gospels, but it is not a Jesus confined to the Gospels'—in other words to the limitations of his life on earth (Auguste Valensin, 1961, p. 255). The term 'the cosmic Christ' occurs in E. L. Mascall, *Christian Theology and Natural Science* (1956) p. x: '*Hebrews, Ephesians and the Cosmic Christ*' (second ed., 1957).

49 'Christianisme et Évolution' (1945). To Père Auguste Valensin, 31 December 1926. To the Abbé Breuil, 13 December 1952: 'If only I were Pope for just long enough to write *one* encyclical on "the universal Christ" . . .'

50 *CM*, p. 23. To M. Teillard-Chambon, from New York, 8 November 1953 (*LT*, p. 347). 'Note sur le Christ Universel' (1920). He thought that the universal Christ had been particularly well understood, in the seventeenth century, by Lallemant and Surin: To L. Zanta, 25 January 1924. Cf. M. Blondel to Auguste Valensin, 5 December 1919, where he notes the lack of an 'integral realism that brings the metaphysics of Christianity into harmony with mysticism lived by the saints—by the faithful, even' (*Archives*, p. 130).

51 Peking, 29 October 1943: 'Tomorrow, after my Mass that Christ the King may grow into the universal Christ.'

52 *Conscience et Logos* (1961), p. 237; cf. pp. 223–4, where Père Teilhard is referred to. Cf. Romano Guardini, *The Lord* (London, 1956), p. 433.

53 See, for example, *MM*, pp. 34, 70, 75, 196, 226; and on the sacraments, pp. 86–7, 192.

54 Cf. *Dictionnaire de Spiritualité*, vol. 4, col. 1586–1621.

55 To his parents.

56 *MM*, pp. 100–1, 225. Letter of 28 August 1918: 'I don't even find it easy to say mentally the "mass on the altar of all things" that came easily to me in June when I was in the tall woods of Laigue. However, when I can do so a little, I can see the sense of communion growing sharper and deeper. I'll have to write something about that, even more fully worked out than "Le Prêtre"' (p. 230; cf. p. 38).

57 *La pensée théologique de Teilhard de Chardin*, p. 85. This is in fact a normal extension of the thought expressed by St. Augustine in his *Confessions*, bk. 1, c. 10, n. 16: '. . . nec tu me in te mutabis, sicut cibum carnis tuae, sed tu mutaberis in me.' 'May thy mysteries, O Lord,' says the prayer in the liturgy, 'realize fully in us what they contain.' Cf. Jules Monchanin, note on *Eucharist, Paruosia, Glorified Body*: '. . . The Eucharist, that magnetizes the universe, will transubstantiate the universe.'

58 'Le Prêtre'. cf. pp. 125, 126. (*DM*, pp. 103–4) 'Mon Univers' (1924). 'L'Élément universel', p. 10: 'The mystical body of Christ is haloed by a cosmic body.' Several important passages are quoted, with a brief commentary, by N. M. Wildiers, in his introduction to *HU*, p. 14. Cf. Henri de Lubac, *Corpus*

mysticum (second ed., 1949), pp. 276–7. Émile Rideau, s.J., 'Technique et Eucharistie', in *Lumen vitae*, 13 (1958), p. 702: 'The host is a warrant and a promise.'

59 *Introduction*, p. 7. On this type of expression, see Chapter 17.

60 Letter of 27 June 1926.

61 'Social heredity and progress', in *FM*, p. 33. To Père Valensin, 16 March 1931: 'It is impossible not to hope that his countenance be revealed more fully.'

62 'Quelques réflexions sur la conversion de monde' (1936). (The italics are Père Teilhard's.) Letter of 9 December 1933: 'What must Christology develop into if it is to remain itself?' 'Note on progress' (1920): 'Christ already risen but still unimaginably great', in *FM*, p. 24. To Père Sertillanges, 4 February 1934: 'I often think that our humanity, which has without doubt become much more adult than it was two thousand years ago, needs, in some way, a "renaissance" of Christ . . . Our Christ should be able to embrace and illuminate today's almost limitless developments. *Neque longitudo, neque latitudo, neque profundum . . .*' 'Comment je crois', p. 20: 'The whole problem is to *preserve* in Christ . . . etc.'

63 'Super-Humanité, Super-Christ, Super-Charité, de nouvelles dimensions pour l'avenir' (Peking, August 1943), etc.

64 'Le Christ évoluteur' (1942): 'An astonishing confluence, indeed, of the evidence of faith and the demands of reason. What appeared to be a threat becomes a magnificent confirmation. Far from conflicting with Christian dogma, the enormous advances Man has just secured in Nature will have the effect (if they are carried to their natural conclusion) of conferring . . . etc.'

65 'Comment je vois', p. 11.

66 'Comment je crois', p. 7; cf. p. 12. 'Life and the Planets' (1945) in *FM*, pp. 97–123. On Père Teilhard's 'third infinite' or 'third abyss', see *MPN*, p. 23; 'Un sommaire de ma perspective' (1954); 'Comment je vois' (1948), no. 1; 'Place in the universe' (1942), in *VP*, p. 216; 'l'Atomisme de l'Esprit' (1941) p. 3, etc.

67 *Esquisse*.

68 Letter of 22 February 1920.

69 Letter of 28th April 1954. The word is no more disconcerting than such traditional expressions as 'the growth of the mystical body'. Cf. 'La Vie cosmique' (24 March 1916): 'The mystical Christ has not attained his full growth—nor, in consequence, the cosmic Christ.' See Chapter 9.

70 Aix, 6 May 1889. Cf. Teilhard, 8 August 1919 (*MM*, p. 300).
Again with Teilhard, Blondel sees 'the incorporation of all the
beings that make up the universe in a chain that is continuous
with the *Verbum caro*, who draws and assumes in himself the
whole of created reality'; unpublished text, dictated in 1941.

71 To L. Zanta, 28 January 1936.

72 Pierre Leroy, s.j., in *LT*, p. 43.

73 *Énergie* (1937).

74 'L'Âme du Monde' (Epiphany, 1918).

75 Letter of 15 August 1936.

76 'Le Prêtre'. Père Teilhard was fond of the prayer, '*Jesus sis
mihi mundus verus*' (30 July 1918, *MM*, p. 223). Letter of 10
January 1926: 'If I cease to believe desperately in the animation of all things by Our Lord . . . the World, that hitherto
has held me up, will engulf me, or crush me, or simply fall
into dust in my hands.'

Chapter 7: The Phenomenon of Man

1 *PM*, p. 30 (Preface); cf. p. 169.

2 To the Abbé Henri Breuil, 15 December 1939: 'I am working
every day on my book on Man that I began tentatively two
years ago. It is progressing steadily and I believe I am getting
it into its final shape.'

3 This is the case with the three works quoted as examples. Should
the *Periarchon* be taken as a first attempt at a theological
summa? Is the *Proslogion* purely a rational composition or does
it presuppose a basis of faith? And if so, what faith? Is the
Contra Gentiles a purely philosophical work of apologetics, or
is it, even in the early books, already theological? We should,
however, note that some of the difficulties experienced by commentators are derived not so much from the novel character of
the work in question as from distinctions in which there is an
element of novelty and with which we have not so far been
familiar.

4 In 1948, in the preface to 'Comment je vois', Père Teilhard
admitted that his earlier writings (of which the most important
is *The Phenomenon of Man*) presented a combination of 'scientific and para-scientific' views.

5 On *The Phenomenon of Man*, see Louis Barjon, s.j., 'Le
monde en expansion, Pierre Teilhard de Chardin', in *Monde
d'écrivains, destinées d'hommes* (1960), pp. 211–43; J. L. Rus-

sell, S.J., 'Teilhard de Chardin: The Phenomenon of Man', in the *Heythrop Journal*, vols. 1 and 2 (1960 and 1961), M. de Tollenaere, S.J., 'De mens in Teilhards Wereldvisie', in *Streven*, 9 June 1956, pp. 820–8; Moeller, review of the German translation, in *Tübinger Theologische Quartalschrift* (1961), pp. 360–3.

6 *PM*, p. 169 note. *Esquisse* (Peking, 4 May 1936), p. 1: the problem is to discover, if such exists, the directive significance of evolution, and this must be done without leaving the domain of scientific facts.

7 *PM*, p. 29.

8 Père Teilhard was well aware that such an objection might be raised. See Chapter 15.

9 Address to the Pontifical Academy of Science, 11 November 1951 (*Acta Apostolicae Sedis*, 1952, p. 52). Ibid: 'How could a scientist avoid thinking in terms of philosophy?'

10 He was later to re-emphasize this point. Thus, on 25 July 1952, he wrote to Père François Russo: 'Since I am trying to define an axis of energy "transversal" to that of Entropy, I am obviously speaking purely as a "physicist" (and not as a metaphysician)—remaining, as I always do, resolutely on the plane of the phenomenon. In the whole of this article, I have been trying not to (refusing to) go beyond the plane of "appearances". Otherwise, I would not be writing in the *Revue des Questions Scientifiques*. You can stress that as much as you like. It is the whole basis of my purpose and of my thought.' See Chapter 15.

11 *PM*, p. 29. '*The Phenomenon of Man*', *QS*, November 1930: 'By the expression "The Phenomenon of Man" we mean here the empirical fact of the appearance in our universe of the power of reflection and thought' (in *VP*, p. 161). 'I would remark that our viewpoint here is purely methodological' (*Ibid*, note). This position has been well analysed by Gustave Weigel, S.J., in 'The Phenomenon of Teilhard de Chardin', in *The World of Chardin* (1961), pp. 157, 161.

12 Similarly, *MPN*, p. 13: the reader is told not to look for 'an exhaustive definition of man', the book is 'simply an attempt to specify his "phenomenal" features . . .'

13 Letter of 11 May, 1923.

14 'Comment je vois.' Preface. 'Foundations', in *VP*, p. 135.

15 *PM*, pp. 291–9; The Abbé Paul Grenet has well noted the type of structural connexion Père Teilhard is concerned with: '. . . and it is here that Christianity's offer fits in'. Similarly,

M. Jacques Mettra, in *Travaux et Jours* (Beirut, July–September, 1961, p. 16) writes: 'The "Christian phenomenon" comes to meet the "human phenomenon", to confirm its "significance" —to give it its whole significance.

16 See also *PM*, p. 313: 'Is it really sure that, for an eye trained and sensitized by light other than that of pure science, etc.'

17 After having carried as far as possible the natural considerations that seem to him to indicate the direction in which happiness should be sought, he concludes by showing that a 'complete solution' to the problem of happiness can be found only in an explicit appeal to Christian faith. *Cahiers*, pp. 68–70. Cf. Chapter 4, n. 23.

18 'Comment je vois', n. 21–4.

19 *PM*, p. 30.

20 Mgr Bruno de Solages, 'La Pensée chrétienne face à l'évolution', address given on 18 November 1947 at the formal reopening of the Institut catholique of Toulouse (from the *Bulletin de littérature ecclésiastique*, October–December 1947). This is the best general study of Père Teilhard's work, as represented essentially by *The Phenomenon of Man*.

21 This is well explained by Père de Tollenaere in the article already quoted from *Streven* (above, n. 5).

22 *Esquisse, CM*.

23 *PM* Foreword, p. 35. One writer has taken this as a reason for criticizing Père Teilhard on the grounds that in writing the book 'he deliberately overlooked or affected to overlook . . . all that God has been concerned to teach us through his Revelation about these vital problems.' G. Bosio, s.j., '*Le Phénomène humain* dans l'hypothèse de l'évolution integrale' in *Civiltà cattolica* (17. 12. 1955). The same criticism could be levelled against all books that deal with man from a scientific or philosophical point of view, including all the textbooks of natural philosophy officially approved by the Church. All treatises on natural theology 'affect' similarly 'to overlook' the light thrown by Revelation on the existence of God. See Chapter 8, p. 84.

24 On this question of method, see also *VP* pp. 161–2, *AM*, pp. 271–3, etc.

25 *MPN*, p. 15.

26 *Esquisse*. 'Man's Place in the Universe, reflections on complexity' (Peking, 15 November 1942) in *VP*, p. 216.

27 'Hominization' (6 May 1923), in *VP*, pp. 51–2.

28 We shall return to this point, looking at it from a complementary angle, in some critical comments, chapters 15 and 16.

Chapter 8: Scientist, Prophet, and Mystic

1 *MD*, p. 119. (*DM*, p. 96) Cf. letter of 17 December 1922: 'this word "equilibrium" being applicable to the two symmetrical, but diametrically opposed, realities reverting to a higher or a lower centre.'

2 *PM*, pp. 302–4, etc. 'Singularities', in *AM*, pp. 208–70.

3 *PM*, pp. 164–83, 281. *MPN*, p. 14. 'The natural units of humanity' (*Études*, 5 July 1939) in *VP*, p. 193. To Marcel Brion: 'At this modest level (of the phenomenon) what dominates my view of things is the metamorphosis that man obliges us to impose on the universe we live in as soon as (in conformity with the best in what science suggests) we decide to consider him as forming an integral, innate part of the rest of life . . .' Marcel Brion, 'Rencontre avec le Père Teilhard de Chardin', *Nouvelles littéraires*, 11 January 1951. 'Man's Place in Nature' (in *VP*, p. 180), the 'appearance of the *power of thought*' represents a 'discontinuity of the first order'.

4 Jean Rostand, *Ce que je crois* (1953), p. 19: 'How could I believe that anything essential could belong exclusively to a single one of the millions of species that inhabit the earth?'; p. 60: 'We have the feeling of being the only valuable curio in nature's vast collection of bric-à-brac . . . but what right have we to claim such special treatment? and can we decently and seriously believe that we are of more importance, in this immense and inexhaustible nature, than any other of our life-companions?'

5 Cf. 'La Centrologie' (1944), no. 33.

6 Cf. Gaston Milhaud, 'Science grecque et science moderne' in *Études sur la pensée scientifique* (1906), p. 273. Alfred Loisy, *Journal* (25 June 1909): 'Looking at things from the point of view of experience, there is no more reason for accepting the immortality of men than there is for that of fleas, ants, snakes or asses. They are all parasites on the earth, they emerge from it, go back to it, and form one with it . . . Man must be oddly naïve or wildly conceited to imagine that he has a right to special consideration from God.' Quoted in *Alfred Loisy, sa vie, son oeuvre*, by A. Houtin and F. Sartiaux (ed. Émile Poulat 1961), p. 129.

7 'La Centrologie', loc. cit.

8 'Comment je crois' (1900–34), p. 7: 'We are told that it is childish and conceited for man to solve the world in terms of himself. But is it not a scientific truth that there is no thought, in the field of our experience, other than human thought? Is it our fault if we coincide with the axis of things?'

9 'La Convergence de l'Univers' (1951), p. 3. *CM*, p. 29. To the Abbé Gaudefroy, 16 January 1927: 'I am planning a book about Man . . . considered as the greatest telluric and biological event on our planet. I am more and more convinced that we are as blind to the human layer on the earth as our ancestors were to the mountains and oceans. This consideration is gradually coming to dominate all my scientific thought.' 'La réflexion de l'énergie', *QS* (1952), p. 485: '. . . a new species of life.'

10 'Singularities', in *AM*, p. 209.

11 *PM*, pp. 163, 232–4, 243. 'Sinanthropus Pekinensis' (*QS*, 20 July 1930) in *AM*, p. 67. 'Some Reflections on Progress,' 1942, in *FM*, p. 68, etc. 'Turmoil or genesis?': 'Human Reflection is not an epiphenomenon of the Organic World, but the Central Phenomenon of vitalization' (*FM*, p. 218). Cf. *VP*, pp. 158–9. Letter of 29 September 1918: '. . . Psychological introduction: getting one's mind accustomed to discerning the phenomenon of man.'

12 Letter of 23 June 1935. 'The Cone of time' (1942) in *FM*, pp. 83. As early as 1870 R. Wallace was writing in *On Natural Selection*: '. . . a grand revolution was effected in nature, a revolution which in all the previous ages of the earth's history had no parallel, for a being had arisen who was no longer necessarily subject to change with the changing universe—a being who was in some degree superior to nature, inasmuch as he knew how to control and regulate her action, and could keep himself in harmony with her not by a change in body, but by an advance of mind', p. 325.

13 'La Convergence de l'Univers', p. 3.

14 'Comment je vois' (28 August 1948), p. 15.

15 To M. and S. Bégouën, 8 January 1929, in *LT*, p. 150.

16 Cf. 'Palaeontology and the Appearance of Man', 1923, in *AM*, p. 49.

17 'The Phenomenon of Man' (1930) in *VP*, p. 161. 'Singularities', in *AM*, p. 209. 'Hominisation' (1923), *VP*, pp. 66–79.

18 'Comment je vois.' 'Évolution de l'idée d'évolution', *Bulletin de l'Union catholiques des scientifiques français*. (1950): 'It might seem that after Galileo man lost his privileged position in the

universe . . . he is now in process of recapturing his leadership' (*VP*, pp. 246–7). *La Centrologie*, n. 17: 'Mankind encloses within its moving circle the still unshaped future of things.'

19 Clement of Alexandria, *Paedagogus*, bk. 1, c. 2, n. 6. (ed. M. Harl, *Sources Chrétiennes*, vol. 70, p. 121).

20 'Singularities', introduction, in *AM*, pp. 209–10. Cf. S. Strasser, 'Évolution et Mystère', in *Le Mystère* (*Semaine des intellectuels Catholiques*, 1959), p. 109: 'The idea of a cosmic development that culminates in the appearance of mind, conscious of itself, is precisely the theory of evolution stripped of the anti-spiritual, anti-religious and anti-clerical garb in which we know it.'

21 É. Borne, 'Biologie et humanisme', in *Qu'est-ce que la vie?* (*Semaine des intellectuels catholiques*, 1957), p. 164.

22 *La Pensée théologique de Teilhard de Chardin* (1961), p. 34.

23 'Philosophie de la nature et la méthode chez le Père Teilhard de Chardin', *Archives de philosophie*, 20 (1957), p. 33. A similar opinion will be found in Père Sertillanges, *L'idée de la création* (1945), p. 152, n. 1.

24 In a comment on an essay (originally intended for the review *Scientia*), which was one of the preliminary sketches for *The Phenomenon of Man*. 'The fundamental idea in the essay is acceptable to Thomist philosophers. Holding that the spiritual soul is created only *in corpore* (in a body) and can operate only with the collaboration of matter, they thereby admit the existence of a "noosphere" attached to the rest of the World by the necessary correlations. In their view, accordingly, there is . . .' (From a letter from Père Teilhard to Père Auguste Valensin, 29 September 1928.) Père Teilhard was saying the same in May 1920: 'The soul cannot be created *outside* a world, because it can exist only by acting within a subject of action fitted to it (this action consisting in *unifying* around itself a Universe that, without the soul, would fall back into plurality).' See Chapter 18 and Appendix 4.

25 M. De Tollenaere, s.j., 'De mens in Teilhards Wereldvisie', in *Streven* (9 June 1956), pp. 820–8.

26 For the study of the 'phenomenon' discloses 'the human paradox' (*PM*, p. 168).

27 *PM*, p. 88, 108–9. On orthogenesis, see also *VP*, 248–55, 268–74; *AM*, p. 215.

28 'L'Union créatrice.' *PM*, p. 169; p. 171: 'a mutation from zero to everything'. 'Comment je vois', n. 7, etc.

29 Louis Cognet, op. cit., pp. 66, 98. Cf. On the other hand,

Sertillanges, loc. cit., commending Teilhard's choice of words: 'When you cross a threshold, you do not interrupt your walking; but since there is a threshold, we have here to introduce the notions of continuity and newness, of evolution *de plano* and transcendence.'

30 *PM*, pp. 170, 171.

31 Letter of May 1920.

32 Père Olivier Rabut, O.P., *Dialogue avec Teilhard de Chardin*, p. 142: 'Teilhard put it very well when he said ' "God makes things make themselves according to their own laws—which is completely Thomist" '. See also pp. 125–6: 'Between life and spirit there is a hidden (though limited) opposition simultaneously with a relative continuity. The passage to a higher level, the change of state of which Teilhard speaks (the threshold of reflection), explain this double aspect.' Earlier, Père Pierre Charles had written, in a note to Père Teilhard's article on 'The Formation of the Noosphere' (*QS*, January 1947), p. 7: 'Just as palaeontology does not abolish the creation, and just as embryology does not stand in the way of a first cause, so the description of the Noosphere and its biological culmination in no way contradict the transcendence of God, or Grace, or the Incarnation, or the final Parousia.'

33 A note in 'Man's place in the Universe' (1942) speaks of 'creative pulsations' which are the principle behind the successive levels of evolution (in *VP*, p. 225).

34 'Comment je vois', n. 7. note.

35 *PM*, pp. 30, 169. n.

36 *La Vie et l'âme de Teilhard de Chardin* (1947), p. 181: 'readers of *The Phenomenon of Man* will have to be on their guard here against an inaccurate interpretation . . . It is not that we have the least doubt about Père Teilhard's complete orthodoxy on the point in question, but that his language may not perhaps be sufficiently explicit: and Père Bosio's criticism makes it clear that the danger of misunderstanding is by no means imaginary.'

37 In apologetics, Père Frédéric Bouvier, an ardent disciple of Père de Grandmaison who left Ore Place to become editor of *Études* just when Père Teilhard arrived. In dogma, Pères Harent, Chossat and Le Bachelet. In Scripture, Pères Albert Condamin and Alfred Durand, etc. Père Bouvier, killed in the 1914 war, never had the chance to give his best. He was, with the well-known Père W. Schmidt, S. V. D., co-founder of the study-weeks in religious ethnology, and brought Père Teilhard

to the first of them (Louvain 1922). Père Teilhard greatly enjoyed it, and wrote a report of it for the *Correspondant* (November 1912).

38 To his parents, 13 July 1910, 16 January 1911, 4 December 1911. At the end of his philosophy, in Jersey, he gave the panegyric on St. Thomas Aquinas; telling his parents the news, he said, 'I am sorry that Papa has never been able to read the *Summa*; but I was glad to know that he thought about it' (6 March 1905).

39 19 June 1926 (*LT*, p. 127); 17 April 1923 (ibid., p. 66).

40 To his parents, Paris, 5 February 1913.

41 'La Centrologie', introduction.

42 Cf. Georges Morel, *Études*, vol. 304 (1960), pp. 81–2, 85. This article, on the other hand, correctly indicates certain essential lines in Teilhard's thought. We should anticipate here a possible misunderstanding: mystics are, in one sense, the most metaphysical of men; but metaphysical analysis, in so far as it is a formal discipline, is not always their concern.

43 To Père Auguste Valensin, 13 October 1933.

44 *Les nouvelles littéraires*, 11 January 1951.

45 *PM*, pp. 29–30, 34–5. 'Man's place in the universe', in *VP* pp. 216 ff. In his writings of a more general character, such as 'L'Esprit de la Terre', he spoke of 'spiritual cosmogony' (to the Abbé Gaudefroy, 25 May 1922). Bruno de Solages, loc. cit.: 'Every treatment from the scientific point of view that concerns not one part of the real but the whole of it, necessarily takes on a philosophical character: But it does not thereby become metaphysics or theology.'

46 Letter of 21 August 1919 (*MM*, p. 302).

47 In this connexion, the metaphysical inquiries of Père G. Fessard, studying man in history and distinguishing the different planes of historical reality, are a valuable corrective and completion of Père Teilhard's scientific inquiries. Cf. Abel Jeannière, 'La Triple Dialectique de l'histoire', *Archives de philosophie* (1961), p. 246.

48 'La Centrologie', introduction. *Esquisse*, p. 4. However, he took this law to be 'capable of extrapolation, in a suitable form, to the totality of space and time'.

49 Letter from New York, 1953.

50 Quoted from Père Dubarle and Père d'Armagnac, in *Archives de philosophie*, 1957, p. 18. On Teilhard's phenomenology, see G. Crespy, *La Pensée théologique de Teilhard de Chardin* (1961), Chapter 1. See Chapter 15.

51 From an article in *Le Monde*, 7 July 1960.

52 'Comment je crois' (1934), p. 5.

53 'Comment je vois' (1948), n. 2.

54 *PM*, pp. 285, 266. In these passages he is concerned with the fundamental mystical attitude, with the natural 'roots' or 'preliminary expressions' of mysticism. At the same time he is at pains to show that there are mystical systems that are specifically very different and even in opposition to one another. See Chapter 14.

55 'Foundations', in *VP*, p. 132.

56 The word is used here to denote primarily an attitude of the soul, not a form or degree of prayer.

57 Letter of 13 December 1918, in *MM*, p. 268.

58 *CM*, 1. 'Le Christianisme dans le Monde' (1953): 'passion for Unity'. Earlier, in 'Mon Univers' (1918), we read that his view of the world was initially an experience 'more of the mystical order'; 'at a secondary level, it was included in a certain ascesis (= ascesis of the "total effort") and a certain philosophy (= a philosophy of union)'. Ibid.: he is 'conscious of having always, in everything, aimed at attaining something of the absolute'.

59 'The Pyx' in *HU*, p. 50.

60 'Mass on the World', in *HU*, pp. 25–6.

61 To L. Zanta, 15 October 1926.

62 The word 'poetry' has been too loosely used in connexion with Père Teilhard's writings. The Abbé Blanchard, op. cit., says, more correctly: 'The closer the thought conforms to the truth of a Universe, itself pure and exuberant poetry, the more the thought too will be a source of poetry, showering poetry on the entranced reader' (p. 46).

63 Letter of 25 May 1938: '. . . in the impression I feel of the love of a God who seems to me continually greater than all the forms in which our moral teaching and our theology present him to us.'

64 See above, Chapter 5, 'La Grande Monade' (1916), etc.

65 26 November 1952 (Cuénot, p. 354). Cf. *LT*, p. 334. In spite of this, Père Guérard des Lauriers (loc. cit., p. 239) writes: 'Père Teilhard promises "the Golden Age": this is the indispensable complement without which his "facile solution" would have no appeal.'

66 N. M. Wildiers, *Teilhard de Chardin* (1961), p. 13. The exaggerated use of capitals as initials, which has sometimes been held against Père Teilhard, is not so much a mark of a certain

pomposity as the normal professional practice of the natural scientist, as for example in the classifications of Linnaeus.

67 Émile Rideau, s.j., *Revue de l'action populaire* (1959. November), p. 1151. After the remark quoted earlier Père Teilhard continues: 'I told myself that now perhaps I was capable of so using the first language as to make it fairly express what the other contains but puts into words that most people can no longer understand' (*LT*, p. 127).

68 On the inclusion of the problem of God in the science of evolution, see Chapter 16.

Chapter 9: The Element of Novelty

1 'Le Coeur du problème' (29 October 1949): 'the urgent necessity for Christian faith in the Above to incorporate the human neo-faith in an Ahead'.

2 *Oeuvres politiques, morales et mêlées* (Geneva, 1621), p. 932.

3 Henri Bergson, *Creative Evolution* (London, 1911), p. 363.

4 Cf. Albert Béguin, *La Prière de Péguy* (1942).

5 *MD*, pp. 81–2. (*DM*, p. 54) Letter of 19 June 1916 (*MM*, p. 103).

6 'Foundations' (1926): 'evolutionism . . . expresses the incursion into all our scientific views of a better understanding of the nature of organic time' (*VP*, p. 141). Cf. p. 128.

7 Ibid., p. 152; p. 128: 'History is gradually invading all the disciplines.' This is now a commonly accepted notion. 'Everything,' writes Père D. Dubarle, 'goes to show that a certain number of large material structures, in which the ancients saw the guarantee of an essential stability possessed by reality, are in fact, themselves too, caught up in becoming and, to the extent that they are, are functions of a dynamism that a briefer and less sophisticated experience was unable to discern' (*Vie intellectuelle*, March 1956, p. 22).

8 'The cone of time' (Peking, 13 February 1942), in *FM*, p. 88. 'The future of man seen by a paleontologist' (1942), ibid., p. 70.

9 *PM*, p. 271.

10 On this continuation, see the remarks, inspired by Père Teilhard, of Georges Belleville in 'Le Christ vie des croyants', *Cahiers universitaires* (April–May 1958), pp. 410–12, in connexion with technological civilization.

11 *MD*, p. 61. (*DM*, p. 29).

12 See, however, *MD*, pp. 55–6, 60. (*DM* pp. 22–3, 29).

13 This comparison was made by Père Maurice Pontet in a lecture on *Le Milieu Divin*. See also his 'Evolution according to Teilhard de Chardin' in *Thought*, 36 (1961), pp. 167–79. Cf. letter of 15 March 1916: 'Something of this mysterious Whole that is matter must pass, through the Resurrection, into the World of heaven, my efforts on behalf of human progress being even (perhaps?) the necessary condition for the development of the New Earth.'

14 'The transformist question' (5 June 1921) in *VP*, p. 7.

15 'Note on Progress' (1020) in *FM*, p. 24. 'The spiritual power of matter' (1919): 'So many things which had once distressed or revolted him—the speeches and pronouncements of the learned, their assertions and their prohibitions, their refusal to allow the universe to move . . .' (in *HU*, p. 66). Letter of 6 October 1932: 'Some very odd people sit in the seat of Moses today' (with some of whom, indeed, he was only too familiar).

16 In *The World of Chardin* (1961), p. 163; p. 162. 'It is well to remember that faith must not be identified with theology. The direct object of faith, the dogmas of the teaching Church, must not be identified with theology. Theology is the human science that explores dogma and faith.' In 1891 Mgr d'Hulst had asked that scientists should be left free to pursue their researches along their own lines; in the *Dictionnaire apologétique*, vol. 4 (col. 1844–7), Père de Sinéty was still concerned to dispute this.

17 'Darwinisme et Catholicisme' (1914). 'Le Darwinisme au point de vue de l'orthodoxie Catholique' (1921), etc. Cf. On the same lines, Ernest C. Messenger, *Evolution and Theology* (Louvain thesis, 1931), *Theology and Evolution*, by various writers, ed. Rev. E. C. Messenger (1950), which is dedicated to the memory of Canon de Dorlodot. Teilhard himself sometimes refers to the theory of 'seminal causes'.

18 Guillaume de Conches (1080–1145), *De Philosophia mundi*, bk. 1, c. 22 (*PL*, 172, 55–6).

19 C. Boyer, s.j., *De Deo creante et elevante*, ed. altera (Rome, 1933), pp. 187–8, 210, etc. *Id. De Deo creante et elevante Synopsis scolastica* (Rome, 1929), pp. 142–62: 'Deus plasmavit corpus primi hominis a materia inorganica', etc.; *Cursus philosophiae*, vol. 2 (1936, pp. 191–7). In the third edition of the first of these (1940), and still more in the fourth (1948), a more moderate view is expressed. On these modifications, see *Theology and Evolution*, pp. 155–71, 'A Roman Theologian on Evolution' (by Messenger).

20 In 1947, Père F. M. Bergougnioux replied to this in a carefully argued little book, with a preface by Cardinal Saliège, *Progrès ou Régression?*

21 G. Vandebroek and L. Renwaert, s.j., In *Nouvelle Revue théologique*, 73 (1951), pp. 348, 351. Cf. *Theology and Evolution*, pp. 211–16. For the present position, from both the theological and the scientific point of view, see Karl Rahner, s.j., *Hominisation: the Evolutionary Origin of Man as a Theological Problem* (*Quaestiones Disputatae*, 13) (London, 1965), Louis Richard, p.s.s., *Le Mystère de la Redemption* (1959), pp. 221–30.

22 As, for example, in the careful articles of V. Marcozzi, s.j., and M. Flick, s.j., in *Gregorianum*, 1948, pp. 343–416. The position had already been discussed by Père Boyer in E. Amann, *Dictionnaire de Théologie Catholique*, vol. 15, col. 1394–5.

23 *MPN*, p. 65: 'In its exact geographical localization and morphological forms, the hominizing mutation will always elude us . . . Palaeontology can distinguish species only at the *group* stage, and that always at some considerable distance from their point of origin; the question of an original single *couple* (monogenism) has no scientific relevance.' Cf. *PM*, pp. 186, 187. Père Bosio is critical of Teilhard's attitude: 'We can find in the book no hard and fast attitude to the existence at the origins of mankind of a single couple' (*art. cit. Docum. cath*, vol. 53, 1956, col. 122). We might equally well ask whether the Church would teach that monogenism is a scientifically established fact. Cf. C. d'Armagnac, s.j., 'Épistémologie et Philosophie de l'évolution', *Archives de Philosophie* (1960), p. 162: 'It is obvious that palaeontology will never be able to settle the question of the number of individuals forming a stock at a given moment.'

24 'Monogénisme et monophylétisme, une distinction essentielle à faire' (1950). Cf. E. Boné, s.j., 'Polygénisme et Polyphylétisme, orientation présente de la pensée scientifique en matière de l'apparition de l'Homme', *Archives de Philosophie* (1960), pp. 97–137. The author is a member of the Institute of Geology in the University of Louvain and Professor at the Jesuit Scholasticate, Louvain-Eegenhoven.

25 'Autour de Galilée,' *Bulletin de l'Union Catholique des scientifiques français* (July–August, 1961), p. 14.

26 Mgr Bruno de Solages, loc. cit. Cf. D. Dubarle, 'La Science, miroir du destin de l'homme' in 'L'Homme devant la science', *Rencontres internationales de Genève* (1952), pp. 131–63.

Teilhard, 'What should we think of transformism' (1930): 'Evolution is as capable as the theory of fixed species, if not more so, of investing the universe with that greatness, depth and unity which are the natural climate of the Christian faith' (*VP*, p. 159).

27 Cf. Langmead Casserly, *Retreat from Christianity* (London, 1952), p. 21: 'During the last two centuries, sometimes because of the dogmatism and insensibility of not a few scientists or, quite as often, perhaps more often, because of the stupidity of many theologians, such (conflicts) have repeatedly . . . become an actuality.'

28 É. Gilson, *The Philosopher and Theology* (New York, 1962), pp. 217–18.

29 Cf. R. Guelluy, op. cit., p. 31.

30 Cf. Littré, quoted by Renan, *Discours et Conferences*, p. 89: 'The heaven of theology has vanished, and in its place has appeared the heaven of science.'

31 'What should we think of transformism?' (1930), in *VP*, pp. 157–8.

32 On board the *Cathay* (8 September 1935, *LT*, p. 207) in connexion with an article he had just written on 'The Discovery of the Past'. He continues, 'Isn't it an odd thing that the very object of my work should fade into the background as it yields me its fruits?'

33 Letters of 18 January and 15 October 1936. To the Abbé Gaudefroy, 14 February 1935.

34 Letter of 8 September 1916, in *MM*, p. 124. To L. Zanta, 1924: 'The Earth, in all its present and its past, is growing more and more dim to me. It is the future that fascinates me.' Letters of 1 March and 20 April 1948 (Cuénot, pp. 280–1). 'La Réflexion de l'énergie', *QS*, 1952, p. 488.

35 *Archives*, p. 150; second Memorandum for Maurice Blondel. 'L'Atomisme de L'Esprit' (1941).

36 *Dialogue*, p. 132.

37 Émile Rideau, s.j., 'Technicité et Eucharistie' in *Lumen Vitae*, 13 (1958), pp. 691–2. Cf. Paul Claudel, *Conversations dans le Loir-et-Cher*, p. 105: 'Everything could continue still in the same way, if it was simply a matter of carrying on with history and going every morning like our ancestors to see what orders have turned up. But don't you feel that a summons has gone round, that something that must be achieved has become necessary, and that if it is to be achieved we can no longer dispense with a common understanding that knows no limits?'

38 Letter of 4 August 1916. *MM*, p. 116. 'God wishes us . . . to help him.' Genesis 1. 28. Cf. Psalms 8. 6–8.

39 *MD*, p. 53. (*DM*, p. 21) Cf. Letter of 13 November 1918 (*MM*, p. 251).

40 'La Parole attendue' (1950). This is what he calls also 'detachment through action', *MD*, p. 70. (*DM*, p. 40).

41 Versailles Week, 1947. Some months before his death he was thinking of writing a new essay on this subject.

42 *Archives*, p. 137. 'I feel that I would welcome with joy the assurance that I can truly let go of everything . . .' (p. 138).

43 'There seems to be no justification for a phase of detachment, as called for by Père Teilhard. Christian detachment is based on reasons that are permanently operative and always hold good. The obligation, therefore, is imperative constantly and not in alternate periods . . . (In Christian ascesis) no trace can be found of this alternating rhythm advocated by Père Teilhard, in which the succession of detachment and attachment recalls André Gide's Ménalque, who refrains from satisfying his hunger until the last possible moment in order the better then to enjoy earthly nourishment' (Louis Cognet, *Le Père Teilhard de Chardin et la pensée contemporaine*. (1952), pp. 166–7; cf. pp. 168–70).

44 *CM* (1950).

45 'La parole attendue', *CM*, p. 25.

46 *MD*, p. 99. (*DM*, pp. 73–4) 'Le Prêtre': 'simultaneously'. Letter of 10 June 1917 (*MM*, p. 195), etc. Cf. Robert Guelluy, *Vie de foi et tâches terrestres* (1960), p. 160: 'the love of God must make us both involved and detached, profoundly concerned with earthly realities and profoundly detached from everything that happens'.

47 'Forma Christi' (1918).

48 Letter of 18 January 1917 (*MM*, p. 172). *HU*, p. 27.

49 *MD*, pp. 97–8, (*DM*, p. 72) 'The sense of man is already a summons to renunciation' ('Le sens humain').

50 'The New Spirit' (1942), in *FM*, p. 95.

51 Père Teilhard, quoted by F. Russo, in the article 'Homme' (*Catholicisme*, fasc. 20, col. 885). Hans Urs von Balthasar, *Science, Religion and Christianity* (tr. Hilda Graef), p. 47.

52 Letter of 5 February 1917 (*MM*, p. 181), etc. R. Guelluy, op. cit., p. 9: 'Faith does not excuse us from continuing to build. . . . We must still build, but with a new soul . . . we must give ourselves completely to what is being made, attaching ourselves to God alone.'

53 He spoke, too, of what is in a way an embryonic form or preparatory stage of this, the 'impassioned disinterestedness' which is the ideal characteristic of the modern scientist. 'La Mystique de la Science', *Études* (March 1939), p. 926.

54 'Note sur la notion de perfection Chrétienne' (1942). Claude Tresmontant quotes this passage in his *Introduction à la pensée de Teilhard de Chardin* (1956), pp. 104–5. Cf. L. de Grandmaison, retreat note: '(I foresee) that the command of God's Providence will probably commit me to a road in which I shall have wholeheartedly to give up this attachment without giving up the studies and relationships and affections from which it derives; I shall have to aim at success without prizing it, and put all my energies into tasks that I love without becoming enslaved to them, and love greatly without ceasing to love purely—and that means living in the fire without being burnt, living in the world without being of the world—and I can see that this is completely beyond my strength.' Jules Lebreton, *Le Père Léonce de Grandmaison* (1932), p. 130.

55 'Comment je crois' (1934), beginning. To Père Valensin, 12 December 1919.

56 Letters of Holy Saturday 1922, and 27 June 1926.

57 To Père Victor Fontoynont, 15 March 1916.

58 Letter of 27 June 1926.

59 This, he said, 'is the great task that in my view is the only one that now matters'.

60 'Réflexions sur le bonheur' (1944), *Cahiers*, p. 69.

61 'Some reflections on progress' (30 March 1941) in *FM*, p. 81.

62 'Le phénomène spirituel' (from the Pacific, March 1937) in *L'Énergie Humaine*.

63 'Note sur la notion de perfection chrétienne.'

64 'L'Atomisme de l'Esprit' (1941), p. 39. Cf. Gilbert of Hoyland, *In Cantica*, sermo 4, n. 8: '*Circuibo civitatem, universa pertingens, universa petransiens . . . donec pateat plenior aditus, ut intrem in sanctuarium Dei . . .*' (*PL*, 184, 31 BC).

65 To Père Victor Fontoynont, 22 July 1916.

66 Versailles conference, August 1947.

67 *CM*, p. 8.

68 To Père Victor Fontoynont, 26 July 1917.

69 *CM*, p. 24: 'All Père T. did, as it happened, was to tell me that the God of the Cross looked for the "natural" development of my being just as much as for its sanctification, without explaining how or why. But that was enough for me to get hold of the

right end of the stick. And I came safely out of that affair . . .'

70 'Quelques réflexions sur la conversion du monde', p. 2. 'The New Spirit', in *FM*, p. 96.

71 Cf. 'La Centrologie', n. 15. In 1936 (March 4) he writes of the 'rarified atmosphere' of Peking.

72 To the Abbé Gaudefroy, Peiping, 7 October 1929.

73 Letter of 31 December 1926. To M. Teillard-Chambon, 2 March 1952: 'Interiorly, the interest of my life is concentrated more and more on the effort to find and if possible to give voice to the final formulation, in which I wish to express the "soul" of my twofold vision of the Upward and the Forward' (*LT*, pp. 323–4). To L. Zanta, 28 August 1926: 'One consideration that gives me patience is this: even though we should not succeed, in our lifetime, in exteriorizing what we see, it would still be a great deal to have served God as a field of experiment for this wonderful alliance of the loves of Heaven and of Earth.'

74 Letter of 4 July 1920.

75 'Life and the Planets' (Peking 10 March 1945) in *FM*, p. 123. Letter of 25 January 1955.

76 On several occasions he quotes from one or other of these to support his view, as, for example, in 'Super-Humanité . . .' (1943).

77 We find a similar reference, as early as 1916 in 'La Vie Cosmique'. Cf. M. Blondel to J. Wehrlé, Aix, 9 May 1904: 'Mankind's endeavour to integrate Christ in cosmology can never be checked . . . Otherwise Jesus Christ would not be the Word.' On the nature of Blondel's 'pan-Christism' see the study by Henri Brouillard in his *Blondel et la religion* (1961), pp. 160 ff., and Jean Rimand, 'Vie spirituelle et philosophie, Maurice Blondel (*Christus*, 1962).

78 Letter of 21 January 1917, in *MM*, p. 173.

79 'L'Étoffe de l'Univers' (1953). 'L'élément universel' (1919), in *Écrits*.

80 *Esquisse* (1936). First memorandum to M. Blondel (*Archives*, p. 135).

81 *CM*.

82 'Note sur le Christ universel' (1920). Correspondingly: 'if some are to begin and others are to continue to believe, we must place before men the figure of the universal Christ.'—In the article 'Jesus Christ' in the *Lexikon für Theologie und Kirche*, 5, col. 955, Fr. Karl Rahner names as one of the es-

sential tasks for today's theological reflection the constitution of a *Kosmische Christozentrik*.

83 'Social heredity and progress' (1938), in *FM*, p. 34.

84 *CM*, Introduction (1944). 'Le Christ évoluteur' (1942). Letter of 17 September 1919: 'The universal transforming Christ,' (*MM*, p. 307). From this is derived Père Teilhard's bold, if sometimes oversimplified, synthesis between Christianity and evolution. At the same time he rejects any Concordism between science and religion, which are 'two different meridians on the mental sphere'; what he wishes to establish between them is a 'coherence', for 'these two different meridians must necessarily meet somewhere at a pole of common vision' (*Les Études philosophiques*, 1955, p. 581). Cf. 'Comment je crois', p. 21: 'Christ, by giving direction to the world, makes evolution possible.'

85 'Christ, rédemption et géocentrie.' *HU*, p. 24. Letter to the V. Rev. Fr. Janssens, 12 October 1951: 'He *in quo omnia constant* and whom the Society has taught me to love' (quoted in *LT*, p. 42).

86 'Mon Univers' (1918).

87 'Science et Christ (ou analyse et synthèse)' (27 February 1921), p. 13. For an explanation of the concluding words, see Chapter 16. There is no confusion of the two; for Teilhard, in Claude Cuénot's happy phrase, 'Christ is the heart of the world, but the world is not Christ': in G. Crespy, op. cit., p. 59, n. Cf. Col. 1. 17, with the commentary of Père Joseph Huby, *Les Epîtres de la capitivité* (in the series *Verbum salutis*, 1935), p. 42: 'He is the dominating centre and keystone of the universe . . . the prime source of beings, he is also their principle of cohesion and harmony; he makes of the created world a "cosmos", an ordered Universe, by giving it a direction, a value, and relating it to an end.'

88 Saint-Germain-en-Laye, 23 September 1947 (*LT*, pp. 294–5). Cf. Eugène Masure, *Bulletin des anciens élèves de Saint-Sulpice* (15 November 1931), p. 581: 'Christ is not only the bearer of an eternal message which comes as a fresh shock to every man in turn; he is also he in whom mankind finds an unlooked-for answer to the problem of its organic unity.'

89 'Mon Univers' (1918).

90 Letter of Holy Saturday 1922, shortly after the oral examination for his doctorate. Cf. a fine passage in 'Le Christianisme dans le monde' (1933) on Christ 'who is never found wanting',

and on his 'boundless capacity for fitting into the whole physical and psychological order of our universe'.

Chapter 10: Evolution and Freedom

1 'Recherche, Travail et Adoration' (1955).

2 'L'Esprit de la Terre' (from the Pacific, 1931), in *L'Énergie Humaine*.

3 'Some reflections on progress' (1941), in *FM*, p. 78.

4 'Comment je vois' (1948) n. 17. 'La Centrologie' (1944), n. 28. 'The Human rebound of evolution' (1947): 'an *irreversible* rise towards the *personal*', in *FM*, p. 207, etc.

5 'Directions and conditions of the future' (1948), ibid., p. 237.

6 Ibid., pp. 232, 235.

7 'La Centrologie', n. 1.

8 To Marcel Brion (*Nouvelles littéraires*, 11 January 1951). *PM*, p. 311. 'Les propriétés expérimentales de l'Humanité', end. 'Hominization' (1923), in *VP*, p. 77, etc. Cf. Emmanuel Mounier, on technical progress: 'If he can choose the worse, it is because his destiny is the better, because he can travel the high roads along which life proceeds only in danger and drama.' (Quoted by F. Russo, *Technique et Conscience religieuse*, 1961, p. 18.)

9 *Esquisse* (1936), 'L'Union créatrice', (1918): 'Moral effort is the continuation, in our souls, of the same dynamism that produced our bodies.' For the meaning of this sort of 'continuation', see Chapter 17.

10 'L'Atomisme de l'Esprit' (1941), p. 35. Letters of 1 January 1917 and 29 January 1917, in *MM*, pp. 160, 176. 'L'Esprit de la Terre.' 'Turmoil or Genesis' (1948), in *FM*, p. 220. Similarly, ibid., pp. 19, 72, 183, 212.

11 'La Centrologie', n. 31. 'Comment je vois', n. 16.

12 Paul Claudel, *Le Repos du septième jour*, act 3 (*Théâtre*, La Pléiade, vol. 1, p. 778).

13 *Contra epistolam Fundamenti*, c. 1 (Bibl. augustinienne, vol. 17, p. 392).

14 Letter of 14 August 1917, in *MM*, p. 201.

15 'Deuxième Instruction pastorale à l'occasion du cas de conscience', *Oeuvres*, Paris ed., vol. 4, p. 10.

16 *Troisième Reponse au livre premier des Réflexions de M. Arnauld*, p. 264.

17 Cf. George Crespy, *La Pensée théologique de Teilhard de Chardin*, pp. 155-6. One may say, in fact, with Pastor Crespy, that in one sense evil 'no longer exerts the same pressure in an organized, as it did in a chaotic, world' (ibid). It is no longer, however, a question of 'evil' in the same sense. The organization that overcomes chaos by leading up to consciousness, and then to greater consciousness, may on the contrary be considered (and still following Père Teilhard, with whom we cannot but agree on this point) as increasing the evil of suffering, and as making possible the evil of sin (since moral freedom is born with consciousness and grows with it): the progress even of organization can be effected under the banner either of adherence or of revolt.

18 Cf. St. Bonaventure, in *Hexameron*, collatio 16, n. 30 (*Quaracchi*, vol. 5, p. 408).

19 'Mon Univers' (1924), *FM*, p. 307, Letter of 1 January 1917, in *MM*, p. 160.

20 *MPN*, p. 120. 'Faith in Man', 2, 'Power and ambiguity', in *FM*, pp. 187-8. 'At each epoch in history, the last men to arrive have always found themselves in possession of an accumulated heritage of knowledge . . . that is to say faced with a more conscious choice between fidelity and infidelity to life, between good and evil' (*VP*, p. 75).

21 'Note on Progress' (1920) in *FM*, p. 21. Cf. J. P. Blanchard, op. cit., p. 30: 'As regards man-the-species—man-the-species, mark you—Père Teilhard's attitude is one of unshakeable optimism.'

22 *FM*, pp. 37, 57-60, 73-4, 181, 188-9, etc. 'Basis and foundations of the idea of evolution': 'the world ripe for conversion', in *VP*, p. 141.

23 On the consequences of the free act, see a fine passage, marked by the influence of Blondel, in an essay dating from 1919. 'Les noms de la matière': 'initially, it is hardly at all a decision that we take . . . but the situation is soon completely different. As time goes by and we diverge from the directions that have been eliminated by our choice—as secondary options emerge from our option, and the lives that surround us become involved in this ramifying axis—a most complicated structure of existences builds up, and a situation spreads through, and becomes established in, things that we are now powerless to check. Something is born through us, that is independent of us. We have become the slaves of our own freedom' (in *Écrits*).

24 'Formation of the noosphere' (1947) in *FM*, p. 182.

25 'Basis and foundations of the idea of evolution' (1926) in *VP*, p. 137.

26 Op. cit., p. 185; p. 229: 'he makes freedom and responsibility the supreme human value'.

27 'The human rebound of evolution' (1948), in *FM*, pp. 196, 201, 203–4.

28 Towards the end of the last century there was a similar distortion of the chapter in *L'Action* (1893) in which Maurice Blondel deduced in its correct place the *necessity* of the idea of *freedom*; cf. p. 357: 'option is the necessary form in which a will imposed upon itself takes possession of self.'

29 Technology, consciousness, and the necessity of moral and even religious choice are all correlated: 'Place de la Technique dans une Biologie générale de l'Humanité' (lecture given 16 January 1947). M. A. Vandel quotes two works in which a similar view may be found: F. Leenhardt, *L'évolution, doctrine de liberté* (1909), and Gustave Mercier, *Le Dynamisme ascensionnel* (1949), *Revue de Théologie et de Philosophie* (1960), pp. 99–103.

30 'Some reflections on Progress' (Peking, 22 February 1941) in *FM*, p. 61. 'Palaeontology and the appearance of man', in *AM*, p. 33. Père Émile Rideau, in reviewing the French edition of the latter, rightly notes that 'far from the future of man being determined by automatic inevitability, Teilhard constantly insists that there must be a free option for greater unity' (*Revue de l'Action populaire*, November 1959, p. 1150).

31 Ibid., p. 96, 'Faith in Man', (1947), in *FM*, p. 187.

32 'Le Prêtre' (1918), *HU*, pp. 135, 123.

33 *MD*, p. 146. (*DM*, p. 128).

34 *FM*, p. 19, n.; pp. 57, etc. *MD*, pp. 141, etc. (*DM*, p. 122).

35 'Formation of the Noosphere' (1947) in *FM*, p. 182.

36 'The Grand Option' (1939) in *FM*, p. 57. 'Basis and foundations of the idea of evolution', in *VP*, p. 141: 'and this will be, more than ever, the world ripe for conversion'.

37 'Note on Progress', in *FM*, p. 19.

38 'The Grand Option', loc. cit.

39 'Note on Progress', in *FM*, p. 19.

40 Letter of 29 December 1919.

41 M. Louis Cognet, op. cit., p. 192, starts by quoting only the elaboration of this first hypothesis, and concludes, 'None of this, unfortunately, can be found in traditional eschatology.' He adds, however (p. 193), 'The objection has such force that Père Teilhard could not neglect it. In his later writings he puts forward

a second hypothesis'; but this produces only the comment (pp. 194–5) that 'it fits very badly into the general curve outlined by his system; it is much more like a concession than a profound dialectical deduction'.

42 *PM*, pp. 288–9. Cf. O. Rabut, op. cit., pp. 150–1: 'There will be no irresistible grace, such that mankind could welcome it with open arms without having to overcome the difficulties of making a choice. Even when evolutively mature, the world still has the duty of choosing, and the temptation will have increased correspondingly.' This is an excellent summary, and faithfully reflects Père Teilhard's view. On the other hand J. Galot, in an article on *The Phenomenon of Man*, writes, 'This view of the Universe fails to consider man's freedom of choice when confronted with God, in answer to the divine gift of grace.' (*Nouvelle Revue théologique*, 78 (1956), p. 180. (One could not expect to find a theory of grace in *The Phenomenon of Man*, but it deals explicitly with the question of the freedom of option.

43 'Directions and conditions of the future' (1948) in *FM*, pp. 236–7. 'Formation of the Noosphere', ibid., p. 183.

44 'Hominization' (1923), in *VP*, p. 75.

45 'Faith in Man', in *FM*, p. 188. Cf. 'La Mystique de la Science' (*Études*, March 1939, vol. 238, p. 735). 'Science et Christ' (1921). Cf. Pope Pius XII, Christmas message, 24 December 1955: 'Like the builders of the tower of Babel, they dream of an inconsistent "divinisation of man" that would meet all the demands of physical and spiritual life' (*Docum. cath.*, 1956, col. 1). Cf. Address to Italian Christian workers' associations, 7 June 1957: 'Will technology make man into a demiurge?' (*Docum. cath.*, 7 July 1957).

46 'Note on progress', in *FM*, p. 19. One may judge from this what importance, if any, we should attach to Fr. G. Bosio's question (in the article quoted from *Civiltà cattolica*, *Docum. cath.* 1956, col. 122): 'In this evolutionary philosophy, in which there is talk of God, and religion, and Christianity and man's destiny, what place is there for the supreme evil, the disorder of the will that rebels against the divine will?' Prof. Roger Garaudy relies on this opinion of Fr. Bosio's, in his *Perspectives de l'homme* (1960), p. 201.

47 *HU*, p. 121.

48 To L. Zanta, 22 August 1928.

49 'The grand option' (3 March 1939) in *FM*, p. 57. 'Some reflections on progress' (1941): 'We can advance much further still, provided we are clear about the direction in which progress lies

and are resolved to take the right road' (in *FM*, p. 61). In this sense Père Teilhard would have accepted what Mgr Maurice Nédoncelle so rightly calls 'the spiritual penury of collective development and its history' (*Recherches et Débats*, 17, 1956, pp. 123–40). See below, Chapter 13.

50 'Spiritual repercussions of the atom bomb' (1946) in *FM*, p. 148. Reply to *Esprit* questionnaire (no. 125, August–September 1946, p. 246); p. 245: 'In the common activity of scientific research, two opposed mystiques, two different spirits can again be recognized, and they must inevitably again come into conflict with one another.'

51 'Mon Univers' (1918).

52 'The human rebound of evolution' (1948) in *FM*, pp. 202–4. It is in this sense (as the context makes clear) that we should understand the phrase 'moral progress' in this passage (p. 204). Cf. *MPN*, p. 120, on 'the action and pressure of the ever-increasing and ever-fallible sum total of all our "liberties"'.

53 'Mon Univers' (Tientsin, 25 March 1924), *FM*, p. 307. The grand option: 'A final cleavage is necessary to separate absolutely, in a pure state, the conflicting spiritual tendencies which are confusedly intermingled in the present world, at the heart of human freedom.' (*FM*, p. 45), see above, p. 128.

54 'Note on progress', in *FM*, p. 19. 'Certain final revolts of mankind' may be of particular gravity (1947).

55 *MD*, p. 80. (*DM*, p. 52).

56 *HU*, pp. 60, 62.

57 One obviously cannot expect to find a treatment of sin properly so called in works that deal basically with physics, biology and cosmology, and which neither can nor should include it.

58 *MD*, pp. 146–9. (*DM*, pp. 128–31).

59 'The Monstrance', in *HU*, p. 49. 'Mon Univers', *FM*, p. 307.

60 *MD*, pp. 85, 88, 103. (*DM*, pp. 57, 61, 77).

61 *MD*, pp. 147, 148–9. (*DM*, pp. 129–131). 'Mon Univers' (1924).

62 'La Vie cosmique' (23 March 1916), in *HU*, p. 76. Retreat notes. Père Teilhard was not putting it too strongly. His attitude reflects that of many of the saints. 'Christian hope is by its nature boundless. The universal will to salvation has set the seal on its proof in Christ' (Xavier Tilliette, s.j., *Existence et littérature* (1962), p. 141).

63 Louis Cognet, op. cit., p. 131. Cf. 114: 'He refuses to personalize evil, preferring to leave it as a metaphysical [*sic*] abstraction, or even to reduce it to more than a mere inertia in the mechanism of the world.' P. 115: 'There is nothing in evil but

an indispensable condition of evolution, in other words, in short, of creation.' This is to confuse 'evil' with the possibility of evil (if it is a matter of moral evil), or the sinful act with its antecedent conditions.

64 'Comment je vois', n. 31 note. *MD*, p. 82. (*DM*, p. 54).

65 'Christianisme et évolution' (1933).

66 'Le Néo-humanisme et ses réactions sur le Christianisme' (21 September 1948). 'L'Étoffe de l'Univers' (1953). 'Comment je vois'. *Esquisse*.

67 Some of Teilhard's explanations seem to be an exact reproduction, in evolutionary language, of St. Augustine's words, *Contra Secundinum*, c. 12: '. . . Inclinationem ab eo quod magis est, ad id quod minus est, malum esse dicimus.' (We say that evil is a tendency from what is more to what is less), (*Bibl. august*, vol. 17, p. 578). Augustine, however, recognizes, as did Teilhard, that properly speaking there is no moral evil without the consent of the will: 'malum . . . cui anima consentiendo voluntarie peccat' (evil . . . by the consent of the will to which, the soul sins), (c. 13), and that this evil arises therefore from the will itself: 'Ecce unde est malum, a propria scilicet voluntate.' (It is from that, i.e. the person's own will, that evil comes), (c. 19, p. 694).

68 *Nova et vetera* (1957), p. 259.

69 Similarly, we cannot say that St. Thomas reduces sin to a mere inattention because he explains the possibility of an angel sinning, by 'non-consideration' of the higher good (*Contra Gentiles*, bk. 3, c. 110), nor that he confuses moral evil and physical evil because he first gives a generic definition of them. 'Peccare nihil est aliud quam declinare a rectitudine actus quam debet habere, sive accipiatur peccatum in naturalibus, sive in artificialibus, sive in moralibus' (*Prima*, q. 63, a. 1). It is only reasonable to say the same, elementary though it is, in Père Teilhard's favour: he, too, gives a generic definition of evil; he then says that 'there is only one evil; disunity', but at the same time he distinguishes very clearly between simply physical and moral evil, which becomes such when 'it affects the free regions of the soul' ('Mon Univers').

70 Louis Cognet, op. cit., p. 119.

71 J. Galot, in *Nouvelle Revue théologique*, 78 (1956), p. 180. The author bases his conclusion on the fact that 'the word "sin" does not occur' in *The Phenomenon of Man*. The same might be said, surely, of many works, even of a less scientific character, by eminently Catholic writers.

72 Mgr Charles Journet, 'Note sur le Milieu divin', in *Nova et vetera* (1958), p. 227.

73 *Multitude*, end: 'Nevertheless, in contrast with this spiritualized Multitude, there will be some part of being handed over, in full life, to disorganization—there will be spirit that falls prey to the multitude. Faithless creatures, stubbornly and deliberately cut off from God, will suffer the heart-rending conflict with a Multitude aroused and swarming at the heart of their immortal substance. Forced, while fully conscious, to suffer the agony of non-being, they will struggle in an impotent effort to dissolve into dust. And in them, too, Unity will triumph.' 'Les Noms de la matière' (1919), p. 7: on 'the "deathless worm" of a decomposition that can never kill', to which carnal vice and pride doom the soul, in *Écrits*.

74 Letter of 4 June 1933.

75 See in de Lubac, *Catholicism*, Chapter 1, passages from Irenaeus, Gregory of Nyssa, Augustine, Fulgentius, Maximus the Confessor, Anastasius the Sinaite, Paschasus Radbert, etc. Cf. Origen, *In Ezechielem*, hom. 9, n. 1 (ed. Baehrens, p. 405).

76 *Multitude*. Cf. Origen, *In Leviticum*, hom. 7, n. 2: 'Ubi vero venit qui dispersa colligeret et qui dissipata conjungeret, consocians os ad os et juncturam ad juncturam, aedificare caepit sanctum corpus Ecclesiae.' ('When he came who was to gather together what is scattered and join up what is broken down, fitting bone to bone and joint to joint, he began to build the holy body of the Church'.) (Ed. Baehrens, p. 380. Cf. Ez. 37. 7–8, etc. . . .)

77 John 11. 52.

78 Hebrews 13. 20.

79 See above, pp. 113, 115, 116. 'Hominization' (1923): 'Born with the intellect, the temptation to revolt must constantly change and *grow* with it' (*VP*, p. 75).

80 For some time he was attracted by a hypothesis ('pre-cosmic') inspired by St. Gregory of Nyssa, and developed with enthusiasm by his friend Père Pierre Charles. According to this, an 'original Multiple' was born from the dissociation of an already unified being (the first Adam); then came a first phase of 'involution', of spirit in matter, 'an evidently non-empirical phase'. 'Mon Univers' (1924). 'L'Union créatrice' *Écrits*. See above, Chapter 1, note 25.

81 *Le Christ évoluteur* (1942).

82 *MD*, p. 148. (*DM*, p. 130).

Chapter 11: Nature and Grace

1 'Human unanimization' (1950), in *FM*, p. 288. 'Esquisse d'une dialectique de l'esprit' (1946), pp. 3–4. Cf. M. Blondel, *Itinéraire philosophique* (1928), p. 262: '. . . Everything seems to be produced from below; but in reality everything proceeds from above', and the metaphor of the keystone. Cf. M. Méry, 'Plan de l'Être de M. Blondel', Introduction, *Giornale di Metafisica* (1961), p. 543.

2 Letter of 14 August 1917, in *MM*, p. 202.

3 'Mass on the World', in *HU*, pp. 21. Letter of 29 March 1917: 'God alone, and no personal effort' can give us the vision and strength to seek him in all things (*MM*, p. 191).

4 *CM*, hence the methodological preoccupation described in Chapter 7, above.

5 To M. Teillard-Chambon, 7 August 1950 (*LT*, p. 303).

6 To L. Zanta, 25 January 1924.

7 Letter of 15 October 1916, in *MM*, p. 133. Cf. 20 October 1916 (p. 135): 'We have to prove to others and ourselves that the core of our power to love is not rooted in selfishness but comes from God and leads to God . . . Remember Françoise [his sister, a Little Sister of the Poor] and her old folk.'

8 Letter of 1 December 1919. (Quoted by the French editor in *MD*, p. 93. *DM*, p. 67) 'Note sur le Christ universel': 'Created man's slow effort becoming divinizable *in opere* and not only *in operatione*.'

9 *Archives*, p. 151.

10 *MD*, p. 110 n. (*DM*, p. 86).

11 *FM*, pp. 35, 36. To Max Bégouën, 8 April 1930: he encourages him by reminding him that his personal effort is needed, 'at least indirectly, by the body of Christ'.

12 Versailles conference, 1947. Letter of 17 November 1917: 'Technology (i.e. the arrangement and super-arrangement of Matter), has an essentially spiritual role: it is a necessary, though not a sufficient, condition of Man's spiritual maturity.'

13 'Turmoil or genesis?' (1948), in *FM*, pp. 223–4 (our italics). For a fuller explanation of this passage, see Chapter 12.

14 Letter of 20 October 1949.

15 Letter of 7 August 1950, in *LT*, p. 303.

16 Letter of 15 July 1950 (Cuénot, p. 272).

17 Cf. to Père Auguste Valensin, 21 December 1926: 'I think

that a properly conducted study of mankind would bring out, almost scientifically, this truth (known to us for very many years, but still expressible in new terms) that belief in some God is an almost physical factor of balance and progress for the human layer—for the Noosphere, as we say with Le Roy. One could, I am sure, bring to light important natural preparations for Revelation and the Incarnation.'

18 Second memorandum for Maurice Blondel (*Archives*, p. 155).

19 First memorandum (ibid., p. 139).

20 'Social heredity and progress' (1938), in *FM*, p. 34.

21 'Christianisme et évolution' (1945). 'Basis and foundations of the idea of evolution' (Ascension Day, 1926), in *VP*, p. 138.

22 'Comment je crois', n. 21, note.

23 'Trois choses que je vois', p. 21 n. Earlier, in 1920, we find in 'A note on progress': 'Without the process of biological evolution, which produced the human brain, there would be no sanctified souls; and similarly, without the evolution of collective thought, through which alone plenitude of human consciousness can be attained on earth, how can there be a consummated Christ? In other words, without the constant striving of every human cell to unite with all the others, would the Parousia be physically possible?' (*FM*, p. 22). 'The Heart of the problem' (1949) ibid., p. 267 n.

24 'Comment je crois'. (1934).

25 *Teilhard de Chardin* (1961), p. 114; p. 102. Cf. *PM*, p. 298 n.

26 *Dialogue avec Teilhard de Chardin*, pp. 143, 167. Étienne Borne has noted, in a more general way, this mental kinship with St. Thomas: *Cahiers*, 2, p. 160. Cf. Charles Péguy, *Un nouveau théologien*, p. 192, on 'the intimate and deep-seated connexion between culture and faith', and 'the basic sustenance provided for faith by culture'.

27 'La Mystique de la Science' (*Études*, March, 1939, vol. 238, p. 739), St. Thomas, *De veritiate*, q. 27, a. 6, ad primum; a. 5: 'Gratia proportionatur naturae ut perfectio perfectibili': *In Boetium de Trinitate*, q. 2, a. 3: 'Natura praeambula est ad gratiam'; *Prima*, q. 1, a. 8, ad 2^m, etc.

28 *Adversus Haereses*, bk. 4, c. 5, n. 1. (Migne P. G. 7, col. 983 B.)

29 Address to Italian Catholic youth, 19 March 1958 (*AAS*, 50, p. 212, Acts of H. H. Pius XII, vol. 20, p. 192). Quoted by Chauchard, op. cit., p. 133.

30 To Père Valensin, 8 December 1919.

31 Letters of 7 November 1918 and 20 September 1915 in *MM*,

pp. 249–69. 'The natural units of humanity', in *VP*, p. 195: 'the metamorphoses of life', p. 207, etc. Cf. 'L'Étoffe de l'univers', p. 1.

32 *HU*, p. 78. Letter of 2 February 1916, on how men suffered during the war: 'Why must it be that their agony should lack the element of adoration and oblation through which the wearisome task of co-operating with life is transfigured and made intelligible?' (*MM*, p. 92).

33 *Archives*, pp. 151–2. It will be noted that, according to Ernout and Meillet, *Dict. étym. de la langue latine* (1932), under the word *summa*, '*consummo* is akin to *consumo*, with which, in late Latin it tends to be confused'. Cf. L. Richard, *Le Mystère de la Rédemption* (1959), p. 70 n.

34 To L. Zanta, 3 October 1923.

35 To the Abbé Gaudefroy, 15 August 1923.

36 *MD*, pp. 152, 122. Cf. pp. 125–6, 131–2, 136, 140, 150. (*DM*, pp. 136, 100. cf. pp. 104, 111–2, 116, 121, 133) 'Some Reflections on Progress, (1941), in *FM*, p. 80.

37 Quoted by G. Crespy, art. cit., p. 308. 'La Mystique de la Science', loc. cit., p. 740.

38 *MD*, p. 110 n. (*DM*, p. 86).

39 See above, Chapter 8. Père Guérard des Lauriers, *Revue Thomiste* 56 (1956), p. 524: 'Why include under the same name two things so different, and even opposite, as continuity and discontinuity?'

40 *MD*, pp. 131–2. (*DM*, p. 112).

41 *MD*, pp. 102–3. (*DM*, p. 78) *PM*, pp. 88, 90. *Multitude*: 'Who can describe the agony of this metamorphosis?' In another context, cf. *Énergie*, p. 22; on the 'metamorphosis' in the man of the future, 'of certain ancient powers', etc.

42 *MD*, pp. 82, 85, 87; p. 79: 'a specific power of knowing and loving whose transfigured term is charity, but whose roots and elemental sap lie in the discovery and the love of everything that is true and beautiful in creation'. (*DM*, pp. 55, 57, 59, and 71.

43 Moreover, Père Teilhard was more careful than many other writers not to conceive the supernatural as a sort of 'supernature' that formed a 'complete and finished organism' (*MD*, p. 152, *DM*, p. 136).

44 See H. de Lubac, *Exégèse médiévale*, vol. 1 (1956), pp. 344–6. Jean Mouroux, *The Mystery of Time* (New York, 1964), (1962), 'Supernatural finality calls for a universe to be transfigured, and natural finality is a receptiveness of, and an appeal

for, this transfiguration.' Cf. the words in the Ordinary of the Mass, before the offering of the chalice.

45 *Études*, February 1962, p. 160, 'Signification de Teilhard de Chardin'.

46 Mgr Charles Journet, *Nova et vetera*, July–September 1958, pp. 224–6; cf. *Divinitas*, 1959, pp. 339–44.

47 *Revue Thomiste*, 1958, p. 517. The author would seem to be less happy in his regret that Père Teilhard 'does not make it sufficiently clear by what mystery of death and resurrection this is to be achieved'.

48 *HU*, pp. 30–1. *MD*, p. 88, (*DM*, p. 61): 'We have not yet crossed the critical point of our excentration, of our reversion to God. There is a further step to take: the step that makes us *lose all foothold within ourselves. Oportet illum crescere, me autem minui.* ("He must grow greater, and I must grow less.") We are still not lost to ourselves. What will be the agent of that definitive transformation? Nothing other than death.' 'The Grand Option': 'Before passing into the Beyond, the World and its elements must attain what may be called their "point of annihilation"' (*FM*, p. 56). To Père Valensin, 12 December 1919. On elevation to the supernatural, and its gratuitous character, see also a passage in 'Mon Univers' (1924): 'What precisely constitutes the "generous" character of the present world is that the place of the universal Centre has not been accorded to some supreme intermediary between God and the universe, but is occupied by the Godhead itself, which thus introduces us, *in mundo et cum mundo,* to the triune bosom of its immanence.'

Chapter 12: The Transfiguration of the Cosmos

1 Retreat notes, 1941, and 1943 (Peking).

2 See above, Chapter 11, p. 148–151. 'La Centrologie', n. 9: 'critical point of centration'. 'The Phenomenon of Man', in *VP*, p. 166. Cf. *Esquisse*: The successive deaths which are 'critical points scattered along the road to Union'. 'The heart of the problem': 'a certain critical point of collective maturity' (*FM*, p. 267). 'L'esprit de la terre', p. 11.

3 *PM*, p. 168. We shall have to bear this in mind later, see Chapter 17. Péguy was using this same metaphor at the same time as Teilhard. Cf. *Clio*, p. 269. 'There are critical points of the event just as there are critical points of temperature.'

4 See St. Augustine's commentary in *Contra Faustum Manichaeum* bk. 17 and 18; and our *Exégèse médiévale*, vol. 3, pp. 131–6.

5 1. Cor. 7. 31. Rom. 8. 22. We should note also 2 Cor. 3. 18: 'Nos vero omnes, revelata facie gloriam Domini speculantes, in eamden imaginem transformamur' ('And we all, with unveiled face, beholding the glory of the Lord, are being changed into his likeness'), and 1 Cor. 15. 51–2 (ἀλλαγησόμεθα—'we shall be changed'). On the meaning of σχῆμα and μορφή in St. Paul see P. Henry, *Dictionnaire de la Bible*, supplément art. *Kénose*, vol. 5, col. 21–2.

6 St. Ambrose. Cf. Origen, *In Leviticum*, hom. 1, n. 4 (Baehrens, p. 286), etc.

7 *In ascensione Domini sermo* 5, n. 12 (*PL*, 183, 321 A). Cf. *In psalmum qui habitat, sermo* 17, n. 5: 'Sancti . . . a Domini spiritu transformantur' ('the saints . . . are transformed by the spirit of the Lord') (253 A).

8 1 Cor. 15. 44.

9 Letter of May 1920.

10 *MD*, p. 132. (*DM*, p. 112). 'The human rebound of evolution', in *FM*, p. 198. 'Life and the Planets,' ibid., p. 123, etc. About the same time Charles Maurras was praising 'the finest of Catholic dogmas, the dogma that promises the resurrection of the body', but this was only to interpret it from the aesthetic point of view: 'If the youth who is mourned enters into eternity, he undergoes no metamorphosis'; in the concept of Greek art death does not 'transform'; it 'preserves and perpetuates' the glory of a beautiful immortal body': 'Corps Glorieux', *L'Illustration* (Christmas 1926). Cf. Paul Valéry, *Introduction à la méthode de Léonard de Vinci*, 1 (1919), pp. 187–9, where he admires, but interprets wrongly, the Church's teaching on the 'restitution of the flesh'.

11 *MD*, p. 151. (*DM*, p. 134). *HU*, p. 37.

12 *De excessu fratris sui*, bk. 2. (*PL*, 16, 1354). St. Cyril of Jerusalem, *Catechesis* 15, c. 3–4 (*PG*, 33, 873 A, 875 A), etc.

13 Bernard of Morval (Cluny, twelfth century), *De contemptu mundi* 1. v. 39, 43. Cf. Pseudo-Isidore, *Liber de variis quaestionibus*, c. 86 (ed. Vega-Anspach, p. 262).

14 St. Ambrose Autpert, *In Apocalypsin*, bk. 9 (Magna Bibliotheca Vet. Patrum, vol. 13, col. 628–30).

15 St. Jerome, *In Amos*, bk. 2, c. 5. (*PL*, 25, 1043 AB) Filaster, Haer. 80, n. 7–8. (*Corpus Christianorum latin*, vol. 9, p. 251.) Isaac de l'Étoile, sermon 54 (*PL*, 194, 1874 A), etc.

16 St. Hilary, *Tractatus in Psalmum*, 55, n. 12: 'fit in eo demutatione potius quam creatione, quod novum sit'. (*PL*, 9, 362 A); cf. *In Matthaeum*. c. 10, n. 24 (976 c.).

17 See, for example, among many others, St. Leo the Great, Sermon 51 (*PL*, 54, 310 c); St. Isidore of Seville (*PL*, 83, 943); St. Bruno of Segni, *In Isaiam*, c. 18 (*Spicilegium Casinense*, vol. 3, p. 196); Joscelin of St. Bertin, *Liber confortatorius*, bk. 4 (ed. H. Talbot, p. 112); Hervé du Bourg-Dieu, *In 1 Cor.* (*PL*, 181, 850): Anselm of Laon, *In Apoc.* c. 21 (*PL*, 162, 1575 C); Hugh of St. Victor, *Miscellanea*, bk. 1, tit. 81 (*PL*, 177, 516 B); St. Martin of Léon, *In. Apoc.* C. 21, sermo 2 (*PL*, 209, 404 BC), Absalon, sermon 49 (*PL*, 211, 381–2); Otto of Freising, *Chronicon*, bk. 8, c. 9: nature is 'commutanda et transfiguranda' (*Monumenta Germaniae historica, Scriptores*, vol. 20, pp. 281–2), etc.

18 *MD*, p. 152. (*DM*, p. 135).

19 Letter of 8 December 1939 (Cuénot, French edition, p. 300).

20 Letter of 15 February 1940 (ibid.).

21 *MD*, pp. 136, 88. (*DM*, p. 116, 61) Letter of 30 October 1929 (*LT*, p. 160).

22 'The Mass on the World', in *HU*, p. 25.

23 Retreat note, 1941; eighth day, Parousia.

24 *Énergie*, cf. p. 38. 'The human rebound of evolution', in *FM*, p. 198.

25 To the Abbé Gaudefroy, 11 October 1936. See Chapter 16.

26 'The heart of the problem' in *FM*, p. 260 f.

27 To Père Russo, 21 November 1952: 'In sound and strict biology, the probabilities for the future are not on the side of a milleniarism nor of an ageing of the species (Eddington, etc.) but on that of a critical point of convergence.' This whole attitude, he notes, runs counter to 'communist Messianism'. To the same, 23 December 1952.

28 'Mon Univers' (1924). 'Comment je vois' (1948): there will be a 'final emergence'. *PM*, p. 287: 'a reversal of equilibrium'.

29 'Comment je vois', n. 19.

30 'Cuénot, pp. 55–6; cf. 457. He writes, however, to Père Valensin, on 13 October 1933: 'I am working in the direction not so much of an "idealist" transposition as of a "spiritualized transposition" of the universe.'

31 Cf. H. de Lubac, *Aspects du Bouddhisme*, vol. 1 (1951), pp. 136–40, 186–90 (*Aspects of Buddhism*, London, 1953). Newman, *Christ hidden from the world*, Sermon XVI, Parochial Sermons (Oxford, 1839).

32 *MD*, p. 149. (*DM*, p. 131) Cf. Paul Claudel, *Le Repos du septième jour*: 'One and the same fire burns in a threefold dwelling—it is the same fire that nourishes us in life, that is in heaven the splendour and fusion of the blessed, and is the agony and burning of Hell' (*Théatre*, La Pléiade, vol. 1. p. 757). Cf. St. Isidore, *De natura rerum*, C. 15 (Fontaine, 229).

33 'L'Esprit de la Terre', end, in *L'Energie humaine*. Cf. above, Chapter 5.

34 *MD*, pp. 150, 151. (*DM* p. 133–4) 'Mon Univers', *FM*, pp. 306–7. There is not the least resemblance between this concept of the Parousia and the crude fantasy which M. Louis Cognet sees in it, when he says, op. cit., p. 189, 'I cannot help being reminded of the ideas, very little known in France, of Fedorov, for whom the resurrection of the dead will itself be the ultimate product of scientific research working hand in hand with charity: if we love our dead sufficiently, we may well find some way in the end of bringing them back to life.'

35 Yves de Montcheuil, *Leçons sur le Christ* (1949), p. 175.

36 M. Goguel, *Revue d'histoire et de philosophie religieuses*, 1935, p. 347. Cf. J. Huby, *Épître aux Romains* (new ed. by Stanislas Lyonnet), p. 301.

37 'Le Christique'.

38 'L'atomisme de l'esprit' (1941), pp. 26–7.

39 'Comment je vois', n. 24. 'L'activation de l'énergie humaine' (1953). 'Trois choses que je vois': this will be 'the parousiac flash-point'.

40 'Mon Univers.' *FM*, p. 307. 'Trois choses que je vois' (1948).

41 *MD*, p. 151. (*DM*, p. 134). 'La Place de l'homme dans l'Univers' (1942), p. 13. To the Abbé Gaudefroy, 7 October 1929: 'I believe that the internal tension of spirits (even if it is not exteriorized) must play a great part in the coming of the true Kingdom of God.'

42 E. Fuchs, 'Le Phénomène, présentation et critique de la pensée du Père Teilhard de Chardin', in the *Bulletin du centre protestant d'études*, ed. by J. de Senarclens, P. Bonnard, J. Derous (Geneva and Lausanne, December 1958), pp. 3–23.

43 He confines himself to a single reference, with no further details, on page 3, to the title of *Le Milieu Divin*, saying that 'on his own admission (Père Teilhard) had made no very profound study of theology, and his personal spiritual interests directed him more towards problems of asceticism and Christian mysticism than towards dogmatic questions'.

44 Similarly, in the first memorandum for Maurice Blondel, we find 'death, night, turning back (*retournement*)' (*Archives*, p. 135).

45 P. 22: 'Christian eschatology envisages a rupture—and how profound a rupture!—since it is effected through a judgement that consists in a putting to death and a resurrection.' The reality of death, judgement and resurrection is not in dispute. But to say that the end of the world is 'a putting to death' is to use language that is foreign to Catholic tradition, and it is not surprising that Père Teilhard does not use it or its equivalent: although he had no objection to the word 'rupture'.

46 *Divinitas*, 1959, p. 234, n. 29, p. 242.

47 The question arises only in the case of the final generation. Teilhard speaks of a 'turning about that is like a death' (cf. 'La Grande Monade': 'happy the world that is to end in ecstasy!') —which echoes St. Paul, 1 Cor. 15. 51 and 1 Thess, 4. 15–17.

48 *Dialogue avec Teilhard de Chardin*, p. 156, with references to *MD*, pp. 151–2. (*DM*, pp. 134–5).

49 *Moralia in Job*, bk. 17, c. 9, n. 11 (*PL*, vol. 76, col. 16). St. Bernard, in connexion with man, *De diligendo Deo*, c. 10, n. 28: 'Manebit quidem substantia, sed in alia forma, alia gloria, alia que potentia.' ('The substance will remain, but in another form, another glory, another potency.') Père Teilhard more than once refers explicitly to the Greek Fathers, for whom Christ 'uplifts and saves the totality of matter by sanctifying spirit'. 'The New Spirit', in *FM*, p. 94, etc. Cf. Paul Claudel, 'the earth is risen again . . . the same but made new' (*La Cantate à trois voix*).

50 They were anticipated in this by one line of modern scholastic philosophers. Thus Lessius, *De summo bono*, bk. 3, c. 8 (ed. Hürter, pp. 539 and 554–5); Drexelius, *De aeterno damnatorum carcere et rogo*, c. 4 (Munich, 1630), etc.

51 In particular in relation to the pleasures of the table and sensible expression of married love.

52 For example Matt. 22. 30; 1 Cor. 6. 13; Apoc. 21. 22–3.

53 Saint Cyril of Jerusalem, *Catechesis*, 19. C. 18: . . . μᾶλλον δε, ὡς οἶδευ ὁ ἀυιστῶυ κὺριος (*PG*, 33, 1040A). Honorius, (ed. Endres, p. 152.) Cf. St. Chromacius of Aquilea, *In evangelium Matthaei tractatus* 3. c. 6, v. 5: 'Tunc autem videbimus eum, accepta immortalitate, in caelestem gloriam transformati (CCL, vol. 9, p. 400) ('then, we shall see him, once we have received immortality and been transformed into the glory of heaven'.)

St. Augustine, *Contra Adimantum*, c. 12, n. 5: 'Jam non caro et sanguis erit, sed in corpus caeleste mutabitur.' ('It will not be flesh and blood any more but will be transformed into a heavenly body'), (*Bibl. August*, vol. 17, p. 276). St. Maximus, *Ambigua* (*PG*, 91, 1076 BC). St. Bernard, *De diligendo Deo*, C. 15, n. 39, commenting on 2 Cor. 5. 16 (*PL*, 182, 999 AB), etc.

54 J. J. Surin, s.J., *Autobiographie* (Lettres, ed. Michel-Cavallera, vol. 2, p. 38).

55 If some of St. Augustine's presentations are more material than those of other Fathers, they still do not justify the conclusions arrived at by the theologians whose views we are questioning.

56 *Compendium theologiae*, c. 158. Thus St. Thomas does not base the essence of his position on an obsolete system of physics: even though it is true that this 'physics' is an assistance to him in commenting on the text of 1 Cor. 7. 31. Cf. ibid., c. 172.

57 Letter of 6 January 1917, in *MM*, p. 162.

58 Cf. 'Les noms de la matière' (1919), pp. 11–12: 'One can conceive a state in which everything in us that is now blind and rigid compulsion, would become flexible balance, mobile and conscious.'

59 Letter to Père Laberthonnière, 2 December 1915 (Cl. Tresmontant, p. 234).

60 See Chapter 19.

61 *De Genesi ad litteram*, bk. 1, c. 19, n. 39 (*PL*, 34, 261).

62 *In 2 Sent*. dist. 12, q. 1, a. 2. *Summa*, Prima, q. 68, a. 1.

63 To Père Auguste Valensin, 8 December 1919. This is what the liturgy calls 'terrena despicere et amare caelestia'—to despise the things of earth and love the things of heaven. Cf. 'Mon Univers' (1924): The world must 'lose its visible form, in us and in its totality': it 'can reach God *in Christo Jesu* only by a complete recasting in which it must appear to be lost in its entirety, with no perceptible compensation (of the terrestrial order)'.

64 1 Cor. 15. 51.

65 Fragment *De resurrectione* (*PG*, 11, col. 98 CD).

66 *In Matt*. XII, 30 (ed. Klostermann, p. 671). *De principiis*, bk. 1. c. 6, n. 4: '. . . Si enim mutabuntur caeli, utique non perit quod mutatur; et si habitus hujus mundi transit, non omnimodis exterminatio vel perditio substantiae materialis ostenditur, sed immutatio quaedam fit qualitatis atque habitus transformatio . . . In hoc fine si qui materialem naturam, id est corpoream, penitus interituram putet, nullo omni genere intellectui meo occurrere potest, quomodo tot et tantae substantiae vitam agere ac subsistere sine corporibus possint . . . Certius tamen qualiter

et habitura sit res, scit solus Deus, et si qui ejus per Christum et Spiritum sanctum amici sint.' 'If the heavens are changed, what is changed certainly does not perish; and if the form of this world passes away, one should by no means see in that an annihilation or disappearance of material substance, but a change of quality and transformation of form . . . If anyone believes that, in this end, material, that is to say corporeal, nature is to perish entirely, it is utterly impossible for me to understand how so many and so large substances could subsist without bodies . . . God alone knows for certain both how this will happen and whether any of us, through Christ and the Spirit, are his friends' (ed. Koetschau, pp. 84–5). See also, arguing against the return of a 'sensible Paradise', Nicetas Stethatos, treatise on the 'new heaven and new earth' (*Sources Chrétiennes*, vol. 81, pp. 508–15).

67 Gennadius, *De ecclesitiasticis dogmatibus*, c. 6 (*PL*, 58, 982 D).
68 Phil. 3. 20–1.
69 Apoc. 21. 5. Cf. Romans 8. 19–22.

Chapter 13: Personalism

1 'Panthéisme et Christianisme', pp. 2–3. *Énergie*, p. 63. *CM*, beginning.
2 'La Vie Cosmique', *Écrits*.
3 Letter of 9 October 1916, in *MM*, p. 130. Shortly afterwards he wrote 'La Vie Cosmique'; letter of 4 October 1917 (ibid., p. 206).
4 Père Guérard des Lauriers, O.P., 'La Démarche du Père Teilhard de Chardin, réflexions d'ordre épistémologique', in *Divinitas*, 1959, pp. 250, 256–7.
5 *MD*, p. 113. (*DM*, p. 90).
6 See above, Chapter 5.
7 'Réflexions sur le bonheur', *Cahiers*, p. 70.
8 It is Teilhard, again, who says that 'on this earth we are cut off, we are hamstrung', and refers in this connexion to the *Phaedrus*: 'Panthéisme et Christianisme', p. 2.
9 'Note on progress' (1920). Hence, in 'The grand option' (1939), 'optimism of withdrawal or optimism of evolution' (*FM*, pp. 11, 43). In 'The cone of time' he says of Christian detachment that it is 'no longer a withdrawal but an act of emerging' (*FM*, p. 96).

10 Letter of 28 December 1916, in *MM*, p. 158. Cf. 5 August 1917 (ibid., p. 199).

11 Quoted in *FM*, p. 307.

12 Letter of 1 September 1926, in *LT*, pp. 132–3.

13 Cf. *MD*, pp. 99, 104. (*DM*, pp. 74, 79).

14 *PM*, p. 272.

15 *Énergie*, 'Centrologie', nos. 15, 24, 30.

16 *FM*, p. 123.

17 Similarly in 'Comment je vois' (1948), etc.

18 'The end of the species', in *FM*, p. 302.

19 *Esquisse* (1936).

20 'La Vie Cosmique' *Écrits*: Christianity is 'a religion of persons, the religion of souls'. At the final term he posits not simply 'a harvest of souls' but 'a world of souls'. 'Palaeontology and the appearance of man' (*AM*, p. 57). 'Mon Univers', 1924. 'The true evolution of the world takes place in souls, and in the union of souls'. Wedding address, February 1948: 'Far from being fragile and accidental, it is souls alone that progress infallibly and alone are destined to endure.' February 1929: 'This personal treasure the centre within every soul, is imperishable' (*LT*, p. 151). 'La crise présente' (*Études*, 20 October 1937, p. 163). 'La mystique de la science' (1939, *Études*, vol. 238, p. 741). 'The fulfilment of the Universe' coincides 'with the access of individual souls to a higher, and distinct, centre of personality' (to L. Zanta, 24 January 1929). Cf. *MM*, pp. 64, 180, etc.

21 Letters of 25 February 1929 and 15 August 1936.

22 'L'esprit de la terre' (1931), *L'Énergie Humaine*.

23 Letter of 23 September 1934, in *LT*, p. 205. He adds an English title, 'Why and How'. Cf. 6 July 1934, to Père Jouve: 'In my view, the Personal is again dominating the whole evolution of things.'

24 Letter of 15 November 1935, in *LT*, p. 216.

25 To Max Bégouën, 26 September 1937, from Peking (*LT*, p. 232).

26 'The human rebound of evolution' (1948), in *FM*, p. 207.

27 *Énergie*.

28 'La Crise présente, réflexions d'un naturaliste' (*Études*, 20 October 1937, pp. 163–4). Mgr Charles Journet has taken a sentence from this article, as also from one published in 1945 in the *Cahiers du monde nouveau*, that might well give the reader a false impression of the general meaning of both (*Divinitas*, 1959, p. 336, n. 19).

29 Loc. cit., p. 164.

30 *PM*, pp. 254–72; 'The Grand Option' in *FM*, pp. 59–60. 'Le Sens de l'Espèce chez l'Homme' (1949).

31 *PM*, p. 207; cf. p. 290. Letter to Max Bégouën, 11 November 1929; all our energies must 'bring God the homage of the world' (*Cahiers*, p. 24).

32 Letter of 3 May, 1953.

33 *Esquisse.*

34 To M. Teillard-Chambon, 18 October 1940, in *LT*, p. 269.

35 Cf. Claude Cuénot, 'Pierre Teilhard de Chardin, sa vie mystique à Pékin', 1936–46, in *Rencontre Orient-Occident*, vol. 3 (May–December 1957), p. 3.

36 *CM*, 1950.

37 *Esquisse, PM*, p. 257.

38 Cf. Einstein, *Out of My Later Years* (London, 1950), pp. 26–7.

39 'Comment je crois', p. 23. 'L'Esprit de la terre', p. 33.

40 *Journal d'une mission ouvrière*, p. 36.

41 'Some reflections on Progress' (Peking, 1941), in *FM*, p. 75. 'The natural units of humanity' (*Études*, 5 July 1939): 'Just as man . . . will lose the courage to construct and go on seeking, so he will have no more strength to conquer the inner antipathies which separate him from the joys of unity unless he finally becomes conscious that he is drawing near, together with the universe, not only to something but to Someone' (*VP*, p. 215). 'Comment je crois', p. 24.

42 Letter of 15 August 1936.

43 'Hominisation et spéciation', *Revue des Questions scientifiques*, 90 (1952), p. 438, in *VP*, p. 256.

44 *Esquisse.* Other references in Cuénot, pp. 377–380.

45 Letter of 17 April 1923 (*LT*, p. 67).

46 *HU*, p. 120. Letter of 17 September 1919: 'I felt once again the longing to live only as a force or a living idea, so completely would the influence of the *unum necessarium* animate me—to live completely depersonalized—"in him, seen in all things"' (*MM*, p. 307).

47 *HU*, p. 32. First memorandum for M. Blondel: '. . . The fulfilment of the world is consummated only through . . . a turning back, an excentration and a quasi-depersonalization of the monads' (*Archives*, p. 135; cf. p. 141).

48 Letters of 23 September and 8 October 1917 (*MM*, pp. 203, 209). '. . . through the utter annihilation of my ego' (*HU*, p. 32). Later, he puts it even more definitely, 'positive annihilation' (15 February 1940). Cf. *La perle évangélique*, 'our

whole salvation consists without doubt in this nothingness', and countless similar expressions. J. P. Camus, *Défense du pur amour*, p. 492: 'This word "extinction" occurs as frequently in Scripture as the word nothing or nothingness. . . . Only a stranger to France could fail to understand the word, and only a novice in the spiritual life would be ignorant of its mystical significance' (H. Bremond, vol. 11, p. 197). Fénelon, *Manuel de piété*: 'It is by the extinction of my own limited being that I shall enter into your divine immensity.'

49 Phil. 2. 7: *exinanivit semetipsum.*

50 Memorandum for M. Blondel, *Archives*, pp. 135–6.

51 To L. Zanta, 15 April 1929.

52 Letter of 16 July 1929 (Cuénot, p. 210 n.).

53 *LT*, p. 159.

54 8 October 1933. *Esquisse*, p. 52: 'I do not think that there is any better, or even any other, natural centre to the total coherence of things than the human person. Starting from this complex mesh in which the soul is linked with the body, the Cosmos unravels as we look back, and ahead in accordance with a simple law that satisfies both intelligence and action.

55 *Énergie* (1937). Pascal called God 'the universal being'. *Pensées*, section 17 (ed. Jean Steinmann, 1961, p. 229).

56 'Some reflection on progress' (1941), in *FM*, p. 79. The universe increasingly exhibits an 'organized heterogeneity' (*VP*, p. 222).

57 *Esquisse.*

58 *Énergie*, *PM*, p. 262: 'Through neglect of this universal rule many a system of pantheism has led us astray to the cult of a great All in which individuals were supposed to be merged like a drop in the ocean or like a dissolving grain of salt. Applied to the case of the summation of consciousness, the law of union rids us of this perilous and recurrent illusion.'

59 *Méthode et Principes du Père Teilhard de Chardin* (1961), p. 15.

60 'The Grand Option', in *FM*, pp. 52–7. *MPN*, pp. 114–15. 'All science teaches us that on the level of the "simple life" union differentiates the elements it brings together. At the stage of reflection, as we discover by self-observation, it personalizes us'. (*AM*, pp. 269). 'La Centrologie', nos. 27 and 28. Cf. Léopold-Sédar Senghor, in *Cahiers*, vol. 3 (1962), pp. 35, 56–7.

61 'Life and the Planets' (1945), in *FM*, p. 119. *PM*, p. 258; p. 260: 'to think it, undergo it, and make it act, it is *beyond* our souls that we must look'.

62 *Esquisse*.

63 *HU*, p. 35. *Introduction*, p. 22: 'This, one should be careful to note, is not a restriction or a weakening but, on the contrary, a perfection and an accentuation of the idea of unity.' The connexion between the universal and the personal is explained in the present writer's *Catholicism* (London, 1950), Chapter XI, pp. 177–92.

64 *PM*, p. 263: 'It looks as though we have lost both respect for the person and understanding of his true nature.' *Esquisse*, p. 16: 'The source of our resistance to the collective is to be found in the illusion that makes us persist in identifying "personal" with "individual".' *Énergie*, p. 42.

65 'La Centrologie', no. 27, c. n.

66 Cf. Henry Bars, commenting on J. Maritain: 'we still have no more than a germ of personality' (*La Politique selon Jacques Maritain*, 1961, p. 29).

67 See above, Chapter 8. He was well aware that there is a 'false anthropocentrism' (*PM*, p. 35). In a letter from Peiping, 29 April 1934, he explains his attitude to both: 'Nothing is more ambiguous than the accusation of *anthropocentrism*. False anthropocentrism is the sort that attributes human properties to animals below us, *without any correction*—and to the Divine, above us. But there is another anthropocentrism, legitimate and undeniable—which consists in attributing value, *starting from ourselves*, to a Universe *of which we form a part* (not simply because we are included in it, but because its development takes place through us). The whole difficulty lies in making ' "corrections by analogy" '. It is the old scholastic truth—but given new expression in the light of Duration'.

68 Victor Delbos, unpublished manuscript, quoted by M. Blondel, 'Un interprète de Spinoza, Victor Delbos', in *Chronicon Spinozanum*, vol. 1 (1921), pp. 295–6.

69 'Comment je crois', p. 12. Similarly, J. A. Cuttat, answering the charge that some Eastern thinkers may bring against the Christian faith: 'An anthropomorphic God?—by no means; homocentric Universe and theomorphic man. Moreover, it is in the mystical body of Christ that the personalization of the Cosmos is completed and "realised" '. (In his forthcoming *L'expérience chrétienne, est-elle capable d'assumer la spiritualité orientale?*)

70 *Énergie*.

71 *Summa Theologiae*, 2a, 2ae, q. 64, a. 2: 'Omnis pars naturaliter est propter totum; . . . quaelibet autem persona singularis com-

paratur ad totam communitatem, sicut pars ad totum.' Cf. 1a
2ae, q. 109, a. 3.

72 'La Crise présente', *Études*, 20 October 1937, p. 163.

73 To Marcel Brion. M. Brion, 'Rencontre avec le Père Teilhard
de Chardin', *Les Nouvelles littéraires*, 11 January 1951.

74 To Marcel Brion, loc. cit.

Chapter 14: God All in All

1 'La Centrologie', no. 7.

2 Peking, 22 November 1936. *Esquisse*.

3 Letter of 4 May 1931, in *LT*, pp. 177–8.

4 'Quelques remarques pour voir clair sur l'essence du sentiment
mystique' (Winter, 1951).

5 Letter of 20 November 1918, in *MM*, p. 256.

6 'Comment je vois', n. 33 *MD*, p. 117. (*DM*, p. 94).

7 'La Route de l'Ouest' (1932). 'Comment je vois', no. 37:
'Christian mysticism is "The higher and personalized form of
the mysticism of the West".'

8 See the Abbé Monchanin's lecture, extremely personal and extremely Teilhardian, on 'Forms, life and thought' ('Formes, vie
et pensée') included in *L'Abbé Jules Monchanin* (1960), pp.
162–75; also his study of the Christian and Hindu views of
time ('Le temps selon l'hindouisme et le christianisme') in *Dieu
vivant*, p. 14.

9 Letter of 29 April 1934. Jacques-Albert Cuttat, op. cit., similarly finds a system of thought that is 'spatial and extensive in
type' in both 'eastern and mystical' intellectualism and 'western
and philosophical' intellectualism: he sees both combined in
the work of René Guénon, which adds an 'extreme Cartesian
precision to eastern spirituality'.

10 'La Crise présente', *Études*, 20 October 1937, vol. 233, pp.
163–4.

11 To L. Zanta, 7 August 1923. To the Abbé Breuil, 1 October
1923. 'Quelques remarques' (1951).

12 This essay was first published in Paris in 1950, by Robert Aron
in the *Revue de la pensée juive*, and later in Japan in the
Monumenta Nipponica. Cf. Cuénot, pp. 297–320.

13 Cf. 'La Vie cosmique', *Écrits*: 'And as I allowed myself to
drift towards the Centre, ever more diffuse and without tension,
I found that the light of life was growing dim in me.'

14 L. Cognet (op. cit., p. 160) finds Père Teilhard's distinction 'completely arbitrary'.

15 'Comment je vois', no. 33. He notes 'the extreme confusion' that runs together or identifies the 'Inexpressible' of the Vedanta with that of St. John of the Cross; no. 27: it is 'love that enables us to distinguish' these two inexpressibles. 'Quelques Remarques' (1951).

16 *Dialogue*, p. 178. Cf. p. 172. Nevertheless, L. Cognet has not hesitated, again, to say that Père Teilhard sees in the dogma of the communion of the saints 'some ill-defined extinction of the limits of the person'; and emphasizes his disapproval by contrasting with Père Teilhard's view the 'extremely firm personalism' on which the dogma rests. Mgr M. Nédoncelle, on the other hand, shows that personalization is the precise contrary of a hardening of the limits of the person: *Conscience et Logos* (1961), in particular, pp. 9 and 133.

17 Jacques-Albert Cuttat; in addition to his *La Rencontre des religions* (1957), see his 'Dialogue chrétien avec l'Orient spirituel', in *Choisir* (Fribourg and Geneva, 24 October 1961); an article in which the fullness of the author's grasp would have delighted both the Abbé Monchanin and Père Teilhard.

18 Père Bosio, s.j., sought to apply to Père Teilhard the words of the encyclical *Humani generis* aimed at those who 'do not hesitate to show that they favour the *monist* and *pantheist* hypothesis of a universe undergoing a perpetual evolution' (Père Bosio's italics.) (*Civiltà cattolica*, 17 December 1955: *Docum. cath.* 1956, col. 117). Père Teilhard, in fact, never ceased to combat such an 'hypothesis'. No doctrine is more strongly opposed than his to this sort of 'perpetual evolution'.

19 Père Guérard des Lauriers, loc. cit., pp. 222–8.

20 Letter of 27 July 1915. To Marcel Brion. 'Comment je crois', pp. 14, 17. *CM*, p. 7 'false pantheism'; *MD*, p. 116. (*DM*, p. 94).

21 Réflexions sur deux formes inverses de l'esprit' (25 July 1950).

22 'Panthéisme et Christianisme', p. 1.

23 *Énergie*.

24 *Esquisse*.

25 'Mon univers' (1918). Cf. *Énergie*, p. 25: on the antiquity of 'pantheistic aspiration towards a universal communion'.

26 *Esquisse. HU*, p. 26. 'Panthéisme et Christianisme', p. 6.

27 'Panthéisme et Christianisme', *passim*.

28 'La Vie cosmique', *Écrits*. Cf. John Lafarge, S.J., in *America*, November 1960.

29 'Comment je crois', p. 36.

30 'L'élément universel' (1919) in *Écrits*. Cf. J. Monchanin, 'De l'esthétique à la mystique', (1955), pp. 37–8, 45–6.

31 'Le Milieu mystique' in *Écrits*, *MD* (see Chapter 20), etc. It would not, accordingly, be quite accurate to say without qualification, that 'to designate his position, he adopts the term pantheism'. (G. Crespy, op. cit., p. 58).

32 Père Valensin agreed with him: letter of 28 August 1919 (*MM*, pp. 303–4). 'The difficulty is to keep within the truth, and not, in order to contradict Spinoza, refute St. Paul.' The 'pantheism' of the poets is 'a psychological force' and contains a part of 'lived truth' (17 December 1922).

33 Letter of 17 December 1922. 'Life and the Planets' (1945), in *FM*, p. 120.

34 'Panthéisme et Christianisme.' What he rejected, under the name of 'juridicism', was 'the exclusive analogy of human social relations (taken in their artificial content)'. 'Mon univers' (1924).

35 *MD*, p. 57.

36 *PM*, p. 294. 'Panthéisme et Christianisme': 'Indeed, what evolutionist pantheist has ever spoken of the All with more splendour than Paul speaking to the first Christians?'

37 'Réflexions sur deux formes inverses d'esprit', p. 6.

38 *Esquisse*. On the term 'monist', see 'Comment je crois', p. 12. *Énergie*: 'Towards a Christian monism.'

39 Coined, it would seem, in the eighteenth century by the English writer John Tolland. Even about 1830 it was not in use in French: cf. Saint-Beuve, *Causeries du Lundi*, 29 October 1849, on Lamartine's *Raphaël*. It soon came into common usage. The nineteenth-century deists applied it on more than one occasion to the Catholic doctrine. Renouvier applies it to Thomism. The rarely-used 'panentheism' lends itself to similar confusion.

40 *De falso traditionalismo*, n. 4 (Denzinger-Rahner, 1952, p. 463, n. 1652). The word is here taken from a passage by Augustin Bonnetty, who accused the modern scholastics of falling, through their method, into *naturalismum et pantheismum*.

41 Letter of 13 March 1932. 'La Centrologie', no. 4: 'cosmogenesis through centrogenesis', etc.

42 Marcel Méry. 'Les deux dialectiques de Blondel', *Annales de la Faculté des Lettres d'Aix*, 34 (1961), p. 15. Cf. M. Blondel',

La Philosophie et l'esprit chrétien, vol. 1 (1944), p. 281, on 'The doctrine of the universal Mediator': 'All that part of the truth which pantheism had glimpsed through the development of speculative reason up to knowledge of the third degree, is completed, given warmth and life by this panchristism which allows each one to retain his own originality and loveableness while at the same time raising him up so that he may enter into what we may call "the blazing furnace of charity".'

43 'The Grand Option', in *FM*, p. 53. *PM*, p. 309. *Énergie*, pp. 46–66. 'Centrologie', no. 29. 'The Pyx', in *HU*, pp. 53–4 n. Cf. Roger Leys, s.j., in *Balisage*, University Journal (Louvain, special number, March–April, 1961). *Le Point Oméga*, etc.

44 *De Trinitate*, bk. 4, c. 7, n. 11 (*PL*, 42, 895–6). Cf. Origen, *In Leviticum*, hom. 7, n. 2 (ed. Baehrens, p. 378). *Periarchon*, bk. 1, c. 6, n. 2, quoting John 17. 22–3. Eph. 4. 13. 1. Cor. 1. 10 (ed. Koetschau, p. 82). St. Gregory of Nyssa, in 1 Cor. 15. 28 (*PG*, 44, 1316 B, 1320 C) etc.

45 Hans Urs von Balthasar, introduction to Le Visage de l'église, translated from St. Augustine by Camelot and Grumel, Paris, 1958.

46 *Registrum*, vol. 1, p. 333, St. Ambrose, *Epist.* 30, c. 14: 'ut fiat in omnibus omnia Christus'—that Christ may be all in all. *De fide*, c. 183, etc.

47 *In Psalmos paenitentiae* (*PL*, 79, 658).

48 *De divisione naturae*. He qualifies it more precisely: 'naturae integritate permanente'–'the integrity of their nature remaining'–'naturarum igitur manebit proprietas'–'the characteristic quality of their nature will therefore be unimpaired'. Cf. Paul Vignaux, *Philosophie au moyen âge* (1958), p. 20. Étienne Gilson, in *Beiträge Baümker*, vol. 3 (1935), p. 191. In the twelfth century, Hugh of St. Victor was more perceptive or more indulgent than the nineteenth-century historians of medieval thought were to be.

49 *Ad Fratres de Monte Dei*, bk. 2 passim (*PL*, 184, 345 A, 348–9, 352 B). *In Cantica*. n. 77–8, 107, 128 (M.–M. Davy, pp. 106, 136, 160). Cf. Gilbert of Stanford, *In Cantica*, bk. 5 (Leclercq, *Studia anselmiana*, 20, p. 230).

50 *De diligendo Deo*. c. 15 n. 29: 'Totus perget in Deum, et deinceps adhaerens ei, unus cum eo spiritus erit'–'All spirit will proceed to God and thereafter, cleaving to him, will be one with him.' (*PL*, 182, 998 D). Sermo 80 *de diversis*, n. 1: 'Unitas spiritualis est, quae nos conjungit Deo'–'There is a unity of the spirit, which joins us to God' (183, 699 A). *In*

Ps. qui habitat, sermo 14, n. 3: 'Factus est ipse tecum caro una: te quoque secum faciet spiritum unum'—'He is made one flesh with you: and he will make you too one spirit with himself' (240 B), etc. 1. Cor. 6, 17, the scriptural passage most frequently quoted by St. Bernard.

51 We find the same accusation of pantheism and confusion in Julio R. Meinvielle, 'La Cosmovision de Teilhard de Chardin', in *Estudios Teologicos y filosoficos*, vol. 2 (Buenos Aires) pp. 107–34. In all his interpretations the author relies primarily on Père Guérard des Lauriers. Those who seek union with God, Louis Lavelle has written, 'should beware of meriting the accusation of pantheism; but the others should equally beware of making the accusation too hastily'. 'Le Théisme et le panthéisme' (*Le Temps*, 8 February 1939).

52 *Énergie.* 'Mon Univers' (1924).

53 Letter of 17 December 1947. In 1924, in Tientsin, it was with these same words of St. Paul that he ended his 'Mon Univers' (*FM*, p. 308). Cf. letter of 2 February 1916 (*MM*, p. 93). *Introduction* (1944), p. 1, etc.

54 Letter of 17 December 1922. He could, too, have pointed out that St. Paul speaks of the members of Christ as a single new man. At the entrance to the Institute of Geobiology that he had founded with Père Leroy in Peking in 1940 and dedicated to Christ the King, Père Teilhard had put up an inscription: 'ut sit Deus omnia in omnibus'.

55 Cf. 1 Cor. 15. 26, 27, 28, *FM*, p. 309.

56 In proof of the materialist monism professed by Père Teilhard, Père Guérard des Lauriers quotes the phrase 'to be all, to be fused with all', referring to *CM*, p. 8. Père Teilhard's actual words are 'To be all, fuse myself with all'. That, however, is not the really important point. Père Guérard des Lauriers omits to quote what follows. It continues: 'This is the mystical act to which, following poets and Hindu mystics, I would logically have been drawn by an innate and imperative need to find my level, by access not, I insist, *to others*, but *to the Other* —had not there chanced, just in time, to germinate in me, like a seed come from I know not where, the idea of evolution, etc.' The criticism mistakes for Père Teilhard's own thought, and for the expression of his own principle, the temptation that he says he was in time to avoid, the danger he explains his escape from, the mistake that he time and time again refuted.

Chapter 15: A Reversal of Method

1 Cf. L. Malevez, *Nouv. Revue théologique*, 79 (1957), p. 591.
   L. Cognet, op. cit., p. 22.
2 He expresses similar thoughts, this time in connexion with historians, in a letter of 31 January 1953 (Cuénot, p. 345).
3 Cf. Albert Vandel, 'L'importance de "L'Évolution Créatrice" dans la génèse de la pensée moderne', *Revue de Théologie et Philosophie*, 10 (Lausanne, 1960). Thus Lamarck, 'as later Bergson and Teilhard de Chardin were to assert, saw the true criterion of progressive evolution in psychic faculties' (p. 88). Others are referred to by name in G. Crespy, op. cit., Ch. 1.
4 To Max and Simone Bégouën, Peking, 9 May 1940, in *LT*, p. 263.
5 To M. Teillard-Chambon, New York, 22 November 1952 (*LT*, p. 334).
6 'The Cone of Time', in *FM*, p. 82.
7 'The Planetization of mankind', in *FM*, p. 126. In 'Man's Place in the Universe' in *VP*, p. 216, he goes so far as to say, in a somewhat extreme metaphor: 'I confine myself . . . to the field of facts, that is to say to the domain of what can be touched and photographed.'
8 As for example in connexion with tool-making at Choukoutien and its relation to Sinanthropus. Letter of 26 March 1932: 'I have made the Geological Survey of Peking back-pedal, in time . . . etc.' Writing to the Abbé Breuil, 25 March 1932, he refuses to draw any conclusions without 'indisputable positive proofs'. 'I recognize that certain details in the Nihowan deposits could be explained by Man. But they can *also* be explained in other ways. And, with something so new, we cannot afford to commit ourselves to any "ambiguity".' To the same, 8 May 1932: 'I am persecuting Pei to be more meticulous in his stratigraphy.'
9 *PM*, pp. 257–258.
10 Ernest Renan, *L'avenir de la science*.
11 Letter of 10 January 1920.
12 To the Abbé Gaudefroy, 14 January 1924, in connexion with the study of the Earth.
13 *PM*, p. 35.
14 'Comment je crois', p. 6.

15 *HU*, p. 24.

16 'La mystique de la science', *Études*, vol. 238 (March 1939), p. 734.

17 *PM*, foreword, p. 35. 'The future of man seen by a palaeontologist' (Peking, 22 February 1941), in *FM*, p. 65.

18 From a letter to Teilhard, 3 December 1952 (Cuénot, p. 393). This, though expressed differently, seems a fair reflection of Père Teilhard's view.

19 *Énergie*, 'Science et Christ, (ou analyse et synthèse)' (lecture, 27 February 1921): analysis by itself can introduce us only to 'an infinitely dissociated world', to 'a swarming of elements governed only by statistical laws of large numbers and chance'. All this stems 'from a fundamental error in outlook'.

20 *PM*, foreword, pp. 35–6; p. 55. Letter of 17 December 1922: some people regard 'all other beings (except man) as lacking any "within" . . . without asking themselves whether this notion of purely "external" being is even thinkable'.

21 'The human rebound of evolution' (*QS*, 20 April 1946), in *FM*, p. 210.

22 'Turmoil or genesis?' (*L'Anthropologie*, September 1948), in *FM*, p. 218.

23 *Esquisse*. On analysis and synthesis in the study of living forms see 'The transformist paradox' (1925) in *VP*, p. 96.

24 *Esquisse*, *PM*, p. 33, to Père Valensin, 13 October 1933: 'You know that my "hobby" [he uses the English word] is to prove that science is marking time, and turning its back on religion, simply because it has never tried to integrate thought into its series.'

25 'L'esprit de la terre' (1931) in *L'Énergie Humaine*. Cf. M. Blondel, *L'Action* (1893), p. 95: 'The universe focuses its rays in him (man).'

26 1929 (*LT*, p. 151). To L. Zanta, 24 January 1929. 'The Movements of Life' (1928): 'Entropy is the name that physics give to that apparently inevitable fall by which collections of corpuscles (the seat of all physico-chemical phenomena) slide, by virtue of statistical laws of probability, towards an intermediate state of diffuse agitation, a state in which all exchange of useful energy ceases on our scale of experience.' It is 'the decline or diminution of utilizable energy' (*VP*, pp. 149, 167).

27 'Le Christique', p. 3.

28 'The Phenomenon of Man' (1930), in *VP*, p. 172. 'La Convergence de l'univers' (1951), pp. 5–6.

29 To M. Teillard-Chambon, 6 September 1953 (*LT*, p. 344).

30 Letter of 25 February 1929. Earlier, in 1921, he has said: 'Reality eluded us, and was constantly drawing still further away from us with each fresh analysis, just as a light eludes a man who tries to catch its reflection. We have in fact been moving in the direction in which everything breaks down . . . If we are to reach the luminous, solid, zone of the world, it is no use travelling towards what lies deepest below us or furthest behind us; we have to make our way towards what is most interior in the soul and most new in the future' ('Science et Christ').

31 C. d'Armagnac, s.J., 'De Blondel à Teilhard, nature et intériorité', *Archives*, vol. 21 (1958), pp. 298–312. Blondel seeks also to show how 'interiority and exteriority meet' and 'how there is continuity from knowledge of the object to knowledge of the subject' (*L'Action*, p. 88). He speaks similarly of 'methodological phenomenism'; but in 1963 he notes that 'phenomenology' would be more appropriate.

32 'Philosophie de la nature et méthode chez le Père Teilhard de Chardin, *Archives*, vol. 20 (1957), pp. 19–39.

33 *La Vie intellectuelle* (March 1956), p. 15. He is speaking of accepted usage 'at the level of physics', and Père Dubarle recognizes that 'the process of a biologist's thought can never be reduced to that of the pure physicist'; Père Teilhard 'correctly applied the lesson on method that the practice of his own science taught him in relation to the realities of the biological field' (p. 14).

34 'La Centrologie', no. 30, etc. *Énergie*.

35 Cf. Henri Gouhier, *Bergson et le Christ des Évangiles* (1961), pp. 27–37.

36 He does not, however, speak of 'panpsychism', and it will be noted, as it is by J. Blanchard (op. cit., p. 42), that he would not accept the word.

37 'Man's place in the Universe' (1942) in *VP*, p. 225. 'La Centrologie', no. 8, etc. These terms are obviously inadequate (though one would be hard put to it to improve on them) but they are suggestive. In *La Connaissance de l'univers* M. Jean-E. Charon similarly distinguishes an 'elementary' and a 'complex' psychism (pp. 135–53). He praises Teilhard for having discovered elementary psychism and so opening a door 'to a new view of things'. Nevertheless I do not believe that the explanation he gives conforms completely with Teilhard's thought.

38 'La Centrologie', n. 1–2, n. 8–17. 'Un sommaire de ma vision phénoménologique du monde' (1954). Cf. Jean Mouroux, *The Mystery of Time* (New York, 1964).

39 *PM*, pp. 53–66, etc.

40 'La Convergence de l'Univers' (1951), p. 5.

41 *Esquisse*: 'In this I am not introducing any judgement of absolute value. I am not trying to find out whether a more conscious being is *absolutely* better than a less conscious. All I am doing is to record (a succession, etc.).' p. 53: 'The notion of absolute best does not enter into the working out of my scheme, either explicitly or implicitly, nor do the notions of causality or finality. All that I am asking the positivist thinkers of today to consider is an empirically observed law of recurrence, a rule of succession in duration.'

42 'The human rebound of evolution', in *FM*, p. 210.

43 '*Le parallélisme psychophysique et la métaphysique positive*' (1901): Biology and the sciences of man 'observe and experiment without there ever being at the back of the scientist's mind any question of arriving at a mathematical formulation'. (*Écrits et Paroles*, vol. 1, p. 141); cf. the comment of Henri Gouhier (*Bergson et le Christ des Évangiles*, p. 43): 'With biology, it is a new type of intelligibility that calls for understanding; a further clarity is added to mathematical clarity . . . the evidence is of two types, according to whether it *demonstrates* truth or discloses reality.'

44 'The Phenomenon of Man' (1930) in *VP*, p. 174.

45 To Père Valensin, 4 July 1920. Cf. Letter of 15 October 1926: 'Geologists, I know not why, study all the concentric spheres that make up the earth except one: that formed by the layer of thinking beings. To scholars specifically interested in man, geology is a closed book. What we have to do, therefore, is to unite the two points of view. (Cuénot, p. 70–71).

46 *Rapport* (1867): 'That a searching study of the phenomena of life must oblige positive science to broaden its scope and go beyond the pure mechanism it has been confining itself to for the last three centuries, is a possibility that we are now beginning to envisage, even though the majority refuse to admit it' (quoted by Gouhier, op. cit., p. 33).

47 Jean Baruzi. *Leibniz et l'organisation religieuse de la terre*, p. 227.

48 See in particular 'L'atomisme de l'esprit, un essai pour comprendre la structure de l'étoffe de l'univers' (Peking, 13 September 1943); 'Centrologie', no. 31. It will be remembered that Leibnitz, in connexion with this very 'double infinity' of Pascal, said that it 'is only an approach to my system' and that it must

be understood that 'the whole of matter is organic throughout'. *Iné, dits. Théologie*, 20, fol. 213 recto.

49 *PM*, p. 53. Père d'Armagnac (*Archives*, vol. 20, p. 14) rightly notes that this short introduction to Chapter 2 of the *PM*, which is earlier in date than the foreword to the book added in March 1937, undoubtedly brings out more clearly the originality of Teilhard's method. See also 'Un sommaire de ma perspective "phénoménologique" du Monde' (1954), *Les Études philosophiques* (1955), p. 569.

50 Père P. Malevez has some wise comments on this matter. 'We have to recognize,' he writes, in 'La Méthode du Père Teilhard de Chardin' (*Nouvelle Revue Théologique*, 79, 1957, p. 592), 'that there is no trace in *The Phenomenon of Man* of the main themes which have emerged from the whole great phenomenological movement. There is no hint of what constitutes the essence of the phenomenological method and its results; no rejection of the natural attitude which, according to the phenomenologists, disguises consciousness from itself; no reduction nor ascesis that allows the mind to recover and rediscover itself in its function as the universal giver of meaning. The subordinate themes themselves are also absent. Particularly notable is the lack of any apparent awareness of the personal drama of the "existent".' Père Malevez sees in this a 'deficiency' and concludes from it that *The Phenomenon of Man* is curiously unmodern (p. 586). He would have liked to find in Teilhard the themes of Husserl and Merleau-Ponty. These complaints would seem to be based on an ambiguity. One might equally well complain at not finding Teilhard's cosmological themes in Husserl and Merleau-Ponty. Why should either one of these two concepts of phenomenology be taken as the standard by which the other is judged? It would be better to recognize that the same word is differently applied in each case, and try to understand, and so judge, each work on its own. Père Teilhard said explicitly: 'My phenomenology is not the phenomenology of Husserl and Merleau-Ponty.' No doubt he had better things to do than to give us variations on Husserlian themes. For Blondel's phenomenology, cf. Henri Bouillard, *Blondel et le Christianisme* (1961), Ch. 3, in particular pp. 165–72. E. Minkowski's phenomenology, which studies 'anthropocosmic solidarity' (*L'idée de l'univers*, second congress of the Société de Philosophie française) represents a use of the word intermediate between the two.

51 Letters of 29 April 1934 and 3 December 1954.

52 C. d'Armagnac, s.j., *Archives* (1957), pp. 5–41.

53 *Bergson et nous*, p. 214.

54 D. Dubarle, o.p., 'A propos du Phénomène humain', *La Vie intellectuelle* (March 1956), pp. 17–19. O. Rabut, op. cit., p. 15: 'In different forms, and giving it a new significance, he returns to the Aristotelian notion of nature as something which develops and expands'; p. 40: 'he rediscovers, in personal terms, far-reaching Aristotelian intuitions; I believe he is right in showing that there is an internal aspect in things.'

55 Bruno de Solages, *La Pensée chrétienne face à l'évolution*, loc. cit.: 'In so far as one can enclose so modern a thought in ancient structures, it must be admitted that his fundamental outlook is what Aristotle called physics and the Schoolmen call cosmology. It involves, in considering the whole of the real, the objective point of view that is proper to science, the presentation of a systematic account of it and the distinguishing of its essential laws and postulates.' See also Paul Grenet, *Teilhard de Chardin* (1961), p. 118.

56 Aristotelian hylomorphism, he says, represents 'the projection of modern evolution on a world without duration' (*VP*, p. 129 n.). Cf. 'Singularities of the human species', in *AM*, p. 208.

57 'What should we think of transformism?' in *VP*, p. 154.

58 'L'esprit de la terre' (beginning). *PM*, p. 281.

59 C. d'Armagnac, *Archives* (1957), p. 7: 'In this case, as with Descartes, for example, or Hegel, the method, in its novelty and importance, is inseparable from the system.'

60 'No thinker,' writes P. Chauchard, op. cit., p. 16, 'has been so little understood . . . this is because his point of view is so new . . . that one is at loss to know how to place him.'

61 François Russo, s.j., 'L'oeuvre scientifique du Père Teilhard de Chardin', in *Choisir* (Fribourg, 14 December 1960): 'Starting from extremely detailed and extensive analyses, and with no break in the development of his thought, Père Teilhard rises to views of great width that lead us to a deeper understanding of life.'

62 Nicholas Berdiaev, *The Meaning of the Creative Act*.

63 Since very often, as J. P. Blanchard says (op. cit., p. 103), 'in the subconscious of the purest scientist there lurks a philosopher'.

64 'Mon univers' (1924). 'Les Noms de la Matière' (1919). Moreover, 'an analytical observation of phenomena cannot enable

us to attain God': 'Note sur les modes d'action divine dans l'Univers' (January 1920).

65 *Esquisse* (1936). For some time he had seemed to accept a more pronounced dualism. The human soul 'entirely synthetic in its activities, escapes science, the essence of which is to analyse things into their elements and material antecedents. Only insight and philosophical reflection can find it' (*AM*, p. 57). 'How the transformist question presents itself today' (1921): 'To decide whether the movement of evolution is intelligible in itself, or if it requires a progressive and continuous creation implemented by a prime mover, this is a question that belongs to metaphysics.' At the same time, he goes on to add: 'transformism, we must tirelessly repeat, imposes no philosophy. Does this mean that it does not hint at one? Of course not' (*VP*, p. 23).

66 *Énergie*. 'The human rebound of evolution', in *FM*, pp. 206–7. S. Strasser, 'Évolution et Mystère', in *Le Mystère, Semaine des intellectuels catholiques* (1959), pp. 105–9.

67 'La Centrologie', no. 33. 'Mon Univers' (1924).

68 As, in fact, is already being said: and it is a pleasure to find oneself in agreement on this point with Père Jean Daniélou: cf. *Études* (February 1962), 'Signification de Teilhard de Chardin'.

69 C. d'Armagnac, 'Épistémologie et philosophie de l'évolution', *Archives*, vol. 23 (1960), p. 154. See also an important study by Fr. Smulders, s.j., 'Evolutieleer en Toekomstverwachting bij Teilhard de Chardin', in *Bijdragen* 21 (1960), pp. 223–80; p. 259; Teilhard's science is less abstract than what is now generally understood by the word—a point that is of cardinal importance for the understanding of his thought. Cf. p. 237, note, 10: we necessarily think of every individual unity by analogy with our own experience of unity, and a distant *analogatum* of human consciousness is to be found in all matter.

Chapter 16: Faith and Intelligibility

1 *Balisage*, special number (Louvain, 1961), p. 31. In his 'Note sur le Christ universel' Père Teilhard called on theologians to 'explain this eminently Catholic notion of Christ the Alpha and Omega'.

2 *PM*, pp. 251, 260; p. 259: 'Because it contains and engenders

consciousness, space-time is necessarily *of a convergent nature.*
Accordingly, its enormous layers, followed in the right direction, must somewhere ahead become involuted to a point—which we may call *Omega*—which fuses and consummates them integrally in itself.'

3 'La Centrologie', n. 18–19.

4 *PM*, pp. 262–72. 'L'esprit de la terre' (1931) *L'Energie humaine. MPN*, p. 121, etc. Cf. Paul Chauchard, *L'Être humain selon Teilhard de Chardin*, pp. 145–61.

5 Cf. 'The formation of the noosphere' (*QS*, January 1943), in *FM*, p. 181.

6 *PM*, pp. 53–66, 262, 271. *MPN*, p. 121. Père Pierre Charles, reflecting the influence of his friend Teilhard, spoke of 'the aspiration that raises up the world, unconscious of its destiny, towards the universal term, towards the Omega of all reality'. 'Dante et la Mystique', *Revue néo-scholastique de Philosophie* (1921), p. 139.

7 *Esquisse.*

8 'Basis and foundations of the idea of evolution' (Bay of Bengal, Ascension Day, 1926), in *VP*, pp. 133–6. See Chapter 18.

9 Cf. A. D. Sertillanges, quoting St. Thomas; H. de Lubac, *Sur les chemins de Dieu* (1955), pp. 168–71. St. Thomas, *Ia*, q. 32, a. 1; *In Boetium de Trinitate*, q. 5, a. 4.

10 To L. Zanta, 15 April 1929.

11 *PM*, p. 270.

12 'La Centrologie', n. 25, 32. 'Hominization', in *VP*, p. 79.

13 And he knows even more indisputably that 'scientific transformism, strictly speaking, proves nothing for or against God . . . It presents us with an anatomy of life, certainly not a final reason for it'. 'The transformist question' (1921), in *VP*, p. 23. Evolution, however, is another matter.

14 *MPN*, p. 116. 'La Centrologie', n. 3: 'a certain pole or focus of universal synthesis'.

15 'Comment je crois' (1934), pp. 2, 8. This is what contemporary philosophers would prefer to call belief.

16 On 3 December 1954 he was to write that what seemed to him 'most vital' in his 'hyperphysics' was its 'energetic side'.

17 'Singularities of the human species', appendix, in *AM*, p. 271 'Comment je crois', pp. 9–10. On immortality in Omega, see 'Centrologie', n. 25.

18 'Contingence de l'Univers et goût de survivre' (1 May 1953).

19 'Man's place in the Universe' (1942), in *VP*, p. 216.

20 Letter of 31 January 1955 (Cuénot, p. 354). M. Jean Rostand

thinks that in this connexion Teilhard 'underestimates man's instinctive and affective forces. The impetus that has carried him to his present position cannot be arrested by any abstract certainty, however disappointing that certainty may be'. (*Le Figaro littéraire*, 18 March 1961. *Que deviendra l'homme sur la terre?*) The force of Père Teilhard's supposition, it is clear, rests entirely on his general theory of the evolution of reflective consciousness and on the progressive predominance of 'true action'—a notion akin to his notion of 'research'.

21 'Comment je vois' (1948), n. 18. 'The end of the Species' (1948): only this 'hunger for *more-being* . . . can preserve the thinking earth from the *taedium vitae*' (in *FM*, p. 303).

22 'La Centrologie', n. 17. 'The directions and conditions of the future' (1948): 'The regressive cases of indolence (search for *well*-being as opposed to *more*-being) . . . (*FM*, p. 230 n.).

23 *Énergie*. What impels us forward is not simply a fatal instinct. To believe that would be to misunderstand 'the real crux of the problem of man'. 'If it is directed mainly towards the lesser evil, Life takes cover in a protective sheath—becomes "encysted" we might say: It has no need to press on.' Mankind is born not from an effort to *survive* but from a will for *fuller-living*.

24 'Comment je crois', p. 10. 'Man's Place in the Universe', in *VP*, p. 221–2.

25 'L'activation de l'énergie humaine' (6 December 1953): 'There will be no physical lack: but what about courage? what about spiritual impulse? what about psychic resources?'

26 'Man's Place in the Universe', in *VP*, p. 230. *PM*, p. 230. *Énergie*, p. 40. To the Abbé Gaudefroy, 14 February 1925. 'Comment je crois', p. 11: 'Before setting out tomorrow on the great adventure from which its consummation is to emerge, the human mass will have to collect itself together in its entirety and examine once and for all the value of the impulse that drives it forward', etc.

27 'Comment je crois', p. 10. With Blondel he associates Édouard Le Roy, whose effect came later and was not so decisive. At the same time, while Blondel's influence remains recognizable, Teilhard's thought develops on different lines.

28 Père Rabut's objection in this connexion may perhaps derive not so much from a more rigorous conception of science as from a mental attitude with an existential tinge (op. cit., pp. 103–4).

29 'La Réflexion de l'énergie', *QS* (20 October 1952), p. 495.

30 'L'esprit de la terre', in *L'Énergie Humaine* etc.

31 To L. Zanta. *Esquisse*.

32 'Comment je vois' n. 20 note. See below, p. 209.

33 Cf. 'The formation of the Noosphere' (1947) in *FM*, p. 180. It is the mind that refuses to entertain the idea of total death.

34 'The human rebound of evolution', in *FM*, p. 201. Cf. Jean Rostand, *Ce que je crois* (1953), pp. 75, 77: 'That intellectual dissatisfaction is our portion, that we must resign ourselves to living—and dying—in darkness and anxiety, that is one of the things of which I am certain . . . This certainty of the final extinction of all human values cannot fail to appear desperately disappointing to some—including, I must confess, myself—but I believe that it must ultimately be accepted and "controlled" . . .' The transition from one 'certainty' to another will be noted.

35 *Énergie. PM*, p. 254.

36 In 'Science et Christ' (1921) he had criticized 'extreme pragmatists', i.e. 'the utilitarians'.

37 On 'What is truly exceptional in the essence of the phenomenon of thought' see 'Turmoil or genesis?' in *FM*, p. 219. 'It becomes more and more necessary to us, in order to live, to *understand* man.' ('The phyletic structure of the human group', *Annales de Paléontologie* 37 (1951), in *AM*, p. 132.)

38 Letter of 7 November 1915, in connexion with Paul Bourget's *Le Sens de la Mort* (*MM*, p. 78). To L. Zanta, 3 October 1923: 'Don't allow yourself to be intimidated or influenced by what X or Y may say to you in criticism of the intelligence as opposed to mysticism . . .'

39 'Comment je crois', p. 10. 'Mon Univers' (1918): 'I have always aimed, in everything, at attaining something of the Absolute; otherwise I would never, I believe, have had the courage to carry on.' 'Formation of the Noosphere', in *FM*, p. 180.

40 Peking, 1945 Retreat. 'Comment je crois.'

41 *PM*, p. 284: 'Man will continue to work and to research so long as he is prompted by a passionate interest. Now this interest is entirely dependent on the conviction, strictly undemonstrable to science, that the universe has a direction and that it could—indeed, if we are faithful, it *should*—result in some irreversible perfection.' 'Le Christianisme dans le monde' (1933), pp. 5–6: 'Mankind will have lived just long enough to be certain that the world could not offer it the only thing that made life worth the trouble of living. That, it would seem, is a hypothesis that must be eliminated, since it would reduce the

universe to absurdity.' 'Turmoil or genesis?' (1948), in *FM*, pp. 225–6. Étienne Borne was closer to Teilhard than he realized when he wrote ('Biologie et Humanisme', *Semaine des intellectuels catholiques*, 1957, pp. 167, 168): 'Man will hesitate between the final purpose and the absurdity of life . . . The world disclosed to us by biology is a world in movement and incomplete, a pathetic world patient of two interpretations, offered either by tragic pessimism or by dramatic optimism. Its meaning is both present and absent, hidden and exposed.'

42 'Comment je crois', p. 9.

43 'Singularities of the human species,' appendix, in *AM*, pp. 208–273. *PM*, pp. 267, 269–70. 'La Réflexion de l'énergie', *QS* (1952), p. 495.

44 *PM*, pp. 267–8. Here Père Teilhard echoes the early Jesuit missionaries who related the Buddhist nirvana to *materia prima*. 'Sur deux formes inverses de l'esprit' (1950): the eastern mystic 'seeks to attain the undifferentiated zone of prime "stuff" (the Aristotelian "prime matter"?) in which opposition disappears and everything is identified with everything in the basic substance common to all things'. See above, Chapter 14. H. de Lubac, *La Rencontre du Bouddhisme et de l'Occident*.

45 'L'union créatrice' (in 'Mon Univers').

46 *Esquisse*. See above, Chapter 11, n. 1, 2. 'Esquisse d'une dialectique de l'esprit' (1946): 'If it is seen as we ascend from our side of things, the apex of the evolutionary cone (Omega point) stands out at first on the horizon as a focus of simply immanent convergence. But, if we look more closely, it is clear that if this focus is to hold together it presupposes, behind it, and deeper than it, a transcendent, divine nucleus.'

47 Letter of 19 January 1929 (*LT*, p. 151). *AM*, p. 272. *Energie*, *PM*, p. 272. Further, 'the world is infused, from the humblest level of belief in God, with an irresistible attraction' 'Foundatione', 1926, in *VP*, p. 139). On the attributes of Omega, see 'Centrologie', n. 20–4.

48 'Comment je vois', n. 24. 'L'esprit de la terre' in *L'Energie humaine*: 'We have followed the cosmic spiritual phenomenon *from within*, by the way of simple immanence. But now the very logic of that way obliges us to stand outside and recognize that the current that raises up the world must be conceived not so much as a mere internal impulse, but as a *tide*.'

49 St. Thomas, *Summa Theologiae*, Ia, q. 2, a. 3: 'Ergo necesse est devenire ad aliquod primum movens, quod a nullo move-

atur: et hoc omnes intelligunt Deum'; 'et hoc dicimus Deum', etc. ('Therefore we necessarily arrive at some prime mover, itself unmoved: all men understand this as God'; 'and this we call God.') Cf. Père A. D. Sertillanges' explanations in the *Revue des Jeunes* edition, pp. 341–2, 347.

50 'Un front humain spirituel', in *La Table Ronde* (June 1955): cf. Cuénot, bibliography, no. 178.

51 'Man's place in the universe', in *VP*, p. 231.

52 'On the probable coming of an ultra-humanity' (1950), in *FM*, p. 279.

53 11 May 1923, in *LT*, pp. 70–1: 'I believe, in fact, that this is a fundamental option of all thought, a postulate which cannot be proved but from which everything is deduced.' See above, p. 345, n. 41.

54 Claude Cuénot, 'Teilhard de Chardin et les philosophies', in *La Table Ronde* (June 1955), p. 37. 'Basis and foundations of the idea of evolution': 'faith in a supreme centre of personalization, concentration and cohesion, the only point at which the salvation of the universe can be conceived' (in *VP*, p. 141). Cf. The fourfold 'I believe' in 'Comment je crois', and the three 'basic options' in 'Trois choses que je vois' (1948), pp. 2–4.

55 M. de Tollenaere, loc. cit., p. 317. *PM*, pp. 232–4. About 1923 to 1924, at a time when his ideas on this question had not finally crystallized, he wrote to L. Zanta: 'I feel, as you do, that it would be possible, metaphysically, for the universe to mark time, and for Mankind's efforts to vanish into nothingness. As you again, in considering this question on its own, I would be inclined to hesitate about what will remain of our consciousness after death—But there you are: I have seen and experienced that there can be no coherent life without an abounding faith in a universe whose whole movement urges us to a supreme Union. All I want to do in future is to live that faith and make it real. To satisfy it, I believe fiercely in some sort of progress, and those who deny it I regard as pernicious heretics. And, to still my anxiety about the "beyond", I close my eyes in the arms of the Greater being who draws me along. I do not think that anyone who has always professed his trust in the Energy that drives the World has anything to fear from it. On the other side we shall be something very new. But it will still certainly be us, in a better form.'

56 *Introduction*. Cf. 'The end of the species', where he concludes that there must be 'the expectation of some revelation', etc.

57 'Comment je vois', n. 28.

58 *PM*, p. 313. It is thus with the hope of 'the final success of hominization' (p. 308 n.), with the idea of original sin (p. 312), and the determination of the attributes of Omega. It is in a context of faith that Omega can be identified with Christ or that one can see the Church 'as the central axis of universal convergence and the exact meeting point that springs up between the Universe and Omega Point': 'Comment je vois'.

59 J. L. Russell, s.j., '*The Phenomenon of Man*' (two articles) in *The Heythrop Journal*, vols. 1 and 2; vol. 2, January 1961, p. 13. '. . . When all legitimate criticism has been made, it seems to me that Teilhard's vision of the universe as an unity in which all things are orientated towards the final consummation in the Mystical Body of Christ is both reasonable and important. His ideas should, at the least, be a stimulus and inspiration to philosophers and theologians for many years to come.'

60 *PM*, foreword, p. 35.

61 To the Abbé Breuil, 25 May 1923 (in *LT*, p. 73). Cf. the moving declaration dated from Nanking, 10 April 1934: 'In my distress following Black's death, and in the stifling atmosphere of "agnostic" condolences that surrounded it, I swore to myself, on the body of my dead friend, to fight more vigorously than ever to give hope to man's work and inquiry' (*LT*, p. 202).

62 'Basis and foundations of the idea of evolution', in *VP*, p. 140. There is no scientific formula that will automatically eliminate 'the fundamental tragedy of uncertainty, of the support that vanishes, of the answer that never comes' (Diary, 16 February 1948).

63 Art. cit., pp. 106–7. In Teilhard, in fact, 'mystical experience comes first', and he seeks to clear a road that will lead others to faith; but it does not follow that his faith enters into the logical assumptions in his argument and that his procedure ceases to be a 'phenomenology'. It is perhaps an exaggeration to say that because of this, *The Phenomenon of Man* often seems 'unintelligible to non-believers'; and it is certainly untrue to say that it is 'regarded as heretical by the Catholic hierarchy.'

64 *PM*, pp. 35, 40.

65 Cf. To L. Zanta, 24 January 1929.

66 *CM*, 3.1, The Heart of Jesus: 'That spark through which my universe, still only *half* personalized, was to succeed in becoming amorized and so centred.'

67 'Le Christique', p. 8.

68 'Le Sens humain' (1929), Chapter 4.
69 'Comment je vois', n. 36, 37.

Chapter 17: Neologisms and Analogies

1 Rabut, op. cit., pp. 209, 189, 157–8.
2 Letters of 5 August 1936 and 2 February 1920.
3 *Introduction* (1944), p. 11.
4 X. Le Bachelet, art. 'Apologétique', in Père A. d'Alès, *Diction-naire apologétique*.
5 'Comment je crois', p. 16. Nevertheless, Père Teilhard did not contest the miracle, but allowed it its place.
6 'Le Christique' (1955). 'As soon, on the other hand, as the Universe, through a cosmogenesis orientated on a Christic Omega, assumes for us the form of a really convergent whole . . .'
7 *Esquisse*. 'The Cone of Time': 'The transposition of all human values', in *FM*, p. 89.
8 *Esquisse*. 'Quelques réflexions sur la conversion du monde', p. 8 'Comment je vois', n. 37. 'Le Christique', p. 13.
9 'L'atomisme de l'esprit', p. 34. We should, however, note (p. 36) that he qualifies this to some extent: 'No, contrary to the general opinion, charity is not out of fashion, not obsolete.' And in 'Panthéisme et Christianisme' he says, more correctly, that the charity preached by Christ, if properly understood, 'has nothing in common with our philanthropy'.
10 'Comment je crois', p. 19; p. 12: 'At first blush, Christian-ity had disappointed me in its narrow representation of the world and in its failure to understand the role of matter.' To interpret this 'disappointment' correctly, one should bear in mind the literary genre to which the essay belongs and its dialectical construction.
11 'Le Christianisme dans le monde' (1933).
12 'Le Milieu mystique', in *HU*, p. 91.
13 *Introduction*, pp. 7, 18. *MPN*, p. 120. 'Comment je vois,' n. 38, 'Life and the Planets', in *FM*, p. 119. See in particular 'La Centrologie', n. 17. *VP*, p. 134 n., on the miracle of 'super-creation or super-animation'. Cf. M. Blondel, commenting on a letter in which Laberthonnière said to him (20 October 1923) that God 'makes us into persons': 'That is true—but not the whole truth. God is super-person—and we have to super-

personalize ourselves' (*Correspondance philosophique*, ed. Claude Tresmontant, 1962, p. 314.

14 Letter of 29 May 1953.

15 'Le Christique', 'L'atomisme de l'esprit', p. 39. 'Le sens de l'espèce chez l'homme' (1949). *CM*, p. 4: 'neo-milieu of vision and action'. To the Abbé Breuil, 31 January 1955: 'What is really thrilling is the access to atomic energy which brings with it (in my opinion) the dawn, at the other end (at the other pole), of a Christic neo-energy.'

16 'Comment je crois', beginning. 'La Crise présente' (*Études*, 20 October 1937, p. 164): 'Christianity may tomorrow be called on once again to save the World.'

17 *MD*, p. 145. (*DM*, p. 127).

18 *HU*, pp. 68–9.

19 Cf. Henri de Lubac, *Sur les chemins de Dieu*, pp. 122–3, 304.

20 To the Abbé Gaudefroy, 14 July 1934.

21 *PM*, pp. 116–18. 'Zoological evolution and invention' (1947) in *VP*, pp. 234–6. Cf. Ed. Le Roy, *La Pensée intuitive*, 2, *invention et vérification*. Earlier: Ravaisson, *Rapport sur la philosophie en France au XIXᵉ siecle* (1867); Lachelier, *Le Fondement de l'Induction* (1871).

22 'The transformist paradox' (1925) in *VP*, pp. 96–7. Letter of 10 July 1916: while he realizes that 'the moral and social development of humanity is indeed the authentic and "natural" consequence of organic evolution', on the other hand he sees that 'all moral perversions are found in embryo in the most "natural" of activities' (*MM*, pp. 110–11).

23 'Singularities of the human species', in *AM*, p. 208. As P. Chauchard well notes (op. cit., p. 124), Teilhard points out that 'the historian and the sociologist, immersed in the often incoherent vicissitudes of history, are not sufficiently removed to be able to see the true significance of human history'.

24 Letters of 23 April 1929 and 11 December 1952. 'In one way or another anthropology cannot fail to become a prolongation of physics' (Cuénot, p. 347). On civilizations, *MPN*, pp. 86–7.

25 September 1952 (Cuénot, p. 357). To Abbé Breuil, 18 February 1952 and 13 December 1952. He sometimes had some sharp things to say in this connexion: to Père Russo, 4 January 1953: 'For heaven's sake, a real vital Science of Man—and let's get rid of the literary men, the archaeologists and the historians!'

26 Letter of 21 September 1952 (Cuénot, p. 350).

27 'Un problème majeur à résoudre pour l'Anthropologie' (30 December 1951).

28 'Transformation et prolongement en l'homme du mécanisme de l'évolution' (14 November 1951).

29 Written shortly after 'La Vie cosmique' (20 September 1916).

30 To Père Russo, 30 April 1953.

31 'La Centrologie', n. 26. He envisages 'concrete modalities' that vary with the different phases of 'zones', n. 32.

32 In R. Garaudy, *Perspectives de l'homme* (1959), pp. 204–5.

33 *CM*, 'Le Christianisme dans le monde', p. 2, etc.

34 *CM*, p. 18. He may have had in mind here the metaphor in *Creative Evolution* 'I am speaking of a centre from which worlds would spring like rockets from an immense pyrotechnic set-piece.'

35 *PM*, p. 289.

36 *Énergie. Esquisse d'une dialectique de l'esprit, Introduction.* 'Turmoil or genesis?' in *FM*, pp. 223–4.

37 Letters of 9 November 1948 and 4 October 1950. See below, Chapter 20.

38 Letter of 14 March 1954 (Cuénot, p. 367).

39 'Remarques sur les flexures continentales de Chine.' *Bulletin de la Soc. géol. de France* (1946), p. 501.

40 Cf. M. de Tollenaere, art. cit. (end).

41 *CM*, p. 7.

42 *MPN*, p. 62: The appearance of man 'produces a profound alteration in the governance of evolution', etc. 'The natural units of humanity', in *VP*, p. 192.

43 'The natural units of humanity', in *VP*, pp. 197–8. *MPN*, p. 73.

44 'Formation of the noosphere', in *FM*, p. 158.

45 Ibid., pp. 159–60, 164–5. 'The Singularities of the human species', in *AM*, p. 208.

46 Here, as has been pointed out more than once, we meet one of the most pronounced differences between Teilhard's view and Bergsonism. For Bergson, it is true, as for Teilhard, 'the creation of species ends with our own', and 'with humanity something comes to an end, because something else begins'. But Bergson and Teilhard do not both see this 'something' in quite the same way. (Cf. H. Gouhier, *Bergson et le Christ des Evangiles*, pp. 99–102). It is true, again, that for both, 'psychic existence' and spiritual life are 'concentration', while matter and 'physical existence' are 'release of tension' and 'dispersion' (compare, for example, *Creative Evolution*, pp. 210–216 and *Énergie*, p. 41). Bergson, however, envisages only individual concentrations, not the concentration of the Noosphere. At the same time, we should not exaggerate the contrast. While there

is indeed a difference, and a considerable difference, there is no contradiction properly speaking. It is not *secundum idem* that Teilhard speaks of convergence where Bergson speaks of divergence. In *Creative Evolution*, Bergson speaks of the three lives, vegetative, instinctive, and rational, as 'three divergent directions of an activity that divides as it increases', for life is an urge, and the 'essence of an urge' is to launch out in divergent directions (hence the celebrated metaphor of the pyrotechnic explosion). He does not really consider the problem of a diverging or converging evolution within the third life. However, see below, Chapter 18, p. 230. 'La Réflexion de l'énergie', *QS*, 1952, p. 485, n. 3. *CM*, p. 8.

47 'Note sur le Christ universel' (1920). This would not seem to justify the statement that 'Teilhard emphasizes the homogeneity of spirit and nature', or that he puts forward, at least by implication, 'the principle of the homogeneity of being', as Mgr Journet writes, in *Nova et Vetera*, (1958), pp. 229, 230.

48 *Esquisse* (1936), 'Le Phénomène spiritual' (1937), on Spirit: 'Its supreme simplicity is made up of a prodigious complexity.' This may be compared with the notion of eternity, which can be arrived at by suppression or condensation or 'concretion' of duration (one or other being appropriate according to the idea of duration initially conceived). Cf. Bergson. *Introduction to Metaphysics*, on 'a duration that becomes more taut and concentrated, becomes progressively more intensified: at the extreme limit you would have eternity'. *Creative Evolution*, p. 315, on the Absolute: 'Like us, but in certain aspects infinitely more concentrated and gathered up in itself, it endures.'

Chapter 18: Creation, Cosmogenesis, Christogenesis

1 Mgr Charles Journet, in *Nova et Vetera* (1960), p. 313.

2 Père Guérard des Lauriers, o.p., 'La Démarche du Père Teilhard de Chardin: réflexions d'ordre épistémologique', in *Divinitas*, a. 3 (1959), pp. 227–8. 'The monism is thus so radical that it removes being; it even removes creation.' The author admits in a note that the passages on which he is commenting are 'particularly difficult' (though fuller quotation would have eased the difficulty). He adds that 'they may be the result of a momentary straying of the imagination'. His commentary on them, on which his criticism is essentially based, is none the less objectively untenable.

3 'Comment je vois', p. 18. 'The irreversible and self-sufficing presence of a first Being', etc.

4 'Basis and foundations of the idea of evolution', in *VP*, p. 131 n.

5 *Multitude*. Cf. 'Comment je vois.'

6 'Mon Univers' (1924): 'The one is not born from the fusion into itself of the elements it associates'; if they are to be 'raised to a higher level of being' in a human body, these elements must be 'grouped by the soul'. See above, Chapter 8.

7 'L'Union créatrice' (1917–18). 'La Centrologie', n. 27a. *Nothing* was italicized by Père Teilhard. We do not, accordingly, have to 'postulate, as a preliminary, the multiple side by side with the One': M. Georges Crespy (op. cit., pp. 114, 118–19), has appreciated this and explains it well.

8 'L'Union créatrice.' 'Les Noms de la Matière' (Easter 1919). 'Multitude' (26 February 1917) 1, 'Le néant de la multitude'. 'In this view,' says Père Guérard des Lauriers (op. cit., p. 260 n. 80), 'it is impossible to see how one can avoid the existence of an eternal matter *a parte ante*.' Père Teilhard, it should be noted, was aware of the difficulty and explained how it may be avoided.

9 'In Milton's view, the divine desire for expression gave birth to the universe which in consequence was not created *ex nihilo*, but from the divine essence itself, *prima materia*, abyss, boundless space, uncreated Night, Chaos' (Serge Hutin, *Les Disciples anglais de Jacob Boehme*, 1960, p. 68).

10 'Note sur la notion de transformation créatrice' (about 1920). Cf. Cuénot, bibliography, p. 451, II.

11 Letter of 20 October 1919. From this experiential point of view, no beginning to the universe can be envisaged, since every phenomenon, when analysed, sends us back to an earlier phenomenon, and so on indefinitely. 'No object is scientifically intelligible to us except as the end of an unlimited series of earlier states' ('Panthéisme et Christianisme'). But, 'whether our space and time have an ascertainable limit or not in no way affects the operation of a higher force, the property of which is precisely that it is applied to the global totality of the world, past, present and future' ('Bases and foundations of the idea of evolution', in *VP*, pp. 134–5). This is exactly what the Thomist theory holds. Again, 'it does not at all follow from the fact that the temporal beginning of the world is, from the phenomenal point of view, not to be found, that the notion of an ontological beginning of the universe has no objectivity' (ibid.): 'The absence

of all empirical beginnings . . . has a more modest and very different meaning' (ibid., p. 131). Cf. Jean Mouroux, *The Mystery of Time* (New York, 1964), Chapter 2: 'Every beginning is impatient of clear understanding: we always grasp things that have begun, never pure beginning.'

12 'Mon Univers' (14 April 1918), *MD*, p. 62. 'Centrologie', n. 26. Cf. S. Strasser, 'Évolution et Mystère', in *Le Mystère* (*Semaine des intellectuels catholiques*, 1958, p. 112). 'One could even say that evolution *is* creation in so far as it unfolds in space-time and gives birth to new forms of existence.'

13 'Note sur la . . . transformation créatrice.' Letter of 21 December 1919, in connexion with an article by Père Maurice de la Taille (*Recherches de science religieuse*, 1919): 'His general principle, which seems to me very sound, is this very principle of "creative transformation"—which explains, without any break in the cosmic structure, life after matter, thought after instinct, Revelation after rational inquiry, the new Earth after the old, etc.' The analogy indicated with the idea of the 'critical point' will be noted. See above, Chapter 12, p. 132.

14 To Père Valensin, May 1920. 'Les Noms de la Matière', p. 2. At the same time, being 'perfectly centred', by virtue of the very complexity of the body it dwells in, the human soul 'can survive the dissociation of the elements it assembles . . . It is immortal'.

15 Quoted in a letter to Père Valensin, 29 September 1928. See above, Chapter 8, p. 95. Cf. St. Thomas, *De Potentia*, q. 3, a. 10.

16 'Comment je vois' (1948), n. 26–7 and *Note*: 'It is evident that the term "plura" cannot hold good for God in the case of Trinitization.'

17 *De l'esthétique à la mystique* (1955), pp. 92–5 (written about 1930): it was to this mystery, again, that the Abbé Monchanin's thoughts turned on his death-bed, as we know from a note dictated by him on 20 September 1957, commenting on the thought of St. Denis of Alexandria: 'The monad unfolds into the triad without growing in stature, and the triad gathers itself into the monad without impoverishment.' On the light on the mystery of the Trinity received by reason, see Abbé de Tourville, *Lumière et Vie* (1924); and earlier, for example, the Capuchin Père L. F. d'Argentan's *Conférences théologiques et spirituelles sur les grandeurs de Dieu*, 10ᵉ conférence.

18 'Comment je vois', n. 29 and appendix. 'La Centrologie', n. 27.

19 'L'Union créatrice' ('Mon Univers'). 'Comment je vois.'

20 For example in 'A note on progress' (1920), *FM*, p. 23. On pp. 22–3, however, we see quite clearly both the connexion in conditioning and the difference in order.

21 'Some reflections on progress' (1941) in *FM*, p. 79.

22 *HU*, p. 25 'La Foi qui opère': 'if Christ is born, without any violation of nature's law, in the heart of the world', it is 'through the working of faith' that this is effected (*HU*, p. 138). In 'Comment je crois' (1934), p. 21, we may note, as an example of awkward or overcondensed expression, the phrase 'the world, around me, becomes divine'.

23 It is in the same sense that classical theology speaks, for example, of the physical causality of the sacraments.

24 *Énergie*. To Père Valensin, 2 February 1930. It was about the same time that Père Émile Mersch, s.j., to take but one example, was writing his books on the mystical body, bringing out, in accordance with tradition, its physical and not simply its moral reality: *Le Corps mystique du Christ*, vol. 1 (1933), introduction, pp. xxiii–xxv.

25 *CM*, p. 25.

26 Letter of 27 May 1923. 'The transformist question' (*Études*, 20 June 1921): 'Christ is the end supernaturally but physically marked out as the consummation of humanity' (*VP*, p. 23).

27 *Archives*.

28 *Pedagogus*, bk. 1, c. 6. (*Sources chrétiennes*, 70, p. 188.)

29 See above, Chapter 9. On the 'confluence of Heaven and the world', see *CM*, III, 2, the universal Christ. When, however, he writes (ibid., p. 9), 'The primacy of Spirit, or, what comes to the same thing, the primacy of the future', he is perfectly right from the point of view he is adopting at the time. What he is doing is to affirm, in opposition to materialist Entropy, 'the emergence of a force of "complexification" that is everywhere under pressure in the universe' (ibid., p. 16).

30 'Mon Univers' (1918).

31 That such an appearance is deceptive, we have as warrant, among others, the explanations he gave to his friend Père Auguste Valensin, who had mentioned to him the doubt referred to.

32 O. Rabut, op. cit., p. 158; pp. 141–2: 'There is no doubt that on some important points Teilhard needs to be *completed* . . . There are passages where a greater exactness of expression is indispensable but is lacking. Such explanations, however, as are necessary do not impair his thought. Sometimes the vocabulary is ambiguous, some expressions are unfortunate, and sometimes

the development is insufficient. These are shortcomings that we must regret; but under this deceptive appearance we can distinguish some extremely sound seminal intuitions that can introduce new vigour into Christian thought.' On the idea of the evolution of the world, as orientated towards Christ, see Karl Rahner, s.j., 'Problèmes actuels de Christologie' (tr. Michel Rondet), in *Études théologiques*, 1 (1959), pp. 136–8.

33 'La Crise présente', *Études* (20 October 1937).

34 Newman, *The Theory of development in Religious Doctrine* (sermon of 1843, Oxford, feast of the Purification); 'Essay on the development of Christian doctrine', 29. It should be borne in mind that Père Teilhard did not wish all his essays to be published or circulated. He regarded a number of them as simply a way of setting his bearings, of marking out stages of a mind that was constantly in movement. They should therefore be read now more as documents that enable one to study a thought that is feeling its way than as the expression of a fully developed system.

35 *HU*, p. 70.

36 'La Maîtrise du Monde' (1916).

37 *CM*: The universal Christ: the conflicts.

38 Cf. Letter to Père Sertillanges (Peiping, 4 February 1934): '*Neque longitudo, neque latitudo, neque profundum . . .*' I imagine that St. Thomas would recognize himself in the gay audacity with which you are daily seeing them grow a little greater before our eyes.'

39 Abbé Joly, *Saint Paul et l'Apocalypse* (1949), p. 188.

Chapter 19: The Legitimacy of Teilhard's Extrapolation

1 N. M. Wildiers, *Teilhard de Chardin* (1961), p. 55.

2 To M. Teillard-Chambon, New York, 2 March 1952 (*LT*, p. 323). To the same, 5 April 1946: 'The first war started me on the ladder. This one has cut clean across my life, but I have a better grasp of certain distinct central points, and to these I wish to devote all that is left to me of life' (*LT*, p. 291).

3 To Abbé Breuil, Peking, 12 August 1941 (*LT*, p. 284).

4 To M. Teillard-Chambon, 4 December 1951 (*LT*, p. 321).

5 'Le Christique', p. 1. 'La Réflexion de l'énergie', *QS*, 1952, p. 64.

6 'The transformist paradox' (1925), in *VP*, p. 87. 'Du Cosmos à la cosmogénèse' (15 March 1951). Ms. note (26 February

1950). Earlier, in 'Bases and foundations of the idea of evolution', he had said: 'the real transformist question is not just a simple dispute over detail that can be decided in the course of an osteological discussion' (*VP*, p. 141). To Père Valensin, January 1923: 'We have nothing that can take the place of Evolution.' Cf. G. Weigel, s.j. in *The World of Chardin* (1961), p. 157: 'Evolution . . . is as evident to him as the existence of the cosmos we see.'

7 'Note sur l'essence du transformisme' (1935).

8 'Evolution of the idea of evolution' (1956), in *VP*, p. 245.

9 Letter of 23 March 1930. Letter of 29 September 1929: 'For a long time now I have had more than enough of the transformist controversy.' See above, Chapter 9, nn. To Abbé Breuil, 13 December 1952: 'I haven't been able to find out what was said in Quebec at the Catholic symposium on Evolution (*sic!* These good people have been meeting to discuss the question of finding out whether the earth revolves).'

10 'Turmoil or Genesis?' (1948): 'We have now entered the battle' (*FM*, p. 221).

11 *CM*, 'The Heart of the Problem' (1949): 'In one form or another, something that is ultra-human is coming to the front' (*FM*, p. 263).

12 *Esquisse*.

13 Letter of 20 April 1948. This 'idea is more and more becoming my scientific platform'.

14 'La Crise présente, réflexions d'un naturaliste', *Études* (20 October 1937).

15 *PM*, pp. 251, 287. 'The grand option' (1939) in *FM*, p. 60. 'The conic transposition of action' (1942): 'We see Mankind extending . . . beyond the individual: it coils in collectively upon itself above our heads, in the direction of some sort of higher-mankind' (*FM*, p. 89). 'La Convergence de l'univers' (1951), on complete co-reflection: 'one single immense mirror, in which the face of the self-reflecting universe may one day be seen'.

16 *PM*, p. 168.

17 'Life and the planets' (1945), in *FM*, p. 113; p. 154: 'The demon of immobilism.'

18 'L'atomisme de l'esprit' (1941), p. 16. 'Transformation et prolongement en l'homme du mécanisme de l'évolution' (19 November 1951).

19 'The phyletic structure of the human group', in *AM*, p. 150, 'The Planetization of Man', in *FM*, p. 134.

20 *PM*, p. 88. Letter of 9 January 1917, in *MM*, p. 166.
21 'Croyez-vous en l'homme?' (1956), pp. 26–9.
22 'The planetisation of man', in *FM*, p. 133.
23 'Que deviendra l'homme sur la terre?' *Le Figaro littéraire*, 18 March 1961.
24 *Esquisse*. 'Union made us men by organizing the confused forces of matter the control of a thinking mind. It will again make us "supermen" by making us elements governed by some higher soul.' Cf. *Énergie*, p. 15: Is not the humanity of today 'already organically, in relation to the neolithic earth, a true super-humanity?'
25 This was the title of an essay he was planning in 1953 (*LT*, p. 337). 'The Singularities of the human species', in *AM*, pp. 208–70. Cf. the article by Père A. Jeannière in the *Revue de l'Action populaire* (January 1962), 'L'avenir de l'humanité d'après Teilhard de Chardin'.
26 *PM*, p. 251–2. *MPN*, pp. 114–15.
27 'Singularities of the human species', in *AM*, p. 224.
28 *PM*, pp. 251, 248.
29 Letter of 30 March 1955. 'The Heart of the Problem.'
30 'L'atomisme de l'esprit', pp. 19, 24.
31 *PM*, p. 251 (our italics).
32 'Singularities of the human species', in *AM*, p. 208.
33 'The human rebound of evolution' (*QS*, 20 April 1948), in *FM*, p. 212.
34 *PM*, pp. 148–9. 'La Convergence de l'Univers', pp. 4, 8: 'The organo-physic threshold of reflection', 'psychogenic convergence of the Universe'. 'Comment je vois', n. 31: Christ 'the ultimate psychic centre of concentration'. *FM*, p. 120, God, 'the cosmic psychic centre', etc.
35 'Man's place in nature' (1932), in *VP*, p. 181.
36 'Le Phénomène spirituel' (1937).
37 Cf. *PM*, p. 163.
38 St. Thomas, *Contra Gentiles* 2, c. 81, n. 5. Cf. Jean Mouroux, *The Mystery of Time*. (New York, 1964): 'Time (both in consciousness and in the world) exists only for a mind that is rooted in eternity and vivified by it. If incarnate consciousness opens up time, it is because it is itself open to eternity, and because it can thus imitate, in its own finite degree, the creative act itself. Ultimately it is because there is in it a point of emergence into eternity that there is also available to it a point of deployment into temporality without ever being lost in it.' It was this 'point of emergence into eternity' that Père Teilhard

did not always *fully* appreciate. See, however, *Réflexion de l'énergie*, p. 482.

39 *CM*, pp. 18–19. 'Comment je vois.'

40 Cf. 'L'atomisme de l'esprit', p. 27, etc.

41 'The planetization of mankind', in *FM*, p. 132. *MPN*, pp. 100–1. To put it in yet another way, does the extension (or, if you prefer, the tightening) of the network of objective relations in itself necessarily entail a deepening of personal relationships?

42 'La Convergence de l'Univers', p. 7.

43 *PM*, p. 251.

44 On this final 'schism', see 'Mon Univers' (1924), *FM*, p. 307, etc. See also above, Chapter 10.

45 *Dialogue avec Teilhard de Chardin*, pp. 89, 95.

46 'L'énergie d'évolution' (24 May 1953), in a comment on recent works by Charles Galton-Darwin, Julian Huxley, G. Gaylord Simpson, and others.

47 *Études*, May 1946, p. 166.

48 *CM*, 'Esquisse d'une dialectique de l'esprit'.

49 *PM*, p. 267 n. This note clears up the ambiguity of such expressions as 'personal universe' or 'personality of the universe'.

50 'On the probable coming of an "ultra-humanity"' (1956) in *FM*, p. 278.

51 'Esquisse d'une dialectique de l'esprit.' 'L'unanimisation humaine' (1950). See above, Chapter 16.

52 'L'atomisme de l'esprit', p. 29.

53 'Life and the planets', in *FM*, pp. 119–20. 'Centrologie', no. 29. Letter of 30 June 1948, 'Directions and conditions of the future': the only desirable unification is that which is effected not by an imposed technique of 'social arrangement' but by a union of love (*FM*, p. 235–6).

54 *CM*, p. 19 n.

55 'La Convergence de l'univers', p. 5, on 'the existence of some critical and final point of ultra-hominization, corresponding to a complete reflection of the Noosphere upon itself'.

56 'On the probable coming of an "ultra-humanity",' in *FM*, p. 279. 'Comment je vois', no. 24.

57 *CM*, p. 19. 'From the pre-human to the ultra-human' (1950), in *FM*, pp. 296–7. 'Ultra-human' and 'transhuman' are, as usual, sharply distinguished.

58 For example, in 'Comment je vois', no. 16, he explains that 'totalization certainly does not mean immobilization'; 'within unified mankind two sorts of movement are still conceivable'— which seems to imply a continued terrestrial duration. Never-

theless, a little later, the 'human mass' is said again to be 'in process of folding-back upon itself', which implies that totalization itself is not complete. His thought, however, becomes unambiguously clear if it is looked at in the light of 'The Christian phenomenolon', no. 24.

59 'La Crise présente', *Études* (20 October 1937).

60 'Life and the planets', in *FM*, pp. 118–19. *PM*, pp. 254–7, etc.

61 *Énergie.* 'Science et Christ, (ou analyse et synthèse).'

62 'Comment je vois', no. 4.

63 'The grand option', in *FM*, p. 54.

64 'Phyletic structure of the human group', in *AM*, p. 154; cf. p. 156.

65 'Turmoil or genesis?' in *FM*, p. 226.

66 Cf. letter to the Abbé Breuil, 25 May 1953 (*LT*, 73). Between 'the zone of the human' or reflective and 'the zone of the ultra-human' or co-reflective, there would accordingly be more continuity than Père Teilhard appears to allow: 'L'étoffe de l'univers.' Cf. Léopold Sédar Senghor, *Cahiers*, vol. 3, p. 47.

67 'La montée de l'autre' (Peking, 20 January 1942): 'I have no personal illusions about the incredible element in my hypothesis . . .' Even in such rare passages, it could, moreover, be possible that Père Teilhard had in mind, without making it quite clear, the supernatural reality of the mystical body.

68 'Comment je vois', no. 25. 'Réflexions sur la compression humaine' (1953), p. 6. 'Le Dieu de l'évolution' (1953): 'It is always, of course, dangerous to predict or extrapolate.'

69 'Trois choses que je vois' (1948). 'Conditions and directions of the future', in *FM*, pp. 236–7.

70 Op. cit., p. 188.

71 Charles Duquoc, O.P. 'Eschatologie et réalités terrestres', in *Lumière et Vie* (November–December 1960), pp. 5, 8.

72 Cf. St. Irenaeus, *Adversus Haereses*, bk. 4, c. 5, n. 1. (*PG*, 7, 983 B).

73 Loc. cit., p. 19.

74 To the Abbé Gaudefroy, 31 December 1923. To L. Zanta, 25 January 1924.

75 Letter of 24 June 1934.

76 *Esquisse*, p. 26. Retreat notes, *passim.* 1939: 'Day of entry into the Presence', etc., 1948: 'The Sacred Presence. *Jesus solus, solus Jesus!*' Again in 1954, '. . . The Presence. Take up my dwelling again in Christ Jesus.'

Chapter 20: Teilhard's Picture of the Christian

1 Cf. 'Le Christique' (1955): 'The neo-humanisms of the twentieth century are dehumanizing us under too low a heaven.'

2 *MD*, pp. 116, 119. (*DM*, pp. 93, 96–7). Père Guérard des Lauriers' version of this is very different, loc. cit., p. 234: 'According to Père Teilhard, the perfect Christian must be monist, pagan, quietist' [*sic*]. This comment is derived from a mis-reading of the 'Mass on the World' (*HU*, pp. 26–7). He attributes to Père Teilhard the exact opposite of what he says. Referring to 'three of the most formidable passions that can unlock the human heart'—the passions of the monist, the pagan and the quietist—Père Teilhard shows how the Christian extracts from each one of them that portion of the truth which they corrupt, and gathers it up in 'a wonderful synthesis' in which 'they rectify each other as they mingle'. But, what the Christian experiences, he makes clear, 'is not the absorption of the monist . . . nor the emotion felt by the pagan . . . nor the passive self-abandonment of the quietist . . .' (p. 26). The line Père Teilhard follows is found in most of the great apologists, ever since Clement of Alexandria; cf. *Stromata*, bk. 1, ch. XIII, n. 57: 'Truth is one, falsehood has a thousand ways of going astray . . . the philosophy of the barbarians and the Greeks has dismembered the eternal truth; this is no longer the dismemberment of the Dionysus of myth, but that of the eternal Word of Revelation. If we gather up the scattered fragments and reconstitute their unity, we shall see, without danger of error, you may be sure, the whole word, the truth.' Père Guérard des Lauriers adds, it is true, that the perfect man according to Teilhard must 'master all this and so make it one'.

3 *MD*, p. 116. (*DM*, p. 93) At the end of *PM*, which does not appeal to the light of revelation, he speaks only of converging on 'Some One'.

4 *Le Repos du septième jour* (*Théâtre*, La Pléiade, vol. 1, p. 786).

5 *MD*, p. 134; pp. 96–7. (*DM*, p. 114, pp. 70–71). In a letter to his parents (16 June 1912), written after a visit to the Charterhouse at Parkminster in Sussex, he admires 'the forceful affirmation of the supernatural represented by the life of these men'; those who refuse to see anything but human progress will say that this life 'is no use at all; and it is not a bad thing

that it should be possible for this to be said, in this sense, about some people, in the Church: in that way, there can be no possible misapprehension'. Cf. H. H. Pope John XXIII, address to the international congress of the Reformed Cistercians, Rome, 20 October 1960, quoting Pius XI: 'In truth, it is these most pure and exalted souls who, by their suffering, their love and their prayer, practise in silence within the Church the most universal and fruitful apostolate.'

6 *MD*, p. 134. (*DM*, p. 114).

7 See a lovely passage on the Immaculate Conception in a letter of 5 December 1916 (*MM*, p. 149).

8 Cf. Henri de Lubac, *exégèse médiévale*, vol. 3 (1960), pp. 188-92.

9 Quoting these lines, Pastor G. Crespy (*Revue de théologie et de philosophie*, 1959, p. 298, n. 2) detects in them 'strangely "Protestant" overtones (*cum grano salis*)'. Even though offered with a grain of salt, and allowing for the fact that 'Protestant' is in quotation marks, it seems an odd remark. However, we can welcome the agreement it indicates.

10 Cf. 'Le Milieu mystique', *Écrits*, on the contemplative: 'Seeing the mystic immobile, crucified or rapt in prayer, some may perhaps think that his activity is in abeyance or has left this earth: they are mistaken. Nothing in the world is more intensely alive and active than purity and prayer, which hang like an unmoving light between the universe and God. Through their serene transparency flow the waves of creative power, charged with natural virtue and with grace. What else but this is the Virgin Mary?' (*HU*, p. 154). And, we may add, what better commentary could there be on the ancient traditional saying, 'Prius concepit mente quam ventre'—'She conceived in the mind before she conceived in the womb'. Cf. St. Leo, first Christmas sermon: '. . . prius conciperet mente quam corpore' (*PL*, 54, 191 B); Rupert of Deutz, *In Cantica*, prologue (*PL*, 168, 838); St. Augustine, *De Virginitate*, c. 3 (*PL*, 40, 358); St. Thomas, *3a*, q. 30, a. 1, etc.

11 Similarly he describes the very pure and very positive ideal of the religious state in general in this sentence from 'Le Prêtre' (1919): 'by practising the counsels of perfection, to salvage through their self-denials all the heavenly fire imprisoned within the threefold concupisence of the flesh, of avarice, of pride: in other words to hallow, through chastity, poverty and obedience, the power enclosed in love, in gold, in independence' (*HU*, p. 129).

12 October 1923 (*LT*, p. 101).

13 'The spiritual value of a man, the range of his influence depends on the degree of reality that God has assumed for him: not the degree of speculative or even affective perfection, but, I repeat, the degree of reality' (quoted by Cuénot, p. 391).

14 'Réflexions sur le bonheur' (1944), *Cahiers*, p. 69. 'Mon Univers' (1924).

15 Letter of 26 July 1923, in *LT*, p. 83. Cf. Robert Guelluy, *Vie de foi et tâches terrestres* (1960), pp. 130–1: 'What the Gospel asks of us is not to ignore what God has put into his creation, but not to be enslaved to it by an attachment that is a manifestation of the instinct for pleasure.' See also letter of 8 December 1918 (*MM*, p. 262).

16 *Multitude*, in *HU*, p. 125.

17 *MD*, pp. 123, 133, 137. (*DM*, pp. 100, 113, 118.) *PM*, p. 295.

18 Cf. *MM*, pp. 55, 76, 114, 123, 173.

19 Letter of 10 January 1926: 'Further, this faith must be maintained with a jealously guarded fidelity.' He was constantly concerned to show that his ideas made him 'as faithful as any man to the ancient attitude' (16 May 1925). Letter of 13 December 1918: 'to wait in all loyalty for God's own hour' (*MM*, p. 269). To his father, 20 December 1911: 'The only true peace and consolation is the consciousness of having done one's best to remain faithful to the end.'

20 Letter of 15 October 1915: '*All* is vanity, you see, except *holding on loyally*' (*MM*, p. 76). Prayer in 'Le Milieu mystique' (1917) *Écrits*: 'Lord, if the Spirit is ever to shine in me, if I am not to succumb to the temptation that lies in wait for every bold act, if I am never to forget that *You alone* are to be sought through all things, you will send, when you know best, loss and disappointments and pain.'

21 *MD*, p. 139. (*DM*, pp. 119–120). To L. Zanta, 28 August 1926: 'All that matters is to be faithful in the hands of God.' Cf. Max Bégouën: 'Père Teilhard had the freshness of soul of the little children who are promised that theirs shall be the Kingdom of God because they constantly marvel at the splendours God reveals to them' (*La Table Ronde*, June 1955, pp. 63–4).

22 *MD*, pp. 151, 154. (*DM*, pp. 133, 138) Cf. Maurice Blondel, *Journal*, 29 May 1890: 'Right into the heart of the wood of Les Puits . . . and there I kissed the divine earth, in love for this poor matter, so lovely, so transfigured in Christian eyes.'

23 *MD*, pp. 61, 140 (*DM*, pp. 30, 121). 'The Mass on the World', prayer: 'Lord, Yes, at last . . . I have found one to whom I can whole-heartedly give this name' (*HU*, p. 33). *CM*: 'In a universe which was being revealed to me as in a state of convergence, you had assumed, in virtue of your Resurrection, the place of sovereign dominance as the total centre into which all things are gathered.' 'Mon Univers', p. 19: The Resurrection 'marks Christ's effective assumption of his functions as the universal centre'. We find the same note in 1955, in the conclusion of 'Le Christique'; cf. letter of 10 June 1924: 'It's Whitsun week, and I like to think that "the spirit of Christ has filled the earth", as the Church says at this season' (*LT*, p. 117).

24 Ulrich of Cluny, *Consuetudines*, quoted by Dom Jean Leclercq in his *Théologie de la vie monastique* (1961), p. 457.

25 'La Nostalgie du front', *Écrits*, 20 November 1917.

26 The other great wind that passed over his life, he says, was the wind of Asia: *CM*, p. 26.

27 'The spiritual power of matter' (*HU*, p. 66): 'Thus at long last he had found a *point d'appui*, he had found refuge, *outside* the confines of human society' (ibid.).

28 'The Mass on the World', in *HU*, pp. 21–3. *CM* (p. 25). Second memorandum for M. Blondel (*Archives*, pp. 151–3).

29 *CM*, p. 23. 'Le Milieu mystique', in *HU*, p. 78. To L. Zanta, 15 October 1926: 'Once we have this fire and this light, we can go everywhere, finding light and nourishment in everything.' 'Le Prêtre': 'I must . . . spread abroad the fire you have given me.'

30 Letter of 30 May 1925. Cf. Luke 12. 49: 'Ignem veni mittere in terram, et quid volo, nisi ut accendatur?'—'I came to cast fire upon the earth, and would that it were already kindled!' It will be noted that that text is the Communion antiphon for the mass of St. Ignatius Loyola. Cf. St. Augustine's commentary on it, *Contra Adimantum*, c. 13, n. 3 (*Bibl. Aug.*, vol. 17, pp. 282–4). On fire in Origen, see de Lubac: *Histoire et Esprit*, pp. 235–6. St. Gregory, *In. evang.* hom. 33 (*PL*, 76, 1241 B).

31 Letter of 11 June 1927, in *LT*, p. 140. He felt, however, an equally strong pull back to geology through 'an insatiable need to maintain contact (a contact in communion) with what is a sort of root or universal matrix of beings'.

32 To Abbé Bréuil, 23 October 1923, in *LT*, p. 104. Cf. *MM*, p. 36: 'So far as I can remember my own self, I have always lived in a forward-looking tension.'

33 To Joseph Teilhard de Chardin, 25 July 1939, in *LT*, p. 242.

34 Letter of 25 February 1929, explaining his expedition to Abyssinia.

35 Letter of 26 April 1926, in *LT*, p. 123.

36 Letter of 1934, in *LT*, p. 206.

37 *CM*; his 'interior adventure into the quest for the heart of things' (p. 17).

38 Letter of 17 December 1922. Letter of 29 June 1916, 'May our Lord, then, preserve deep in our souls this impulse towards progress and fuller being—and may he at the same time direct this deep-rooted urge towards himself alone' (*MM*, pp. 106–7).

39 Letter of 12 July 1940, to M. Teillard-Chambon, in *LT*, p. 265.

40 'Le Milieu mystique', in *HU*, p. 80.

41 To Max Bégouën, 11 November 1929 (*Cahiers*, 2, p. 4). Letter of 5 April 1927: 'If you only knew how impossible it has become for me to take pleasure in anything! Sometimes, I feel that there is nothing left in me but a force that drives on towards all that can be attained of the superhuman, or totally human.' Again: 'my sole ambition is to be laid among the foundations of what is to grow' (quoted by M. Teillard-Chambon in the introduction to *LT*, p. 59).

42 Letter of 30 December 1929.

43 Letter of 4 October 1917, in *MM*, p. 207.

44 *MD*, p. 112. (*DM*, p. 89). Letter of 18 January 1936: 'I am less and less able to do without Christ (and even my life of "prayer" is tending to become more regular and intense).'

45 Cf. Letter to M. Teillard-Chambon, 9 May 1940 (*LT*, p. 264). 'Le Milieu mystique': 'Just as the mystic does not fall into pantheism by following his innate desire for the universal, so he does not become inert by giving way to his predilection for passivity.'

46 Preface to 'L'énergie spirituelle de la souffrance' (1951), p. 12. in *L'Énergie Humaine*. Letter of 1936: 'Her loss created a sort of universal solitude around me that affected all the elements of an interior world of which I had gradually made her a part. She and I thought together in everything that concerns spiritual activity and the interior life.'

47 On Père Teilhard as 'the exemplary and constantly submissive religious' see the tribute of the Abbé Henri Bréuil, *Le Double Miracle dans le cas Teilhard* (*Cahiers*, 2, pp. 137–8), and P. Grenet, *Teilhard de Chardin* (1961) pp. 78–84. See

also his letter of 13 April 1940, in Cuénot, p. 244–5; the evidence quoted by Cuénot, p. 405; and *Archives*, p. 140, n. 4.

48 Letter of 16 January 1927. Letters of 19 and 30 May 1925.

49 Letters of 16 March 1921, 13 April 1940, and 29 September 1929.

50 Letter of 18 September 1948, about the offer of a Chair at the Collège de France.

51 To L. Zanta, 7 May 1927.

52 To Père Raymond Jouve, Peking, 6 July 1934. To Père Valensin, 29 September 1929: 'I repeat: I am ready for anything (except intellectual disloyalty), and in particular for being "buried away".' Towards the end of his life, his General was able to tell him what a joy it was always to find in him a frank and trusting son, always animated by the same supernatural feelings.

53 Letters of 7 November 1926 (*LT*, p. 134), and 31 December 1926: 'Even if this book is never to be published, writing it will have served to focus my ideas.—I have one other ambition: somehow or other, to have it approved and authorized—so that I could feel with more assurance that the spirit of the Church was with me.'

54 Letter of 31 December 1926. To the Abbé Gaudefroy, 27 February 1927: 'I wish I could dispel the cloud that hangs between Rome and me.'

55 'Mon Univers' (14 April 1918). Letter of 3 October 1918, in *MM*, p. 244. He was confident, however, that 'substantially, the experience is orthodox, since I was told so again—and since I have St. John and St. Paul on my side—and have, moreover, a whole mass of postulates and interior satisfactions that can hardly be misleading.'

56 'Forma Christi' (22 December 1918): 'Show him once more the inaccuracy or error in the terms in which he is trying to express his "experience", and he will patiently try to find some other way of putting it. But he will still retain his vision.'

57 Letter of 13 December 1918, in *MM*, p. 269.

58 1955 (Cuénot, French edition, p. 142).

59 Letters of 13 April 1940, 11 January 1920, 12 October 1951.

60 Letter of 25 May 1938: not that this implies any fatalism, for he adds: 'but it will happen if we do not fight.'

61 'Le Christique' (March 1955). 'Comment je crois', introduction. *CM*, 11. p. 1, 'Le coeur de Jesus.' 'Mon Univers' (1924).

62 But even this realization could take a poignant form: letter of 26 September 1952 (Cuénot, p. 367).

63 'Le Sens humain' (1929). To Père Valensin, 14 May 1922.

64 'Directions and conditions of the future', (*FM*, p. 236). Here he has directly in mind the forces of liberty that can compromise 'the success of anthropogenesis', and it is for that reason that he even adds 'and of uncertainty'. But the element of indetermination derives also from his desire to lead the unbeliever step by step towards total truth, which is revealed only in faith. See above, Chapter 19.

65 *MD*, p. 70. (*DM*, p. 39) 'La pensée du Père Teilhard de Chardin' (by Teilhard himself) in *Les Études philosophiques*, 1955, pp. 57–81.

66 Letter of 22 August 1925. See above, Chapter 7, pp. 63–4.

67 Paris, 6 October 1932. 'Bases and foundations', in *VP*, p. 138.

68 'En regardant un cyclotron', in *Recherches et Débats*, April 1953. 'The end of the species', in *FM*, p. 303. Cf. a passage dating from 1933: 'In their search for a name to give the unknown God who they vaguely feel must exist, the Gentiles look to us.'

69 'Les conditions psychologiques de l'unification humaine' (Paris, 6 January 1949), *Psyché* (1955), p. 80. Cf. *FM*, pp. 286–7.

70 'Mon Univers', p. 1. 'Comment je crois', introduction. His friend Auguste Valensin shared this attitude; see his *Autour de ma Foi*, preface (1948).

71 'Comment je crois', p. 10.

72 Cf. Retreat note: 'May Christ-Omega keep me *young* A. M. D. G.!—(What better argument for Christianity . . . than an enduring youthfulness drawn from Christ-Omega) (*HU*, p. 99).

73 'Monde chrétien, monde moderne', in *Esprit* no. 125 (August–September 1946), p. 255. 'La Maîtrise du monde et le Règne de Dieu' (1916), Ch. 11: 'Le heurt.' 'La Mystique de la Science' (1939; *Études*, vol. 238, p. 139): 'Quite accidentally, because of the materialist explanation it gave of the evolutionary process recently disclosed in the universe, the religion of science presented itself as hostile to the God of the Gospel. The natural reaction of the adherents of the Gospel to this provocation was to condemn it', etc.

74 'Barrière de la mort et co-réflexion' (5 January 1955), appendix.

75 Holy Saturday, 1922. Letter to Père Russo, 4 January 1953. 'L'Âme du Monde' (1918). He does not wish the Cross 'to

become a sign of *false contradiction*': G. Crespy. op. cit., p. 110.

76 'Quelques réflexions sur la conversion du monde', p. 4. 'What should we think of transformism?', in *VP*, p. 160.

77 *La Semaine d'ethnologie religieuse de Louvain*, in *Correspondant* (10 November 1912), vol. 249, p. 560. 'What should we think of transformism' (1930): 'It is now necessary to take the offensive' (*VP*, p. 157).

78 Letter from Peking, 7 January 1934: 'Everyone in the Far East is waiting for a book on the essence of Christianity—or on the Christian point of view—as opposed to Buddhism or Confucianism. It would be translated into every language. But it would have to have the scope and serenity of Bergson's last book.' Cf. 'Comment je crois', p. 177ff., etc.

79 'Turmoil or Genesis?' in *FM*, p. 226. Cf. Newman, *University Sermons*, 11 (13 April 1830), no. 24: 'There is, perhaps, no greater satisfaction to the Christian than that which arises from his perceiving that the Revealed System is rooted deep in the natural course of things.'

80 To L. Zanta, 7 May 1927.

81 *Introduction*, p. 3. See above, Chapters 7 and 16.

82 On Pascal, see 'Le Sens humain', p. 3.

83 In *Travaux et Jours* (Beirut, Université Saint-Joseph, Faculté des Lettres, July–September 1961, pp. 24–7). Cf. Henri de Lubac. *Catholicism* (London, 1950), 'our age dreams of organizing this total humanity by unifying it. From hominization to humanization—that is the dream, but no Catholic could accept it in just that form, nor simply reject it as a pernicious fantasy. But just as the Catholic uses man's aspiration to transcend himself and "make a God for himself", in order to make him accept the death to self that is the indispensable condition for entry into life, so he uses the no less deep-seated, no less "natural" aspiration—often though it may be stifled or diverted—for human unity, in order to lead men of good will to the threshold of Catholicism, which alone is capable of realizing that unity in an eminent sense'. This, it would seem, is precisely what Père Teilhard does. Cf. Fr. Smulders, in *Bijdragen* (1960), p. 260.

84 To M. Teillard-Chambon, Peking, 7 March 1940, in *LT*, p. 261.

85 *MD*, pp. 45, 43. (*DM*, pp. 13, 11).

86 Père d'Ouince was also for a long time Père Teilhard's religious superior at the house in Paris of *Études*. For the text

of his address, see Appendix 6. In 1903 Père Teilhard had asked to be sent to the mission in Armenia, as he told his sister Françoise in confidence. In 1905, when he was sent to teach in Cairo, he hoped that this would be for him 'some small beginning as a missionary' (letters of 16 August 1903 and 28 May 1905).

87 Letter of 19 June 1926, in *LT*, p. 128. Letter of 21 June 1921: 'I am sure that in society around us, there is a point that is vulnerable to penetration by the Spirit of God.'

88 'On the possible bases of a universal human creed', in *FM*, p. 77. 'Quelques réflexions sur la conversion du monde', p. 4: 'A religion of the Earth is in process of formation, in opposition to the religion of Heaven. That is the basic situation—in its gravity, but also in the hopes it holds.'

89 Letter of 9 December 1933. Nevertheless, he was still 'convinced that the Christian faith will again echo throughout the world': 2 January 1948. To Père Valensin, 18 January 1936: 'Something great is now being born in the heart of the Church, something that will contagiously convert the earth.' During his last years, he could not help reflecting on some reverses suffered by the Christian apostolate in France: was there not in that, he asked, a 'terrible warning?' (14 January 1954).

90 'Le Coeur du problème' (1949).

91 Letters of 1922, 1926, 1928, 1930. 'Christologie et Évolution' (1933).

92 Today, as always, the primary cause of the impotence he deplored is surely the weakness of the Christian impulse in ourselves, the weakness of our faith as part of our lives. It is true, of course, that the two things are closely connected. When Christianity becomes 'humanly lukewarm' (15 January 1954, Cuénot, p. 374) it also becomes lukewarm as Christianity.

93 To Abbé Breuil, 13 December 1952. 'Le Dieu de l'Évolution.'

94 *CM*, III. 2.

95 *Teilhard de Chardin* (1961), p. 90.

96 'Le Coeur du problème' (1949); ibid.: 'In so far as Christianity ceases to embrace the whole Human thing on earth, it loses the sharpness of its vitality and the flower of its appeal.'

97 'The cone of time', in *FM*, p. 92. Letter to Père Schurmans, Peking, 1 December 1940.

98 To M. Teillard-Chambon, Johannesburg, 6 September 1953 (*LT*, p. 344). Letter of 4 October 1950: 'It is only in the Roman stock, *taken in its integrity*, that I can see biological support sufficiently extensive and sufficiently differentiated to operate and maintain the transformation (of humanity) we await.'

99 Letter of 16 March 1921. Cf. letter of 22 August 1925. On 13 March 1932 he wrote that he was coming closer to 'a more loving orthodoxy'. To Abbé Breuil, 25 March 1932: 'In strict loyalty I cannot . . . envisage a Universe without Christ Alpha and Omega. How, then, can I exist without the Church?' To L. Zanta, on the Society of Jesus; 'Even though it is for reasons very different from those of my youth, I am deeply and wholeheartedly attached to it.'

100 To Abbé Breuil, 28 October 1948.

101 Letter of 14 July 1915, in *MM*, p. 59.

102 Letter of 18 September 1948. 'Comment je crois' ends: ' "I am ready, in these conditions, to press on until the end on a road of which I am more and more certain, towards horizons that are more and more shrouded in mist." ' Letter of 21 June 1921: 'Wherever I look, whether towards the nations or towards the visible Church, I can feel no peace except (and there I find it) in the *Pater: Adveniat regnum tuum!*'

103 Letters of 13 July 1925 and 10 September 1933.

104 'Mon Univers' (1918).

105 Letter of 20 April 1948.

106 'Centrologie', introduction.

107 *Archives*, p. 156. Letter of 15 October 1916: 'You feel . . . how complicated these questions are and how they need to be treated in conformity with the mind and living tradition of the Church' (*MM*, p. 132). It was thus that St. Augustine looked to the *viri spirituales* for a criterion.

108 Retreat of 1949. Ibid.: 'Jesus, take me in time, before I spoil anything for you!' ('O Golden Flower' is in English.)

109 She was a girl of great personality and intelligence, and, shortly before, she had started on reading the whole of Plato in Greek.

110 *Soeur Marie-Albéric du Sacré-Coeur* (Little Sisters of the Poor, Rennes, 1914), p. 17. Cf. letter of 28 February 1919 (*MM*, p. 288). There was a great spiritual intimacy between brother and sister. She died in Shanghai on 7 June 1911. See Appendix 3.

111 He wrote to his cousin Marguerite Teillard-Chambon, 13 December 1952: 'Pray to God for me continually, that I may end in such a way that my end may humbly, but distinctly and worthily, set the seal upon my witness' (*LT*, p. 335). Cf. letter of 18 September 1948: 'Pray that I may "make a good end", in conformity with what I have tried to preach: that seems to me more and more the supreme grace.'

INDEX

Above: synthesis with Ahead, 118, 182

absolute: 102, 142, 177, 182, 284; man's demand for, 208; Teilhard's quest for, 16, 102

abyss: of complexity, 196; Pascal's two abysses, 77, 196

action: Christian activity, 305; divinization of activities, 305–7, 309; natural activity, 303; problem of, 206, 307; true, 206

Ahead, 182, 262; synthesis with Above, 118; Teilhard's preoccupation with, 119, 121

Ambrose, St., 155

amorization, 146, 184

analysis, 190–91; scientific, 199

Anselm, St., 82

anthropocentrism, 94, 197, 381

anthropogenesis, 126, 158, 241; cosmogenesis continued in, 108; extension of biogenesis, 221

anthropology, 196; new, 239

anthropomorphism, 197

Aristotle, 197, 202

Armagnac, Christian d', Bd. 96, 194, 197

astronautics, 158

Augustine, St., 35, 110, 128, 137, 163, 164

Bars, Abbé Henri, 43–44, 51

Barthélemy-Madaule, Mme M., 196

Blanchard, Abbé J. P., 174

being: participated, 136; understanding of, 200

Berdiaev, Nicholas, 199, 200

Bergson, Henri, 96, 97, 194, 195; and Teilhard's 'Creative union', 230; differences between Bergsonism and Teilhard's views, 403

Bernard, St., 72, 154, 185, 258

biogenesis, 221

biology, 191, 195, 196, 204; generalized, 221

biosphere, 225

Blondel, Maurice, 78, 164, 193, 197, 206; Teilhard's exchange of views with, 24, 115, 143–44, 149, 235

Boné, Édouard, 22, 30

'Book of the Earth', 62

Borne, Étienne, 95

Breuil, Henri, 124

Buddhism, 45, 60, 179

Brunschvicg, Léon, 56

centration, 177, 184, 202

Centre: natural, 176

centreity, 195

Centrologie, La, 101

cephalization, 223

charity, 183

Charles, Pierre, 24, 99

Chauchard, Paul, 129

chemistry, 191

Crespy, Georges, 76, 96, 327

Christian: fundamental attitude of the, 257, 258; phenomenon, 87, 223

Christ: Alpha and Omega, 77, 124; centre of all things, 135; centre to evolution, 123, 146; centre of world, 124; con-

Image Books

... MAKING THE WORLD'S FINEST
CATHOLIC LITERATURE AVAILABLE TO ALL

OUR LADY OF FATIMA
By William Thomas Walsh
                                    D1—75¢

THE SPIRIT OF CATHOLICISM
By Karl Adam   D2—85¢

DAMIEN THE LEPER
By John Farrow   D3—85¢

A POPULAR HISTORY OF THE CATHOLIC CHURCH
By Philip Hughes   D4—95¢

MR. BLUE
By Myles Connolly   D5—65¢

THE DIARY OF A COUNTRY PRIEST
By Georges Bernanos D6—75¢

THE CHURCH SPEAKS TO THE MODERN WORLD:
The Social Teachings of Leo XIII. Edited by Etienne Gilson
                                    D7—95¢

PEACE OF SOUL
By Fulton J. Sheen   D8—85¢

LIFT UP YOUR HEART
By Fulton J. Sheen   D9—85¢

STORM OF GLORY
The Story of St. Thérèse of Lisieux. By John Beevers
                                    D10—75¢

THE PERFECT JOY OF ST. FRANCIS
By Felix Timmermans
                                    D11—85¢

SAINTS FOR OUR TIMES
By Theodore Maynard
                                    D12—95¢

INTRODUCTION TO THE DEVOUT LIFE
By St. Francis de Sales. Newly translated and edited by John K. Ryan   D13—95¢

THE ROAD TO DAMASCUS
Edited by John A. O'Brien
                                    D14—85¢

JOYCE KILMER'S ANTHOLOGY OF CATHOLIC POETS
With a new supplement by James Edward Tobin
                                    D15—$1.25

BERNADETTE AND LOURDES
By Michel de Saint-Pierre
                                    D16—85¢

THE IMITATION OF CHRIST
By Thomas à Kempis. A Modern Version edited with an Introduction by Harold C. Gardiner, S.J.   D17—85¢

THE EVERLASTING MAN
By G. K. Chesterton D18—95¢

A GRAMMAR OF ASSENT
By John Henry Cardinal Newman with an Introduction by Etienne Gilson   D19—$1.25

BROTHER PETROC'S RETURN
By S. M. C.   D21—75¢

ST. FRANCIS OF ASSISI
By Johannes Jörgensen
                                    D22—95¢

STORIES OF OUR CENTURY BY CATHOLIC AUTHORS
Edited by John Gilland Brunini and Francis X. Connolly
                                    D23—95¢

AUTOBIOGRAPHY OF A HUNTED PRIEST
By John Gerard. Introduction by Graham Greene D24—95¢

FATHER MALACHY'S MIRACLE
By Bruce Marshall D25—75¢

ON THE TRUTH OF THE CATHOLIC FAITH *Summa Contra Gentiles Book I: God. Newly translated, with Introduction and notes by Anton C. Pegis*
                                    D26—95¢

Image Books

... MAKING THE WORLD'S FINEST
CATHOLIC LITERATURE AVAILABLE TO ALL

Image Books

*...making the world's finest
Catholic literature available to all*

VIPERS' TANGLE
by François Mauriac D51—75¢

THE MANNER IS ORDINARY
by John LaFarge, S.J. D52—95¢

MY LIFE FOR MY SHEEP
by Alfred Duggan D53—90¢

THE CHURCH AND THE RECONSTRUCTION OF THE MODERN WORLD: *The Social Encyclicals of Pius XI.* Edited by T. P. McLaughlin, C.S.B. D54—$1.25

A GILSON READER: *Selections from the Writings of Etienne Gilson.* Edited by Anton C. Pegis. D55—$1.25

THE AUTOBIOGRAPHY OF ST. THERESE OF LISIEUX: *The Story of a Soul. A new translation by* John Beevers. D56—75¢

HELENA
by Evelyn Waugh D57—75¢

THE GREATEST BIBLE STORIES
A Catholic Anthology from World Literature. Edited by Anne Fremantle. D58—75¢

THE CITY OF GOD—St. Augustine.
Edited with Intro. by Vernon J. Bourke. Foreword by Etienne Gilson. D59—$1.55

SUPERSTITION CORNER
by Sheila Kaye-Smith D60—65¢

SAINTS AND OURSELVES
Ed. by *Philip Caraman, S.J.* D61—95¢

CANA IS FOREVER
by Charles Hugo Doyle D62—85¢

ASCENT OF MOUNT CARMEL—St. John of the Cross. Translated and Edited by E. Allison Peers. D63—$1.25

RELIGION AND THE RISE OF WESTERN CULTURE
by Christopher Dawson D64—85¢

PRINCE OF DARKNESS AND OTHER STORIES
by J. F. Powers D65—85¢

ST. THOMAS MORE
by E. E. Reynolds D66—95¢

JESUS AND HIS TIMES
2 Volumes D67A—95¢
by Daniel-Rops D67B—95¢

ST. BENEDICT
by Justin McCann, O.S.B. D68—85¢

THE LITTLE FLOWERS OF ST. FRANCIS
Edited and Translated by Raphael Brown. D69—95¢

THE QUIET LIGHT
by Louis de Wohl D70—95¢

CHARACTERS OF THE REFORMATION
by Hilaire Belloc D71—85¢

THE BELIEF OF CATHOLICS
by Ronald Knox D72—75¢

FAITH AND FREEDOM
by Barbara Ward D73—95¢

GOD AND INTELLIGENCE IN MODERN PHILOSOPHY
by Fulton J. Sheen D74—$1.25

If your bookseller is unable to supply certain titles, write to Image Books, Department MIB, Garden City, New York, stating the titles you desire and enclosing the price of each book (plus 5¢ per book to cover cost of postage and handling). Prices are subject to change without notice. I 21

Image Books

. . . MAKING THE WORLD'S FINEST CATHOLIC LITERATURE AVAILABLE TO ALL

THE IDEA OF A UNIVERSITY
By John Henry Cardinal Newman. Introduction by George N. Shuster   D75—$1.45

PLAYED BY EAR: The Autobiography of Father Daniel A. Lord, S.J.   D76—95¢

MY BELOVED: The Story of a Carmelite Nun. By Mother Catherine Thomas   D77—75¢

DARK NIGHT OF THE SOUL
By St. John of the Cross. Edited and translated by E. Allison Peers   D78—75¢

TERESA OF AVILA
By Marcelle Auclair. Translated by Kathleen Pond   D79—$1.45

SAINT PETER THE APOSTLE
By William Thomas Walsh   D80—95¢

THE LOVE OF GOD
By Dom Aelred Graham, O.S.B.   D81—85¢

WOMAN OF THE PHARISEES
By François Mauriac. Translated by Gerard Hopkins   D82—75¢

THE PILLAR OF FIRE
By Karl Stern   D83—85¢

ORTHODOXY
By G. K. Chesterton   D84—75¢

THIS IS CATHOLICISM
By John J. Walsh   D85—$1.25

MEDIEVAL ESSAYS
By Christopher Dawson   D86—95¢

VESSEL OF CLAY
By Leo Trese   D87—65¢

SAINTS FOR SINNERS
By Alban Goodier, S.J.   D88—75¢

THE LONG LONELINESS
By Dorothy Day   D89—85¢

THIS IS THE MASS
By Henri Daniel-Rops. Photographs of Bishop Fulton J. Sheen by Karsh   D90—95¢

THE ORIGIN OF THE JESUITS
By James Brodrick, S.J.   D91—85¢

A POPULAR HISTORY OF THE REFORMATION
By Philip Hughes   D92—95¢

THE RESTLESS FLAME
By Louis de Wohl   D93—85¢

PROGRESS AND RELIGION
By Christopher Dawson   D94—85¢

THE CATHOLIC CHURCH IN THE MODERN WORLD
By E. E. Y. Hales   D95—95¢

THE LIFE OF TERESA OF JESUS: The Autobiography of St. Teresa of Avila. Translated and with an introduction by E. Allison Peers   D96—$1.25

GIANTS OF THE FAITH
By John A. O'Brien   D97—95¢

SCHOLASTICISM AND POLITICS
By Jacques Maritain   D98—95¢

THE SON OF GOD
By Karl Adam   D99—85¢

THE MAN WHO WAS CHESTERTON
Edited by Raymond T. Bond   D100—$1.45

Image Books

... MAKING THE WORLD'S FINEST CATHOLIC LITERATURE AVAILABLE TO ALL

Image Books

A HISTORY OF PHILOSOPHY, Vol. 3:

Late Mediaeval and Renaissance Philosophy, Parts I & II
By Frederick Copleston, S.J.

A magnificent exposition of philosophical thought from Ockham to the Speculative Mystics (Part I), and from the Revival of Platonism to Suarez (Part II).
D136A & D136B—95¢ ea. vol.

CATHOLIC VIEWPOINT ON EDUCATION

By Neil McCluskey, S.J.

A complete, authoritative, and clear-cut presentation of the Catholic viewpoint on a vitally urgent national issue. "Required reading"—*N.Y. Times.*
D149—75¢

MIRACLE AT CARVILLE

By Betty Martin

The story of a courageous girl's triumph over the world's most feared malady. **D150—85¢**

CATHEDRAL AND CRUSADE
(2 volumes)

By Henri Daniel-Rops

A history of the stirring age between the eleventh and fourteenth centuries. "An important work of Catholic scholarship."—*The Saturday Review.*
D154A & D154B—$1.35 ea. vol.

SEARCHING THE SCRIPTURES

By John J. Dougherty

A popular and lucid guide to the reading and study of the Bible, giving historical background and theological explanations. **D151—75¢**

TRANSFORMATION IN CHRIST

By Dietrich von Hildebrand

Presents a profound analysis of the Christian experience and offers a rich new insight into the reality of the Christian life.
D152—$1.35

SECRETS OF THE SAINTS

By Henri Gheon

Four complete biographies in one volume: the Curé of Ars, the Little Flower, St. Margaret Mary, and St. John Bosco.
D153—$1.25

A DOCTOR AT CALVARY

By Pierre Barbet, M.D.

The classic and moving account of the Passion of Our Lord as described by a physician.
D155—85¢

MARY IN OUR LIFE

By William G. Most

A comprehensive and beautifully written study of Mary's importance in one's faith. **D156—95¢**

If your bookseller is unable to supply certain titles, write to Image Books, Department MIB, Garden City, New York, stating the titles you desire and enclosing the price of each book (plus 5¢ per book to cover cost of postage and handling). Prices are subject to change without notice. **I 33**

Image Books

*. . . making the world's finest
Catholic literature available to all*

PRAYER IN PRACTICE
by Romano Guardini
D157—75¢

THE BOOK OF MARY
by Henri Daniel-Rops
D158—75¢

THE PROTESTANT REFORMATION
(2 vols.)
by Henri Daniel-Rops
D159A & D159B—$1.35 ea. vol.

THE SANDS OF TAMANRASSET
by Marion Mill Preminger
D160—85¢

**YOUR CHILD'S WORLD: From
Infancy to Adolescence**
by Robert Odenwald, M.D.
D161—75¢

WE LIVE WITH OUR EYES OPEN
by Dom Hubert van Zeller,
O.S.B. D162—75¢

**BLITHE SPIRITS: An Anthology of
Catholic Humor**
Ed. by Dan Herr and Joel
Wells D163—85¢

ON THE LOVE OF GOD (2 vols.)
by St. Francis de Sales—Trans.
with an Intro. by John K. Ryan
D164A & D164B—95¢ ea. vol.

LIFE OF ST. DOMINIC
by Bede Jarrett, O.P.
D165—75¢

IN SOFT GARMENTS
by Ronald Knox D166—75¢

**THE YEAR AND OUR CHILDREN:
Planning the Family Activities for
the Church Year**
by Mary Reed Newland
D167—95¢

**THE CHURCH IN CRISIS: A History
of the General Councils,
325–1870**
by Philip Hughes
D168—$1.25

**ISRAEL AND THE ANCIENT
WORLD**
by Henri Daniel-Rops
D169—$1.35

**THE SPIRITUAL EXERCISES OF
ST. IGNATIUS**
Trans. by Anthony Mottola,
Ph.D. Intro. by Robert W.
Gleason, S.J. D170—85¢

**A NEWMAN READER: An
Anthology of the Writings of
John Henry Cardinal Newman**
Ed. with Intro. by Francis X.
Connolly D171—$1.45

WITH LOVE AND LAUGHTER
by Sister Maryanna, O.P.
D172—95¢

THE GOLDEN STRING
by Bede Griffiths, O.S.B.
D173—75¢

**A HISTORY OF PHILOSOPHY:
MODERN PHILOSOPHY VOL. 6**
(2 vols.) French Enlightenment
to Kant
by Frederick Copleston, S.J.
D139A & D139B—95¢ ea. vol.

THESE ARE THE SACRAMENTS
Described by Fulton J. Sheen
Photographed by Yousuf Karsh
D174—95¢

**FRANCIS: A BIOGRAPHY OF THE
SAINT OF ASSISI**
by Michael de la Bedoyere
D175—85¢

THE WAY OF PERFECTION
by St. Teresa of Avila
Trans. & ed. by E. Allison
Peers D176—85¢

REFLECTIONS ON AMERICA
by Jacques Maritain
D177—75¢

THE HIDDEN STREAM
by Ronald Knox D178—75¢

IMAGE BOOKS

Image Books constitute a quality library of Catholic writings, broad in human interest and deep in Christian insight. They will include classical Christian writings, devotion, philosophy, education and history; biographies, novels and poetry; and books on contemporary social problems. They represent a planned program of making available to the widest possible audience the finest Catholic literature in attractive, paper-bound, inexpensive editions. They have been selected with these criteria in mind: that they must in every instance be well written, inspiring to the spirit, and of lasting value to the general audience who will purchase them.

The majority of Image Books will consist of reprints made possible through the cooperation of the publishers of the original editions. Occasionally certain much-needed volumes which are not available will also be initiated for this series.

A descriptive catalogue of the Image Books already published may be obtained by writing directly to the publisher. Comments and suggestions from those interested in the series are welcomed by the publisher.